Steve Michel
and Dale Coleman

MacWrite Pro Inside & Out

Osborne **McGraw-Hill**

Berkeley New York St. Louis San Francisco
Auckland Bogotá Hamburg London Madrid
Mexico City Milan Montreal New Delhi Panama City
Paris São Paulo Singapore Sydney
Tokyo Toronto

Osborne **McGraw-Hill**
2600 Tenth Street
Berkeley, California 94710 U.S.A.

For information on translations and book distributors outside of the U.S.A., please write to Osborne **McGraw-Hill** at the above address.

MacWrite Pro Inside & Out

234567890 DOC 99876543

ISBN 0-07-881864-8

Acquisitions Editor
Frances Stack

Associate Editor
Jill Pisoni

Technical Editor
Jeffrey R. Estes

Project Editor
Wendy Rinaldi

Copy Editor
Paul Medoff

Proofreader
Linda Medoff

Indexers
Steve Michel
Dale Coleman

Computer Designer
Jani Beckwith

Illustrator
Susie Kim

Cover Designer
Compass Marketing

Contents at a Glance

Contents

Part III • Recipes

Part IV • Appendixes

Acknowledgments

We depended on the kind support of a number of people while writing this book. Chief among them was Jeff Estes, our able and enthusiastic technical editor. Jeff filled our manuscript pages and CompuServe mailboxes with astute comments about our work, and with valuable tips for wringing the most out of MacWrite Pro. While he is not responsible for any mistakes or oversights in this book, he deserves a great deal of credit for the good and the useful that you'll discover. We are also indebted to Osborne/McGraw-Hill acquisitions editor Frances Stack and her most excellent crew, without whom we are nothing. Ren Risch at Claris Corp. coordinated all of the initial contacts. Others we have relied upon in one way or another include but are not limited to Bob Kermish, Henry Norr, Blair Miller, David Todd, Stephen Howard, Ken Blunt, Edwina Riblett, Mick McCuistion, Steve Phifer, Eric Alderman, Rick Le Page, Elston Gunn, Kurt Carlson, Xavier Raya, Raines Cohen, Bill Clinton, Jennifer Ambrulevich, Michael Britten, Mia Runanin, Shan Carr, Mimi Babcock, Chiqui Linda, and the Albany, California public library.

Introduction

For most long-time Macintosh users, the name MacWrite conjures many and varied memories. As Mac owners since a month after its 1984 introduction, we tend to be nostalgic about the excitement of the early days. At last we were able to see different typefaces (fonts) on screen, and to print documents containing those fonts on a dot matrix printer. How exciting to be able to actually mix graphics and text in the same document and on the same page. The new user interface for the Mac and MacWrite (which used to come free with every Mac) got our juices flowing the most; instead of having to memorize commands as our DOS-based brethren did, we chose commands from always-visible but never cumbersome pull-down menus.

However, the nostalgia is tempered by memories of the sadly underpowered Macintosh and MacWrite we used at the time. The first MacWrite couldn't handle a document of much more than 12 pages, and that first Macintosh included only one 400-Kbyte floppy disk drive; saving a document to a different disk could lead to sufficient time spent swapping disks in and out to cause repetitive stress injury.

It's no understatement to say that the shape of personal computing has changed dramatically since then. Large hard disks are now common, Macintoshes have almost enough memory, and we have scores more documents to keep track of. But one of the biggest changes we see is not so positive. For lack of a better phrase, we call it the dilution of the

Macintosh user interface. Software has become much more powerful than it was just a few years ago, but it has also become more complicated to learn and use; more so, we suspect, than the addition of new features would justify.

Our respect and appreciation for the Mac interface drew us to MacWrite Pro when we were given our first sneak preview in 1990, and we immediately became excited about writing a book about it. While MacWrite Pro is a powerful program, it has retained the essential ease of use that graced the original. In other Mac word processors, we find icons that don't communicate their purpose, commands we don't understand, tools that we never use more accessible than tools we use everyday, and a host of other user interface sins that make us long for the days when software wasn't designed by a committee but was the product of small groups of people who cared passionately about their work.

This is not to say that MacWrite Pro is the perfect word processor because it's not. We disagree with some of the design decisions made at Claris. But overall, we find in MacWrite Pro a very intuitive and deceptively powerful tool. We trust that you will too.

About This Book

This book is divided into four parts.

Part I covers the basics of working with MacWrite Pro—creating, editing, formatting, and printing basic documents.

Part II covers the most powerful aspects of MacWrite Pro. With MacWrite Pro's powerful frames, you can do many of the tasks that were previously in the strict domain of desktop publishing programs.

Part III shows you how to create a range of commonly used documents, from letterhead and envelopes to newsletters and even a product catalog.

Part IV shows you how to customize your MacWrite Pro installation and discusses many other matters related to MacWrite Pro.

PART I

Basics

CHAPTER 1

MacWrite's Workspace

This chapter introduces the fundamental elements of the MacWrite Pro user interface. It explains how the interface works. It also serves as a road map to this book, with pointers to chapters where subjects and techniques are discussed in more detail. It also introduces many of MacWrite Pro's powerful and time-saving features.

A word processor's user interface is arguably its most important aspect. What use is a powerful word processor if the commands are so complicated and obscure that you won't want to explore them? Bruce Tognazzini, formerly Apple's user interface guru, eschewed the vogue term "graphical user interface" in favor of "visible user interface." A graphical user interface uses icons, menus, and dialog boxes to help you get the job done without having to remember cryptic commands. A visible user interface does the same, but with the difference that all of the available tools are immediately, or nearly immediately, apparent. The next step in any procedure should be obvious to the user.

As you explore MacWrite Pro, you'll see that its developers have followed the visible interface model: the tools you need for any specific task are intuitively accessible. You don't need to memorize arcane codes and key combinations, although MacWrite Pro includes a wealth of optional keyboard equivalents to menu commands that you might find can increase your productivity.

We assume throughout this book that you are familiar with the basics of operating your Mac. If you're not, now is a good time to break out the Apple manuals and familiarize yourself with the Mac basics. It's a rewarding adventure, and you'll be able to apply almost everything you learn to MacWrite Pro.

If you've used other Mac applications such as spreadsheets, databases, or especially other Mac word processors, you should be right at home with MacWrite Pro. If you haven't, you will soon discover that many of the techniques and shortcuts you learn with MacWrite Pro apply to other Macintosh applications. This is all doubly true of other applications published by Claris Corp.—there's a great deal of consistency between MacWrite Pro and other Claris applications, such as Resolve (a spreadsheet) or FileMaker Pro (a database).

The Elements of the MacWrite Pro Workspace

All standard Mac applications have several elements in common: a menu bar, windows, and dialog boxes. The *menu bar* contains most of the available commands. *Windows* contain the actual document data. MacWrite Pro *data* is the text you type and the graphics elements you place in the document. Dialog boxes are summoned on those occasions when you need to make a decision about how you want MacWrite Pro to respond to an action.

MacWrite Pro also includes five palettes. *Palettes* are small floating windows that give you access to some features that you otherwise access with menu commands. Palettes are usually a more efficient tool for accessing commands than the menus.

Starting MacWrite Pro

Start MacWrite Pro by double-clicking its icon in the Finder, or by double-clicking the icon for a MacWrite Pro document. You can also launch the program by selecting the MacWrite Pro icon or document and then choosing the Finder File menu's Open command, but the double-click method is usually much more convenient.

Memory Requirements

You can control the amount of memory allocated to MacWrite Pro. Select the MacWrite Pro icon, then use the Finder File menu's Get Info command (or hold down ⌘ while pressing I), which summons the following dialog box:

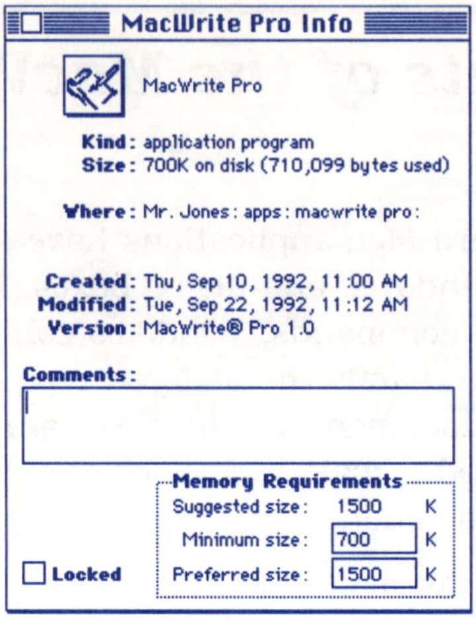

Note The exact dialog box you get may differ in several respects; the created and modified dates, as well as the version number, may be different. Also, the Get Info window shown is from Macintosh System 7.1; this information differs from System 7.0 and 7.0.1, in that you cannot set the minimum size, as discussed next, in the earlier systems.

This dialog box lets you change the following two aspects of MacWrite Pro's memory requirements.

Minimum Size

The Minimum Size number is the absolute minimum of available free memory that must be available when you launch MacWrite Pro. If this much memory is *not* available, the Finder tells you that it cannot launch the application, and gives you the option of quitting another running application to make more memory available. (To find out how much memory is available, use the Finder Apple menu's About This Macintosh command.)

Preferred Size

This is the amount of memory that MacWrite Pro prefers. Initially, it is the same as the uneditable Suggested Size figure. If this much memory is available, the Finder allocates it to MacWrite Pro when you launch the application.

Generally, you should run MacWrite Pro, and all other applications for that matter, with as much memory as possible. More memory means that MacWrite Pro is able to load more of a document into memory at one time so that manipulating the document is much quicker, especially actions such as global Find/Change and reformatting. When it is running in a memory partition lower than the suggested size, MacWrite Pro may also be unable to work with large graphics elements. In this case, it warns you of the condition.

Launching Options

When you launch MacWrite Pro, it reads the contents of a folder called Claris folder, which is located in the System Folder. The Claris folder contains several elements, including XTND file translation filters, AddIts, a font list, and MacWrite Pro Options.

You can also launch MacWrite Pro without loading the contents of the MacWrite Pro Options file by holding down the Option key at launch. The MacWrite Pro Options file contains default document formats and styles; it is discussed in more detail in Chapter 14.

When you launch MacWrite Pro with any of these methods it creates a new document called Document1. You can force MacWrite Pro to open the Open Document dialog box instead by holding down the ⌘ key at launch.

Document Windows

The window in which you type and edit text is called the *document window*. You have a separate window for each open document. When you click in a document window, it comes to the front of any other open document windows.

View of the Page

You can automatically position the open document window either with the mouse or with the commands on the View menu.

Magnifying and Reducing the Display

You can expand and reduce the image of the current page of a document with a click of the mouse. To the left of the horizontal scroll bar at the bottom of the window are two zoom controls, plus an indicator that tells you at what magnification you are viewing the document, as shown here:

Click the left control to zoom out, making the page smaller. Decreasing the image of the page on the screen lets you quickly view the entire page.

The right control zooms in on the document; less of the page is displayed, but the individual elements on the page are displayed larger. This is a particularly handy feature when you want to fine-tune very small page elements, including small font sizes. For example, 12-point Times text is less legible on the Mac screen than many other fonts; Times text in smaller sizes is nearly illegible. Magnifying the document window with zoom in solves this problem nicely.

Successive clicks on these two controls zooms in preset increments. Beginning at 100 percent, which is the normal view, successive clicks on the zoom out control reduces the document page by 50, 33, and 25 percent. From the normal view, successive clicks on the zoom in control increases the image 200 and 400 percent.

The zoom status control, immediately to the left of the two zoom controls, displays the amount the display is magnified or reduced. To fine-tune the percentage of magnification or reduction, double-click the control, which summons this dialog box:

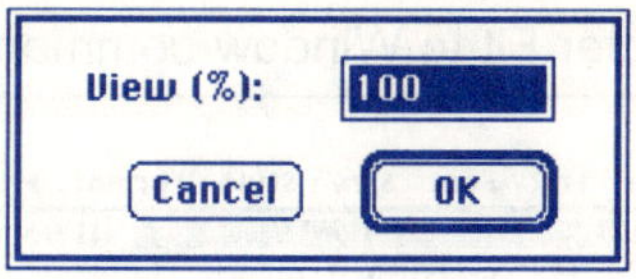

Type the number of percentage of magnification or reduction you need into the View (%) field and click the OK button. The dialog box accepts any integer ranging from 25 to 400.

Fit to Window Shift-⌘-R

The View menu's Fit to Window command automatically reduces the page display to fit within the boundaries of the document window. The keyboard equivalent is Shift-⌘-R. Choosing this command a second time returns the display to the 100 percent view. The two zoom controls and the zoom status control are also active, so after you view the document in the fit-to-window view, you can quickly go to any other size view, instead of returning to 100 percent view. An example of this is shown in Figure 1-1.

Note If the document window is too small to display an entire page in 25 percent view when you choose the Fit to Window command, only the first portion is displayed.

Page Guides

The document display is WYSIWYG (What You See Is What You Get); it displays each page as it looks when printed. A by-product of this feature is that you can see both the body of each page and the page margin. The inside edges of the margins are indicated by a thin gray solid line. (The line is dotted if you are using a black-and-white monitor.) You can modify these margins with the Format menu's Format Document dialog box, or manually by holding down the Option key when the pointer is above a margin boundary and dragging.

FIGURE 1-1

Newsletter after Fit to Window command

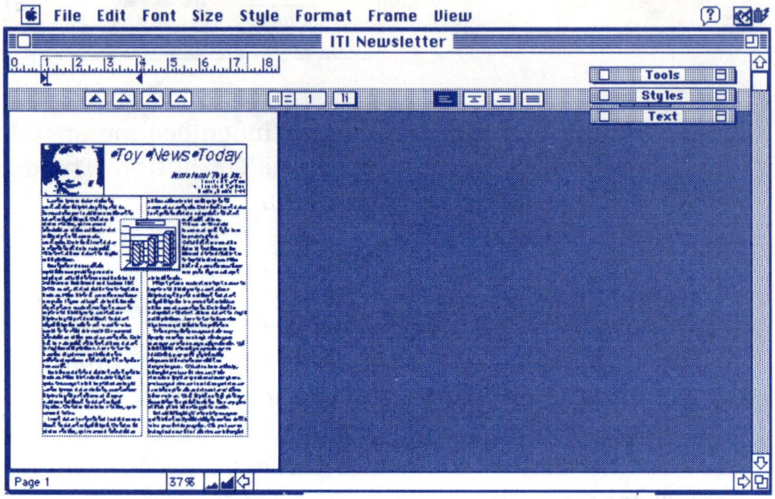

Ruler

The Ruler sets properties of the currently active or selected paragraph or paragraphs. It is discussed in detail in Chapter 4. Use the View menu's Hide Ruler command to hide the Ruler. If the Ruler is not displayed, you can summon it with the View menu's Show Ruler command. This is the standard, unmodified MacWrite Pro Ruler:

Page Number Box

The Page Number box, located in the lower-left corner of the document window, displays the number of the current page. If portions of two or more pages are visible in the document window, that range of page numbers is displayed. If the document is divided into sections (accomplished with the Format menu's Insert Break | Section submenu), the page number box displays both the section number and the page number. For example, page 1 of section 2 is displayed as Page 1, §2.

You can use the Page Number box to move to a specific page by double-clicking it, which summons the Go to Page dialog box:

You can also move to a specific page with the View menu's Go To Page # command.

Note Using either of these methods to go to a specific page does not change the location of the insertion point. If you type a character after moving to another page, the original page containing the insertion point is automatically displayed. If you want to move the insertion point to the new location, use the mouse to position the I-beam cursor to the desired location and click.

There are two other related shortcuts. Double-click on the section number to summon the Format Section dialog box or Option-double-click on either the Page Number box or the Section Number box to summon the Preferences dialog box.

Managing Document Windows

Dealing with more than one or two document windows would be frustrating without some window-management tools. MacWrite Pro provides tools to manipulate windows in almost any fashion imaginable.

Using the Mouse

MacWrite Pro supports the standard Mac document window, mouse-driven manipulation techniques. You can bring any document window to the front by clicking on any portion of it. The area with the horizontal lines at the top of the window, called the *title bar*, is shown here:

In addition to displaying the name of the document, it offers several ways to move and resize windows.

To move a window to a new position, click and drag the title bar.

To close a window with the mouse, click in the *close box*, which is the box on the left of the title bar. If you haven't saved your changes to disk before you click the close box, MacWrite Pro asks you if you want to save the changed document before closing it. If you hold down the Option key while clicking in the close box, all the open windows will be closed. (This mimics the behavior of the Finder.)

On the right of the title bar is a small box containing a second small box called the *zoom box*. Click the zoom box to return the document window to full size any time you have changed its size or position. Clicking the zoom box a second time returns it to its previous size and position. Thereafter, clicking the zoom box acts as a toggle to switch between the current size and position and the most recent size and position.

Note The View menu's Arrange Windows | Zoom command (Shift-⌘-M) has the same effect as clicking the zoom box.

Yet another way to manage document windows is by using the window resize box, which is located in the lower-right corner of the window. Click and drag this box to shrink or enlarge the window. The window remains anchored in its original position relative to the top and right sides.

View Menu

MacWrite Pro adds the name of each document to the end of the View menu as you open or create it. This is the most elementary way to switch between windows. To switch between document windows, choose the name of the document from the View menu as you would any other menu command. Here's an example of how the View menu displays the names of the open documents:

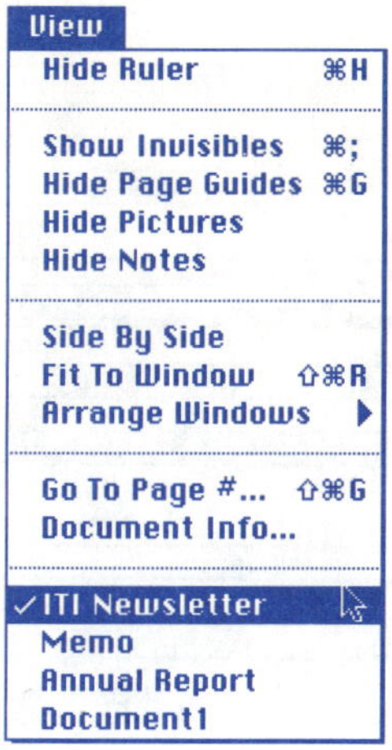

You can also cycle through document windows, one at a time, by pressing Shift-⌘-W.

Tiling Shift-⌘-L

If you have two or more documents open, you can tile them with the View menu | Arrange Windows submenu | Tile command. The keyboard equivalent is Shift-⌘-L. When the document windows are tiled, they shrink and are rearranged so that three windows are displayed on the top level, as shown in Figure 1-2.

Any additional windows are also tiled, but they are behind the front three windows on a 13-inch monitor.

The number of tiled windows MacWrite Pro displays depends on the size of the monitor. For example, MacWrite Pro displays five tiled windows on a 16-inch monitor.

If you have two monitors connected, you have more tiling options. The Preferences Application Tile has a Use Main Monitor Only setting. If this option is checked, windows tile on the main monitor only. If this option is unchecked, windows tile on both monitors. You can override the setting of the Use Main Monitor Only option by holding down the Option key while using any of the tiling commands.

FIGURE 1-2 Three windows as they appear after the Tile command is implemented

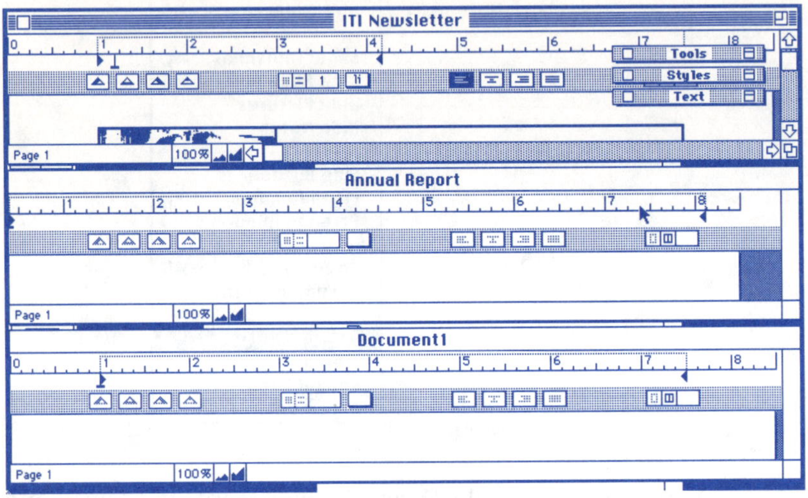

Stacking Shift-⌘-K

Stacking is an alternative to Tiling when you have two or more documents open. To stack windows, use the View menu's Arrange Windows hierarchical menu's Stack command. The keyboard equivalent is Shift-⌘-K. This command arranges the windows so that the title bar and a small portion of the right side of the window of each document are visible, as shown in Figure 1-3.

Stacking windows is probably the most efficient way to switch between multiple document windows when you are working with four or more open documents.

Zoom Shift-⌘-M

Choosing the View menu | Arrange Windows submenu | Zoom command zooms all open document windows between full size and a reduced size. The result is identical to clicking the window zoom box in each window.

FIGURE 1-3

Stacking windows leaves the title bar and a small portion of the right side of each document visible

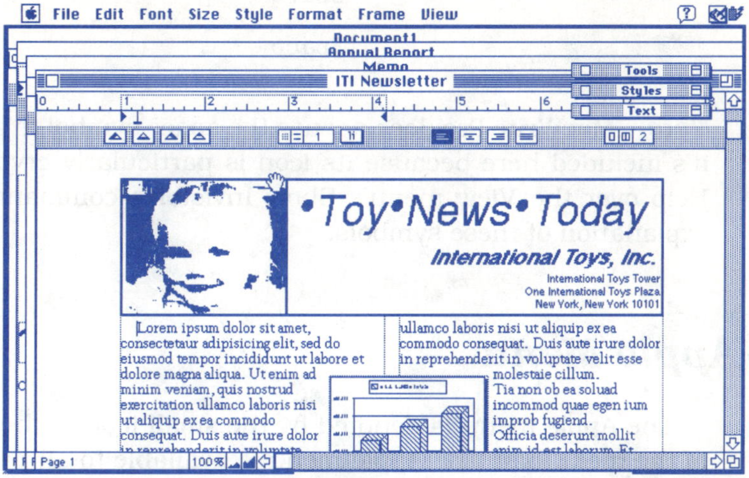

MacWrite Pro Menus

This section is devoted to a general overview of MacWrite Pro's menus. Menu commands are discussed in detail in appropriate chapters.

When the name of a menu command is followed by an ellipsis (...), choosing that command summons a dialog box.

Keyboard Equivalents for Menu Commands

Many MacWrite Pro menu commands have *keyboard equivalents*, key combinations that you can press to activate the menu command. These equivalents are shown to the right of the menu commands. Since Apple made these symbols somewhat cryptic, here's an illustration that shows what they mean:

Command ⌘

Option ⌥

Shift ⇧

Space ␣

Note MacWrite Pro does *not* use the space symbol in any of its menus; it's included here because its icon is particularly cryptic. Use Balloon Help over the View menu's Show Invisibles command for a complete explanation of these symbols.

The Apple Menu

The Apple menu is denoted by the small icon of the Apple at the left of the menu bar. The Apple menu is available to all programs, and can be customized in the Finder very easily. Different applications can add their own items into the Apple menu; these appear at the top of the list, and are separated from others by a line.

MacWrite Pro adds two commands to the Apple menu. The first command, About MacWrite Pro, summons an About MacWrite Pro dialog box that contains the serial number of your copy of the application. It also contains three radio buttons. The Info button changes the display to a description of the system. The Credits button lists the many hard-working people who worked on MacWrite Pro. The About button returns the About MacWrite Pro box to its original state. The OK button closes About MacWrite Pro.

Note The Info screen in the About MacWrite Pro dialog box also performs a useful task behind the scenes. When you use it MacWrite Pro silently purges all unneeded RAM. This can be handy if you are running MacWrite Pro with less than the full amount of memory it prefers, and can speed up program operations slightly.

The second Apple menu command, called Help, summons the MacWrite Pro help system. The keyboard equivalent is ⌘-?. You can also summon Balloon Help with the standard System 7 help icon, which is on the right of the menu bar. Both kinds of MacWrite Pro help are discussed later in this chapter.

Other commands on the Apple menu are determined by the contents of the Apple Menu Items folder in the System Folder. Any items you place into this folder automatically appear on the Apple menu; choosing one of them from the Apple menu causes it to open just as if you had opened it from the Finder. This is a very handy feature.

To take advantage of this feature, first place an *alias* (an icon representing a particular program that points back to the program that you can put in another folder) of MacWrite Pro itself into the Apple Menu Items folder. To do this, make sure the Finder is the frontmost application and then follow these steps:

1. Locate the MacWrite Pro icon (which is probably in a folder called MacWrite Pro).
2. Select the icon, and then choose the Make Alias command from the Finder's File menu. This step creates a new file called MacWrite Pro Alias.
3. Drag this file's icon to the desktop.
4. Next, locate the System Folder and open it.
5. Locate the Apple Menu's Items folder and press ⌘-O to open it.
6. Drag the MacWrite Pro Alias icon into this folder (before or after doing this, you might want to delete the word "Alias" from the name of the alias file).

After you've done this, you can open MacWrite Pro from the Apple menu, no matter what application you are currently using.

As you work with MacWrite Pro, you might find yourself dealing repeatedly with the same document. This is especially true if you take advantage of MacWrite Pro's excellent stationery capabilities (discussed in Chapter 16). You can place aliases of stationery documents into the Apple menu. Then, not only is MacWrite Pro opened when you select one of these items, but so is the specified document. Stationery files for letterheads, interoffice memos, and the like are excellent candidates for this technique.

If you regularly store most MacWrite Pro documents in a single folder, you can put an alias of the folder in the Apple Menu's Items folder so that you can summon it from the Apple menu.

For details on creating and managing aliases, consult the System 7 Reference that came with your Macintosh or System 7 software.

The File Menu

Predictably, the commands on the File menu, shown here, deal with files:

You use these commands to create new documents, open existing documents, merge documents into the current one, save, and print documents. Most of the commands on this menu are standard to virtually all Mac applications.

The Edit Menu

All standard Mac applications contain an Edit menu. It includes items for cutting, copying, and pasting text via the Clipboard. This is MacWrite Pro's Edit menu:

Some of the menu commands contain right-facing arrows at the right. These arrows indicate the menu command is a hierarchical menu. When you pass the mouse pointer over one of these commands, a new menu with additional commands appears. To use one of these submenu items, move the mouse a little to the right as the hierarchical menu appears. The Edit menu uses hierarchical menus for Publish & Subscribe, Spelling, Finding, and Variable functions.

The Edit menu's Preferences command, which lets you customize much of the behavior of MacWrite Pro, is discussed in detail later in this chapter.

The Font and Size Menus

The Font and Size menus contain commands for text formatting. The Font menu contains a list of all the fonts that are installed in the system, optionally presented in their actual face (see the Preferences section later). Choosing a font from the Font menu changes the font of selected text. Choosing a size from the Size menu changes the size of the selected text. Here are the Font menu and the Size menu:

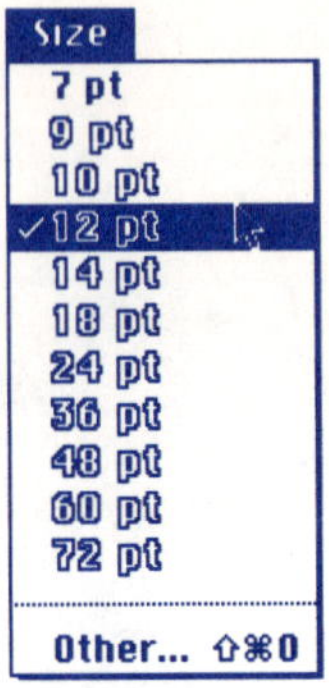

The Style Menu

The Style menu, shown here, contains commands for changing text attributes such as bold, underline, and the like:

This menu also contains various tools to manage MacWrite Pro's more powerful style sheet functions, which are discussed in Chapter 7.

The Format Menu

The Format menu, shown here, contains commands to define the formatting of documents, sections, pages, paragraphs, and tab settings:

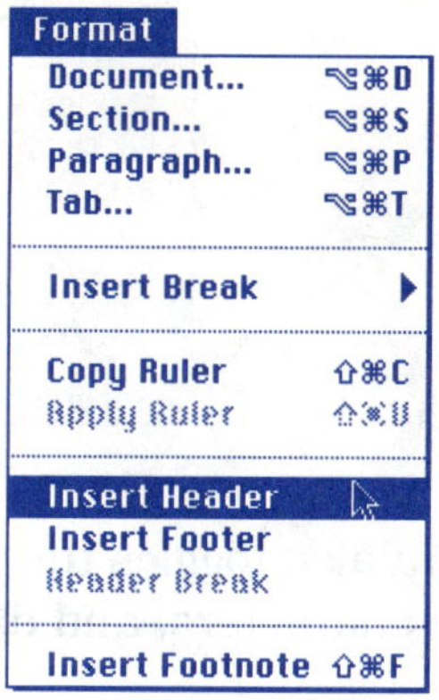

It also contains the commands you use to create and edit headers and footers.

The Frame Menu

The Frame menu contains commands that are the key to opening the doors to MacWrite Pro's powerful desktop publishing features. Frames are used to contain items such as graphics, tables, and text, which are separate from the main "flow" of a document's text.

The View Menu

The View menu, as discussed earlier, provides controls for tiling windows, zooming, and navigating through a document. The View menu is shown here:

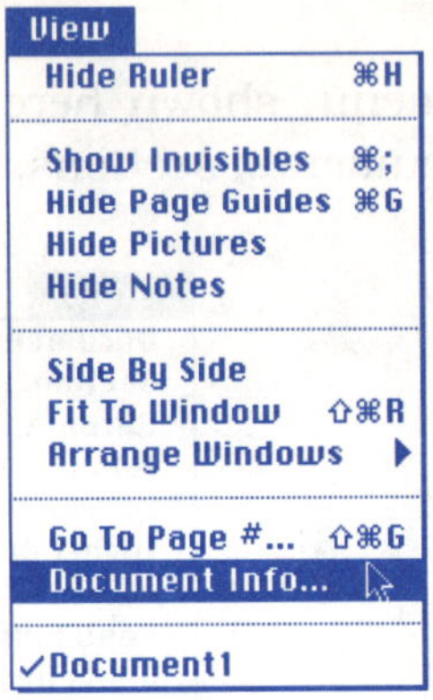

The View menu also toggles the view of page guides in the document, viewing invisible characters, and displaying the Ruler.

The Table Menu

The Table menu only appears on the menu bar when a table is active; it is to the right of the View menu and looks like this:

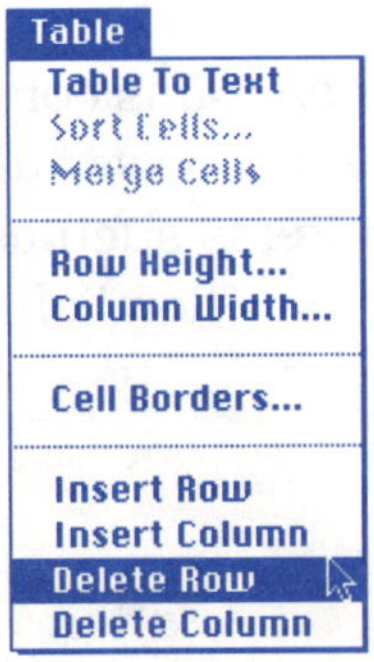

The Table menu contains commands for converting tables to text and back, sorting and merging cells, creating cell borders, and inserting and deleting cells and rolls. The Table menu is described in Chapter 12.

The Notes Menu

The Notes menu only appears on the menu bar when a Note is active; it is to the right of the View menu, as shown here:

The Notes menu contains commands for manipulating Notes and is described in Chapter 15.

Palettes

In addition to its menus, MacWrite Pro gives you another mechanism for issuing commands. This mechanism is the five palettes that float above the document window. That is, the palettes are not hidden when you click in a document window, as are other windows. The five palettes are Tools, Styles, Text, Merge, and Note.

Palettes are handy time savers because they put many relevant options in front of you and are usually more efficient than accessing the same commands via the menus. This is especially true of the Text palette, which contains most of the items that are also on the Font, Size, and Style menus. If you are an experienced Macintosh user, using these palettes takes some getting used to, but is well worth it.

When you start MacWrite Pro, it remembers which palettes were opened, where they were, and if they were collapsed the last time you quit the application. This means you can arrange the palettes according to your work habits once and forget about rearranging them each time you restart MacWrite Pro.

Tools

The Tools palette, shown here, contains controls for working with picture, text, and note frames:

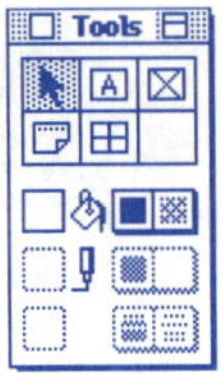

This palette is discussed in Chapter 10. Display it by using the Frame menu's Show Tools Palette command.

Styles

The Styles palette, shown here, controls the creation and management of user styles:

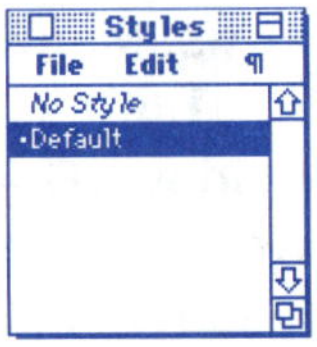

Its use is discussed in Chapter 7. Display it with the Style menu's Show Styles command.

Text

The Text palette formats selections of text; it is discussed in Chapter 3. To show the Text palette, use the Style menu's Show Text Palette command. This is the Text palette:

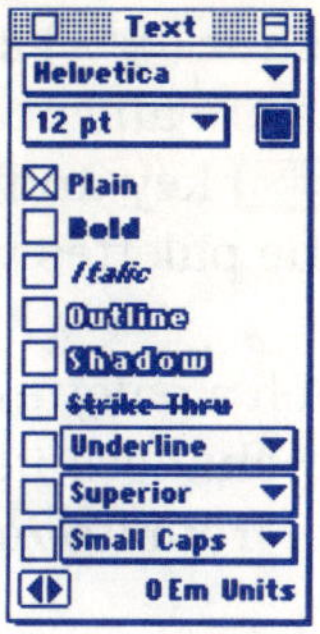

Merge

The Merge palette is used when you are merging data files and text files for such uses as form letters. This palette is discussed in detail in Chapter 13.

Notes

The Notes palette is used only when a Note is active:

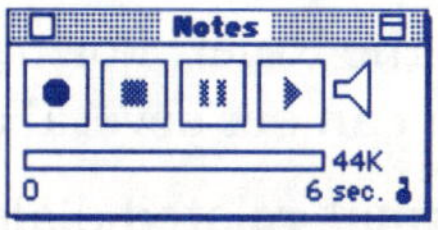

Notes are discussed in Chapter 15.

Palette Behavior

Like other windows, palettes have close boxes and zoom boxes. Close boxes are at the left edge of the title bar, and clicking in them dismisses the palette.

Note If you press the Option key and move, close, or zoom a palette, all of the open palettes are affected. Thus, just as you can close all windows by pressing the Option key and clicking in the close box of a window, so you can close all the palettes with one Option-click.

The point to which a palette collapses is called its *gravity point*. Moving a collapsed palette changes its gravity point, so that the next time you collapse the palette from its zoomed out view, it will collapse to the new gravity point.

Working with Dialog Boxes

Many MacWrite Pro menu commands contain an ellipsis after their names. These commands summon a dialog box. Dialog boxes fall into two broad categories. In one category, MacWrite Pro asks you for some information to complete a command such as Save As. In this case, MacWrite Pro is asking you to specify the name of the file and the location where you want it saved.

In the second category, dialog boxes let you issue several formatting commands at the same time. For example, the Format menu's Paragraph and Character dialog boxes both let you set attributes of text that can also be set using the Ruler, Format, Size, and Style menus. But by using a dialog box, you can set several attributes at the same time.

Most of the format-related dialog boxes include an Apply button. This button applies the changes you've made to the format of the selected text, letting you see what the changes look like without first dismissing the dialog box. This feature lets you experiment with different formatting options before making a decision. If you don't like the new changes, you can then change the settings to new ones or use the Cancel button to dismiss the dialog box and undo all the changes.

Many dialog boxes also have title bars similar to the title bars on standard Macintosh windows. These dialog boxes can be moved around the screen by dragging on the title bar. Dialog boxes without title bars cannot be moved.

Dialog Box Shortcuts

Most MacWrite Pro dialog boxes feature ⌘-key shortcuts. You can display these ⌘-key shortcuts by pressing and holding the ⌘ key when the dialog box is visible, so you need not bother with learning the ⌘-key equivalents before you start using them. This is the Format menu's Document dialog box:

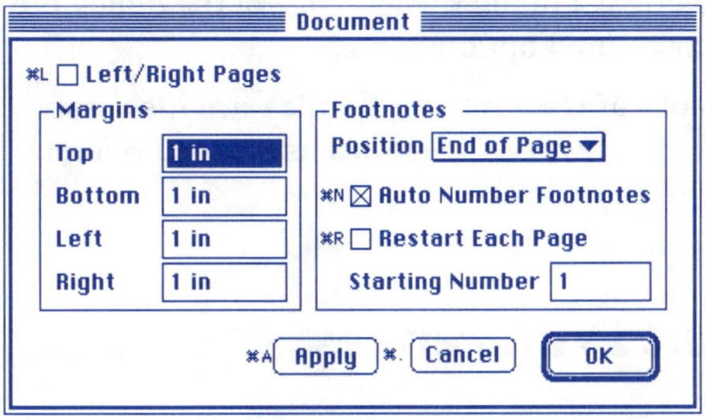

As you become familiar with a dialog box you might find using the keyboard more efficient than reaching for the mouse.

Alert Boxes

Alert boxes are similar to dialog boxes but are usually much simpler, containing only buttons. MacWrite Pro summons an alert box to notify you that a command you have used might have unintended results. For example, if you use the File menu's Save As command to save a document under a different name and a file with that name already exists in the specified folder, MacWrite Pro summons an alert box, confirming the overwrite.

The buttons in alert boxes are supremely intuitive; usually one button to execute the command that summoned the alert box and one button to cancel. MacWrite Pro alert boxes do not have keyboard equivalents.

Customizing the Workspace: Preferences

There are two ways to customize the workspace. The first is the Edit menu's Preferences command; these preferences are discussed next. The second is by saving a special document called MacWrite Pro Options; this method is discussed in Chapter 14.

The Preferences dialog box contains separate *tiles*, available in a scrolling list along the left edge of the dialog box. Click a tile to summon its associated options.

Most of the Preferences tiles are discussed throughout this book in appropriate areas. Here is a list of the Preferences tiles along with a brief description of each.

Document Preferences

The Document Preferences tile, shown in Figure 1-4, has three sections. The top group of items lets you control the units of measurement. For example, if you set the Unit of Measure to centimeters, the format of the Ruler changes to centimeters instead of inches. Most references to measurement throughout MacWrite Pro reflect this setting.

FIGURE 1-4 The Document section of the Preferences dialog box

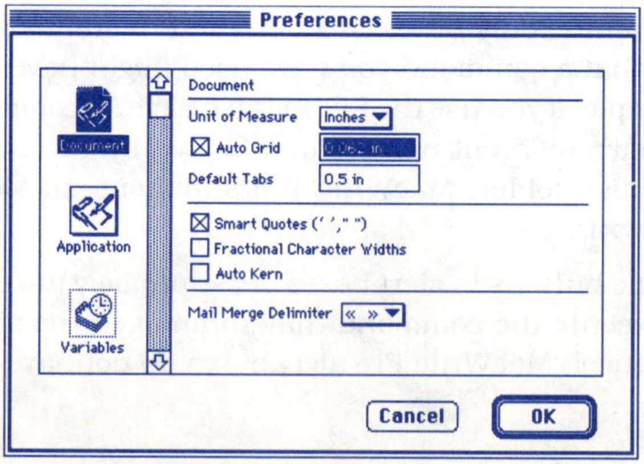

A second set of check boxes lets you specify whether Smart or dumb quotes are used; these are discussed in Chapter 2. Fractional character widths and Auto Kerning are discussed in Chapter 3. (As a general rule, however, you should not enable either of these latter options unless you have a printer with a resolution greater than 72 dots per inch (dpi)). The greater-than-72 dpi category includes all LaserWriters and many other printers such as the Apple StyleWriter. The Apple ImageWriter is a 72 dpi printer.

The Mail Merge Delimiter specifies how merge fields are separated from other text in a document; for more details see Chapter 13.

Application Preferences

The Application tile shown in Figure 1-5 has two sections. In the first section, the name that appears in the User Name is taken from the entry in the System 7 Sharing Setup control panel. This user name is assigned to MacWrite Pro Notes and also appears in the document info dialog box. You can override the assigned name by typing a new one in the User Name field.

The second item in the first group is a check box called Show Font Menus in Actual Typeface. If checked, each of the font names on the Font

FIGURE 1-5 The Application section of the Preferences dialog box

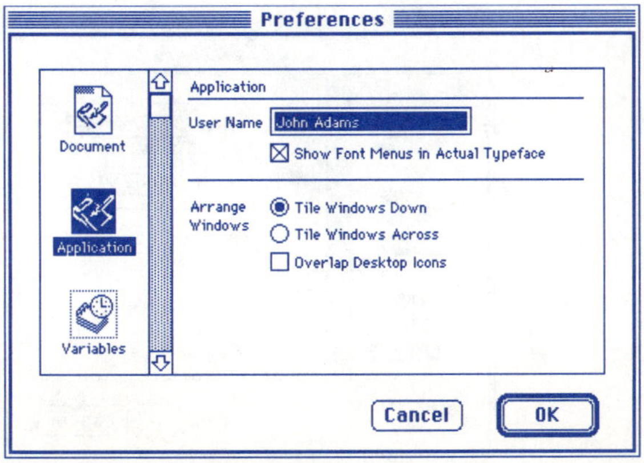

menu are displayed in that font. Uncheck this check box to display the Font menu in the Chicago font. This is discussed in more detail in Chapter 3; this box is checked by default.

The two radio buttons in the Arrange Windows section let you specify how windows are tiled when you use the View menu's Arrange Menus Tile command. In its default state, the Tile Windows Down button is checked.

If the Overlap Desktop Icons box is checked, MacWrite Pro uses the entire width of the screen when opening, zooming or tiling windows. Otherwise, a margin at the left edge of the screen is left, so you can easily switch to the Finder to access a disk icon. We recommend unchecking this box from its default checked state unless your monitor is larger than 13 inches.

Variables Preferences

Variables are used to insert special codes—such as those for the current date or time, or page number—into the document. Items in this tile let you specify the default format for those variables. They are detailed in Chapter 5. The Variables Preference is shown in Figure 1-6.

FIGURE 1-6 The Variables section of the Preferences dialog box

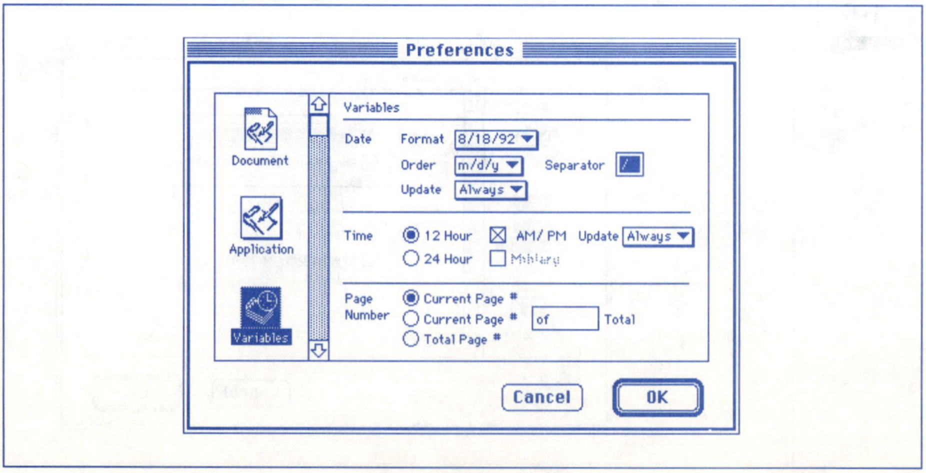

Spelling/Hyphenation Preferences

The Spelling/Hyphenation tile contains a check box to toggle between interactive spelling and no interactive spelling. The Hyphenation section contains a pop-up menu with commands for setting the maximum number of hyphens in a row and fields for entering the smallest word to hyphenate, the minimum number of characters before hyphenation, and the minimum number of characters after hyphenation. There is also a check box to instruct MacWrite Pro whether or not to hyphenate capitalized words. Spelling and hyphenation are discussed in Chapter 8, along with MacWrite Pro's Thesaurus.

Color Preferences

If you have a color monitor, MacWrite Pro can use colors to indicate different elements of the document and interface. The Color tile shown in Figure 1-7 lets you specify which colors are used; it is not available if you do not have a color display, or if your color Mac is set up to black and white or gray/scale mode.

To set a color for an element, hold the mouse button down while pointing to one of the colors. This summons a pop-up menu displaying

FIGURE 1-7 The Color section of the Preferences dialog box

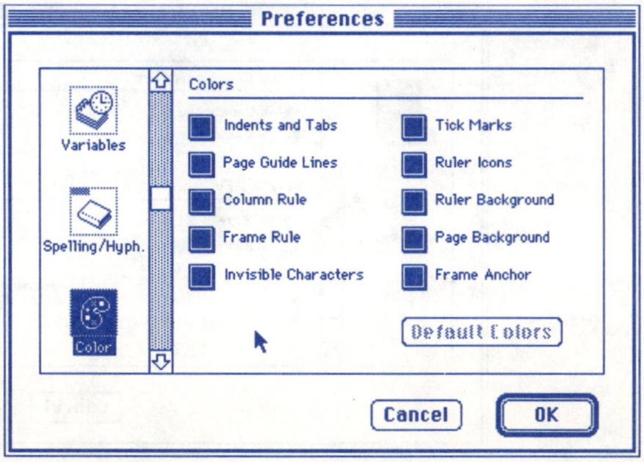

the 81 available colors. While holding down the button, move the mouse pointer to the color you want and then release the mouse button.

Clicking the OK button saves your color choices. The Default Colors button restores all color selections to the default value.

Publishing Preferences

Publishing Preferences govern much of the behavior of MacWrite Pro's Publish and Subscribe capabilities, as shown in Figure 1-8.

Two radio buttons control whether new subscribers are updated automatically or on request only. Two other radio buttons control whether newly published editions are to be sent when the document is saved or on request only. The Publish and Subscribe feature is discussed in Chapter 15.

XTND Preferences

Through a technology called XTND, MacWrite Pro can open files created by a wide variety of other programs, and save to those formats

FIGURE 1-8 The Publishing section of the Preferences dialog box

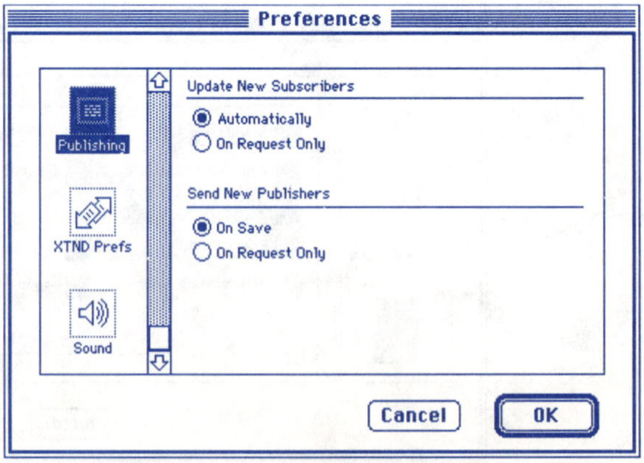

as well. The items in the XTND tile, shown in Figure 1-9, let you set the preferences for any of the translators that have them.

Opening and Saving files using the XTND filters is discussed in Chapter 14.

Sound Preferences

Sound Preferences determine the quality and volume of sound embedded in MacWrite Pro Notes. This Preferences tile contains buttons for selecting good, better, or best sound quality; a field to set the maximum allowed size of sound Notes; and a volume gauge, as shown in Figure 1-10.

MacWrite Pro lets you attach voice comments to notes, and these are discussed in Chapter 15.

Getting Help

MacWrite Pro has two kinds of help, Balloon Help and a more traditional indexed help system that offers you more detailed information about MacWrite Pro features.

FIGURE 1-9 The XTND section of the Preferences dialog box

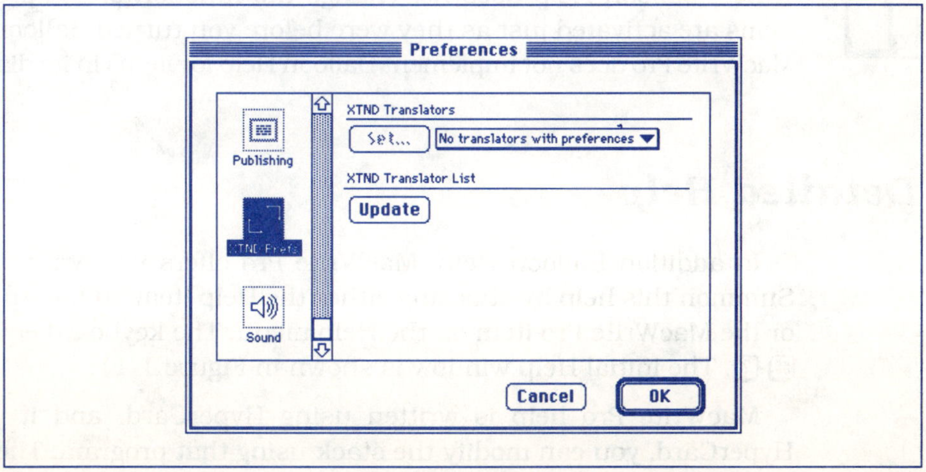

Balloon Help

To enable Balloon Help, choose the Show Balloons command from the Help menu, as shown here:

Note If you are using a version of the Mac operating system earlier than System 7, Balloon Help is not available.

When activated, MacWrite Pro displays small balloons containing help for the first tier of user interface features. As shown here, small comic book-style balloons appear that contain a brief explanation of these features as you point to them.

Note Balloon Help does *not* change the function of the program; all items are activated just as they were before you turned Balloon Help on. MacWrite Pro does not implement Balloon Help for items in its dialog boxes.

Detailed Help

In addition Balloon Help, MacWrite Pro offers its own help system. Summon this help by choosing either the Help item on the Apple menu, or the MacWrite Pro item on the Help menu. The keyboard equivalent is ⌘-?. The initial Help window is shown in Figure 1-11.

MacWrite Pro help is written using HyperCard, and if you know HyperCard, you can modify the stack using that program. The interface

FIGURE 1-10 The Sound section of the Preferences dialog box

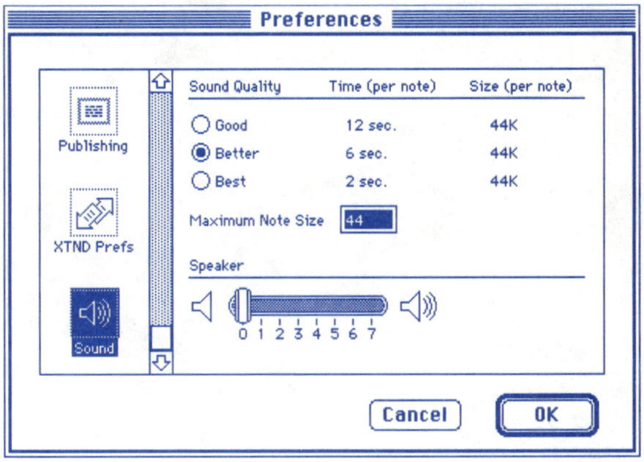

follows standard HyperCard guidelines. It opens in its own window, which you may keep open to switch between Help and the document window. If you are using Help extensively, you might want to keep the Help window open for easy reference.

FIGURE 1-11 The initial Help window

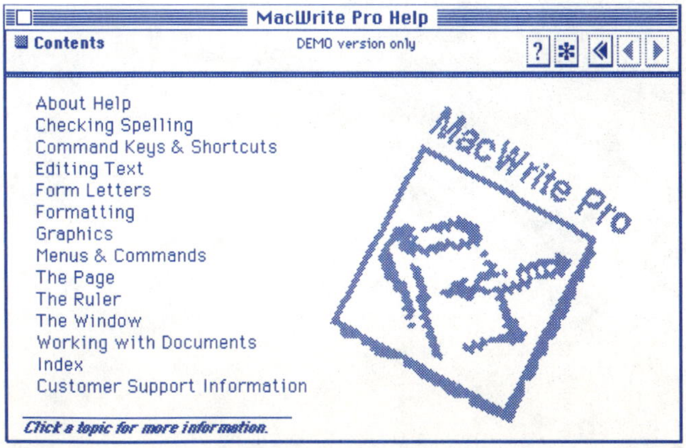

CHAPTER 2

Typing and Editing Text

This chapter discusses typing and editing text in MacWrite Pro. It begins with a basic discussion of typing, goes into the use of both the mouse and the keyboard to move the insertion point and select text, and, finally, describes how you can use certain typographic symbols to improve the appearance of your work on the printed page.

Typing Text with Word Wrap

MacWrite Pro supports a feature common to all word processing programs, *word wrap*. This means that text you type is placed on the current line, and as you reach the end of the line, the program automatically *wraps* new text to appear on the next line.

As you type, you should only use the Return key in three circumstances:

- To end a paragraph
- To end a short line
- To insert a blank line between paragraphs

There are some exceptions to the above rule: Sometimes you want to start a new line, but not a new paragraph, and sometimes you should use paragraph format settings to govern the space between paragraphs instead of inserting a blank line. Both techniques are discussed in Chapter 4.

As you type text, you can backspace over characters using the Del key at the top-right corner of the keyboard (on some keyboards, it may be labeled Backspace). Pressing this key deletes the character to the left of the current insertion point. If text is selected (this will be discussed later), pressing Del deletes the selected text.

Selecting Text and Moving the Insertion Point

The *insertion point* is the point at which text you type is entered into the document—in other words, "where you are now" in the document. When you start a new document, the insertion point is the only item visible on the screen. As you type, text is inserted, and the insertion point moves to the right to accommodate the new text.

The *selection* is any text you have selected. In a sense, it is a "wide" insertion point (or you can say that the insertion point is a selection of no width). Any text you type replaces selected text, and the insertion point moves to the right of that text.

Note What you see when you highlight text depends on several factors. On a Macintosh with a black-and-white monitor (such as the Classic or Powerbook), selected text will be inverted, meaning that it will appear white against a black background. On Macintoshes with color monitors, selected text will remain black, and will be displayed against a colored background. The color of that background is determined by settings controlled by the Color Control Panel. For instructions on using the Color Control Panel, consult your Mac documentation.

Using the Mouse

To move the insertion point with the mouse, move the mouse pointer (an *I-beam*—a thin vertical line with curly "feet" on top and bottom—is the Mac's standard text pointer) to the location at which you want to insert text and click.

You can also select text with the mouse, and there are several techniques for doing so. One of the most basic techniques is to *double-*

click, that is, click the mouse button twice in rapid succession. Double-clicking selects the word at which you are pointing.

You can also *click and drag* to select text. Point to a location at either the beginning or end of the text you want to select, press the mouse button, and while holding the button down, drag across the text to select it. When the text you want to select is highlighted, release the mouse button.

Selecting by clicking and dragging is useful, and there are many occasions when it's the best method. However, there are a number of shortcuts that let you automatically select ranges of text with varying numbers of mouse clicks:

Mouse Click	Selection
Double-click	Single word
Triple-click	Single line
Four-click	Paragraph
Five-click	Entire document

Double-clicking is generally easy to do, but you may need to practice triple-clicking and beyond before they feel natural.

Note If nothing happens when you try these clicking techniques, you probably need to click faster. The allowable time between the clicks can be adjusted from the Mac's Mouse Control Panel.

If you want to select the entire document, you have seen two ways to do so, both of which are rather cumbersome. You can start at the beginning of the document and click and drag through the entire document, which can be very awkward in a long document, or you can five-click within it, which can be tricky. There is an easier way: the Select All command on the Edit menu. When you choose Select All or press its keyboard equivalent, ⌘-A, the entire document is selected.

Using the Keyboard

Navigating with the mouse, as easy as it is, is not always the most efficient way to move the insertion point. Just moving your hand from the keyboard to the mouse can be enough of an interruption to cause you to you lose your train of thought. MacWrite Pro offers several keyboard shortcuts for jumping around the document.

The Mac keyboard has a set of directional arrow keys. These arrows point up, down, to the left, and to the right. Different keyboards have different layouts for these keys.

Note The arrow keys do not move the mouse pointer. Instead, they move the insertion point directly.

The arrow keys do pretty much what you think they would do. The ↑ moves your insertion point up one line, the ↓ moves it down one line. The ← and → move the insertion point to the left or right one character at a time.

When moving the insertion point up or down, MacWrite Pro attempts to maintain the current horizontal position on the line. If the insertion point is in the middle of a line that extends across the page, and the line above it also extends across the page, using the ↑ takes you to the same point on the previous line—that is, it puts it at approximately the same number of characters from the left edge as it was previously. If, on the other hand, the line above is shorter than the current line, the insertion point is placed at the end of the line. If you press the ↑ again and the line above the short line is longer, the insertion point is again placed at the same number of characters from the left edge as it was with the longer line.

Making Bigger Keyboard Jumps

You can also use the keyboard alone to make bigger jumps through your text.

MacWrite Pro uses two modifier keys with the arrow keys to let you make larger jumps. These are the Option and ⌘ keys. To use them, hold down the modifier key before you press the arrow key.

The effects of the modifier keys are shown in Table 2-1.

TABLE 2-1 Effect of Modifier Keys When Used with the Arrow Keys to Move the Insertion Point

Arrow Key	With Option	With ⌘
←	Previous word	Left margin
→	Beginning of next word	Right margin
↑	Beginning of paragraph	Beginning of document
↓	End of paragraph	End of document

Navigating Through a Document

Navigating through a document is different from moving the insertion point or selecting text. Navigation lets you view different portions of the document without altering the selection or insertion point. There are a couple of ways to move through the document, using either the keyboard or the mouse.

Scrolling

Chances are, if you are familiar with the Mac, you already know how to use the *scroll bars*, the shaded bars that you see on the right and bottom edges of the document windows. MacWrite Pro gives you both vertical and horizontal scrolling. Mostly you will scroll through documents vertically, but horizontal scrolling is there when you need it.

The *scroll box* is located on the scroll bar. Click and drag the box to move through your document. This technique is fast, but not terribly exact. It's great for going to the beginning, end, or perhaps the middle of your document, but it's only so-so for going to a specific location.

On either end of the scroll bar is an arrow. To scroll through your document approximately one line at a time you click the arrow. The ↓ moves you toward the end of your document, and the ↑ moves you toward its beginning. To scroll through your document one screen at a time, click anywhere in the gray area of the scroll bar between the directional arrow and the scroll box. If you are using an extended keyboard, the [Pg Up] and [Pg Dn] keys perform the same function.

Note Scrolling does not affect the location of the insertion point. If, for example, your insertion point is at the beginning of your document and you scroll to the end of the document, the insertion point stays at the beginning of the document. So, if you start typing after scrolling to the end, the display will jump to the beginning of the document, where the letters you just typed appear.

Navigating with the Keyboard

Extended Mac keyboards contain four keys that you can use to move through the document. These four keys are located above the arrow keys on Apple's extended keyboard, and are part of a cluster of six keys.

They are labeled [Home], [End], [Pg Up], and [Pg Dn]. Here's a rundown of what they do. Remember that they change only the portion of the document that MacWrite Pro is displaying to you; they do not move the insertion point.

[Home]	Scrolls the display to the beginning of the very first page in your document (if you are already there, nothing happens)
[End]	Scrolls the display to the end of the very last page in your document (whether or not it actually contains text)
[Pg Up]	Scrolls the display backward one window in your document
[Pg Dn]	Scrolls the display forward one window in your document

The Go To Page # Command [Shift]-[⌘]-[G]

If you know the exact page number of the location you want to display, you can use the View menu's Go To Page # command (the keyboard equivalent is [Shift]-[⌘]-[G]). This command summons the following dialog box with a field for you to type in the page number.

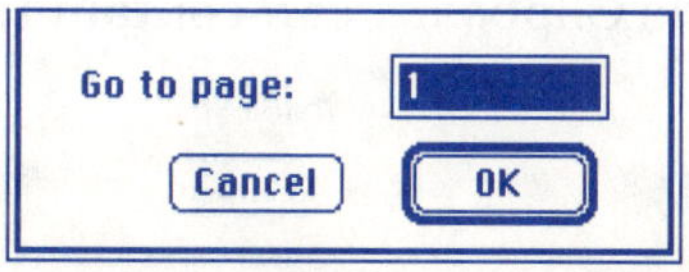

Note You don't actually move your insertion point to the page you've entered, you only view the page.

If you type a number for a page that doesn't exist (such as page 100 in a 90-page document or page 0 of any document), MacWrite Pro beeps and tells you there is no such page.

Note MacWrite Pro has a hidden shortcut for summoning the Go to page dialog box. Double-click the page number display in the bottom-left corner of the document window. This is the same as calling the dialog box from the menu or using the keyboard equivalent.

Copying, Deleting, and Moving Text

The Edit menu contains these five commands for copying, deleting, and moving text: Undo, Cut, Copy, Clear, and Paste. Undo is discussed in the next section.

Use Cut, Copy, Clear, and Paste to delete or move selections of text. These commands are the tools you will use. Here's a rundown of how to use these commands:

Cut ⌘-X

The Cut command (key equivalent: ⌘-X) deletes the selection and places it on the Mac's *Clipboard*. The Clipboard is a storage facility in the Mac's memory. Use this command when you want to move some text to a different location in the document, or even to another document or application, since the contents of the Clipboard remain when you quit an application. The Clipboard can contain text or graphics.

Copy ⌘-C

The Copy command (key equivalent: ⌘-C) places the selection in the Clipboard just like the Cut command, but doesn't disturb the original selection. Use this command when you want to clone a selection to another location in the document or to another document or application.

Note Since the Clipboard can only contain one item at a time, both Cut and Copy have the effect of destroying the previous contents of the Clipboard.

Clear Del

The Clear command (keyboard equivalent: Del) deletes the selection without placing it in the Clipboard.

Paste ⌘-V

The Paste command (key equivalent: ⌘-V) places the text or graphic in the Clipboard at the current insertion point. If you have text selected instead of just an insertion point, the selection is replaced with the contents of the Clipboard. The Paste command has no effect on the contents of the Clipboard; that is, it simply places a copy of the text at the insertion point, without removing it from the Clipboard.

Viewing the Clipboard

You can see what's in the Clipboard with the Edit menu Show Clipboard command. This opens up a window that displays the current contents of the Clipboard. If you are doing a lot of editing with many copies and pastes, you can leave this window open, and resize the main document window, as shown here:

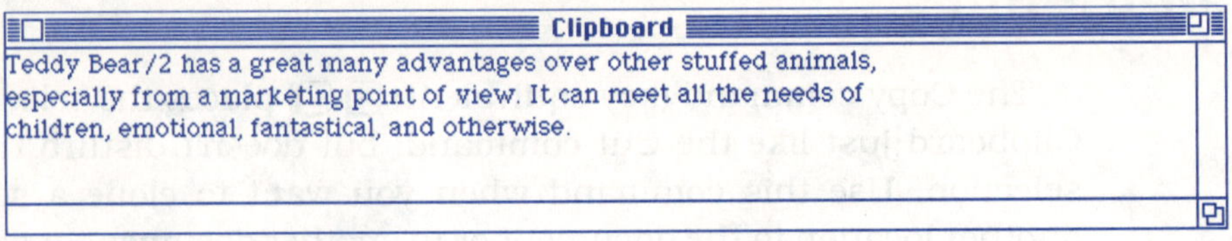

The Clipboard window is constantly updated, always showing the current contents of the Clipboard.

Styles and the Clipboard

In most instances when you move text between applications with the Clipboard, you move just the text, not the styles. So, if you select a block of text that contains, for example, several words in boldface or italic and then paste the block of text into a document created by another application, that style information is lost. However, when you paste text to another location within MacWrite Pro (whether it's a different spot in the same document, or another document) style information is retained.

Note There is an exception to this generality. When you move text via the Clipboard between a MacWrite Pro document and a document created by another Claris Corp. application, style information is retained.

Undo ⌘-Z

Like all law-abiding Mac applications, MacWrite Pro supports the Undo command (key equivalent: ⌘-Z). MacWrite Pro remembers the last action you took that affects text in your document and lets you reverse its action. Actions like scrolling through the document, or choosing menu commands such as Show Clipboard that don't alter the contents of document, aren't "undoable."

The name of the Undo command changes as you issue commands. For example, if you change the font of some text, the name of the Undo command will change to Undo Font Change, as shown here:

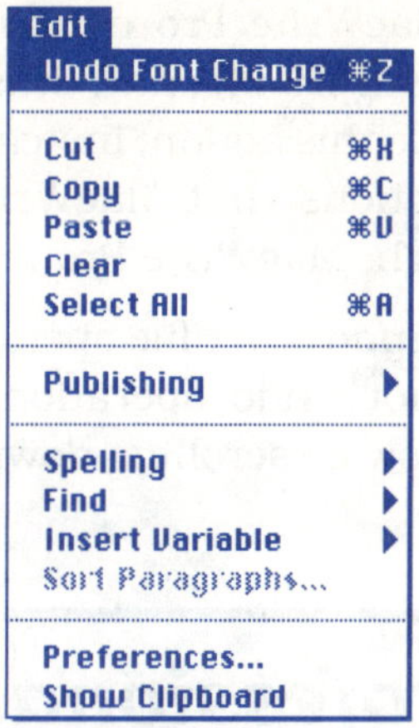

If you execute Undo Font Change, its name on the menu will change again, this time to Redo Font Change, as shown here:

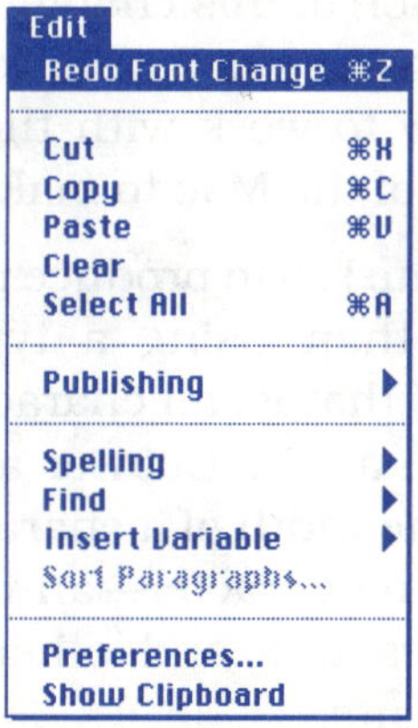

Executing the command at this point will redo the original command, in this case a font change.

Note For most users, this change of the name of the menu command is just a curiosity, but if you are using the Undo command with a macro program such as CESoftware's QuicKeys, this will have to be taken into account.

What Cannot Be Undone

There are certain actions that you can't undo, even with MacWrite Pro. These include consequential actions, such as closing a document without saving. That MacWrite Pro cannot Undo closing a document without saving it is not surprising, and thus MacWrite Pro doesn't warn you that you cannot Undo this action; instead you are asked to confirm the action. Before other actions that MacWrite Pro cannot undo (such as global changes), though, MacWrite Pro warns you.

You cannot undo other file operations, such as Save, Save As, or Print. Also, you cannot undo operations that don't relate to text, such as resizing a window or scrolling down.

Producing Professional-Looking Documents

The next portion of this chapter takes a slightly different approach to typing and editing in MacWrite Pro than you've seen so far. Instead of a reference to how to work with the program, it shows you how to use special features of the Mac to make your type look better.

Using MacWrite Pro to produce printed documents on the Mac is quite a bit different than using a typewriter. Typewriters generally use *monospace* type, that is, all characters have the same width. With a few exceptions (such as the Courier and Monaco fonts), this isn't the case with the Mac. The width of a character on screen and on the page varies from character to character—an i takes up less room than an m. This section discusses this and other aspects of producing aesthetically pleasing documents.

Double Spaces

The chief habit to break when you switch from a typewriter (or some more primitive word processors) to MacWrite Pro is that of typing two spaces after the period at the end of a sentence. On a typewriter, this is desirable because spaces and periods take up the same amount of space, and the extra space is needed to help guide the eye to the beginning of the next sentence. With proportionally spaced fonts, this extra space is not needed. This is a tough habit to break. In Chapter 6, you will see how to use the Find and Change function to strip the extra spaces from your document.

Accented Characters

The Mac lets you type special accented characters using the Option key. Table 2-2 gives a summary of these keys.

Note Words containing special accented characters are flagged as misspelled by MacWrite Pro's spelling checker. Chapter 3 explains how to use available foreign language dictionaries with documents that contain text in both U.S. English and other languages.

In addition to accented characters, there are a number of characters that you can type that don't appear on the keyboard. Use the KeyCaps desk accessory to see them. Consult the user's guide for your Mac to learn how to use KeyCaps.

Smart Quotes

Typewriters usually only have two sets of quotes—the single and the double quote. These quotes are vertical marks, and don't "curl." That is, the same characters both open and close a quotation. Quotation marks that curl in matched opening and closing sets are called *smart quotes*.

TABLE 2-2 Producing Accented Characters on the Mac

Accent Mark	Key Combination
Grave accent (\`)	Option-\` then the character to be accented; e.g., Option-\` E would be è
Acute accent (′)	Option-E, then the c aracter (e.g., é)
Circumflex (^)	Option-I, then the character (e.g., î)
Tilde (~)	Option-N, then the character (e.g., ñ)
Umlaut (¨)	Option-U then the character (e.g., ü)
C with a cedilla: Ç	Option-C

Unfortunately, producing smart quotes is cumbersome on Mac keyboards (it may be cumbersome on Macs, but on IBM compatibles, it's almost impossible). To type an opening double quote, you use the nonintuitive Option-[keyboard combination. That's not so bad, but to produce a closing double quote, you don't use Option-] as you might expect, but Shift-Option-[. To produce an opening single quote, use Option-], and Shift-Option-] produces a closing single quote.

Fortunately, MacWrite Pro includes its own Smart Quotes feature. You can turn it on with the Preferences command on the File menu.

Note Even at its advanced age, the Mac is still more advanced in many respects than some of the large systems that many of us encounter. So if you use MacWrite Pro to, say, compose a message for an online service such as CompuServe or America Online, smart quotes will be displayed by a seemingly unrelated character, usually a U. As a result, you and your fancy MacWrite Pro typographer quotes aren't going to look so smart displayed on one of these systems.

If you know ahead of time that your document is destined for a non-Mac system, use ⌘ - ' and ⌘ - " as you type to override the Smart Quote Preference setting. For a good way to "stupidify" existing smart quotes in a MacWrite Pro document, see Chapter 6.

Dashes

When you learned to type, you learned to use two hyphens, as in --, to replace the regular em dash that's used in typeset materials. An *em dash* is approximately as wide as the capital letter M in the type size currently in use; the *en dash* is as wide as the capital N in the type size.

On Mac keyboards, the hyphen and underscore characters are to the right of the 0 above the letters.

Most Mac fonts, however, do feature the em dash and en dash characters. To type the em dash, hold down the Option and Shift keys, and press the underscore key—the same one that produces the hyphen. To produce an en dash, hold down Option and press the hyphen key.

Use an em dash within a single sentence the way you would normally use a dash, when a sentence has a logical break. Use an en dash to represent the mathematical minus sign (–32°) and between numbers that indicate a range (rows 5–9, the years 1969–1973). In most other instances, use the standard hyphen, produced by pressing the hyphen key.

Ligatures

A *ligature* is a special single character that takes the place of two other characters, making for a nicer-looking document. Two of these are supported on the Mac, and they are shown in Table 2-3.

Italics

Typewriters generally do not feature different type styles without cumbersome replacement of type elements (wheels or balls). Thus, when you learned to type, you learned to use underlining to indicate italics. Since the Mac can italicize characters, you will want to take advantage of this feature. Use underlining only where a good style manual (such as the *Chicago Manual of Style* or the *Random House Handbook*) specifically recommends underlining. Italics and the formatting of characters are discussed in Chapter 3.

Punctuation

Remember to keep punctuation in the same style as the characters preceding it. For example, if a word is in italics and it is followed by a comma, be sure that the next character, whether it's a space, period, or a comma, is also in the italics style. This keeps the spacing regular.

TABLE 2-3 Using the fi and fl Ligatures on the Mac

Ligature	Replaces which letters	How to Type
ﬁ	f i	Shift-Option-5
ﬂ	f l	Shift-Option-6

Fractional Character Widths

Use Fractional Character Widths to kern pairs of characters in increments less than a point wide. Higher resolution printers such as Apple's LaserWriter and StyleWriter and the Hewlett-Packard DeskWriter can print within a fraction of a point. So if you will be using a higher resolution printer, the printed output looks better with Fractional Character Widths turned on.

Note Standard Mac screen resolution, 72 dpi (dots per inch), lacks the precision to accurately display text with the Fractional Character Widths turned on. As a result, in 100 percent view, text will not be displayed accurately. You may also find that the screen is redrawn more slowly, especially if you are using one of the slower Macs. You can turn the option off while editing and then turn it on just before printing. For fine tuning just before printing, select a higher resolution view, such as 200 percent. To learn how to use the different view resolutions, see Chapter 1.

Set Fractional Character Widths in the Documents tile of the Preferences menu.

Ellipses

On a typewriter, you normally type three periods (...) for ellipses. Ellipses are used to indicate deletions from printed material. To produce real ellipses rather than retro imitations, use Option-:.

Summary

MacWrite Pro features a powerful typing and editing environment. Many of the skills you learned in this chapter will come in handy with almost any Mac application that deals with text.

To effectively and efficiently edit the text of a MacWrite Pro document, you need a comfortable understanding of the basic editing tools. In this chapter you learned about the three MacWrite Pro cursors (insertion point, I-beam, and pointer) and how to move about your text with both the mouse and the keyboard.

You learned several ways to navigate through documents using the keyboard, the mouse, and MacWrite Pro's Go To Page # command.

The very powerful concept of text selection is described, along with related techniques such as copying, cutting, and moving text both within a single MacWrite Pro document and to documents created by other applications.

The Mac lets you use many text elements previously limited to professional typographers. These include accented characters, smart quotes, em and en dashes, italics, and ellipses.

CHAPTER 3

Formatting Characters

One of the several things that make MacWrite Pro the tool of choice for word processing is the flexible and very powerful way it lets you format your documents. Four levels of formatting are available:

- *Character formatting*, discussed in this chapter
- *Paragraph formatting*, discussed in Chapter 4
- *Section formatting*, discussed in Chapter 5
- *Document-wide formatting*, discussed in Chapter 5

Formatting characters means applying style to individual characters in your document—it is easy to do. For example, you can make specific words **bold**, *italic*, underlined, or any combination, such as ***bold and italic***. Individual characters can also be in different fonts, or typefaces, from the text around them, or in different sizes (for an in-depth discussion of fonts on the Mac, see Appendix D). This chapter shows you how to apply styles to characters as you type (select the font, size, or style and then type) or as you edit your text (select the text you want to format and then apply the formatting).

Formatting Characters in MacWrite Pro

MacWrite Pro gives you a great deal of control over how characters appear in your final document. First, there's the standard set of Mac format capabilities: different fonts; sizes; and styles, such as bold, italic, underline, outlined, and shadowed text. MacWrite Pro also has a few capabilities that are rarely, if ever, found in other Mac word processors. These capabilities include the ability to specify that a particular portion of text is in a foreign language (at last, a method for spell checking multilingual documents), several different kinds of underlining, and control over the horizontal spacing of text.

In keeping with its flexible, visible user interface, MacWrite Pro also gives you different sets of tools, some of which overlap, for formatting characters. All character-formatting commands are available on the Font, Size, and Style menus, and many of the commands also have keyboard shortcuts. Additionally, as you saw in Chapter 1, MacWrite lets you display a Text palette, which includes all the formatting commands. As you become more skilled at using MacWrite Pro, you'll probably find yourself using the keyboard shortcuts for applying styles as you write, but for editing you'll find the Text palette very handy. If you place it on the right edge of the window about halfway between the top and the bottom, its formatting commands will never be too far from your mouse.

The Font Menu

The names of the available fonts are listed on MacWrite Pro's Font menu. You can tell MacWrite Pro to display each font on the menu as it is displayed in your document when you use it. If you need to turn this feature on, go to Preferences, select the Application tile, and check the box for the "Show Fonts in actual typefaces" option. The Font menu then looks like this:

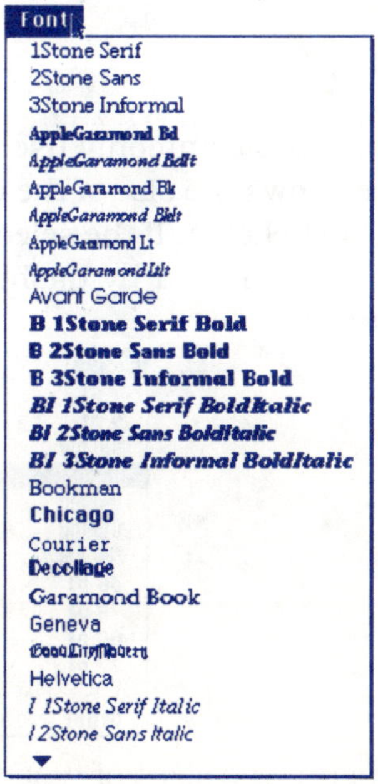

This technique takes the guesswork out of selecting a font. You can temporarily reverse this setting by holding down the Option key when selecting the Font menu. For example, if you have set MacWrite Pro to display the actual typefaces on the menu, hold down the Option key when selecting the menu to display all the font names in the standard Macintosh menu font (Chicago).

The display of actual typefaces has a couple of drawbacks. Some fonts, for example Zapf Dingbats, don't contain recognizable characters, so it's up to you to interpret those strange characters on the Font menu. Some decorative fonts, also, do not include any lowercase letters. In these cases, you won't be able to read the font listing. This feature can also slow down the display of the Font menu, especially if you're using MacWrite Pro on a Mac Plus or Mac Classic, although MacWrite Pro will display the Font menu faster after the first time you ask it to display the menu.

The Font menu does not include keyboard equivalents. The best way to choose a font is to either choose it from the Font menu or from the Text palette.

The Size Menu

The Size menu lists commonly used type sizes; a check mark next to a particular size shows the size of the currently selected text. To select a listed type size, just click it. If the selection contains text of several sizes, all those sizes are indicated by dashes next to the type size. The Size menu is shown here:

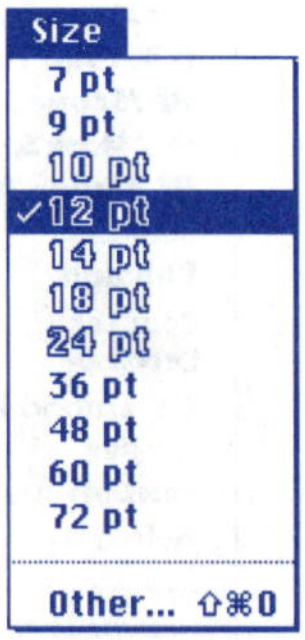

In the Size menu, the sizes of type that are currently available to the system are shown in outline type. So, for example, if you have a bitmap of Times 12 installed in your system, the 12 will appear outlined; if Times 14 is not installed, that size will be shown in plain text. TrueType fonts are shown in all the available sizes.

You can use the Shift-⌘-> and Shift-⌘-< keyboard equivalents to make selected text larger or smaller. These shortcuts change text sizes in increments equal to adjacent commands on the Size menu. For example, the sizes adjacent to 12 points on the Size menu are 10 points and 14 points. When your text is larger than 72 points, these shortcuts adjust the text size in 24-point increments. MacWrite Pro will also let you increase and decrease font sizes by single-point increments with the Shift-Option-⌘-< and Shift-Option-⌘-> keyboard equivalents.

If one of the sizes of type on the Size menu is not right for you, use the Other command to summon the Font Size dialog box, shown here:

You can enter any number from 0 to 500 (points) in the Font size dialog box. You are not limited to whole numbers, either. For example, if a line is a little too wide at 26 points, try 25.5. You are, however, limited to quarter-point increments. Click OK or press Enter or Return to enable your choice and return to the document; click Cancel to ignore your entry and return to the document.

The Style Menu

Figure 3-1 shows MacWrite Pro's Style menu and the corresponding Text palette, which includes most of the same capabilities. This section describes the first 11 items on the Style menu (through the Character Spacing item) plus Custom Styles; the remaining items concern Style sheets for paragraph formatting and are detailed in Chapter 7.

The Style menu and the Text palette contain essentially the same tools. Choosing a command from the Style menu has the same effect as clicking in a box on the Text palette; it turns the style on or off for the selected text. If a particular style on the Style menu is in effect for the selected text, a check mark appears next to that style name; in the Text palette, an x appears in the check box next to the style name. If a selection has more than one style, small dashes appear next to the style name instead of check marks.

FIGURE 3-1 MacWrite Pro's (a) Style menu and (b) Text palette are alternative tools for character formatting

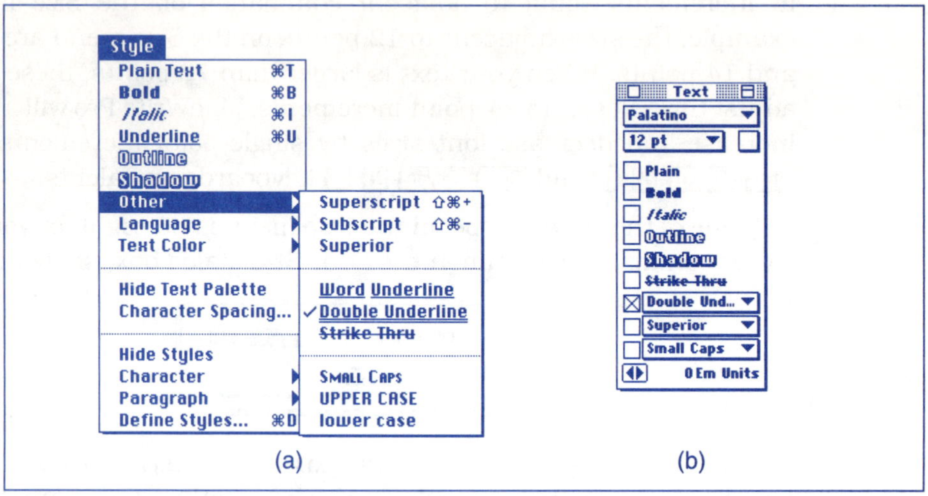

The following sections describe the entire range of commands on the Style menu.

Plain Text ⌘-T

When text is formatted as plain text, it has no special formatting. If you are using paragraph styles, this command means that the text takes on the background formatting of the paragraph it belongs to. (To learn about the power of paragraph styles, see Chapter 7.)

Bold ⌘-B

Bold text is typically used in headlines or for special emphasis of specific words in text. Use it sparingly because blocks of bold text are difficult to read. The Bold style has the traditional ⌘-B keyboard equivalent.

Bold and italic styles are a special case for fonts; there are several ways that bold and italic characters can be drawn on the Mac. This is how they differ.

When you installed PostScript fonts in your system, you may have noticed that there are several versions of the font. For example, the Stone Serif font comes in various styles: Stone Serif, Stone Serif Bold, Stone Serif BoldItalic, and Stone Serif Italic. Other fonts might have some other versions. If you are using one of these fonts and choose a Bold style, the Mac automatically uses the Stone Serif Bold font for drawing the text. However, you don't see that the font has changed when you look at the Font menu. If you're using a bitmap only or TrueType font, the Mac determines what to do with the text using an *algorithm*. That means that the programming code inside the machine that draws fonts determines what to do with it. If it's a bitmap font, the Mac makes all the lines 1 or more pixels wider. If the font is a TrueType font, the font definition includes instructions about how to make the font bold—differing numbers of pixels are added to the lines in the font in accord with the design of the font. So, if you're using a PostScript font, you can sometimes get a little better control over the appearance of the font on screen by changing the font used for a word instead of using the Style menu.

Italic ⌘-I

Italic text (what is normally underlined when you are typing on a typewriter) is tilted to the right a certain amount. As with bold text, use italic text sparingly—it's difficult to read in large blocks. Check a good style guide, such as *The Chicago Manual of Style*, or the *Random House Handbook*, to find out how to use italic type effectively.

When using the italic style, don't forget that punctuation immediately following italicized text should be in italics as well. This includes periods, commas, hyphens, semicolons, colons, question marks, and exclamation marks. The first space after an italicized word should be in italic also; this is necessary to prevent italic characters from colliding with adjacent, normal, "upright" characters. The keyboard equivalent is ⌘-I.

Underline ⌘-U

The Underline command underlines the selected text or turns underlining on for characters being typed. The keyboard equivalent is ⌘-U.

Underlining is usually used in manuscript preparation to indicate text that is to be typeset in italics. If your text is to be prepared by you or others using a Mac for typesetting or final printing, use italics instead of underlining. If your manuscript is going to a copy editor or typographer for separate typesetting, use underlining.

Note that the Underline command differs between the Style menu and the Text palette. When you choose the Style menu Underline command, MacWrite Pro underlines each word, including the spaces between words.

Three additional kinds of underlining options are found on the Other submenu of the Style menu. These are

- *Word Underline*, which underlines each word but not the spaces between them
- *Double Underline*, which works just like the Underline command except that it puts a double underline under each word and each space between each word
- *Strike Thru*, generally used to indicate proposed deletions from text, which draws the underscore through the characters and spaces in the selected text

You can't select Word Underline and Double Underline at the same time. If you find this a limitation, you can use MacWrite Pro's powerful Find command (see Chapter 6 for details on how to do this) to create the same effect. (This technique involves some extra work, so if you're considering turning to Chapter 6 to find out how, you might want to consider a more judicious use of your underlining tools.)

These options are arranged differently on the Text palette. The Strike Thru style has its own check box, and the Underline style is on a pop-up menu that lets you choose between regular underlining and the other styles.

Outline and Shadow

The Outline command and the Shadow command are both located in the Style menu and the Text palette. These styles are normally used only for decorative effects, so use them sparingly. They work best in headline text in documents such as party invitations or informal newsletters.

Other

The Other command is actually a submenu (indicated by a right arrowhead) that pops out when you are holding down the mouse button on its name in the Style menu. If you continue holding the mouse button while you slide the mouse pointer to the side, you can select one of these options. You have already read about the underline commands on the Other submenu.

Superscript Shift-⌘-+, Subscript Shift-⌘--, and Superior The Superscript, Subscript, and Superior commands are on the Other submenu. The keyboard equivalent for Superscript is Shift-⌘-+ and for Subscript it's Shift-⌘--. There is no keyboard equivalent for Superior.

These styles aren't used very often, but when you need them, you're glad they're there, as they help give your document a polished, professional look. Superscript and subscript are most commonly used for footnotes or in specific expressions ($E=mc^2$, H_2O), or for marketing ($Aliens^3$). MacWrite Pro also automatically creates superscripted footnote references for you each time you use the Format menu's Insert Footnote command. Both these styles add more space to the line height above or below the line containing the super- or subscripted text. The superscripted or subscripted text is moved up or down half a line from the other text (that is, if the line is 12-point text, the character is adjusted by 6 points either way).

Superior text works in much the same way as superscripted text, but the size reduction and the amount by which it raises the superior text is different. It raises the baseline and reduces the size of the selected text to a third of what it was before.

Small Caps, Upper Case, and Lower Case The Small Caps, Upper Case, and Lower Case commands are also on the Other submenu. Small Caps is a special text style in which uppercase letters are standard height and lowercase letters are represented by upper case characters one third smaller. Large chunks of text formatted with the Small Caps style can also be hard to read, but it can be quite pleasing when used carefully in, say, a letterhead.

The Upper Case and Lower Case style commands are straightforward. Affected text is changed to match the command, for example, "ALL UPPERCASE" and "all lowercase." These two commands are very useful, and after you develop the habit of using them, you will likely find yourself longing for an Initial Caps command to round out the set.

Language

The Language command (actually a submenu of commands) is unique to MacWrite Pro and, if you deal with more than one language in a single document, you'll find it exceptionally handy. Unlike other character styles, which control the appearance of text, the Language command controls how MacWrite Pro's spelling checker treats the text. If you're working in the United States, you probably have the English-US dictionary, but Claris Corp. offers a variety of other language dictionaries, as well. If you have purchased, say, the French dictionary, you can effortlessly check the spelling of a bilingual English and French document. All you have to do is tell MacWrite Pro which portions of the text are in French. Then when you run the spelling checker, MacWrite Pro will automatically use the appropriate dictionary as it checks your spelling.

You apply the Language style the same way you apply other styles: Select the text and then choose the appropriate dictionary from the Style menu's Language submenu. MacWrite Pro checks to see which language version of the Mac operating system you are running and then it sets the default language accordingly. In North America this usually means that MacWrite Pro defaults to the English-US dictionary.

The Language menu's None option also affects how the MacWrite Pro spelling checker deals with your text. When you apply the Language None style to text, the spelling checker ignores and does not check that text. If you are working on a document that contains lists of acronyms or nonstandard abbreviations that you don't want to add to your user dictionary, just apply the Language None style; thereafter the spelling checker will skip those words.

Text Color

In typography, "text color" refers to how heavy or light text is on the page. Text color has a different definition in MacWrite Pro. Choose the Text Color submenu from the Style menu to see the Color palette.

Selecting one of those colors applies that color to the text. (The same options are also available on the Text palette.) When running in 256-color mode or greater, MacWrite Pro's Color palette gives you 81 color options. When running in 16-color mode you get 16 color options, and when running in 4 or 1 color mode, you get a list of 8 color names. If you are working on a black-and-white Mac, you can still assign one of the 8 colors listed by name on the menu. When the document is then printed on a color printer or viewed on a color Mac, your color selections will be displayed in the color you have selected.

If you are working on a grayscale monitor, you'll get to select from shades of gray unless you change the display to 4-bit mode or 1-bit mode. In this case, you get the same list of 8 color names you get when working in 4-bit and 1-bit color mode. (These options are accessed through the Monitor Control Panel. See the manual that came with your Mac for a complete explanation.)

Unless you have a color or grayscale printer or are preparing documents to be printed as slides or read on screen, you probably won't use Text Color too often.

Caution Watch out for the white color—it makes your text invisible on the screen and on the page.

Character Spacing (Kerning)

Character spacing, also known as kerning, adjusts the horizontal space between characters. Character spacing can be accessed from the Text palette or by choosing the Style menu's Character Spacing command, which summons the Character spacing dialog box, shown here:

You can type in any number from –100 to 100, including fractions. Negative numbers move the selected characters closer together; positive numbers move them apart. The default value is 0, which causes MacWrite Pro to use the standard character spacing for the font and size in use.

There are two primary uses for the Character Spacing command. The first is in headlines with large type. You can make pairs of characters such as WA tuck closer together. You can also use character spacing when copyfitting—you can select an entire document, and type in a value such as –1, to see if it shrinks enough to fit the specified area on your page.

Custom Character Styles

Formatting characters or groups of characters in your documents is fairly straightforward once you learn the tools at hand. But what if you regularly need to format text in, say, French Language Helvetica italic? Making three trips to the menu bar or three trips to the tool palettes every time you needed to use this custom style would quickly become tedious. MacWrite Pro's solution to this dilemma is custom character styles that you build yourself.

This feature is discussed in greater detail in Chapter 7. But if you need to use this feature right now, here's how to do it. The last command on the Style menu is Define Styles. The keyboard equivalent is ⌘-D. This command summons the Define Styles dialog box, shown here:

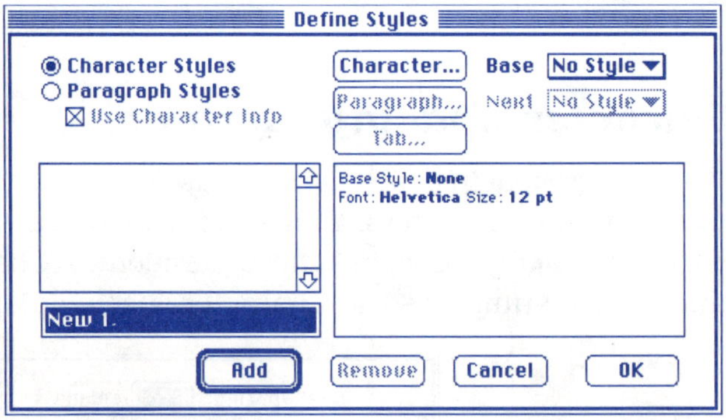

In the upper left of this box you see two main options: Character Styles and Paragraph Styles.

When you first open the Define Styles dialog box, select the Character Styles radio button (located in the upper-left corner) if it is not already selected. Below the Character Styles radio button is a scrolling list box of available custom character styles. If you're dealing with a new document and have a fresh copy of MacWrite Pro, this list will be empty.

To the right you see the Character button. Click once here to summon the Character dialog box. You can also summon the Character dialog box by pressing ⌘-M once the Define Styles dialog is open. (Pressing the ⌘ key at this point will reveal ⌘-*key* equivalents for all the Define Styles buttons.)

It may have seemed like a long journey, but you have finally arrived at the place where you do the actual work of defining your custom character styles. You'll first see pop-up menus for the name and size of the font. Click on the pop-up menu and make your selection. In this example, Helvetica is already selected, and we will accept the suggested 12-point type size.

Below the pop-up font menu is a list of the available style options. These are the same options that are available on both the Style menu and on the Text palette. In this example, you should click to check the Italic option.

Below the list of styles you'll see a pop-up menu for languages. If you're working with the U.S. version of MacWrite Pro, the English-US style will be selected. In this example, you should click on the pop-up menu and select French.

Immediately to the right of the Language pop-up menu is a kerning field. Enter the number of em units (the amount of space the letter m takes up); positive numbers to move the letters apart, and negative numbers to move the letters closer together. This works the same way as the Character Spacing command described earlier in this chapter.

The final option in the Character dialog box is the text color. This works exactly as it does from the Style menu or text palette. Click the OK button to close the Character dialog box.

Clicking the OK button makes the Define Styles dialog box reappear. On the right side of the box is a description of your newly defined style, including font, size, style, and language. The only thing left to do is to give it a name. The field for typing in the name of the new style is already selected, so just type in a name. Giving custom styles that you create sensible names is a good idea. In this example, "French Italic Helvetica" would be an excellent choice.

The name of the new style you have created has now been added to the Style menu's Character submenu. It has also been added to the Styles palette list of character styles.

Custom styles are saved with the document. This means that when you create a new document or open an existing one that does not contain the custom style, your custom style is not automatically available. MacWrite Pro does, however, give you a simple way to access the styles located in other files. The Styles palette File menu has an Open Custom Styles command, which opens a standard Mac file dialog box. Use this command to find the file containing the custom styles you want. When you open this file from the Styles palette, the custom styles in that document are made available in the current or active document, and the names of those newly opened styles appear both on the Style menu's Character submenu and in the Styles palette list of character styles.

If you regularly use a group of custom styles, you should store them in a MacWrite Pro stationery document. (See Chapter 14 for a complete description of MacWrite Pro stationery documents.) This way you can easily manage sets of custom character styles. When you know you will be using a specific set of styles in a new document, open the stationery document containing that set of styles to create a new document instead of using the File menu's New command.

MacWrite Pro Text Preferences

Some of MacWrite Pro's preferences affect how text is styled on screen. Here's a description of the Preferences that affect character formatting. (For a complete description of the Edit menu's Preferences command see Chapter 1.)

Fractional Character Widths

The Fractional Character Widths preference in the Document section of the Preferences dialog box, shown here:

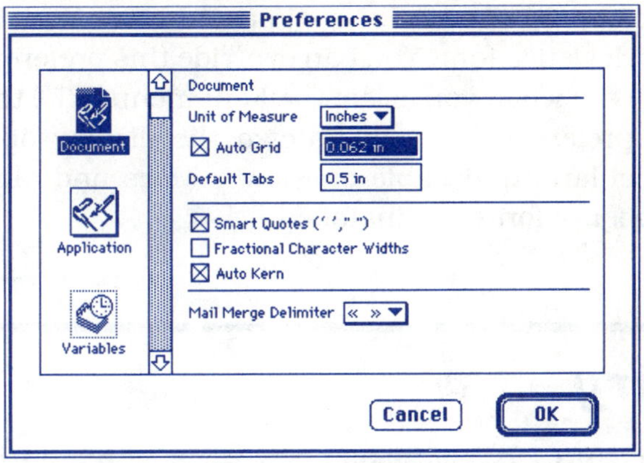

is document specific. If Fractional Character Widths are in effect, MacWrite Pro does a better job of printing proportional fonts. This doesn't affect such monospace fonts as Courier or Monaco. Unless you've zoomed in to view a portion of your document at an enlarged size, you probably will not notice much difference in the way text is displayed with this option.

If you are running on a slower Mac, such as a Mac Plus or a Mac Classic, it's probably a good idea to keep this preference turned off because it may slow things down some. You can always turn it back on for final editing and printing.

Auto Kern

The Auto Kern preference is also in the Document section of the Preferences dialog and is specific to each individual document. Most PostScript and TrueType fonts contain *kerning pairs*—information that lets the program better squeeze pairs such as WA together. If you have turned Auto Kern on, MacWrite Pro will automatically use kerning pairs where appropriate.

Show Font Menus in Actual Typeface

This item is found in the Application Preference tile. If this item is checked, the Font menu will display font names in their individual fonts. For example, the name New York is in New York font, the name Helvetica is in Helvetica font. You can override this preference by holding down the Option key when you select the Font menu. Like the Auto Kern preference, this preference can slow down the display of the font menu, and is particularly noticeable on slower Macs and almost any Mac if a large number of fonts are installed.

Summary

MacWrite Pro gives you four levels of formatting your documents:

- Character
- Paragraph
- Section
- Document

This chapter covers character formatting options. In addition to the standard Mac character formatting options, such as bold, italic, and underlined, MacWrite Pro provides some special tools not found in other popular Mac word processing products.

Character formatting is controlled from the menu bar (Font, Size, and Style are discussed). These same tools are generally available in slightly different formats from the Style and Text palettes.

CHAPTER 4

Paragraph Formatting

This chapter covers paragraph formatting, which is a powerful but easy-to-use method of enhancing the appearance of your documents. Paragraph formats govern such things as line spacing (how much space is allocated between lines vertically on the page), margins, justification, tab stops, and more. Formatting individual characters is covered in Chapter 3.

What Is a Paragraph?

Before revealing all the mysteries of paragraph formatting, it's probably a good idea to agree upon a definition of the term "paragraph." Composition instructors talk about logical organization of ideas and point to the exquisite paragraphs of Flaubert. Alas, word processing is somewhat more mundane than the efforts of nineteenth century French authors. In the world of word processing, the paragraph is the next greater structure of a document above the character. It ranks below the section and then the page formatting. The most general level of formatting is document formatting.

A *paragraph* is any sequence of characters that ends with a return character (the one that is inserted into your document when you press the Return key). A paragraph can go on forever (such as the first one in Garcia Marquez's third novel) or simply represent a blank line and contain no characters at all, except the return character at the end.

A paragraph can have many lines that are generated automatically when MacWrite Pro wraps your text to a new line. You can also create separate new lines manually within the same paragraph by holding down the Shift key when you press the Return key. This is useful when you have many short one-line entries, like a list, and you want to be able to format them all in the same way.

Mechanics: Changing Paragraph Formats

MacWrite Pro includes two main tools for manipulating paragraph formats: the Ruler and the Format | Paragraph dialog box. The Ruler is an interactive, easy-to-use mechanism that lets you directly change such items as indents, text alignment, and line spacing. The Paragraph dialog box also lets you work with these elements, but in a more precise manner; you can type in numbers accurate to one point (1/72 inch). Changes you make to either the Ruler or in the Paragraph dialog box affect active or selected paragraphs. Note that you don't have to select an entire paragraph in order to format it; MacWrite Pro assumes that you want changes made to paragraph settings to affect the paragraph that contains the insertion point ("where you are now"). Taking advantage of this fact can save you a lot of time as you experiment with different paragraph format options.

The Ruler

Most of the time you will use the interactive Ruler to format paragraphs. Ruler settings affect the currently selected paragraph, that is, the paragraph containing the insertion point or selection. The formatting of the currently selected paragraph is reflected on the Ruler, and any changes you make to the Ruler affect the selected paragraph or paragraphs.

If two or more paragraphs with conflicting settings are selected, the Ruler reflects the settings of the first paragraph only, but any changes you make to the Ruler affect all selected paragraphs.

If you need more room on your screen to display your document, you can hide part or all of the Ruler. To hide the Ruler controls, double-click anywhere (except on a button) in the bottom two thirds of the Ruler. This collapses most of the bottom third of the Ruler. You get about one additional line of text display, depending on your font and size. If you need to see the controls again, click anywhere in the Ruler below the rule itself. (If you click above the rule, MacWrite Pro displays the Document formatting dialog box, which is described in detail in Chapter 5.)

If you are not using the Ruler at all, you might as well not have it lying there at the top of the screen cluttering up your display and needlessly taking up space. You can hide the Ruler by choosing the Hide Ruler command from the View menu. If you want to display the Ruler again later, use the Show Ruler command on the View menu (the same command toggles to Show Ruler when it's hidden and to Hide Ruler when it's visible) or the keyboard equivalent, ⌘-H.

The Paragraph Dialog Box

You can also use MacWrite Pro's Paragraph dialog box (select Paragraph from the Format menu) to enter direct numbers for more precise measurements than you can make with the Ruler. The dialog box includes some features that you don't use as often as those on the Ruler. Note that it doesn't include tab settings, which are controlled in the Tab dialog box.

You can use the Paragraph dialog box and the Ruler together. Any changes you make on the Ruler are reflected immediately in the Paragraph dialog box. Any information you type into the dialog box is displayed immediately on the Ruler.

You can summon the Paragraph dialog box by double-clicking on nearly any of the controls on the Ruler display itself, except the tab controls (double-clicking on tab controls summons the Tab dialog box, described later in this chapter). The Paragraph dialog box looks like this:

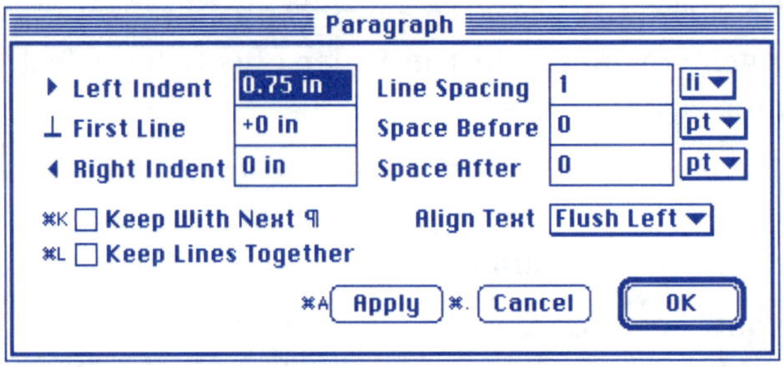

Measurements

The default measurement on the Ruler and in MacWrite Pro dialog boxes is the inch, but MacWrite Pro lets you change the unit of measurement as needed. The available units of measure are inches, inches decimal, picas, points, millimeters, and centimeters. You can change the unit of measurement through the Document tile of the Preferences dialog box (choose Preferences from the Edit menu), as shown here:

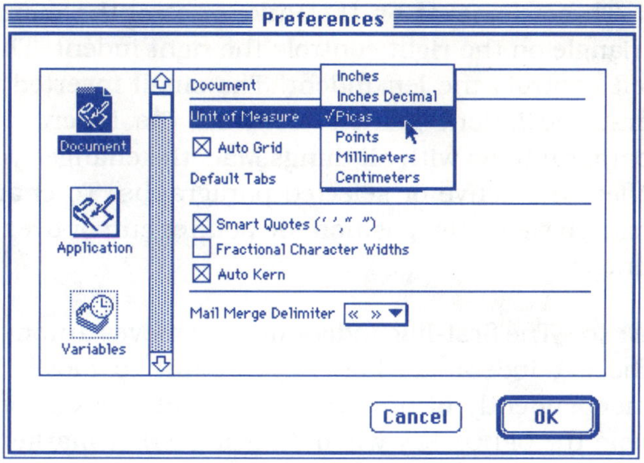

The Ruler, shown in Figure 4-1, starts at the left edge of the page—0, unlike some word processors that make the Ruler relative to the margins you've set up in the document.

Changing margins is part of Section formatting, and is discussed in Chapter 5, but MacWrite Pro's margins are easy to understand and to use.

MacWrite's Ruler

FIGURE 4-1

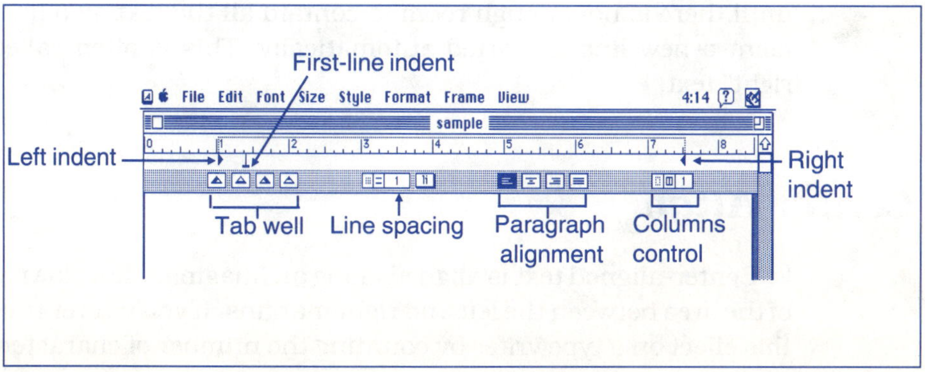

Three elements on the Ruler control the margin settings. The small triangle on the right controls the right indent. The small triangle on the left controls the left indent. The small inverted t-shaped element, the first-line indent marker, controls the indent of the first line of the paragraph. As with all things Mac, the changes you make to the indents affect the active or selected paragraphs. To change any of these three margin elements, position the pointer cursor over the element, click, and drag.

Note The first-line indent marker moves automatically when you move the left indent marker. If you want to move the left indent marker independently of the first-line indent marker, or vice versa, press and hold the OPTION key when dragging either marker.

Alignment

Paragraph alignment governs how paragraphs are aligned horizontally on the page. MacWrite Pro offers four styles of text alignment: left, center, right, and fully justified. Each of these alignment styles is represented by an icon on the Ruler. They are also available from the Align Text pop-up menu in the Paragraph dialog box.

Left Align

Left-aligned text is flush with the left margin and is the standard default. Text starts at the left margin (or indent) and proceeds to the right until there is not enough room to contain all the text on a line, at which point a new line is started automatically. This is often called "ragged-right" text.

Center Align

Center-aligned text is aligned along an imaginary line down the middle of the area between the left and right margins. If you've ever tried to create this effect on a typewriter by counting the number of characters in a line, dividing that by two, and then backspacing from the center, you are going to love this feature! With MacWrite Pro, all you have to do is click the center alignment button, or choose Center from the pop-up menu in the Paragraph dialog box.

Most of the time you won't center paragraphs that are more than a few lines long. Such things as headings, the full text of birthday party invitations or other announcements look good centered. Large blocks of text are difficult to read when centered. Generally, a large type size helps make centered text more readable, as does fairly large line spacing.

Right Align

Right-aligned text is the opposite of left. The left margin is ragged instead of the right and the text is aligned flush right. Right-aligned, like center-aligned text, is much more effective when used judiciously. Some people like to use it for the return address of an informal letter.

Full Justification

Fully justified text has even, flush margins on both the right and left. Unless you are really trying for a professionally typeset appearance in your document and have a 300 dpi (dots per inch) printer such as an Apple LaserWriter or better, you should avoid it. It's more difficult to read than ragged right text. If you do use it, make sure the Fractional Font Widths box in the Preferences dialog is checked; fractional font widths make it easier for MacWrite Pro to space the characters evenly across the page. Most documents look better with the Auto Kern option turned on, too. Character spacing is accessed from the Text palette or by choosing the Character Spacing command from the Style menu. Kerning is covered in Chapter 3.

Full justification works best in narrow columns such as those commonly used in multicolumn newsletters. Some argue, however, that in almost every application left-justified text is easier to read and more attractive.

Indenting Paragraphs

There are three controls for paragraph indenting: left indent, first-line indent, and right indent. All three features are accessible from the Ruler when the Paragraph dialog box is visible.

Left Indent governs how text lines up against the left margin. More specifically, it governs how the second and succeeding lines of a paragraph line up against the left margin. Normally you will leave this set at 0—the left edge of the document margin.

First Line Indent governs how much the first characters in the first line of a paragraph are indented. When MacWrite Pro starts a new paragraph, that paragraph is automatically indented by the amount specified with this control. It's a good idea to develop the habit of using this feature to indent the first line of each paragraph rather than using the old-fashioned tab technique.

You can produce a *hanging indent* (in which the first line falls to the left of the rest of the lines of a paragraph) by making the First Line Indent less than the Left Indent.

One example of the use of hanging indents is a bibliography listing, and the second is a glossary entry. You can also use hanging indents in resumes.

Finally, Right Indent specifies how far from the right edge of the paper the paragraph's actual margin is.

Line and Paragraph Spacing

Line spacing controls the spacing between the lines within a paragraph. *Paragraph spacing* specifies the space between the current paragraph and those before and after it. Line spacing tools are found both on the Ruler and in the Paragraph dialog box. Paragraph spacing options are only available in the Paragraph dialog box.

Line Spacing

Line spacing controls the spacing between lines within the currently selected paragraph. While you can change line spacing with the Paragraph Format dialog box, it's generally more convenient to do it with the Ruler. The only advantage the dialog box has over the Ruler is that it lets you type exact figures, instead of increasing or decreasing the line spacing in preset increments.

The line spacing of a paragraph is called its *leading*. Leading is the amount of space between the lines. By default, MacWrite Pro adjusts the line spacing of a paragraph to make it fit with the largest size of type you have on a line. It also adjusts automatically for superscript and subscript characters (if you use any of the precise measurements, such as picas, inches, or centimeters, MacWrite Pro does not automatically adjust line height for superscripts and subscripts).

The "less" and "more" line spacing buttons behave differently depending on the measurement unit. Here's how they increment, based on the measurement unit:

Measurement Unit	Increment Value
Line	0.5 lines
Point	1 point
Inches	0.01 inches
mm	0.35 mm
cm	0.35 mm (except it's rounded up or down to the nearest integer)

Double Spacing

Double spacing, or a blank line between each line of your text, is an option that you might use often. Many publishers, for example, require double-spaced manuscripts. Select the paragraph or paragraphs you want double-spaced, make sure the measurement indicator is set to li, and click on the more button until it reads 2.

Note The double-spaced manuscript requirement is a holdover from the days when a typewriter was considered a sophisticated writing instrument. Proportional fonts obviate the original need for double-spacing because they allow for tighter spacing and, as a result, greatly improved readability. However, the same publisher that requires double-spaced manuscripts probably also specifies a nonproportional font such as Courier.

Space Before and Space After

Space Before and Space After control the amount of space that precedes or follows the paragraph. In most cases you will set one or the other of these values for a particular paragraph, but not both (what is after one paragraph is before the next). Use these values for paragraphs instead of inserting blank lines between paragraphs because it gives you more control. Later if you need to squeeze more text on to a page, you can adjust these values by small increments globally instead of having to remove blank lines.

You should also not mix adding extra space before or after a paragraph with 1.5 or double spacing within paragraphs. Space before and space after space is added in addition to the line spacing for the paragraph, so this can add too much space between them.

Note Space Before does not affect the first line on a page or column; nor does Space After affect the last line on a page, assuming the paragraph in question starts or ends a page, respectively.

Extra space before and after header paragraphs sets them apart from regular paragraphs. You may want to remove space before or after paragraphs such as long indented quotations, for example, that are closely related to other paragraphs.

If you are using a laser printer or other high-quality printing device, it's a good idea to keep line spacing somewhat tight (that is, 1 line) and set paragraphs apart by adding space before or space after. Again, this gives you more control.

Note If you already know how you want to format the selected paragraph or paragraphs, adjust the necessary settings and click the OK button. You may want to experiment with various formatting options before making a final decision. The Apply button in the Paragraph Format dialog box lets you do just that. To experiment with different settings, adjust the settings and click the Apply button instead. The dialog box stays active, but you can see the results of your formatting settings in the affected part of the document behind the Format Paragraph dialog box. To see more of the document, move the Format Paragraph dialog box to one side by clicking and dragging on its title bar.

Keep Lines Together and Keep With Next ¶

The Keep Lines Together and Keep With Next ¶ options, available only in the Paragraph dialog box, specify how the paragraph is to be treated when MacWrite Pro is repaginating the document.

If Keep Lines Together is checked, all the lines in the paragraph stay on the same page together. Use this only for short paragraphs. If you use it with large paragraphs, you risk leaving a lot of white space at the bottom of a page as MacWrite Pro brings the entire paragraph over to the next page.

Keep With Next ¶ means that the paragraph with this property stays on the same page as the next paragraph. This setting works well with a head (or subhead) and the paragraph it introduces. When you use the Keep Lines Together option this way, you won't have a head at the bottom of a page and the first paragraph that follows it at the top of the next page. Keep With Next ¶ has precedence over Keep Lines Together.

Tabs

Tabs govern the horizontal spacing that is inserted into a line when you press the Tab key. Specific kinds of tabs govern what happens to text you type immediately after you press Tab.

Use Tabs, Not Spaces

If you've been working on a typewriter, you are probably just as accustomed to using spaces to align text as you are to tabs. Sometimes this is just as easy on a typewriter as setting tab stops.

There are several reasons why you shouldn't use this technique on a word processor. First, if you've "hard-coded" spaces into your document, it's very difficult to change the formatting later, especially as regards to tab placement: you will need to delete a mess (this collective noun is used advisedly) of spaces in each line to make things line up correctly.

Second, and more important, most text on the Mac is in a proportional font. Proportionally spaced characters do not give the same width on the line to all characters; thus it is very difficult, if not impossible, to type lines that align correctly if you use spaces rather than tabs.

Working with Tabs

In a new document with no style sheet, MacWrite Pro assigns default tab stops at every 1/2 inch between the margins. These default tabs are not shown on the Ruler. If you create a new tab, all tabs to the left of it are removed, however, MacWrite Pro maintains the 1/2-inch tabs to the right of it.

Note You can change the default tab stops in the Document tile of the Preferences dialog box.

MacWrite Pro has four kinds of tabs, which are shown in Figure 4-2.

Left Tabs

The left tab is the kind of tab a typewriter makes. After you press the Tab key, the insertion point moves to the tab location, and text you type starts at the tab point and moves to the right. This is good for use in small text tables or tables in documents that you intend to transfer to other word processors or other computers. Otherwise, it is much easier to make tables using MacWrite Pro's custom table tool, as discussed in Chapter 12.

FIGURE 4-2 The four kinds of tabs

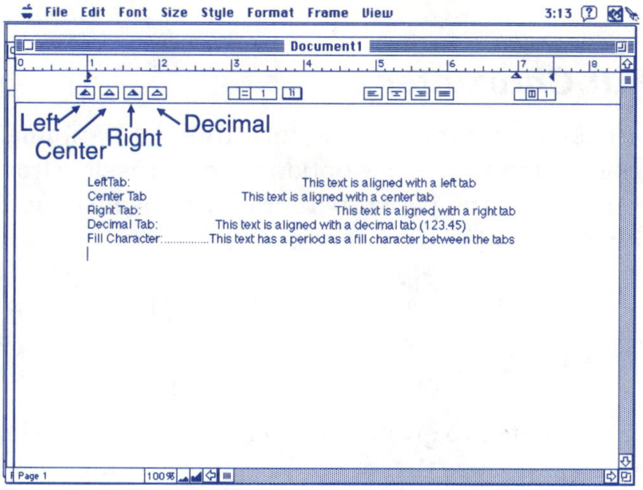

Right Tabs

Right tabs work in the opposite manner from left tabs. After you press the Tab key, text you type is pushed to the left, so that the last character lines up at the tab. It's handy to use this style of tab at the right margin of your document, if you want the characters, especially numbers, to line up with that margin.

Center Tabs

Text you type after pressing the Tab key is centered around the tab point when you use center tabs.

Decimal Tabs

Normally, you use decimal tabs when typing columns of numbers that you want to align on the decimal point. However, you can enter virtually any character into the field to the right of the Align On radio button in the Tab dialog box (see "Setting Tabs"), and have text align with that character. For example, you may want to enter a comma and have text line up with the comma.

Fill Character

The character you type into this field automatically fills the space between tab stops. This option is not accessible from the Ruler. Generally you will use the period here, to create leaders across the page for such things as tables of contents.

Setting Tabs

MacWrite Pro gives you two mechanisms for setting tabs. Most of the time you will use the Ruler, dragging new tab stops from the tab well onto the Ruler or adjusting existing tabs by sight on the Ruler. Remember that tab adjustments affect all the lines in an active or selected paragraph.

For more precision in your tab settings, use the Tab dialog box:

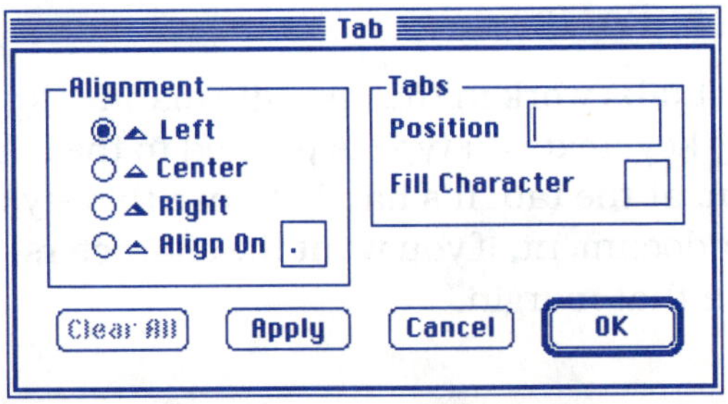

The Ruler stays active behind the dialog box while it's visible, so you don't give up a direct user interface while using it. The dialog also lets you specify some things, such as the align character for decimal tabs and the fill character, that you can't specify with the Ruler. The Tab dialog box also has a Position field that helps you place tabs at exact locations (up to a precision of 1/72 inch).

Note The Tab dialog box has an Apply button that works similarly to the Paragraph Apply button described earlier. You can use it to experiment with different tab settings without closing the Tab dialog box.

Remember that MacWrite Pro includes a separate table tool. This tool, discussed in Chapter 12, is much easier to use than creating tables by hand using tabs.

Note If you are going to create tables using tabs (and there are good reasons for doing so, such as when you intend to eventually export the text of a document to other programs), then use Shift-Return to create new lines in the table. That gives you more control over such things as line and paragraph spacing, as well as margins and tabs while working with a single paragraph.

New Lines and Paragraphs

The RETURN key always generates a new paragraph in your MacWrite Pro document. But sometimes you may want to start a new line without beginning a new paragraph, for example, fixing bad line breaks in a column of text. (Columns are covered in Chapter 5.) You can force MacWrite Pro to start a new line without beginning a new paragraph by using Shift-Return rather than the standard Return where you want the new line to begin.

Another time when you might want to use the newline feature is in the address portion of a letter. By keeping the entire address as one paragraph, you can easily change the indentation or line spacing without having to select the entire address.

The newline feature is also very handy for creating tables and bulleted lists for the same reason.

Copying Paragraph Formats

If you have created a complex paragraph format, you might want to apply that format to a different paragraph, even one in another MacWrite Pro document.

You can do this using the Copy Ruler command on MacWrite Pro's Format menu (shortcut: Shift-⌘-C). In effect, this places a copy of the current Ruler on the Clipboard. The one difference between this command and the standard Copy command is that when you copy a Ruler, the contents of what you might call the "Ruler Clipboard" are not disturbed by other commands, such as Copy and Cut, that place material on the Clipboard. To paste the Ruler into a different paragraph, just click anywhere in that paragraph (it's not necessary to select the return character at the end), and use the Format | Apply Ruler command (or Shift-⌘-V, the keyboard equivalent).

MacWrite Pro also lets you group together character and/or paragraph styles and use them repeatedly throughout a document. These user-defined styles are an extremely powerful tool to help you maintain consistency among repeating elements such as captions, headers and footers, and body text. User-defined styles are described in Chapter 7.

Summary

A paragraph is any group of characters that ends with a return character.

You can use either the Ruler or Paragraph dialog box to change Paragraph formats. The Ruler is quicker, while the Paragraph dialog box gives you more precise control.

When formatting paragraphs, lines as a unit of measurement is usually preferable to inches, picas, millimeters, or centimeters.

Alignment governs how text fills a page horizontally.

Paragraph indenting lets you automatically create indents at the beginning of a paragraph or create a hanging indent. (This is preferable to using a tab character to indent the first line of the paragraph.) Indents also control the left and right borders of the paragraph within the page boundaries.

Use the Ruler or Paragraph dialog box to define the amount of horizontal space a paragraph takes. Use the Apply button to preview the effects your changes will have on the active paragraph(s).

Use Keep Lines Together and Keep With Next ¶ options to control the way MacWrite Pro paginates paragraphs.

Paragraph formats can be copied from one paragraph to another by copying the return character at the end of a paragraph or with commands on the Format menu.

Tabs let you line up text in columns and are useful for shorter tables in those instances when you don't use MacWrite Pro's built-in table feature. Use the Tab dialog box Apply button to preview the effects of your changes.

CHAPTER

5

Formatting Documents, Sections, and Pages

The two previous chapters discussed formatting characters and paragraphs. This chapter deals with formatting a document as a whole, sections within the document, and finally individual pages. It takes a "top-down" approach, dealing with the larger issues of document formatting and working toward the smaller document elements.

Document Formatting

Document formatting options are settings that affect the entire document. These include the size of paper the document will be printed on, whether left- and right-hand pages should be formatted separately, margins, and footnotes.

Paper Size and Orientation

Paper size and orientation are also discussed in Chapter 9 as options for printing, but since paper size and orientation affect an entire document, they are also mentioned briefly here.

The Page Setup dialog box, shown here, contains several items that affect the way a document is printed:

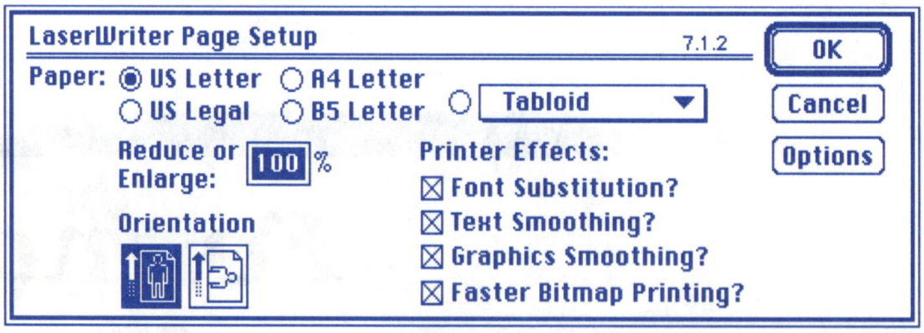

The paper radio buttons are the first controls that affect the formatting of your document. For most printing, choose the US Letter paper size, which is traditionally 8 1/2 × 11 inches.

The Document Format Dialog Box

The Document format dialog box contains the other group of settings that affect the entire document. These settings include Left/Right Pages, Margins, and Footnote Handling. Using this dialog box to set margins is discussed in this section; formatting of footnotes is discussed later in this chapter. You can bring up this dialog box by using the Document command on the Footnote menu, or its keyboard equivalent Option-⌘-D. The dialog box appears, as shown here:

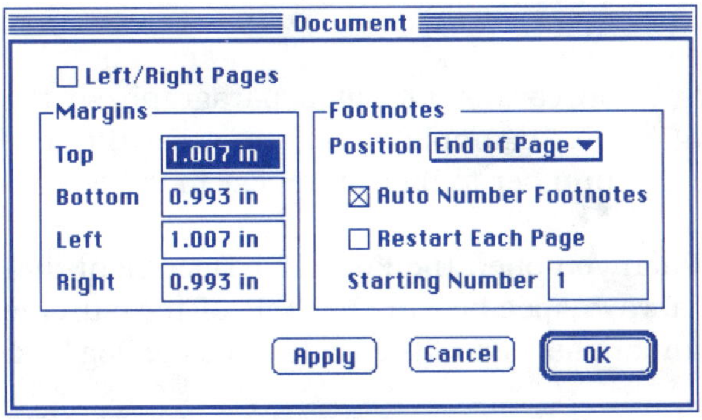

As with most MacWrite Pro documents, you can use the Tab key to move the selection between the various fields (the fields for entering margins and the starting number for Footnotes). The dialog box also features keyboard equivalents that become visible when you hold down the ⌘ key. Here is a table showing the Document box's keyboard equivalents:

Keypress	Clicks This Button
⌘-L	Left/Right Pages
⌘-N	Auto Number Footnotes
⌘-R	Restart Each Page
⌘-A	Apply
⌘-. or Esc	Cancel
Return, Enter	OK

As with most MacWrite Pro formatting dialog boxes, you can use the Apply button to see the effects of new settings in the document window behind the Format Document dialog box. This lets you experiment with some of the settings before you confirm them with the OK button. This is most useful when adjusting margins.

Setting Margins

Margin settings affect the entire document. Margin settings are measured from the edge of the paper as specified in the Page Setup dialog box.

Note You cannot format a paragraph so that text falls *outside* the margins. For example, you cannot set the indent of a paragraph to a negative number to have it appear to the left of the left margin.

When you open the Format | Document dialog box, margin settings are always specified in the unit of measurement you specified in the Document section of the Preferences dialog box, as shown here:

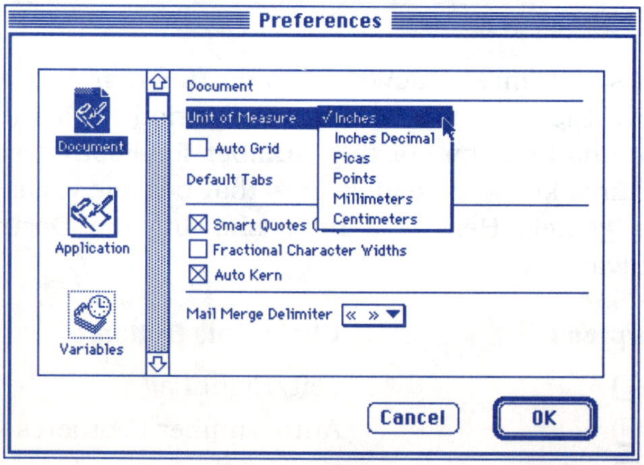

That is, if you have specified inches as your preferred unit of measurement, margin settings will be shown in inches (as will the Ruler); if you have specified centimeters, margin settings will be shown using centimeters, and so on.

You can, however, specify margin settings using any unit of measurement you prefer, regardless of the preferred unit, by including the abbreviation for the measurement unit after the number. Thus, if you want to make your top margin 5 centimeters, you would enter **5 cm** into the Top field. When you reopen the dialog box, the value will be changed to the preferred unit of measurement (in this example, 5 cm would become 2 in). When entering numbers into any of these fields, you do not need to specify a unit of measurement if you want to use the preferred unit. For example, if your preferred unit is inches, you can set the top margin to 2 inches by typing **2** into the Top field.

Direct Setting of Margins You are not forced to use the dialog box to set margins; instead you can directly set the margins by dragging with the mouse.

To do this, make sure that Page Guides are visible (if they are not, select the View menu | Show Page Guides command). Next, point to any page guide, hold down the Option key, and point to a page guide. The mouse cursor will change, as shown here:

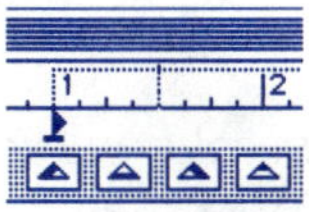

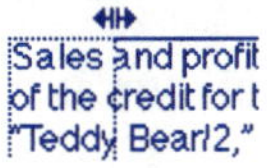

Dragging the top page guide changes the top margin; dragging the left page guide changes the left margin, and so on. As you drag the page guide, a dashed line appears indicating where the new margin will lie. This line appears on both the page itself, and also on the Ruler (when you change a left or right margin). The page number display at the lower-left corner of the window changes to reflect the value of the margin as you change it.

Left/Right Pages

The Left/Right Pages check box determines whether the document is to be treated as if pages were printed on both sides of the paper or not.

Odd-numbered pages become right pages, and even-numbered pages become left pages.

When this button is checked, the names of two of the fields change: Left becomes Inside, and Right becomes Outside. This feature is useful for setting a binding gutter. For example, you can set the Inside margin to 1.5 inches and the Outside margin to 1 inch.

Note Chapter 9 discusses techniques for actually *printing* on both sides of a sheet of paper.

Section Formatting

The section level is the next smaller formatting element after the document level. Sections let you format portions of your document differently than other portions. Sections are useful for a variety of tasks, for example:

- Create *newspaper columns* (columns that move down a page, then snake back up to the top of the next column). Using sections, you can specify that the entire document should be in newspaper columns, or specify that only a portion of the document be in columns.
- Have better control over page breaks. You can use sections to specify that a new page start on the next even- or odd-numbered page. If necessary, MacWrite Pro will insert the necessary blank pages. This is especially useful if you are creating a document to be printed on both sides of a page.
- Suppress headers and footers on the first page of a section (which is usually the first page of a document).
- Force printing of endnotes earlier in a document than the last page.

Dividing a Document into Sections

All documents have at least one section. To create a new section, use the Insert Break submenu on the Format menu to find the Insert Section command. It is easier to use the keyboard equivalent, Option-Enter. When you insert a new section, you can see this section marker placed in your document, providing you have Show Invisibles enabled on the View menu. The section marker looks like this:

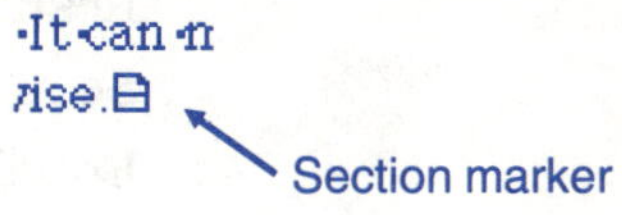

Formatting Sections

Formatting sections is similar to formatting paragraphs, in that the current section is the one containing the insertion point or selection, just like the current paragraph is the one containing the insertion point.

To format a section, place the insertion point anywhere in that section and choose the Format menu's Section command, or use its keyboard equivalent Option-⌘-S. The Section format dialog box appears, as shown here:

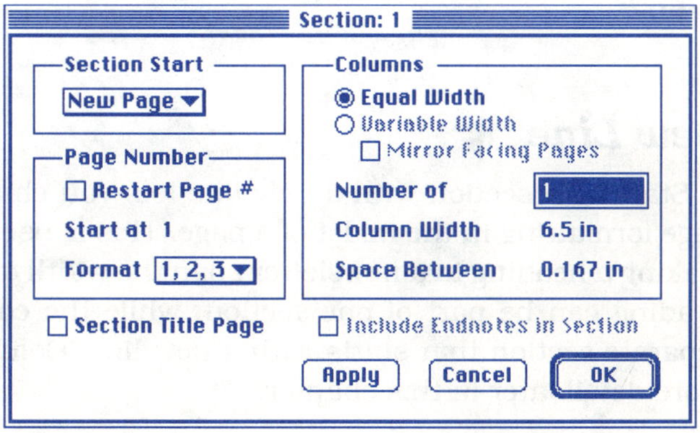

The name of the dialog box contains the word "Section" followed by a colon and a number. The number indicates the number of the section within the document you are editing. If the current selection encompasses more than one section, it will read something like "Section: 1-2."

As with most MacWrite Pro dialog boxes, there are a number of keyboard equivalents for the buttons within it, as shown here:

Keypress	Clicks This Button
⌘-R	Restart Page #
⌘-T	Section Title Page
⌘-E	Equal Width
⌘-W	Variable Width
⌘-M	Mirror Facing Pages
⌘-I	Include Endnotes in Section
⌘-A	Apply
⌘-. or Esc	Cancel
Return or Enter	OK

Section Start

The Format Section dialog box lets you specify how a section is to be separated from the section preceding it with the Section Start pop-up menu.

New Line

Starting a section with a new line lets you change some portions of page formatting in the midst of a page. This is useful as one solution for making a heading in a newsletter span the width of several columns: the heading can be part of one section, while the columns below it are a separate section that starts with a new line. Columns are discussed in more detail later in this chapter.

New Page

The New Page option forces the new section to start on the next page following the end of the preceding section.

New Right Page

The New Right Page option forces the new section to start on the next right page. The next right page ordinarily means the next odd-numbered page. The best use for this is for documents that you intend to print on both sides of the paper. New chapters are an example of portions of a document that should start on a new right page.

New Left Page

The New Left Page option starts the new section on the next left (even-numbered) page.

Navigating by Sections

You can use MacWrite Pro's Find command to quickly jump to the next section in a document. Open the Find dialog box (using the Find command on the Edit | Find/Change submenu or the ⌘-F keyboard equivalent) and press Option-6 in the dialog box Find field. This is especially useful if you have several sections in a document, or your selection or insertion point is currently at the beginning of a long section.

Headers and Footers

Headers are elements that are printed automatically at the top of each page in a document. *Footers* are printed automatically at the bottom of every page in a document. One of the most common uses of headers and footers is to number pages automatically.

Inserting and Editing Headers and Footers

To insert a header, choose the Format menu's Insert Header command. MacWrite Pro creates a space for a header at the top of the page containing the insertion point or selection. Scroll the window if necessary, and place the insertion point within the body of the header itself. Type the text of the header, and then press ⌘-Return to move the insertion point back to the location it was in before you used the Insert Header command. Creating footers works the same way.

Note To create a header or a footer, the insertion point or selection does not have to be located at the first page of the section. Headers and footers *always* apply to the entire section, regardless of where in the section the insertion point happens to be.

As you type text into the header or footer, MacWrite Pro makes the box enclosing it larger or smaller as required to accommodate the text; the box will also adjust itself automatically if you make the text within it larger or smaller. You can manually resize the box containing the header or footer by dragging the handle that appears in the center of its bottom (for headers) or top (for footers).

Note Headers and footers appear *within* the current margins. When setting margins using the Document format dialog box, take into account the size of the headers and footers you will be using. Not surprisingly, larger headers and footers mean that much less text fits on each page.

After creating a header or footer, you can edit it by clicking in it; this causes the header/footer box to open. You can edit a header or footer on any page within the section in which it appears; as with creating it, you need not be at the first page of the section to modify the header or footer.

Left/Right Headers and Footers

If you have set the document format to take into account left and right pages in the Document format dialog box, the Insert Header and Insert Footer commands on the Format menu are transformed into hierarchical menus. These menus let you create new headers or footers that apply only to left or right pages, or that apply to both.

Links Between Headers and Footers

While for most documents you specify separate headers and footers for separate sections, you have the option of linking the header of one section to the header of another section. (You have the option of breaking this link after you have established it, if you need to.)

When you create a new section, that section automatically includes the header and footer from the previous section. For most documents, this is as it should be, since page numbering formats are usually consistent throughout a document.

When you edit a header or footer in a section that is not the first section in the document, the icon of a chain appears above the header or below the footer, as shown here:

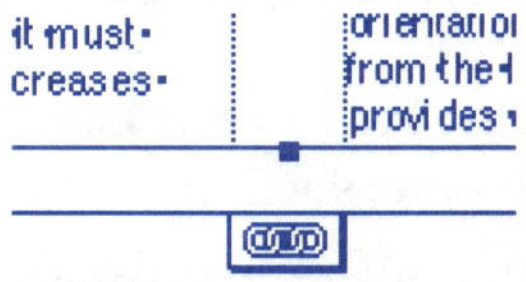

This chain serves as a symbol to notify you that the header or footer is linked to that of the previous section. Any edits made to a linked header or footer apply to the previous section as well.

If you wish to "break the chain" and unlink the header or footer, just click once on the chain icon. The icon will change to one of a broken chain, as shown here:

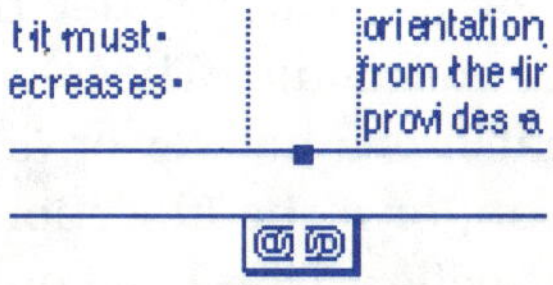

After you have broken the chain, edits to the header or footer will not affect the header or footer in the previous section.

You can also click the icon when it is broken to reestablish the link and thus replace the current header or footer with that of the previous section. In this case, since this operation is not undoable, MacWrite Pro presents a dialog box for you to confirm this action, as shown here:

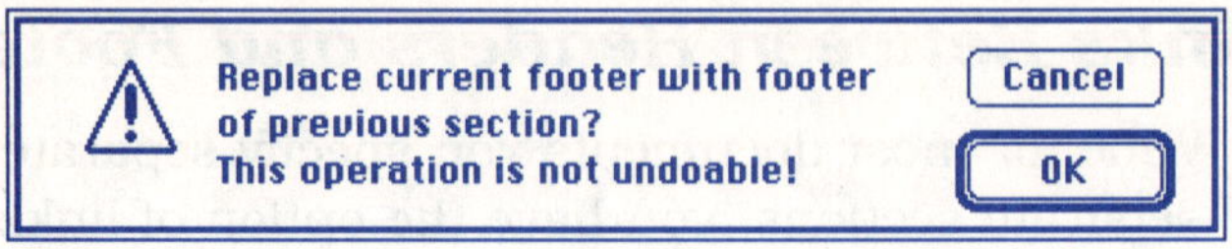

Note As mentioned earlier, headers and footers are linked automatically when you create a new section, providing the previous section had a header or footer defined. If you create a header for the previous section after creating the second section, you can click the icon of the broken chain to automatically pick up the header or footer from the previous section.

Suppressing Headers and Footers

If the Section Title Page check box is checked in the Section format dialog box, headers and footers will not appear on the first page of the section.

When this option is set, the Insert Header or Insert Footer commands are not available when the insertion point is on the first page of a given section.

Removing Headers and Footers

To remove a header or footer, use the Format menu's Remove Header or Remove Footer command. These commands are only available if you are on a page that *has* a header or a footer (that is, if one is defined for the current section, or if the insertion point is not on the first page of a section with the Section Title Page option set).

Header and Footer Styles

When you create a header or a footer, MacWrite Pro automatically creates two *style definitions*, which are rules for formatting portions of the document. These styles are named, appropriately enough, Header and Footer.

Chapter 7 details working with style sheets and shows you how to modify these and other default styles, including changing a style's default conditions, so that headers and footers created in new documents will reflect changes you have made to the default style sheet.

Page Numbers and Other Variables

As mentioned earlier in this chapter, the most common use for headers and footers is page numbering. This is done through the use of *variables*, codes that MacWrite Pro places in your text and then replaces with text. Variables are found on the Edit menu Insert Variable hierarchical menu, as shown here:

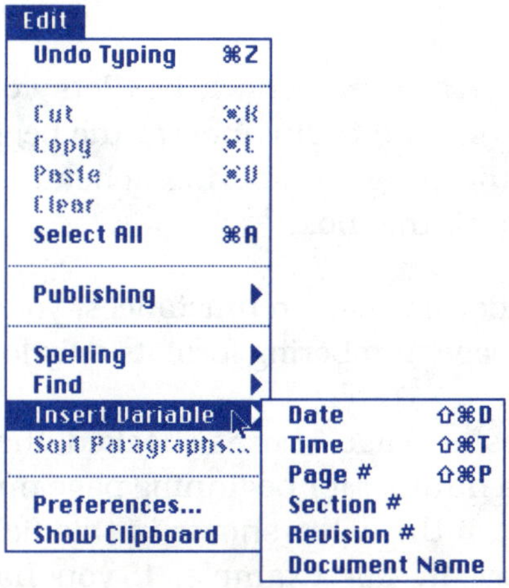

To insert a page number into a header or footer, create the header or footer and then choose the Page command from the Edit menu's Insert Variable submenu, or use its Shift-⌘-P keyboard equivalent. MacWrite Pro will place the current page number at the insertion point automatically.

Page Number Formats

MacWrite Pro includes several different formats for page numbers; these page number formats are most often used for numbering different parts of a document. Use the Section format dialog box to specify the numbering scheme of a section, as shown here:

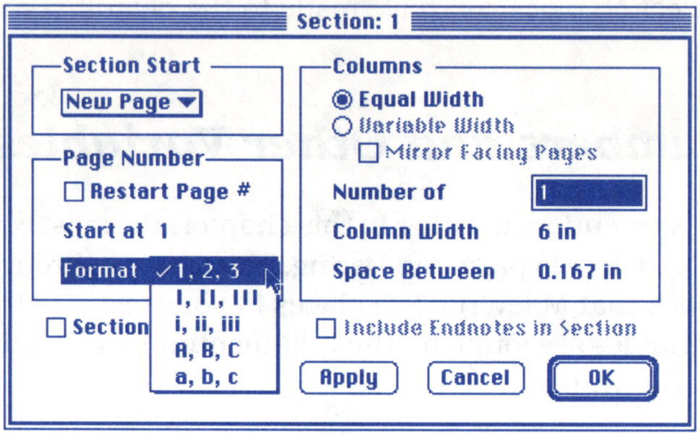

The Restart Page # check box lets you specify whether or not page numbering should begin anew at the beginning of the section. If you are changing the page numbering scheme of a section from the previous section, check this box.

Note Under normal circumstances, you should restart page numbering or change page numbering formats only for sections that start a new page.

If the Restart Page # box is checked, the Start at field is enabled, letting you enter a number for beginning page numbering of the current section. The format of the value shown in this field is tied to the Format pop-up menu below it. For example, if you have the Format set to Roman numerals, you cannot enter a digit into this field.

Note You can also use this field as a Roman numeral-to-Arabic numeral converter (or vice versa). These converters are hard to come by on computers, and are handy for those who do crossword puzzles. If you need to convert a Roman numeral to its Arabic equivalent, set the format to Roman numerals, enter a value into the field, and then change the format to Arabic numerals. For example, set the page number format to one of the Roman formats, enter **L** and then change the format to Arabic numerals. The Roman numeral L is converted to the Arabic 50.

The Format pop-up menu lets you specify the numbering format. The first format uses standard Arabic numerals to number the pages; this is by far the most common page numbering format.

The second two formats, labeled "I, II, III" and "i, ii, iii", let you specify Roman numeral page numbering. This is most often used for sections such as tables of contents, introductions, and the like. The second format, using lowercase Roman numerals, is more common than the uppercase format.

The third set of formats lets you specify alphabetic "numbering" of pages. If a document has more than 26 pages, MacWrite Pro will start over at the beginning of the alphabet on the 27th page, so that the 27th page is labeled AA (or aa), the 28th is labeled AB, and so on.

Inserting Other Variables

You can also insert variables in addition to page numbers into headers and footers (or anywhere else in the document), through the Edit menu's Insert Variables submenu.

Variables Preferences

Most of the variables that you can place in a document can be controlled by the Variables tile in the Preferences dialog box, which is shown here:

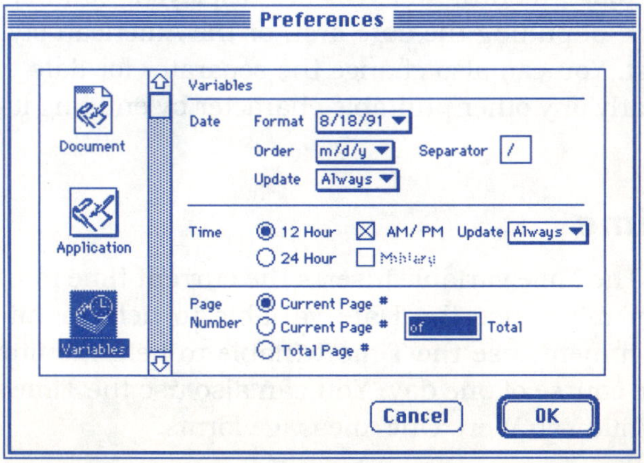

This dialog box is summoned when you choose the Preferences command from the Edit menu. Click the icon labeled Variables in the scrolling icon list to see the Variables settings. The range of settings for each of the types of variables are discussed in their respective sections later in this chapter.

The Update pop-up menu for both the Date and Time items lets you specify whether you want variables updated, and if so, when (at document opening, always, or never).

Note The settings for the Variables preferences are stored with the *current document*, so different documents can have their own date, time, and page number formats. You can use this feature to "freeze" date and time variables when you have completed a document. After you have printed a final version of the document, select the Preferences command, and choose Never from the Update pop-up menus for both the Date and Time variables. This gives you a record of when the document was last printed or modified.

Date

The Date variable inserts the current date as maintained by the Mac. If you are printing revisions of a document over the course of several days, use this variable to help keep track of the different printed versions.

In the Preferences dialog box, the Format pop-up menu lets you choose among five common date formats. You can also specify the *order* in which the date, month, and year are displayed. You might prefer the European style of putting the date first, or the American style of putting the month first. You can also change the separator for date items from a slash (/) to nearly any other printable character by entering it in the Separator field.

Time

The Time variable inserts the current time into the document. Just as you might use the Date variable to help monitor daily revisions to a document, use the Time variable to help monitor multiple revisions in the course of one day. You can also use the Time variable when creating "While You Were Out" message forms.

In the Variables tile of the Preferences dialog box, you can specify whether you want to use 12-hour or 24-hour formats; the default is set to the same setting as Time preference in the General section of the Control Panel. If you are using 12-hour time style, you can specify whether you want AM or PM appended to the time; if you are using the 24-hour format you can specify whether or not to use "military" style. In military style, 9:57 A.M. is formatted as 0957.

Page Number Variables

The Variables tile lets you choose from among three formats for page numbering.

- The default format is Current Page #.
- The second option automatically creates a "page 1 of 10" style format. The first element is the current page number, the second element is a text field that defaults to "of", and the final element is the total number of pages in the section or document.
- The third page numbering option is the total number of pages in the document.

Section

The Section # variable lets you insert the current section number in the document. This is useful if you have a number of sections in the document that are numbered separately (that is, if the Restart Page # box is checked in the Section format dialog box for that section).

In a header or footer, then, you can enter the Section # variable, followed by a dash, followed by the page number variable, to get a display of "1-1" for the first page of the first section (if you do this, make sure that the format of the Page number variable is set to Current Page #).

Revision

The Revision # variable inserts the revision number of the document. Revision numbers are changed automatically by MacWrite Pro each time you close and open a document. Revision numbers are discussed in more detail in Chapter 14.

Document Name

The Document name variable inserts the name of the document into the text. Again, this is useful when you are working on a document and saving different versions under different names. By including the name of the document in a header or footer, you can make sure that the copy you edit on screen is the same one that you marked up from a printout.

Creating Newspaper Columns

Newspaper columns fill down one column and then snake up to the top of the next column, and so on, to the next page. Creating newspaper columns with MacWrite Pro is easily handled using the Section format dialog box.

Notice the portion of the Section format dialog box that deals with columns:

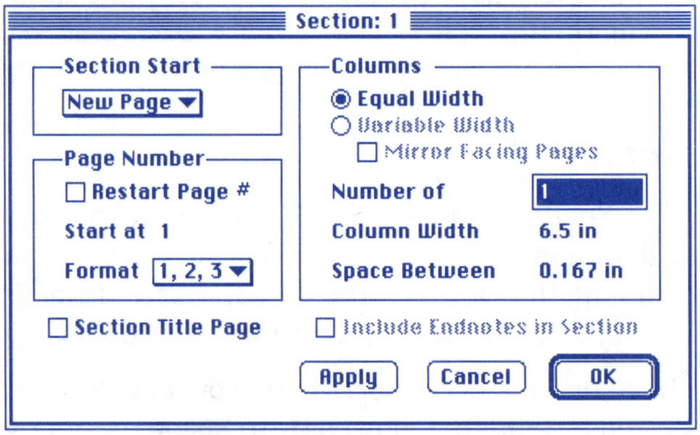

Note Remember that you can use the Apply button in this dialog box to preview changes as you make them.

Creating Columns

To create a section with multiple columns, open the Section format dialog box. In the Columns portion of this dialog box, there is a field labeled "Number of" that you use to specify the number of columns you want. This defaults to 1 for a single column. Type the number of columns you want into this field.

Column Widths

When you create columns, MacWrite Pro automatically inserts values for Column Width and Space Between (spacing between columns is also called the *gutter*) into the appropriate fields. You can type new values if the suggested settings are inappropriate. Column Width and Space Between are dynamically linked: the wider the columns, the narrower the space between them. The default value for the space between the columns is .167 inches.

Changing Column Widths Manually

While typing values into the Column Width and Space Between fields in the Section format dialog box is what you will commonly do, you can also change these values directly, by pointing and dragging.

The following illustration shows the process for changing the widths of columns:

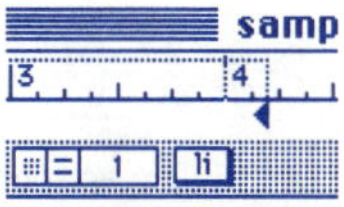

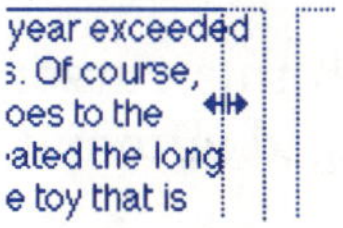

Hold down the Option key and point to the dotted line that defines the edge of the column. The mouse pointer changes to one showing arrows pointing to both the left and the right.

Note When you hold down the Option key, click slightly to the *inside* of the column guide. That is, if you are adjusting the left edge of a column, click slightly to the right of the line; if you are adjusting the right edge of a column click just to the right of a line. Dragging the line itself changes the space between the columns as well as the width of the columns, as discussed below.

As you drag to the left or the right, the dotted lines will follow the mouse. Releasing the mouse button causes the text to reflow into the new column. You cannot drag the margins of the column past the page margins on either side, nor can you drag the margins of a column so that it impinges on another column.

Notice that the page number display at the lower-left portion of the window changes as you drag. If you drag an "inside" portion of a column (for example, the right edge of a column on the left, and the left edge of one on the right), the display will show the new width of the column, labeled with a W. A second piece of information, labeled with a G, shows the width of the gutter, or space between the columns.

If you hold down the Option key while you press the mouse button inside the gutter itself, the cursor changes to the one shown here:

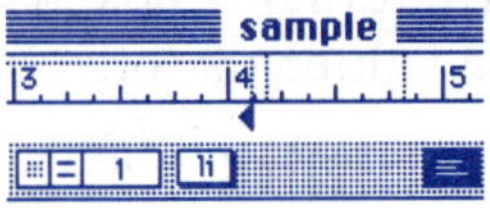

When you drag with this cursor, the width of columns on both sides of the gutter are changed automatically.

Inserting Column Breaks

You can force text to wrap to the top of the next column by inserting a column break with the Column command on the Format menu's Insert Break submenu. This works in the same manner as do Page and Section breaks: text immediately following the break will begin at the top of the next column.

Page Breaks

As you type, MacWrite Pro moves text to different pages automatically. Normally, this mode is preferred. But there are occasions when you need more control over where page breaks occur. MacWrite Pro provides two mechanisms, one manual and one automatic, for controlling page breaks.

Manual Page Breaks

Manual page breaks, also called *hard page breaks*, are explicit instructions you issue to MacWrite Pro to tell it to start a new page at the insertion point. To insert a manual page break, use the Insert Break submenu of the Format menu or the keyboard equivalent Shift-Enter.

Note Unless you are certain that you always want to begin a new page at the insertion point, you should use this judiciously. Editing a document can change the natural page breaks as you insert and delete text. Before printing the final version of any document, you should skim through it to make sure hard page breaks are where you want them to be.

Using Styles to Control Page Breaks

You can also use two Paragraph format options to control page breaks.

The first is the Keep with Next Paragraph attribute. If this option is enabled, page breaks will not occur between the paragraph with this setting and the one that follows it.

The Keep Lines Together option ensures that page breaks do not occur within paragraphs that have this option set. This is best used for short paragraphs (less than ten lines).

Footnotes

MacWrite Pro lets you insert footnotes into your document and uses styles and section formatting to let you control how and where footnotes appear in the document.

Inserting Footnotes

To insert a footnote, use the Insert Footnote command on the Format menu, or its keyboard equivalent, Shift-⌘-F. When you use this command, the following steps happen:

1. A footnote marker is placed in the body of your document at the location of the insertion point. This marker is numbered automatically.
2. A footnote reference is placed at the bottom of the page (by default), and a two-inch rule is placed above it.
3. Your insertion point is automatically placed at the bottom of the page so you can type the text of the footnote itself.

When you finish typing the footnote, press ⌘-Return to move the insertion point back to the location of the footnote marker to continue typing. Later, if you need to edit the text of the footnote, you can click in the footnote area automatically.

Footnote Styles

When you create a footnote, three styles are created automatically for you. These styles are imported from the MacWrite Pro Options file in the Claris folder in your System Folder. For details on changing the default footnote styles, see Chapter 7.

Footnote Paragraph Style

The Footnote paragraph style governs the appearance of the text in the footnote itself. By default this style is the same font as the one used in the default style for your document, is set in 10-point type, and is indented 1/4 inch from the left margin.

Footnote Reference Character Style

The Footnote Reference is the numbered reference in the footnote text itself. The style for the footnote reference is 10-point Helvetica, Superior.

Footnote Marker Character Style

This style is also 10-point Superior text, but the font is the same as the text around it.

Footnote Options

Aside from the options you have for formatting footnotes using the style sheets, the Document format dialog box, shown here, lets you control footnote positioning and numbering.

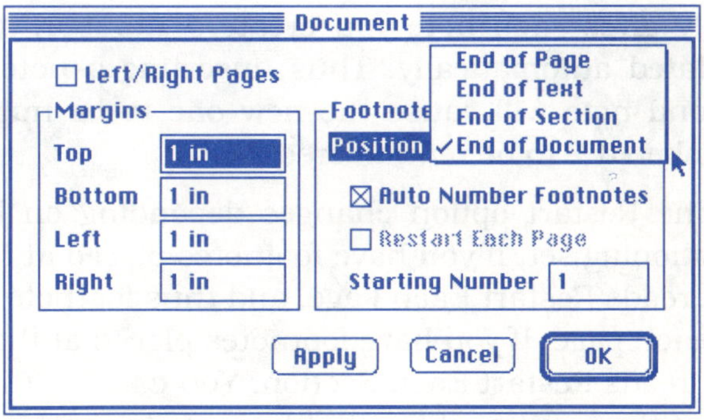

Position

You can choose one of four locations for footnotes: End of Page (the default), End of Text, End of Section, and End of Document.

The default location for footnotes is the end of the page, and is the precise meaning of the word "footnote"—when talking of notes at the end of a document or section, they are called "end notes."

The End of Text option places the footnote immediately after the last line of text in the document. You won't use this option often; it can make typing somewhat slow, as MacWrite Pro calculates all the footnote text positions every time a new line of text is added.

The End of Section option places all the notes at the end of the section to which their markers belong. Their location is actually part of that section, and how they appear on the page is governed by the formatting of the section. If the section start is a new page, the notes will appear on their own page. If the section start is not a new page, the footnotes will be set off from the rest of the section by a two-inch rule, and all the notes will appear before the new section starts at the beginning of a new line.

The End of Document option places the notes on their own page as the last page of the document; no rule appears.

Numbering

If the Auto Number Footnotes box is checked, MacWrite Pro automatically gives each note you create a number, and these numbers are updated automatically. Thus, inserting a note between the first and second note will cause the new one to be numbered 2, and the one numbered 2 to be renumbered as 3.

The Restart option changes depending on how you have footnote positioning set. If you have footnotes placed at the end of the page, this box reads Restart Each Page, and thus footnote numbering starts anew on each page. If you have footnotes placed at the end of the section, the box reads Restart Each Section. You can use the Starting Number field to set the number of the first footnote in each unit.

Deleting a Footnote

To delete a footnote, select the footnote marker in the body of the text, and use the Clear command on the Edit menu or the Delete key to delete it. Deleting the footnote marker automatically deletes the footnote text itself.

Cutting and Copying Footnotes

Just as you can delete a footnote by deleting the footnote reference in the text, so too can you cut and copy footnotes. Copying a footnote marker copies the text of the footnote itself, and pasting text that contains a footnote marker pastes the text of the footnote itself.

You can also select text in the footnote itself for cutting and copying.

Summary

- Document formatting governs the orientation of the text on the page, margins, left and right pages, and footnote positioning.
- Section formatting lets you create columns and restart page numbering differently for different portions of the document.
- Headers and footers are used to number pages, and MacWrite Pro's variables let you insert special codes in your text.

CHAPTER 6

Finding and Changing Text

This chapter starts with a short discussion of performing simple finds: moving to the next instance of a particular word or group of words (also known as a *text string*). It then discusses using the Find and Change functions to alter found text, both the content of the text itself and its formatting. The Find/Change command is a powerful feature, but if you do not use it carefully, you can irretrievably alter a document in an unintended fashion. This chapter also has several useful recipes for such tasks as cleaning up documents you receive from other kinds of computers and giving documents a more professional appearance by using typesetting symbols.

Find Command Basics

MacWrite Pro's Find functions are grouped together in a hierarchical menu on the Edit menu called Find, shown here. It includes four commands: Find/Change, Find Selection, Find Next, and Change.

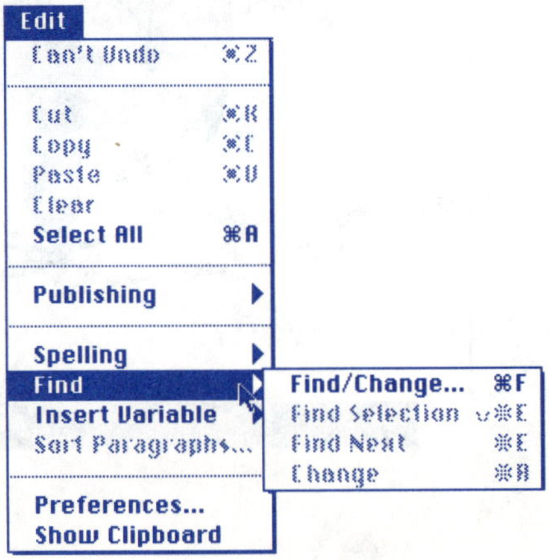

Find Selection Shift-⌘-E

Use the Find Selection command to move to the next occurrence of whatever text you have selected. This command does not summon a dialog box, so it is a very quick way to move through a document.

For example, you may be reading a document on screen that includes a table of contents at its beginning (these are sometimes published online, in sources such as CompuServe or America Online). If the beginning of the document includes a list of the major headings that are in the document, you can use the Edit | Find Selection command to navigate to a specific occurrence of a word or string. Select the headings you want to view, then use the Edit | Find submenu | Find Selection command or the Shift-⌘-E keyboard equivalent.

MacWrite Pro searches for the next occurrence of text that matches the selection. For example, if you select the word "find" in a document, MacWrite Pro will also find "finding," "Finder," and "finds." The Find/Change dialog box, discussed later, will let you specify that only whole words are to be found.

Note All Find operations in MacWrite Pro "wrap around." This means that when the program reaches the end of a document, it continues the search from the beginning of the document. If there is no occurrence of the text you are looking for between the insertion point and the end of the document, both the Find Next command and the Find Selection command take you to the first occurrence of the text you are searching for higher in the document.

Find Next ⌘-E

The Edit | Find Next command repeats the most recent Find command, selecting the next occurrence of the most recently searched for text. It is related to the Find Selection command in that, presumably, the text MacWrite Pro found after performing a Find command is selected, unless you have deselected it by typing or by clicking elsewhere in the document.

Find Next is a handy way to jump repeatedly through a document, looking for instances of the same text. Sometimes online documents, as mentioned earlier, will have various section markings scattered throughout them. These may be special symbols or words. Use the Find Next and Find Selection commands to move quickly from one occurrence of specific symbols or words to the next.

Find Order

When Finding text, MacWrite Pro always starts from the cursor location and proceeds to the end of the document. When it reaches the end of the document, it automatically advances to the beginning of the document and continues the search. You cannot tell MacWrite Pro to reverse the order of the search. One side effect of this behavior is that if there is only one instance of the text for which you are searching in a document, MacWrite Pro keeps selecting that instance each time you click the Find Next button in the Find dialog box.

More Complex Finds: Find/Change ⌘-F

Finding a string of text in a document is a useful tool, and MacWrite Pro has a powerful store of additional tools for manipulating text. These tools are located in the Find/Change dialog box. The basic version of this dialog box is shown here:

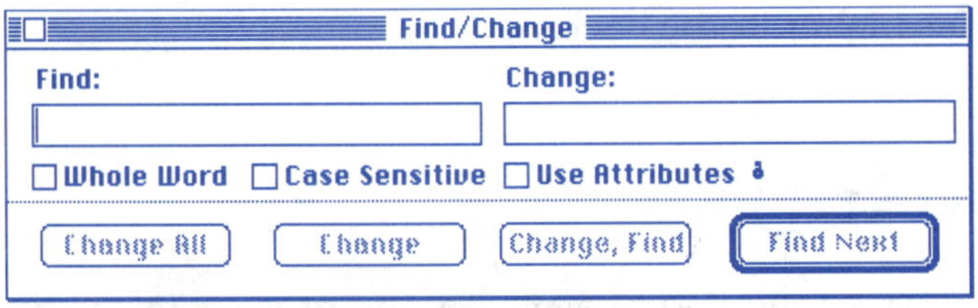

Use the Find/Change command on the Find submenu to summon this dialog box. The keyboard equivalent is ⌘-F.

There are two text edit fields at the top of the Find/Change dialog box. The first field is labeled Find; type the text to search for in this field. If you have previously used the Find or Find Selection commands, the text you last searched for is already entered in the Find field. You can also use the Paste command to place text that is already in the Clipboard into this field.

The Find field, though it only displays approximately 30 characters, can actually contain up to 255 characters—so if you want to find a large string of text, type it in, or select it and paste it into the field.

Note As a rule of thumb, put as much text into the Find field as you can. MacWrite Pro finds larger text strings proportionally faster than shorter text strings, and this helps assure that the text found will be the text you wanted to find.

Changing Text

The Change field is to the right of the Find field in the Find/Change dialog box. Use this field together with the Find field to automatically find a string of text and replace it with another. To do this, type the text you want to change in the Find field, and type the text you want the found text changed to in the Change field.

Note You can navigate between these two text edit fields with either the Tab key or the mouse.

The four buttons at the bottom of the Find/Change dialog box control the Find/Change functions.

Change All The Change All button finds *all* instances of the text you specify in the Find field, and replaces them with the text you specify in the Change field without asking you to confirm them one by one. This action is not undoable, and MacWrite Pro so warns you. Use this button carefully.

Change After MacWrite Pro has located text, the Change button changes the selected text to the text in the Change field. The newly changed text remains selected.

Change, Find The Change, Find button combines the functions of the Change and Find Next buttons; it changes the selection and then jumps to the next occurrence of the text. Click the button again to change this occurrence and jump to the next one.

Find Next The Find Next button locates and selects the next instance (from the insertion point or current selection) of the text in the Find field.

Whole Word Searches

Below the Find field are three check boxes: Whole Word, Case Sensitive, and Use Attributes. The first, Whole Word, lets you specify that only whole words will be found. In the example discussed earlier, when you are searching for the word "find," only that word will be found—"finder," "finding," and "finds" will not be located.

Case Sensitive

Check the Case Sensitive check box to find only strings of text whose case exactly matches the case of the text in the Find field. For example, if you search for the word "find" and have checked the Case Sensitive check box, the word "Find" will not be found, nor will "Finder." A good use for this is when you want to find words at the beginning of a sentence or proper names that might be differentiated from other words. Looking for "Field" with the Case Sensitive box will help you locate only an individual named Field: the field in "Chesterfield" and the field in "fields of grass" will not be found. If a sentence begins with "Field," however, that occurrence will be found because it is capitalized.

Finding with Character Attributes

One of MacWrite Pro's most powerful features is the way it lets you work not just with text when Finding and Changing, but also with the style of the text. In the previous example, you could find instances of "Field" that are in italics.

To enable Finding and Changing text styles, check the Use Attributes check box in the Find/Change dialog box. The dialog box will expand downward, displaying additional buttons, as shown here:

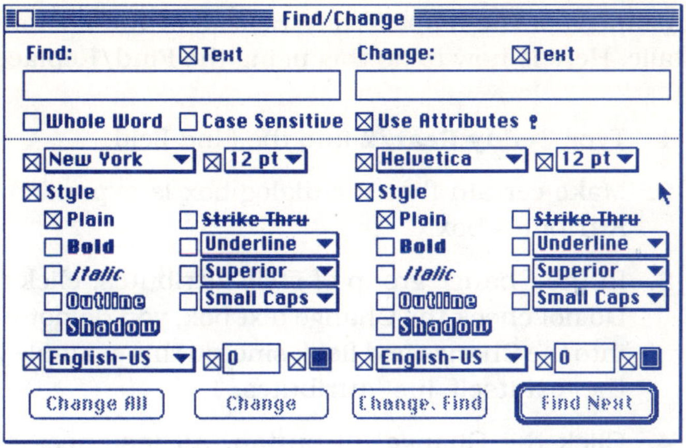

You can switch between the expanded and the lean versions of the Find/Change dialog box using the toggle flag (located to the right of the Use Attributes checkbox label).

This somewhat cluttered dialog box includes the same text formatting options found on the Format menu. The check boxes enable and disable various style formats. The two columns of options under the Find field are controls for defining the style of the text you want to find; the two columns of options under the Change field are controls for the attributes of the text you are changing. If the box next to the pop-up menu listing font names under the Find field is checked, only text of the specified font will be found. It is very important that you only check boxes that pertain to what you want to do. Otherwise, some occurrences of text might not be found—for instance, if the New York font is in the font pop-up and its box is checked, but you don't use New York in the document, no text will be found.

Note If you paste styled text into either the Find or Change field, the corresponding attribute check boxes for that field are automatically updated. For example, if you paste italic Times text into the Find field, the pop-up font menu changes to show Times checked and the italic check box is checked.

This expanded Find/Change dialog box can be used to change the style of text in a document. For example, suppose you want to find all instances of the name Teddy Bear/2 in the document and make them italic. Here is how to do this using the Find/Replace command:

1. Type **Teddy Bear/2** into the Find field.
2. Make certain that the dialog box is expanded, and check the Use Attributes box.
3. In the Change group of style attributes, click the Italic check box. Do not check the Change text box; you do not need to enter any text into the Change text field, since in this example you are not changing the text itself, just attributes.
4. Click the Change All button. All instances of Teddy Bear/2 are changed to italic.

You can also search for text with specific formatting. Here is an exercise that demonstrates how that works by changing all italic occurrences of Teddy Bear/2 from the previous example to bold.

1. Open the Find/Change dialog box (press ⌘-F). Enter **Teddy Bear/2** into the Find field and then click the Italic button below it.

Note You could also copy the italic Teddy Bear/2 from the document, and paste it into the field; if you paste formatted text into the field, and the Use Attributes button is checked, the attributes of the text you pasted are applied to the Find/Change dialog box. This is a terrific shortcut.

2. On the right side of the dialog box, click the Bold button. Do not check the Change field's Text check box. Again, if the Change field's Text check box is active, Teddy Bear/2 is replaced with nothing (deleted) because the Change field is empty.
3. Click the Change All button.

You can also search for any text in a document based solely on its style. So, for example, you could search for any underlined text and change it to italics. Select attributes as in the previous example, but leave the Find field empty and make sure both the Find field's Text check box and the Change field's Text check box are unchecked.

Searching for Special Characters

In addition to finding what you normally think of as "text," MacWrite Pro can search for a wide variety of other characters that are usually part of a document. Many of these characters are very common, for example, the return or the tab character.

Searching for both tab and return characters presents a bit of a problem because both the Tab and the Return key are interpreted by the Find/Change dialog box as commands: the Tab key selects the next field, and the Return key triggers the Find Next button.

One way to search for a character like a tab or return character is to copy it to the Clipboard from a document and then paste it into the Find field. (To see tab and return characters in a document, use the Show Invisibles command from the View menu.)

You can also enter tab, return, and a variety of other special characters directly into the Find field and the Change field. For this purpose, MacWrite Pro implements a special marker character, the backslash (\). This marker character tells MacWrite Pro to interpret any characters that follow it not as the normal characters, but as codes representing other characters. So, to search for a return character, type **\¶**. (Press Option-7 to generate the ¶ character.) To search for a tab character, type **\t**. (To search for the backslash character itself, type **** into the field.) Table 6-1 lists the special characters you can search for using codes.

To use any of these codes, type them or their keyboard equivalents into the Find field in the Find/Change dialog box.

Note If you are working with a document that contains some of the less frequently used special characters, you do not have to worry about remembering obscure keyboard sequences. Instead, use the Clipboard and MacWrite Pro's ability to paste into a Find/Change dialog box text field and its ability to copy and paste between the Find and Change Text Edit fields. For example, if you need to search for the time variable (this is discussed in Chapter 5), first insert the variable using the Edit menu, select it, then use the Cut command to simultaneously remove it from the document and place it in the Clipboard. Then summon the Find/Change dialog box and paste from the Clipboard into the text field.

TABLE 6-1 Using Codes to Search for Special Characters

Symbol	Command Keys	Manual Entry
Tab	⌘-Tab	\t
Paragraph break	⌘-Option-7, ⌘-Return	\Option-7
Page break	⌘-Shift-Enter, ⌘-B	\b
Line break	⌘-Shift-Return	\n
Column break	⌘-Enter	\c
Section break	⌘-Option-6 ⌘-Option-Enter	\Option-6
Page number	⌘-3, ⌘-Shift-3	\#
Footnote	⌘-Option-F	\Option-F
Picture frame	⌘-G	\g
Soft hyphen	⌘--	\-
Date stamp	⌘-D, ⌘-Shift-D	\d
Time stamp	⌘-Option-T, ⌘-Shift-T	\Option-T
Doc name	⌘-Option-2	\Option-2
Revision no.	⌘-Option-R, ⌘-R	\Option-R
Section no.	⌘-Option-3, ⌘-S	\Option-3
Table, note, text frame	⌘-Option-8	\Option-8
Wildcard (char)	⌘-7	\?
Wildcard (mult)	⌘-8	*
Backslash	⌘-\	\\
Smart quote	⌘-'	\'
Smart double quote	⌘-"	\"
Hard space	Shift-Spacebar	\Option-Shift-V
En space	Option-Spacebar	_
Hard En space	⌘-Shift-Option-Spacebar	\Option-J
Nonbreak hyphen	⌘-Option-Shift--	\Option-Shift--
En dash	Option--	\Option--
Em dash	Option-Shift--	\Option-Shift--
Merge break	⌘-M	\m

This technique may seem like a lot of steps, but it is often easier than either memorizing a long list of codes or looking them up.

Wildcard Finds

MacWrite Pro supports two special *wildcard characters* that let you perform more general searches.

The * code lets you search for variable-length strings of unspecified text. Thus, entering **t*e** into the Find text field will locate all words that contain t followed by an unspecified number of characters followed by e. In the sample document, "Teddy," "the," "time," and "advantages" (among others) will be found.

The \? code lets you do single-character wildcard searches. Entering **t\?e** into the Find text field will find "tie," "toe," and "the."

These wildcard characters are very useful tools, even to those among us who have attained spelling perfection. You can use it to find proper names, which by convention obey no spelling rules, and since MacWrite Pro is so well suited for creating and editing documents that contain text in more than one language, these two wildcard tools can help you in editing text in your second, third, or fourth language.

Some Common Find/Change Tasks

Thanks to its rich set of XTND file translation filters, MacWrite Pro excels at importing documents created by other applications, but file translations are rarely perfect. It is often up to you to perform the final fine tuning on imported documents. Here are some handy techniques for performing that fine tuning.

Removing Unwanted Return Characters

Text files imported from other systems sometimes have a return character at the end of every line. This is often necessary for online services, and it is also the MS-DOS convention that plain text files contain a return at the end of every line. Since paragraph formatting information is stored in the return character, editing such a document is nearly impossible in MacWrite Pro without first removing these superfluous returns.

Documents with a return character at the end of each line usually also have two returns at the end of each paragraph. The first step in the process of removing the returns at the end of each line is to preserve the end of paragraph information. If all the returns were removed, you would have to redefine the paragraphs manually. A better procedure is to replace these double returns with a temporary place holder, remove the remaining return characters, and then replace the placeholder characters with actual returns. This is how to do it:

1. Summon the Find/Change dialog box.
2. Type **\¶\¶** into the Find text field. (Press Option-7 to generate the ¶ character.) This instructs MacWrite Pro to search for all occurrences of two returns.
3. Type the temporary placeholder character into the Change text field. The character you use for a placeholder is up to you. Just remember to choose a unique character or string of characters, that is, something that does not appear anywhere in the document. In most cases, a rarely used character such as • (accessed by pressing Option-8) works well.
4. In this procedure attributes are irrelevant, so uncheck the Use Attributes check box.
5. Finally, click the Change All button and then click OK in the resulting alert dialog box.

The following steps remove the return characters.

1. With the Find/Change dialog box open, remove one \¶ from the Find field—all the instances of two return characters have already been removed.
2. Tab to or select the Change field, and enter a space character (by pressing Spacebar).

3. Click the Change All button.

It will usually take MacWrite Pro longer to replace all the returns than it did to replace the double returns (there will be a lot more of them).

At this stage, all the returns, including the ones needed to define paragraphs, have been removed. The following steps will replace the temporary placeholder characters with a return character.

1. Enter the placeholder character (• in the above example) in the Find/Change box's Find field.
2. Tab to the Change field and type **\¶**, the special marker for the return character.
3. Click the Change All button, and OK the warning dialog box.

Converting to Smart Quotes

If you do not have Smart Quotes turned on in the Preferences dialog box, or are working with a document that originated in a program that does not support smart quotes, MacWrite Pro can replace the straight quotes with smart quotes for you. Since MacWrite Pro automatically determines which straight quotes should be opening quotes (they have a space before them) and which should be closing quotes (a space after them), this is a one-step procedure. Enter the straight quote in the Find field and the smart quote in the Change field.

MacWrite Pro always defaults to straight quotes in the Find and Change fields, regardless of the preferences settings. So, when converting straight quotes to smart quotes, press the " key to generate the straight quote in the Find field, and press the ⌘-" key combination in the Change field (\" will appear in the field).

Note It is not a good idea to use a global Find/Change operation when you are smartening quotes; it is difficult to ensure that cases where you want to have straight quotes—such as symbols for inches and feet—are not changed. Only execute a global Find/Change if there are no references to inches and feet in the document.

Converting to Straight Quotes

There are many cases where you do not want to have smart quotes in your document. This includes times when you want to move the document to a different computer (as a text file to an online service such as CompuServe, for example) that does not support smart quotes. If the destination system cannot accept smart quotes, turn the preference off before you begin typing.

To convert smart quotes to straight quotes, press ⌘-" in the Find field (\" will appear in the field). In the Change field press the quote key. Click Change All, and then OK when the alert dialog box appears.

Replacing Double Spaces with a Single Space

Use only one space at the end of a sentence and between words when you are using proportional type on the Mac. A good final editing step is to do a Find/Change to let MacWrite Pro remove all the double spaces and replace them with single spaces.

To remove extra spaces, search for two space characters and replace them with one space. Type two spaces into the Find field and one into the Change field; then click the Change All button. If there are occurrences in the document where you want to have two spaces (though it is hard to imagine why you would want to), use the dialog box to step through the occurrences of double spaces one at a time (Change, Find button), confirming every change before it takes place.

Removing Inappropriate Spaces

You may occasionally encounter documents in which several spaces are used inappropriately as a tool to align or center text. Use Find/Change to find each instance by searching for four or five spaces. This should move you immediately to a location in the document that needs cleaning up. If, for example, the spaces are used to center text, select all the spaces, delete them, then use the Ruler to center the text.

If you encounter a document in which spaces rather than tabs are used to align tables, you can use Find/Change to locate instances of four or five successive spaces, then select the spaces, and replace them with tabs, using the Ruler or the Format Tab dialog box as required. (The Ruler and Format Tab dialog box are discussed in Chapter 4.)

Summary

MacWrite Pro's Find functions are located on the Edit | Find submenu.

The Find Selection command finds the next occurrence of whatever text is selected. This is a quick way to find the next occurrence a text string.

The Find Next command repeats the last Find operation.

The Find/Change dialog box is the tool you use to change every occurrence of a string of text.

Searches can be narrowed based on whole or partial words; case; or any character attribute, including font, size, and style. The Find/Change dialog box can also be used to change the attributes of text without changing the actual text itself.

Searches can include all the special or nonprinting characters a document might contain. These range from common characters such as returns and tabs to less frequently encountered characters such as line breaks, section breaks, and merge breaks. In addition, special wildcard characters aid in pattern matching.

Find/Change helps in cleaning up documents that contain unwanted returns and multiple spaces improperly used for formatting. Find/Change is also handy for converting smart quotes to straight quotes and vice versa.

CHAPTER

7

Formatting with Styles

Previous chapters have covered the ins and outs of formatting both individual characters and paragraphs using dialog boxes, the Ruler, and commands on the Format menu and how you can search for and replace formatting.

Custom styles offer even greater control over the text and formatting styles in a document. They make it easier to apply complex sets of formats to specific text and help you to maintain consistency in those formats quickly and easily throughout a document.

What Is a Style Sheet?

As used in this chapter, a *custom style* is a collection of different format attributes that are grouped together and named. Applying a custom style means assigning that group of attributes to selected text. There are two kinds of custom styles: those that govern only specific ranges of text, which are called *character styles,* and those that format an entire paragraph. Not surprisingly, those are called *paragraph styles.* A *style sheet* is a collection of custom style definitions, stored as part of a MacWrite Pro document. Each document can have but one style sheet, but potentially scores of custom styles.

What Custom Styles Do

Here are some of the advantages of formatting using style sheets.

Enter Several Formats at Once

Custom styles can contain several formats. For example, a user paragraph style might contain ruler settings, tab settings, and character settings that govern font, size, and style of the text. Instead of making several trips to the Format menu to set all these options, you can store them all in a named custom style and apply them to the selected paragraph with a single mouse click.

Reformat a Document Quickly

Style sheets can be copied between documents. If you import into a document a style sheet that was created in a second document, the styles in the first document are replaced by those in the second document. This technique is useful for creating and editing a document that contains many downloadable fonts, and therefore prints more slowly than a document in a single font. You can maintain a set of custom styles in one font that you use for writing and editing a document and a second set of custom styles containing all the downloadable fonts that you use for printing the final copy.

Control Default Formats

By modifying the Default style, which MacWrite Pro automatically opens with, all documents you create will have the same set of formats; when you open a new document, you save time by not having to set up the format of the document from scratch.

Create Standards

Style sheets help you manage sets of custom styles. This is particularly helpful if you are working in an organization in which different work groups produce different sets of documents. You can distribute style sheets to all who need them, ensuring that documents produced by your organization have a consistent, unified appearance.

Automate Typing

Finally, paragraph custom styles can make typing easier. One of the items you can control in a paragraph custom style is the style of the following paragraph. For example, if you define a style called Heading, you can designate that the style to follow this paragraph is the Default style. When you type a heading, assign it the Heading style, and then press Return at the end of the paragraph, the new paragraph will automatically assume the Default style.

Another useful example of this might be a paragraph style for paragraphs that contain a picture. This style might be followed by a Caption style, which would in turn be followed by the Default style.

Two Kinds of Custom Styles

MacWrite Pro supports two kinds of custom styles, governing two different domains, though there is an overlap.

Custom Character Styles

Character custom styles contain the items that can be found on the Style menu. They govern the font, size, and style formats of a group of characters. You typically use character styles to format words within paragraphs, not entire paragraphs.

Custom Paragraph Styles

Paragraph styles use character styles as part of their definitions, and can even use a custom character style to base character formatting on. Paragraph custom styles can also contain all the items that you normally control with the Format Paragraph dialog box and the Ruler.

Where Style Sheets Are Stored

Style sheets are normally stored with the document in which you created them. The benefit of this scheme is that if you move that document to a different machine or send it to a different user, the style sheets are carried with it.

Style sheets can also be stored in a file called MacWrite Pro Options that is stored in the Claris folder inside your System Folder. This allows you to create a set of styles that automatically become part of any new document you create. The MacWrite Pro Options file is discussed in detail later in this chapter in "Creating and Modifying Default Styles."

Creating Custom Styles

There are two ways to define custom styles. The first method can be thought of as "define by example." If you are using this method, you first use standard commands on the Format and Style menus and the icons on the Ruler to format characters or a paragraph, and then create a new custom style based on the resulting style of that text. The second method is to start from scratch and use a Define Styles dialog box to define all the elements of a custom style. You can combine the two methods. That is, you can use the dialog box to add to or modify custom styles that you created by example.

The Styles Palette

No matter which method you use to create custom styles (or, later, to apply and modify custom styles), the Styles palette is the main tool you will use. To open the Styles palette, choose the Show Styles command from the Style menu. The palette will open, as illustrated here:

The Styles palette is unlike the other palettes in MacWrite Pro in that it has its own menu bar, with three pull-down menus. The Styles palette File menu commands perform file functions similar to the main File menu commands on custom styles; its Edit menu commands perform edit functions on styles; the right menu (either ¶ or C) allows you to select the named styles. These menus are discussed later in this chapter.

At the right corner of this menu bar is a small paragraph symbol (¶); this indicates that the palette is listing custom paragraph styles. This symbol toggles the display of custom styles between custom paragraph styles (indicated by the paragraph symbol) and custom character styles, indicated by a C.

The standard Styles palette has two items listed (presuming you have not created any of your own custom styles). Default represents the normal format of your document; it contains the definition for all text you type that is not otherwise styled. The No Style item is for text that is not styled at all.

Creating Custom Styles by Example

Here is how to create a custom style by example, based on the example document shown in Figure 7-1.

The goal is to style the second paragaph, reading "The Advantages of Teddy Bear/2" as a heading. In this example, the heading style will be Helvetica, 14-point, bold, and centered. The following steps show you how to style that text and then define a new style based on it:

1. Select the "Teddy Bear/2" paragraph. You can do this by triple-clicking anywhere in the paragraph.

FIGURE 7-1 A sample document in which to create a new style

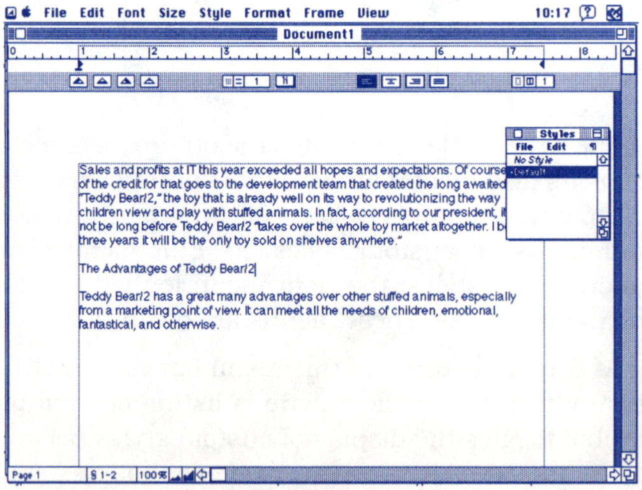

2. From the Style menu, select Bold. All the text in the paragraph is made bold.
3. Select the Helvetica font from the Font menu.
4. Using the Ruler, click the center-text icon.
5. Select 14 from the Size menu.

The paragraph should be in bold Helvetica, in 14-point type, and centered. The newly formatted paragraph is shown in Figure 7-2.

Before continuing, take a look at the Styles palette. With the newly styled text selected, the Styles palette Default style now has a + beside it. That tells you that the selected text is based on the Default style, but has additional formatting.

Here is how to create a style definition based on the text you have just formatted:

1. If it isn't already selected, select some text within the styled paragraph. You do not need to select the entire paragraph; placing the insertion point within the paragraph will do.

FIGURE 7-2 The styled paragraph

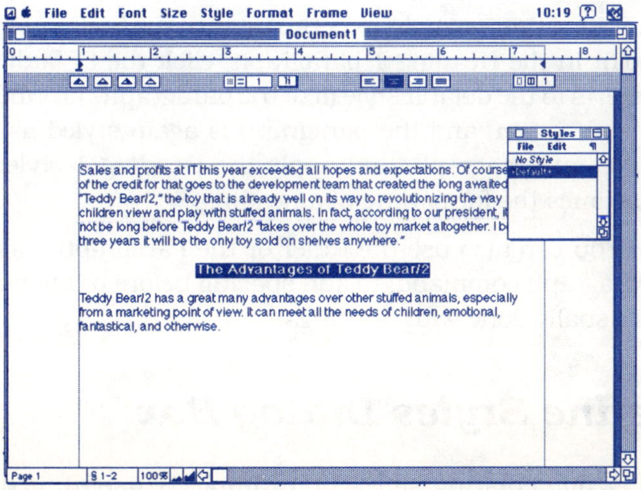

2. Point to the File menu on the Styles palette's menu bar, like this:

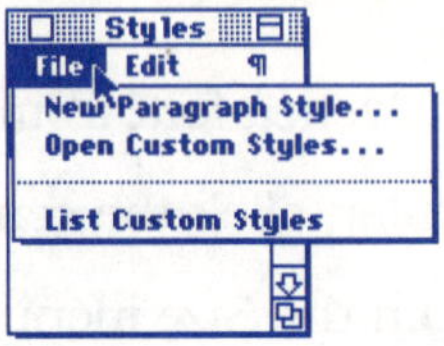

3. Drag down to highlight the New Paragraph Style command and release the mouse. This dialog box appears:

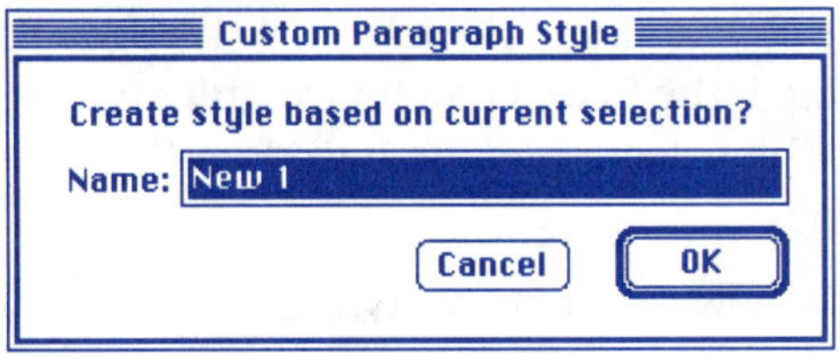

4. Where the text "New 1" appears, type **Heading 1** to name the new style. Click the OK button to comfirm creating the new style.

That's all it takes to create a custom style by example. The Styles palette now shows the Heading 1 style listed below the Default style. When you select text or place the insertion point within the "Advantages of Teddy Bear/2" paragraph, this style name is highlighted.

Using this example, experiment with the Styles palette. With the insertion point in the Heading 1 paragraph, click the Default style: that paragraph reverts to the default style (like the paragraphs around it). Click the Heading 1 style again, and the paragraph is again styled as a heading. Click in a different paragraph, and apply the Heading 1 style; that paragraph now assumes the formatting of a heading.

You can also use the Ruler or the Paragraph dialog box (Format menu Paragraph command) to add spacing before or after the paragraph—which is usually done with headings.

The Define Styles Dialog Box

While creating styles by example is useful, it does involve setting a number of formats and trips to the menu bar. You can use the Define

Styles box, instead, to streamline this process. Open the Define Styles dialog box by choosing Define Styles from the Style menu or using the ⌘-D keyboard equivalent. The Define Styles dialog box is shown here:

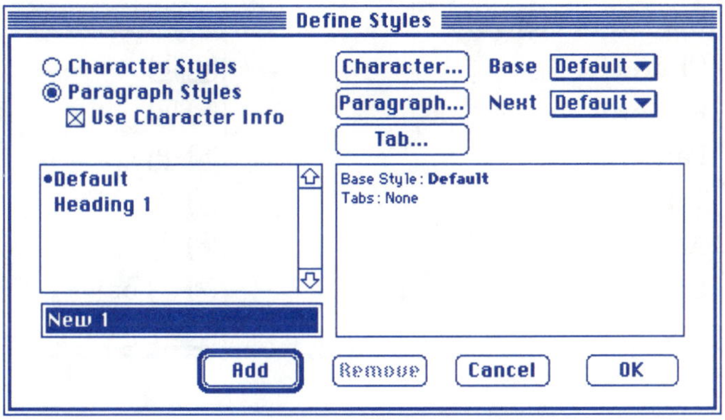

As you can see, this dialog box has a title bar, and is moveable (drag the box by the title bar). This lets you reposition the dialog box on the screen to reveal any selected paragraph behind it. This means you can use the Apply button to test your style definitions before you save them as part of the style sheet.

At the top of the dialog box are two radio buttons, Character Styles and Paragraph Styles. The active radio button—the one that is filled in—determines the kind of style listed below.

As with most MacWrite Pro dialog boxes, you can use the ⌘ key together with other keys to activate buttons. Hold down the ⌘ key, and after a moment these keyboard shortcuts will be displayed in the dialog box. Table 7-1 contains a summary of the keyboard shortcuts for the Define Styles dialog box.

The Add button changes to read Copy if a custom style is selected. The ↑ and ↓ keys select existing custom styles, and the ← and → keys move the insertion point within the field that contains the name of the style you are defining. Standard keyboard shortcuts for Cut, Copy, and Paste (⌘-X, ⌘-C, and ⌘-V, respectively) work in the dialog box as well, to let you copy styles. If you deselect any custom style names, the name New

TABLE 7-1 Keyboard Equivalents for the Define Styles Dialog Box Buttons

Button:	Keyboard Shortcut:
Character Styles	⌘-M
Paragraph Styles	⌘-N
Use Character Info	⌘-I
Character	⌘-H
Remove	⌘-R
Paragraph	⌘-P
Tab	⌘-T
Add	⌘-A
Cancel	⌘-. or Esc
OK	Enter, Return, or ⌘-K

1 appears in the field at the bottom of the dialog, unless there's already a style by that name, in which case New 2 appears, and so on.

Character Styles

Custom character styles format characters only—they do not contain any settings for margins, line spacing, or tabs. As a result, when you click the Character Styles radio button, the Paragraph and Tab buttons and the Next pop-up menu are disabled.

Below the radio buttons is a field listing all the styles of the text currently selected (in this case, character styles). MacWrite Pro does not automatically create default character styles, so unless you have already created some, none are listed.

Here is how to create a new custom character style:

1. Type the name of the custom style you want to create in the field below the list of styles, where the default name "New 1" appears. In this case type **Emphasis**.
2. Click the Character button at the top of the dialog box. A new dialog box appears, as shown here:

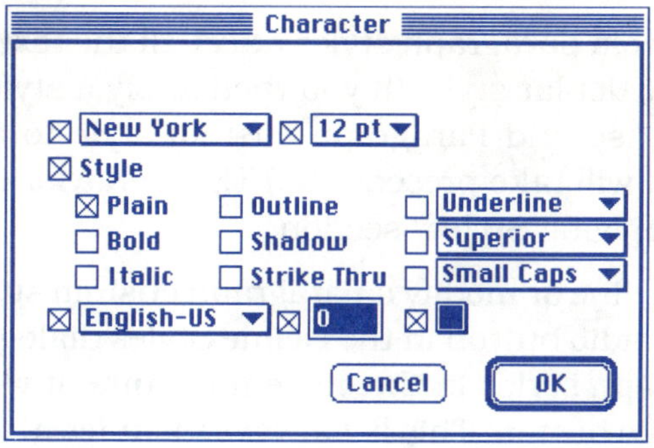

This dialog box includes all the settings you can include in a character style, including Font (accessible from a pop-up menu), size, and style. Character styles are discussed in Chapter 3.

3. For this exercise, hold the mouse down on the font pop-up menu and drag to select Helvetica.
4. Set the size of the text to 14 points.
5. Click the OK button to close the Character dialog box.
6. Click the Add button to add the new style.

Note When you click the new style, the text description window to the right of the field that lists styles details the definition of the style.

Custom character styles need not define all parts of character formatting. In the example, you created a custom style that included the Helvetica font specification. But you may not want to specify a font name for the character custom style; instead you may want the font for a character style to be the same as the text around it. In this case, you need only uncheck the box next to the Font pop-up menu. The same is true of all character attributes: if you do not want them to be part of the style definition, uncheck their boxes.

Base styles, which are used with both character and paragraph styles, are discussed later in this chapter.

Custom Paragraph Styles

Custom paragraph styles affect all the text in the paragraph governed by a particular style. (If you then apply a style from the Format menu or apply a second Paragraph custom style to a paragraph, the last style applied will take precedence.) This behavior is covered in detail below in the "Applying Styles" section.

To define or modify a paragraph custom style, first click the Paragraph Styles radio button in the Define Styles dialog box. A list of all the custom paragraph styles in the current document will appear in the field below the radio button. This list always includes at least the Default style. Later in this chapter you will see how to modify the default style for all new MacWrite Documents.

Use Character Info Below the Paragraph Styles radio button is a check box labeled Use Character Info. If this box is checked, you can define character attributes (font, size, style, etc.) that will then affect all the text in a paragraph of a particular style. If the box is not checked, only paragraph-level definitions—line spacing, tabs, indentation, etc.—apply to that paragraph. When the box is checked, the Character button (the same one used to define Character styles) is active; otherwise, it is disabled.

Paragraph The Paragraph button summons the Paragraph dialog box, shown here:

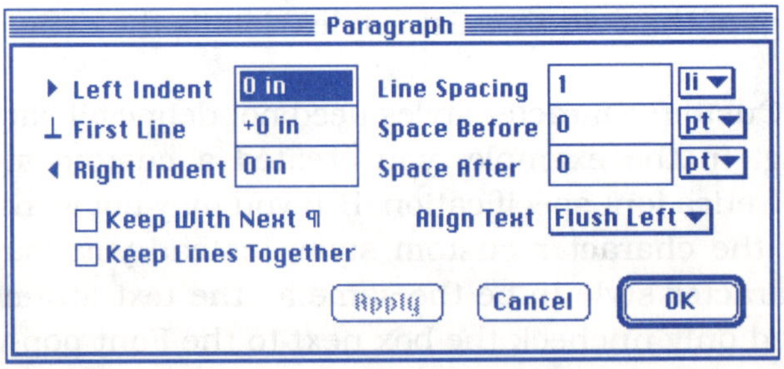

This dialog box includes the same options available when you choose Paragraph from the Format menu. Each element of this dialog box is discussed in Chapter 4.

Entering numbers into the Left Indent, First Line, and Right Indent fields is optional. If the Ruler is visible in the document window behind this dialog box, you can manipulate these values directly by adjusting their icons. As you move the icons, the numbers in the dialog box change automatically to reflect the new icon positions.

Tab Style Since tabs, too, are part of a paragraph style (as mentioned in Chapter 4), you can specify tab settings as part of a paragraph custom style. This is especially useful if you often create tables using tabs (as opposed to using the Table tool). Store the table tab settings as a custom paragraph style.

Clicking the Tab button summons the Tab dialog box:

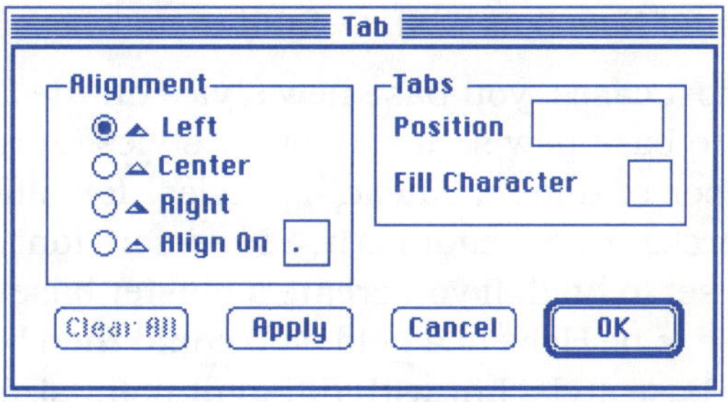

The radio buttons on the left edge of the dialog box let you specify which type of tab you are setting. Enter the location of the tabs into the position field. Consult Chapter 4 for a complete discussion of tabs. While you can move this dialog box around the screen, you *cannot* directly set tabs on the Ruler behind the dialog box. Thus it is more convenient to set tabs using the Ruler or the Tabs dialog box (accessible on the Format menu) to set tabs for a paragraph first and then create or redefine a style based on that paragraph.

Note When you summon the Tabs command from the Format menu, you can directly set tabs on the Ruler while the Tabs dialog box is open, if the Ruler is visible. When you click from within the Paragraph dialog box, you can't.

Base Style Each custom style has a *Base style*—that is, the style on which it is predicated. This means styles inherit all the properties of the Base style. For example, if your Default style is Courier plain text, you can create a character custom style that is Courier bold by creating a new style and clicking the Bold attribute. This new character custom style is automatically Courier because it is based on the Default character style, Courier plain text. If you then change the Default style to Helvetica, all the text that is styled in either the Default style or the new style you created is changed to Helvetica. This technique both saves time and helps ensure document-wide consistency.

In a hierarchy of styles, all formatting is carried through the chain of the hierarchy. Thus if you have a style called New 1 that is based on the Default style, it called a *child* of Default; it shares all the characteristics of Default, except for those that are explicitly defined as being part of New 1. If the style New 2 is based on New 1, it inherits all the characteristics of New 1, many of which are inherited from Default. Changing a characteristic of Default that is not overridden in New 1 or New 2 then changes New 1 and New 2 as well. Default is an *ancestor* of New 1 and New 2.

In most cases, you base new styles on the Default style. But it is also useful to base new styles on other styles. For example, you might have a number of different heading styles, for different levels of subheads. Some prefer to set headings in a sans-serif font such as Helvetica or Avant Garde, set in bold. If you create a master base heading style that defines the style to be Helvetica bold, you could then base the other styles on the master base style, but with different point sizes or margins. Then, if you change the base heading style, all the other heading styles based on it will automatically change accordingly.

Note When you first open the Define Styles dialog box, the Base and Next styles always show the style of the paragraph currently selected.

Next Style The Next style defines the style for the paragraph that follows the one you are typing. This is a very useful feature—you can construct chains of styles.

As mentioned earlier in this chapter, one use of this might involve having a style called Picture, which contains formatting information for graphics. The Picture style could have defined as its Next style a style called Caption, which would contain the caption for the picture. Caption's Next style would probably be the default style.

The Next style has no effect when you are styling a paragraph that you have already typed.

Applying Styles

There are two ways to apply styles when you are typing or editing a document.

Using the Format Menu

New styles that you define are automatically added to the Format menu. Two hierarchical menus—Character and Paragraph—list the custom styles you have defined. Character custom styles are added to the Character hierarchical menu, and paragraph custom styles are added to the Paragraph hierarchical menu.

MacWrite Pro automatically assigns keyboard equivalents to custom styles. The first ten Character styles have the keyboard shortcut in the form of ⌘-Option-*number*. The number range is from 1 through 0 (which represents 10). The first character style you create is automatically assigned ⌘-Option-1, the second with ⌘-Option-2, and so on. Additional character custom styles you create after the tenth one are not assigned keyboard equivalents.

The first ten Paragraph custom styles are automatically keyboard equivalents in the same manner. The form is ⌘-*number*.

You can cut and paste styles in the Styles palette to reorder the listing of styles in these menus.

Using the Styles Palette

You can also use the Styles palette to assign styles. You might find this method easier than using hierarchical menus or remembering arbitrary keyboard equivalents. When the Styles palette is open, the current style (that is, the style that applies to the insertion point or selected text) is always highlighted. You can apply a style to any selection by clicking the style name in the list of styles. At the top-right corner of the palette is an indicator—C or ¶—telling you whether Character or Paragraph styles are being shown. Clicking this indicator switches between the two kinds of custom styles; holding the mouse button down on this item causes a menu to appear that lets you switch between Character and Paragraph styles.

Managing Styles

This section discusses how to use the various mechanisms that MacWrite Pro provides for managing styles, including moving them between documents and creating a descriptive list of the custom styles in a style sheet.

Cutting, Copying, and Pasting Styles

To move a single custom style from one document to another, use the Style palette's Edit menu. This menu contains the same commands—Cut, Copy, Paste, and Clear—found on the main Edit menu. You can use these commands to copy styles selected in the list of styles and paste them into another document.

The Cut command places the selected style in the Clipboard and removes it from the current document. The Copy command places a copy of the current style in the Clipboard, and the Paste command pastes the style in the Clipboard into the current document's style sheet. The Clear command deletes the selected style from the style sheet, a procedure that cannot be undone.

When you cut or clear a style definition, the definition itself is removed from the style sheet, but any text that was formatted with the removed style retains the formatting attributes of that style.

Note When copying styles, MacWrite Pro maintains what you might call a "Style Clipboard" that is separate from the main Clipboard. Cutting or copying a style does not disturb the contents of the main Clipboard or the Ruler Clipboard.

Listing Styles

The List Custom Styles command on the Styles palette File menu creates a new MacWrite Pro document containing a textual description of the styles in the original document. If you are viewing character styles when you select this command (that is, if a C is visible at the top-right corner of the palette), only character styles will be listed; if you are viewing Paragraph styles, only they will be listed.

Note With this feature you can quickly create descriptive listings of all the style sheets used on a particular project or among the members of a work group.

Redefining Styles

You can redefine a custom style in much the same way that you create one by example. You do this by selecting a paragraph of the style you want to redefine, changing its formatting manually, and using the Redefine Style command on the Edit menu of the Style palette.

A good use for this is merging elements of different styles. For example, you may have a header style that you've put a lot of work into, including tab settings, space before, space after, and character formatting. At any rate, you don't want to have to go to, say, the footer style and redefine all these things all over again, by hand. You don't have to. You can merge attributes from a variety of custom styles into a new one as follows:

1. Create a new custom paragraph style.
2. Click in a paragraph that uses the custom style that you want to steal the paragraph (tab) settings from.
3. Copy Ruler (Shift-⌘-C) via Format menu.
4. Click in the paragraph that is using the paragraph style you created in step 1.
5. Paste Ruler (Shift-⌘-V) via Format menu. Note the two custom paragraph styles now share the same paragraph attributes.

6. Click into a paragraph that uses the character style that you want to lift.
7. Create a new Custom Character Style based on this text (assuming that there isn't one already in existence).
8. Click the cursor in the paragraph that is using the paragraph style you created in step 2.
9. Apply the custom character style you created in step 7. Note that the new custom paragraph style now contains all the attributes needed.
10. Redefine Custom Paragraph style.

Opening Style Sheets

The Open Custom Styles command on the File menu of the Styles palette allows you to combine the style sheet of one document with that of another.

For example, you may have created a new document, called A, have it open on the screen, and realize that you want to use the custom styles you have defined in document B. Choose the Open Custom Styles command, and a standard Open dialog box appears. When you locate the document you want, click the Open button, and the custom styles in that document will be merged with those of the currently open document. Any custom styles in document A will be replaced by styles of the same name from document B, but custom styles in document B that have no counterparts (that is, their names do not match) will be left untouched.

Creating and Modifying Default Styles

You can create custom default styles and store them in a special stationery document called MacWrite Pro Options (unless you hold down the Option key when you choose the New command, as discussed in Chapter 14

). This file is stored in the Claris folder inside the System Folder. When you create a new document, MacWrite Pro uses the styles that are defined in the MacWrite Pro Options document if it is available. Here is how to create custom styles that will be available in all new MacWrite Pro documents:

1. Create a new document, and define within it the styles that you want to be part of the default style sheet. You can do this several ways, including copying defined styles from other documents. Make sure that any document settings (such as margins, headers and footers, and the like) are compatible with the way you want your default documents to appear.

Note Any text in the MacWrite Pro Options document will appear in every new document you create. If you do not want text to appear in every new document, do not put any in the MacWrite Pro Options document.

2. Choose the Save As command from the File menu to summon the Save dialog box.
3. In the Save dialog box, select MacWrite Pro Options from the pop-up menu. (The current directory will automatically change to the Claris folder inside the System Folder; the name of the document will automatically change to MacWrite Pro Options.) Click the Save button.
4. Close the open document. (Since you saved as a special stationery document, MacWrite Pro will ask you if you want to save it again, this time as a regular file. Click the No button.)

To test your handiwork by opening a new document, display the Styles palette if it is not already open, and you will see that the new document includes your new default styles. They are now available whenever you create a new document.

Summary

This chapter introduces the powerful concept of custom styles and style sheets. Style sheets can both help you work more efficiently and help ensure stylistic consistency.

There are two kinds of custom styles: Character custom styles and Paragraph custom styles. Character custom styles are combinations of two or more character styles; Paragraph custom styles are combinations of two or more paragraph styles.

Custom styles are stored in a style sheet, which MacWrite stores with the document. If you have a style sheet that you want to have available every time you create a new document, store it in a special stationery document called MacWrite Pro Options that is saved in the Claris folder in your System Folder.

Custom styles are available on the Format menu and on the floating Styles palette.

You can copy and paste styles between documents with the commands on the Styles palette's Edit menu. You can create a listing of the custom styles in a style sheet with the Styles palette | List Custom Styles command.

CHAPTER 8

Reference Tools

MacWrite Pro includes three tools that you can use to help polish your documents: a spelling checker, a thesaurus, and a hyphenation module.

When you install MacWrite Pro, its reference tools are placed into a special Claris folder inside the System folder. MacWrite Pro checks the contents of this folder each time it starts and updates its internal list of the resources it finds there. If you want to add a special dictionary from a third party to MacWrite Pro, drag its icon into the Claris folder. You can also add dictionaries, especially user dictionaries, that are located elsewhere on your hard disk using the Install References command discussed later in this chapter.

Spelling Checker

The Spelling Checker compares words in your document with those in its built-in dictionary, warns you when they don't match, and makes suggestions for correct spelling. The speller can watch what you type and notify you of misspelled words, or you can instruct it to check the spelling of an entire document or a selection range.

You can access the spelling checker (and all the reference tools) from the Spelling submenu of the Edit menu. The Spelling menu is shown here:

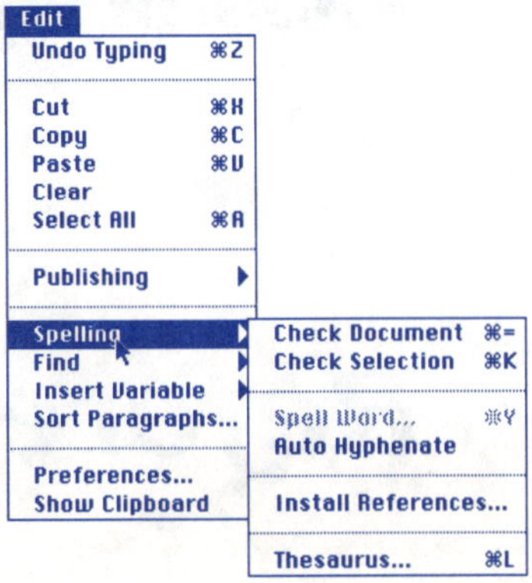

For checking spelling, the three relevant commands on this menu are Check Document, Check Selection, and Spell Word.

Check Document ⌘-=

The keyboard equivalent for the Check Document command is ⌘-=. Use this command to examine every word in your document and compare it with words in the MacWrite Pro built-in dictionaries, any dictionaries you have installed, and your user dictionary. Spell checking begins at the beginning, or top, of your document, no matter where the insertion point or selection is.

Check Selection ⌘-K

Use this command to examine only the word or words you have currently selected. Spell checking begins with the first word in the selection. The keyboard equivalent to Check Selection is ⌘-K.

Note If you have interrupted a check on a document and do not want the check to start over at the beginning, position the insertion point at the location at which you want spell checking to begin, hold down the Shift and ⌘ keys, and press the ↓. All text from the location of the insertion point to the end of the document is selected, and you can then use the Check Selection command to spell-check the new selection.

Spell Word ⌘-Y

Spell Word command is used when you have Spell As You Type enabled in MacWrite Pro's Preferences dialog box. This is discussed later in the chapter. The keyboard equivalent to Spell Word is ⌘-Y.

The Spelling Dialog Box

After you use one of these spelling commands, MacWrite Pro immediately starts checking your document. When it finds a misspelled word, it presents the Spelling dialog box, shown here:

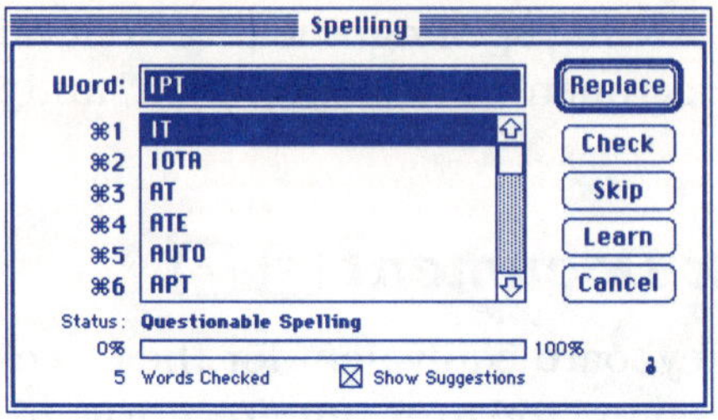

The Word field at the top of the Spelling dialog box shows the questionable word. Below it is a scrolling list displaying as many as six suggested replacements at one time for that word. To replace quickly the misspelled word with one of the suggestions, press the ⌘ key combination shown to the left of the scrolling field. For example, in the preceding illustration, ⌘-1 selects IT, and ⌘-2 selects IOTA.

Note The spelling checker will automatically match the case of a flagged word. Thus if the misspelled word is "Teh," MacWrite Pro will suggest "The" as a replacement.

If you don't want any of the first six words in the scrolling list, you can scroll or page through the list to display more suggestions, if there are any. If you don't want to remove your hand from the keyboard to scroll the list, use the ↑ and ↓ keys.

Note As the list scrolls, the numbers to the left of the Spelling dialog box do not change. Pressing ⌘-1 always replaces the misspelled word with the first word currently displayed in the scrolling list.

You can also type a correct word directly into the Word field and then either click the Replace button or press Return or Enter to replace the misspelled word.

The Check Button The Check button causes MacWrite Pro to check the spelling of the word in the top field; this is useful if you have typed a new word into this field and want to make sure it is spelled correctly before inserting it into your document.

The Skip Button The Skip button tells MacWrite Pro to skip the selected word and all occurrences of that word in the document. For example, in the sample document you can tell MacWrite Pro to skip IPT throughout the document. Skipping applies only during the current spelling check; if you later check the spelling of the document, all flagged words you have previously told MacWrite Pro to skip are flagged as misspelled again.

The Learn Button The Learn button adds the current word to the User Dictionary. This means that it is not flagged as misspelled any time that User Dictionary is used. Later in this chapter you will learn how to manually edit the User Dictionary.

The Cancel Button The Cancel button stops the spelling process and closes the dialog box. When the dialog closes, the last word MacWrite Pro flagged as misspelled is selected in the document.

Status Indicators Directly below the scrolling list of the Spelling dialog box, the Status line tells you what is wrong with the current word (usually it reads "Questionable Spelling").

Below that, a bar indicator shows you how much of the document or the selection has been checked.

Below the status bar indicator, the Spelling dialog box displays how many words have been checked so far.

The Show Suggestions Checkbox The Show Suggestions checkbox tells MacWrite Pro whether or not you want it to indicate suggestions. Unless you are in possession of superior spelling skills, it is a good idea to let MacWrite Pro make spelling suggestions.

The Extended Spelling Dialog Box To the right of the status area is a flip-down button that you use to tell the Spelling dialog box to display more information. The larger Spelling dialog box produced by clicking this button is shown here:

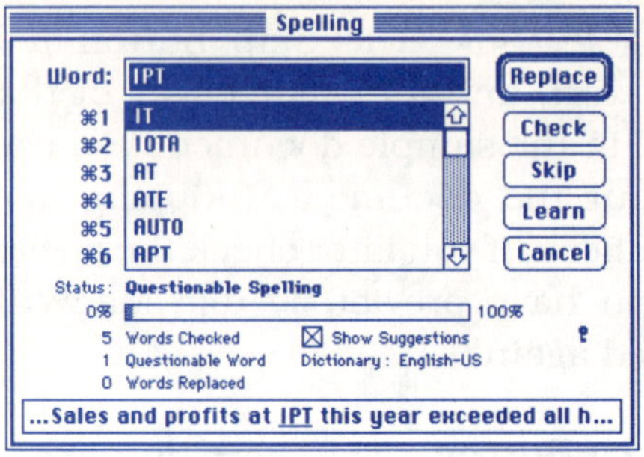

This extended Spelling dialog box gives four additional bits of information. The first tells how many questionable words have been flagged. The second tells which dictionary MacWrite Pro is using for the current word, and the third tells how many words you have replaced. Finally, the extended Spelling dialog box shows you the questionable word in context.

Note The display-flagged-word-in-context feature is especially useful if you are using a small-screen Mac like a Plus, SE, or Classic. If possible, MacWrite Pro scrolls the document behind the Spelling dialog box to display the flagged word in context. If it cannot do so because there is not enough room on the screen, however, displaying the questionable word in context within the Spelling dialog box provides essentially the same the information.

Check While You Type

As mentioned at the beginning of this chapter, MacWrite Pro can also check your spelling interactively as you type. What's more, the price you pay for this, as far as MacWrite Pro being able to keep up with your typing, is not onerous.

Note If you are studying another language, consider purchasing a spelling dictionary of that language to use with the Spell As You Type option. (Additional dictionaries are available directly from Claris customer relations.) You may find that the constant reinforcement of having your misspelled words flagged as you type makes your study time more efficient.

To enable Spell As You Type, use the Preferences command on the Edit menu. Scroll down to and click the Spelling/Hyph. tile, as shown in Figure 8-1.

The top part of this panel governs spelling; the bottom, hyphenation. (Hyphenation is discussed later in the chapter.) To enable spelling as you type, check the box labeled Spell As You Type. When you do so, two radio buttons are enabled. These buttons specify how MacWrite Pro alerts you of flagged words as you type—either with a beep or the flashing of the menu bar. The beep is the system beep defined with the Mac's Sound Control Panel. After you've defined these preferences, close the Preferences dialog box by clicking OK.

Note If you are working in a crowded office and have MacWrite Pro check your spelling as you type, you might want to consider choosing the Flash Menu Bar option, especially if you are a poor typist or speller. Your coworkers will certainly appreciate this small courtesy.

With Spell As You Type enabled, MacWrite Pro looks up each word in its loaded dictionaries immediately after you type it—that is, when you type a space or punctuation mark (comma, colon, semicolon, period, and so on) after typing a string of characters. If the word is not in the dictionaries, MacWrite Pro beeps (or, if directed, flashes the menu bar) to alert you that the word is misspelled. You can then press ⌘-Y to summon the Spelling dialog box. For those who prefer to take the long way home, use the Edit menu, Spelling submenu, Spell Word command to summon the Spelling dialog box.

FIGURE 8-1 The spelling/hyphenation portion of the Preferences dialog box

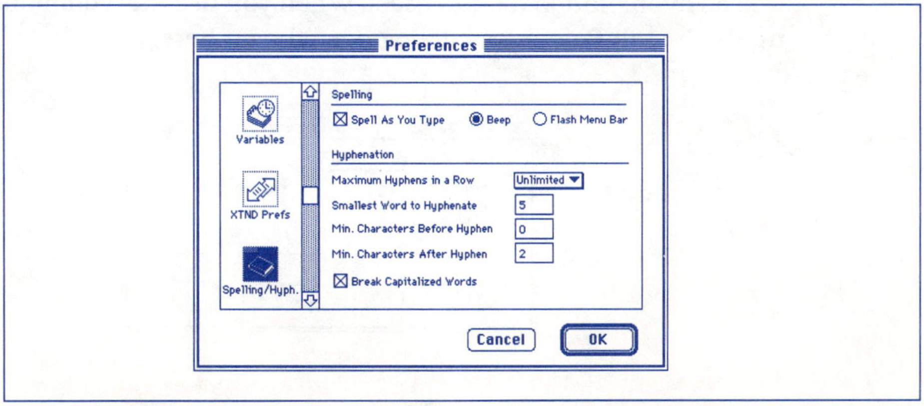

You do not need to summon the spelling document as soon as you are alerted about the misspelled word. You can keep typing until you want to check the word and press ⌘-Y when it is convenient for you to pause. This means that you can complete typing your thought. If, however, MacWrite Pro detects other misspelled words in the interim, only the most recent word is shown in the Spelling dialog box.

Installing and Editing User Dictionaries

When you install MacWrite Pro, it creates a special dictionary called User Dictionary in the Claris folder in your System Folder. All words that you collect with the Add button in the Spelling dialog box are stored in this User Dictionary. Whenever MacWrite Pro encounters a word in a document that is not contained in the main dictionary, it then consults the installed User Dictionary.

In addition to the single User Dictionary, you can also create alternative user dictionaries. You might, for example, create special user dictionaries for words unique to a specific class of documents. If you are creating a cookbook, for example, you could maintain a separate dictionary with abbreviations such as tsp, tbsp, and other food preparation terms. That way, when checking the spelling in your cookbook, these words are not flagged as misspelled, but when checking other documents they are flagged.

The Install References command on the Spelling submenu of the Edit menu (Edit | Spelling | Install References is a good short way to refer to this) is used to maintain user dictionaries and foreign dictionaries (as well as hyphenation dictionaries). When you use this command, it brings up the Install References dialog box, shown here:

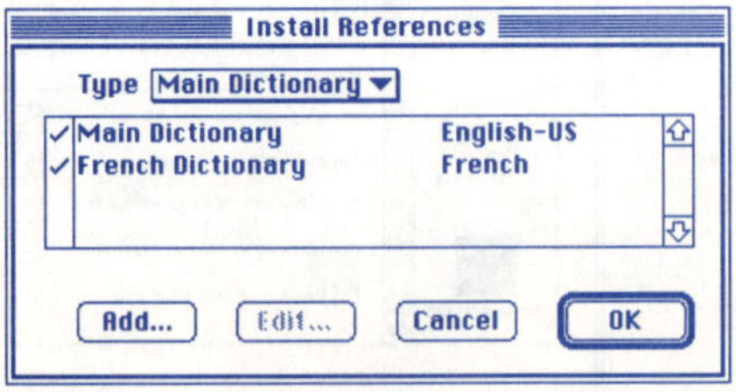

At the top of the Install References dialog box is a pop-up menu that you use to select the type of reference tool you want to modify. The first panel it displays includes the Main dictionaries found in the Claris folder inside the System Folder. Two dictionaries are shown in the preceding illustration: the Main Dictionary of US English and the French Dictionary. If you have purchased and installed additional dictionaries, they are also displayed in the Install References dialog box. Dictionaries with a check next to them are the primary dictionaries consulted when you check your document. The Main Dictionary is always the one used for the main part of your text—that is, text that you have not specified as being in another language. MacWrite Pro checks the Mac system software to determine the primary language. For US users, English-US file is the Main Dictionary. However, if you are using the French version of the Mac system software, the French dictionary is called the Main dictionary, and the English-US dictionary is the one used with words specified as English language style.

Note Only Main Dictionaries—the ones that appear in this portion of the Install References dialog box—are used when MacWrite Pro is spell checking a document.

To maintain your User Dictionary, hold down the mouse button and point to the pop-up list at the top of the Install References dialog box, drag until the User Dictionaries item is highlighted, and release the mouse button. The screen changes to resemble the one shown here, which includes two user dictionaries:

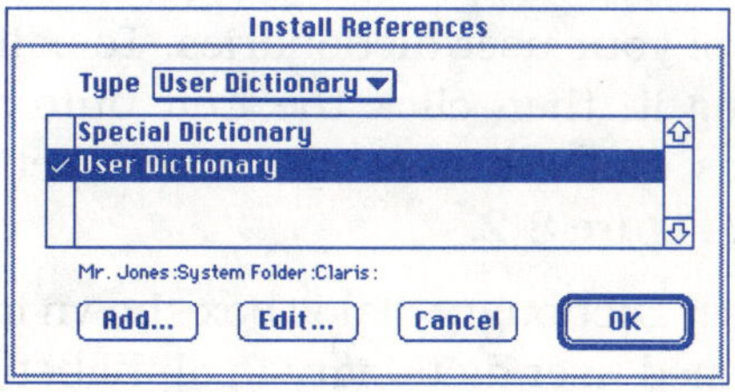

The Install References dialog box shown includes a second User Dictionary, called Special Dictionary. The check mark next to the main User Dictionary means that this is the dictionary that is consulted when you check the spelling of your document, and to which new words are added by the Learn button in the Spelling dialog box.

Note Only one User Dictionary can be active at a time. When you check a second one to tell MacWrite Pro to use it, the other is automatically unchecked.

Normally, the user dictionaries shown in the Install References dialog box are found in the Claris folder inside your System Folder. However, you can use the Add button to specify user dictionaries that are located in other folders. You also use the Add button to create a new User Dictionary. To do so, click Add. The standard File Open dialog box that appears includes a New button, which lets you create a new user dictionary. In most cases you will want to place this user dictionary into the Claris folder inside the System Folder, but you can put it anywhere on any mounted writable storage device. For example, if you are creating a dictionary of special terms for use in one project, then you can keep that user dictionary with the other files that are part of that project.

Note If you click one of the language resources—the Main Dictionary, for example—MacWrite Pro will display the path name below the scrolling list.

Editing User Dictionaries

The Install References dialog box also allows you to modify the contents of your user dictionaries. To edit The User Dictionary, select it by clicking it, then click the Edit button at the bottom of the Install References dialog box. A new User Dictionary dialog box appears, as shown in Figure 8-2.

The User Dictionary dialog box shown in Figure 8-2 displays the words in the named user dictionary in alphabetical order. You can remove any word by clicking it and clicking the Remove button. To add a new word, type it into the field at the bottom of the dialog box and click Add. If the word is already present in the Main dictionary, MacWrite Pro tells you with an alert box.

Even though you can add words to a user dictionary with the Install References dialog box, it is more efficient to use the Learn button in the

FIGURE 8-2 The Edit button lets you maintain user dictionaries

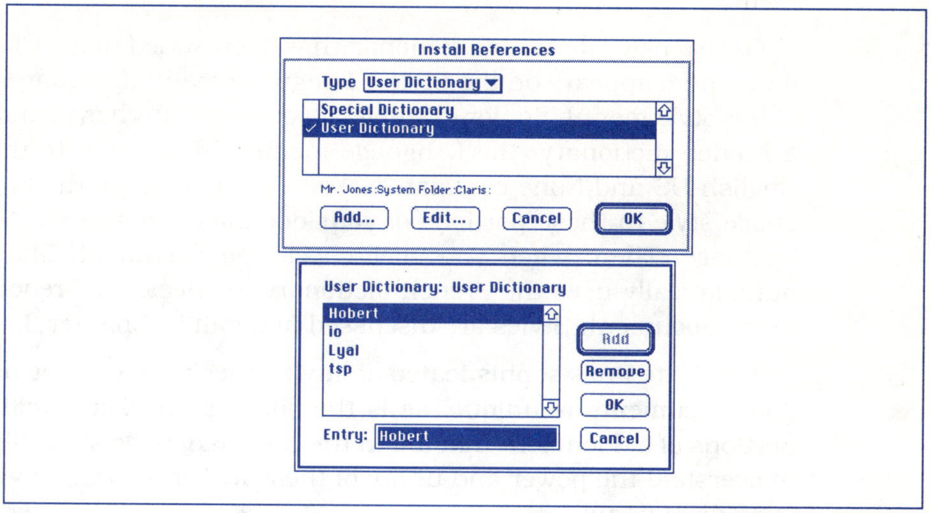

main Spelling dialog box. The best procedure for adding a number of words is to type them into a MacWrite Pro document and then check the spelling of that document. As the program flags these words, use the Learn button to add them.

Additional Main Dictionaries

In addition to the Main Dictionary that you use, MacWrite Pro supports other main dictionaries. Typically, these are dictionaries of foreign languages, but developers can also create dictionaries of special terms, such as legal, medical, or scientific terms. The Install References command lets you add these dictionaries to MacWrite Pro.

To add a dictionary, click the Add button in the first panel of the Install References dialog box. A standard File Open dialog box opens. Use it to locate the dictionary you want.

Normally, the dictionary is located in the Claris folder. Developers who market alternative main dictionaries usually provide them on disks that include Install programs to place them into your Claris folder automatically. Any dictionaries in the Claris folder are used automatically when spelling a document, so you do not need to use the Add button to activate them.

Once a new alternative dictionary has been added to the Claris folder, a new item appears on the Style | Language menu (Language submenu of the Style menu). So, for example, if you have purchased and installed a French dictionary, the Language menu adds French to the existing English-US and None commands. You can then apply the French Language style to those portions of your document that are in the French language. Then, when you spell-check the document, MacWrite Pro automatically uses the French dictionary to check the French portions of the document. Styles are discussed in detail in Chapter 3.

MacWrite Pro's sophisticated ability to check the spelling of multilingual documents is unique, as is the spelling checker's ability to skip portions of a document that are in the None language style. It is difficult to overstate the power and utility of these features to those who deal in such documents.

Spelling Checker Caveats

The spelling checker is not perfect. Its magic is accomplished by comparing words in the document with words in a dictionary. This affects your use of the spelling checker in two ways:

- Just because a word is flagged as misspelled by the spelling checker does not necessarily mean that it is misspelled—just that it is not in the dictionary. This is particularly true of technical or specialized terms (such as legal, medical, and antiquated terms).
- On the other hand, just because MacWrite Pro doesn't flag your word as misspelled doesn't mean that it is spelled correctly. The spelling checker does not take usage and meaning into account. Homonyms, such as "hear" and "here," for example, are beyond the capabilities of the spelling checker. If you type **he quick brown fox**, you have to flag the error yourself. While a spelling checker is a terrific tool for checking obvious spelling errors, it cannot replace careful proofreading by a human.

- ☐ Finally, it is a good idea to review the contents of your User dictionary periodically. It is very easy to add words by mistake when checking a document. Keeping the User dictionary as trim as possible helps to ensure more reliable results.

Thesaurus ⌘-L

MacWrite Pro's thesaurus uses a fairly standard "engine," Word Finder from Microlytics.

Looking up a synonym for a word is straightforward. Here's how:

1. Select the word you want to look up.
2. Use the Thesaurus command from the Edit | Spelling menu or, more easily, press ⌘-L.

   If no word is selected when you give the Thesaurus command, an empty Thesaurus dialog box opens, and you can type any word into the Find: field. This is a handy way to look for that clever phrase as you are typing.
3. MacWrite Pro locates the word in the thesaurus and shows you a list of synonyms, as shown here, in the case of the word "exceeded."

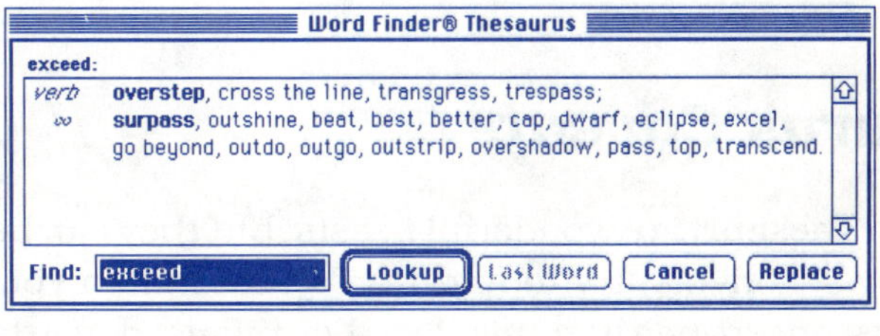

If the word you select is not in the thesaurus, you are presented with a list of words that most closely resemble alphabetically the one selected.

Synonyms are organized by part of speech. Nouns, verbs, adjectives, adverbs, and the like are shown together in the top field of the Thesauras dialog box.

Note The tense of the word is not respected: in the illustration, the word "exceeded" was chosen—a past tense verb. However, all the verbs shown are in the present tense—in this case, "dwarf," "cap," and so on.

To replace "exceeded" in the text with the word "dwarf," double-click "dwarf" in the top portion of the Thesaurus dialog box. You can also click the word "dwarf" (which places that word into the Find field at the bottom of the Thesaurus dialog box) and then click on the Replace button.

There are two ways to fix the tense of the verb:

- In the example, you replaced "exceeded" with "dwarf." But you really wanted to replace it with "dwarfed." After double-clicking "dwarf," the thesaurus dialog box closes, "dwarf" replaces "exceeded," and it is selected. Press the → key to place the insertion point at the end of "dwarf," and type **ed**.
- To fix the tense of the verb before replacing it, click the word "dwarf" (which puts it in the Find field), correct the tense there, and then click the Replace button.

You can also explore the thesaurus by clicking on a word to place it into the Find field and then using the Lookup button. (The heavy outline around the Lookup button indicates that it is the *default button*—pressing Enter or Return chooses it.) This can lead you on a nearly endless pursuit that might increase your vocabulary but do little for your immediate productivity.

Thesaurus Caveats

Thesauri are wonderful beasts, but they can be misused. When looking for synonyms, try to find words that match your style. Nothing is more disconcerting than misplaced or misused words. Keep a dictionary (the old-fashioned, printed kind, containing word definitions) handy, to make sure you are using words meaningfully.

Hyphenation

MacWrite Pro can automatically hyphenate words in a document. The Auto Hyphenate command is, like the other reference tool commands, available on the Edit | Spelling menu.

MacWrite Pro's hyphenation is a combination of dictionary-based hyphenation and guessing based on a simple algorithm. Dictionary-based hyphenation means that MacWrite Pro consults a dictionary of words and syllables to determine how to break words. If there is no match in the dictionary for a word or a syllable, MacWrite Pro attempts to break the word at a join between a consonant and a vowel.

Hyphenation Preferences

The Preferences dialog box contains several items for customizing hyphenation. You can control five aspects of hyphenation through the Spelling/Hyph. portion of the Preferences dialog box, which was shown in Figure 8-1.

Maximum Hyphens in a Row The Maximum Hyphens in a Row pop-up menu lets you specify the number of adjacent lines that can contain hyphens at their ends. Your choices range from 1 through 7, or you can allow an unlimited number of hyphens (which is the default value of this item).

Note Normally you should allow for no more than two hyphens; beyond this, text becomes difficult to read.

Smallest Word to Hyphenate The default for the smallest word to hyphenate is 5 characters long, though a larger value—say, 7 or 8—is preferable. Words with as few as five letters usually do not have multiple syllables to break anyway.

Minimum Characters Before Hyphen Set the Minimum Characters Before Hyphen value to 2 or 3, to help preserve syllables on one line before a hyphen.

Minimum Characters After Hyphen The default for the minimum number of characters after a hyphen is 2. Here's a default that you can live with.

Break Capitalized Words By default, MacWrite Pro leaves Break Capitalized Words checked. How you use this preference is usually determined by your writing style.

Note Most of the time, it is bad form to hyphenate a person's name, though hyphenating cities, product names, and the like is acceptable.

Hyphenating

To tell MacWrite to hyphenate your document, choose the Auto Hyphenate item on the Edit | Spelling menu. MacWrite Pro scans your document and inserts hyphens where it thinks hyphens are needed. As you type with Auto Hyphenate turned on, words are hyphenated automatically.

Note Hyphens inserted into your document by autohyphenation are not the same as hyphens you might insert yourself. You cannot remove these hyphens manually, although you can override automatic hyphenation with Hyphenation Exceptions in the Edit | Spelling | Install References dialog box. Furthermore, Auto Hyphenate is an all-or-nothing feature; it is either turned on for the entire document or turned off for the entire document.

When you make formatting changes to a document—such as margin changes that affect hyphenation, MacWrite rehyphenates the entire document.

When you turn autohyphenation off, all the hyphens that MacWrite Pro has inserted for you are removed automatically.

If you do not want a particular word to be hyphenated, you can press ⌘-- in front of that word. This inserts an invisible character to the left of the word. If you change your mind and decide to hyphenate that word, click to the left of its first character, and use the Del (or Backspace) key to remove it.

Hyphenation Exceptions

While you cannot edit individual hyphens placed into your document by Auto Hyphenate, you can create a *hyphenation exceptions list* of words that you do not want to be hyphenated. This list is fairly easy to edit; but if you have a large number of words you want to add to it, the procedure can be tedious.

1. From the Spelling menu, choose Install References.
2. Choose Hyphenation from the pop-up list that is at the top of the dialog box.
3. Select the hyphenation file that you want to edit. Typically, only one file will be listed. For U.S. users, this file is called US Hyphenation.
4. Click the Edit button, which brings up the Hyphenation Exceptions dialog box.
5. Type the word you want to add to the exceptions list in the field at the bottom and click the Add button to enter it into the list.

You can remove words from the exceptions list by clicking on any that appear in the field in the center of the Exceptions dialog box and then clicking the Remove button.

When you have finished adding words to the Hyphenation Exceptions list, click the OK button to save changes, or click on the Cancel button to close the Exceptions dialog box without saving any changes.

Hyphenation Caveats

As with automatic spelling and the thesaurus, be careful about how you use automatic hyphenation. Make sure that words are hyphenated correctly—for common words, this should not be a problem, as MacWrite Pro's hyphenation dictionary contains most common words. For less commonly used words, however, verify the locations of hyphens with a dictionary.

Be aware of when to use and when not to use hyphenation. Some find that hyphenation is appropriate for formal, professional-looking documents, but not appropriate for less formal documents such as letters and memoranda.

Summary

MacWrite Pro provides three reference tools that help you produce interesting, error-free documents. The tools are

- Spelling checker
- Thesaurus
- Hyphenation

The spelling checker can check an entire document at once, a selected range of a document, or individual words as you type. The spelling checker makes suggestions from the main dictionary supplied with MacWrite Pro. A User dictionary contains correctly spelled words that you use that are not in the main dictionary.

You can augment the power of the spelling checker with specialized dictionaries that contain special terms, such as medical and legal. Foreign language dictionaries are also available. MacWrite Pro is unique in its ability to let you specify the language style of a word or selection of your document, then use the appropriate dictionary when spell checking.

The powerful thesaurus is based on the popular WordFinder Thesaurus from Microlytics. This is an excellent tool for looking up synonyms and related words. Its main limitation is that it only deals with the root of the words in its list; it is your responsibility, for example, to make sure that verbs you select from the thesaurus are in the proper tense.

The hyphenation module can hyphenate automatically as you type or it can hyphenate an entire document at once. It bases hyphenation on its own dictionary and certain rules that you customize with the Spelling/Hyph. tile in the Edit | Preferences dialog box.

CHAPTER 9

Printing

This chapter covers the steps and the various options of the printing process. Because printing is standardized across Mac applications, this chapter is somewhat more basic than the others. But even if you are familiar with printing from other Mac applications, be sure to at least skim this chapter for a tidbit or two that just might be valuable to you.

Using the Chooser

The first step in printing is to use the Chooser desk accessory to tell MacWrite Pro (and the Mac in general) what printer you will be using.

The Chooser desk accessory is shown in Figure 9-1. The left panel shows icons for the different types of printers and similar devices that your Mac knows how to communicate with. In System 7, the Chooser looks through the Extensions folder in the System Folder for these files; in earlier Systems, they are loose in the System Folder. These files are collectively known as *drivers*. Additionally, if your Mac is part of a large network, there may be another scrolling list below the printer icons that shows names of different network zones. If this is the case, consult your Mac user guide for details about zones.

Note If your Chooser is showing a number of printers of a type that you do not use, such as an ImageWriter or StyleWriter, you can safely delete the files that cause these icons to be displayed in the Chooser. The files are located in the Extensions folder in the System Folder (System 7) or in the System Folder on your hard disk. Consult your Mac user manual for details on deleting files.

To select a printer, for example a LaserWriter, click the LaserWriter icon. The names of all available LaserWriters appear in the list to the right. In Figure 9-1, a printer called Mr. Print appears. Click the name of the printer you want to use.

At the bottom of the Chooser are a pair of radio buttons that determine whether or not AppleTalk is active. AppleTalk must be turned on if you are using a printer that connects to your Mac via an AppleTalk or EtherTalk network. Most PostScript laser printers connect via this network connection. If you are unsure, consult the manual for your printer.

FIGURE 9-1 Use the Chooser to tell MacWrite Pro which printer you will be using

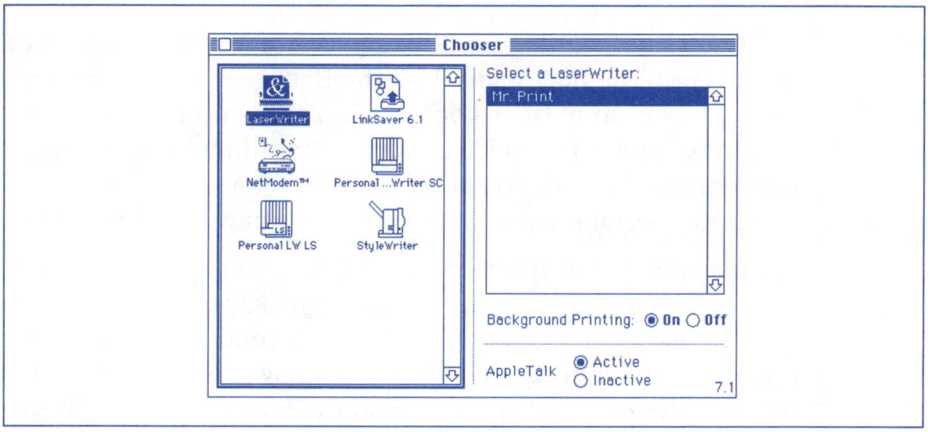

If you choose a printer that connects directly to the Mac (that is, one that does not use a network) such as the StyleWriter, the standard ImageWriter II, or one of the Hewlett-Packard Inkjet printers, the panel to the right will ask you which serial interface port it should use when communicating with the printer, as shown in Figure 9-2. Typically the printer will be connected using the serial interface that bears the icon of the printer on it, but you can use the other serial port if necessary. For

FIGURE 9-2 Click the appropriate icon to indicate how a serial printer is connected

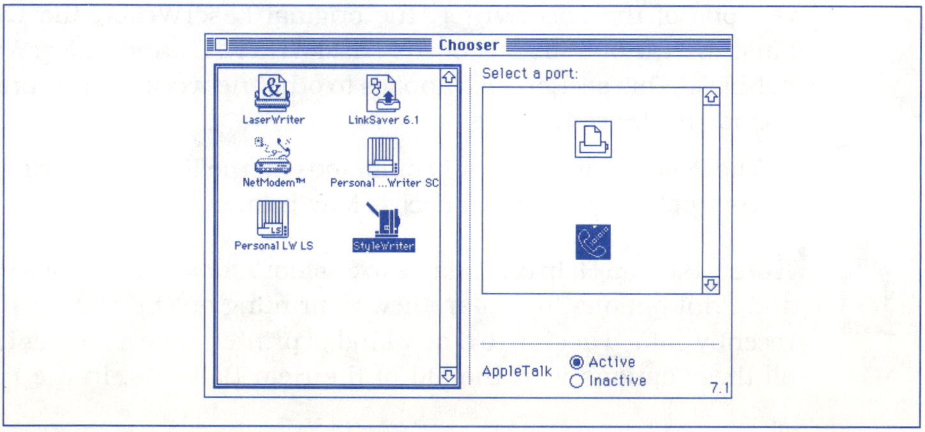

printing purposes, both of the Mac's serial ports are identical. Click the icon to tell the Mac which port your printer is connected to.

Background printing is the ability of your Mac to let you do other things while it prints a document. Use the Background Printing radio buttons near the bottom of the Chooser to turn this option on and off. The Mac currently supports background printing directly only with networked printers and the StyleWriter printer. If you have chosen one of the directly connected serial printers, these buttons may not be enabled.

After you have specified the printer you want, you can close the Chooser. If you have changed printer types, you may be warned that you need to use the File menu's Page Setup command to let currently open applications (such as MacWrite Pro) know that you have chosen a new printer. The Page Setup command in MacWrite Pro is discussed in the next section of this chapter.

Note If you only have one printer, or for other reasons never change between printers, you might never need to concern yourself with the Chooser again.

Printing to the LaserWriter

Apple's LaserWriter family of PostScript printers and compatible models from other manufacturers offer very high-quality output and are considered by many to be the entry-level printers for business use. The LaserWriter's information described in this chapter covers nearly all versions of the LaserWriter: the original LaserWriter, the LaserWriter Plus, the various models of the LaserWriter NT, and "LaserWriter compatibles." This section also applies to other networked laser printers that include PostScript.

The Page Setup and Print commands on the File menu bring up dialog boxes from which you can access Mac printer options.

Note Balloon Help is available in System 7 for all the various Page Setup and Print options. If you are new to printing on the Mac, or if you have recently gained access to a new kind of printer, take a moment to explore all these options with the aid of the Help Balloons. In the Page Setup dialog box prior to System 7, there is a Help button below the Options button.

The LaserWriter Page Setup Command

The Page Setup command on the File menu contains a number of options that govern how a document is printed and, to a lesser extent, how it is formatted. When you choose this command, the LaserWriter Page Setup dialog box appears, as shown here:

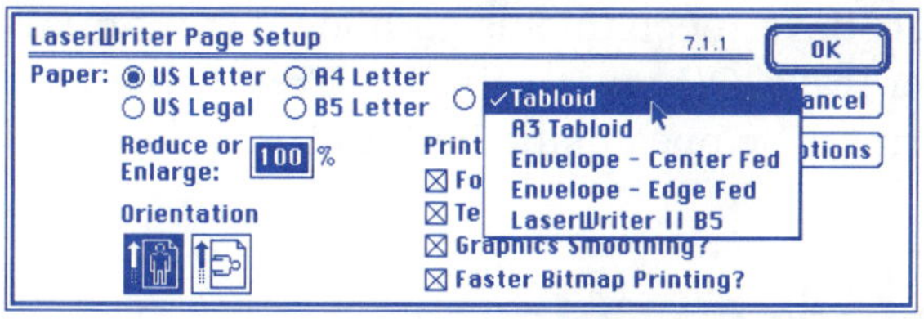

The options on the Page Setup dialog box let you stipulate various specifications about the printer paper. Some of these specifications, such as paper size and orientation, can affect margin settings and page breaks in MacWrite Pro documents. Page Setup settings are stored with the document that is open when you choose the Page Setup command. Note that the figure shows the Tabloid pull-down menu activated to display different sizes of paper.

The top line of the dialog box specifies the type of printer you are using. To the right of the printer type is the version of the printer driver that is being used.

Note Page Setup options are document-wide. They affect every page in the document. You cannot, for example, have both landscape and portrait pages in the same document. Apple has promised to provide a mechanism to let developers add Page Setup options that govern only specific pages in a future version of System 7.

Paper

The five Paper radio buttons, US Letter, US Legal, A4 Letter, B5 Letter, and the Tabloid pop-up list radio button (in System 6 and earlier, it's only a Tabloid button), determine the actual size of the paper. Before printing, make sure the paper in the LaserWriter's paper tray matches the size of the paper specified here.

MacWrite's page margins (see Chapter 5) are specified in distance from the edges of the page. Thus, if you change paper sizes (for example, change from letter paper to legal paper or tabloid), the amount of text that can fit on a page will change. MacWrite Pro automatically makes these adjustments when you specify a different paper size.

Note There are two options in System 7 for envelope printing. The first Envelope option, Center Fed, works well with the NT series of printers, which have mechanisms to allow for manual envelope feeding on the paper trays. Otherwise, use the Edge Fed option. Chapter 16 details how to print envelopes using both of these options.

Reduce or Enlarge

The Reduce or Enlarge text field under the Paper Size options is the control for scaling the page larger or smaller when printed. The advantage of scaling a page with the Page Setup dialog box is that you can decrease or increase the size of the page without having to change margins or font sizes. The scaling control is a convenient way to print thumbnails of a page and an efficient method to create a magnified image of a page.

For example, if you enter **50** in the Reduce or Enlarge text entry field, the entire page will be printed at 50 percent (half) the size that would normally be printed. So instead of a 7 1/2 × 10-inch printing area using a 12-point font, the page is printed in a 3 3/4 × 5-inch area using a 6-point font. The LaserWriter driver supports scaling from 25 percent to 400 percent.

Rulers are automatically scaled to match the settings you specify in the Page Setup dialog box. Using the above example, the Ruler indicates that with a 50 percent reduction, there is twice as much room across the page. Since the page has been reduced to "half" the normal size, twice as much information can be printed on the page—an 8 1/2 × 11-inch piece of paper has a virtual width of 17 inches with a printable area that is14 inches wide.

Orientation

The icon to the left specifies that your document is printed in standard portrait orientation. Landscape printing rotates everything on the page so that it prints sideways.

Note You do not need to change the way paper feeds into the printer to print in landscape orientation.

Font Substitution

The Font Substitution option causes the Geneva font to print as Helvetica, New York to print as Times, and Monaco to print as Courier. Since Apple now includes TrueType versions of all these fonts as part of System 7, leave this button unchecked; when creating a document, use the actual fonts you want to be printed (accept no substitutions). The major problem with font substitution is that Geneva is not exactly equivalent to Helvetica, nor is New York exactly equivalent to Times; differing character widths between these sets of fonts will almost certainly cause differing line and perhaps page breaks in your printed document. If you have just spent a lot of time fine tuning the pagination of a document, your level of disappointment with the results will be notable. You are much better off actually choosing Times as the font in your document than choosing New York and Font Substitution.

Text Smoothing

If the Text Smoothing box is checked, when MacWrite Pro prints bitmap fonts (fonts for which no PostScript file is available and for which there is no TrueType definition in the System), they will look better on the page than they would otherwise. Unless you are using such a bitmap font, you can safely keep it off. You should probably keep Text Smoothing turned off as it slows printing for all documents.

Graphics Smoothing

When printing bitmap graphics, the Graphics Smoothing option smooths jagged edges. MacWrite Pro handles printing bitmap graphics quite well, so you can keep this option turned off, too.

Faster Bitmap Printing

The Faster Bitmap Printing option causes the Mac to preprocess bitmap images before they are sent to the printer. Leave this option turned on.

Options

Further Page Setup options become available when you click the Options button to the right of the LaserWriter Page Setup dialog box. The LaserWriter Options dialog box appears, as shown here:

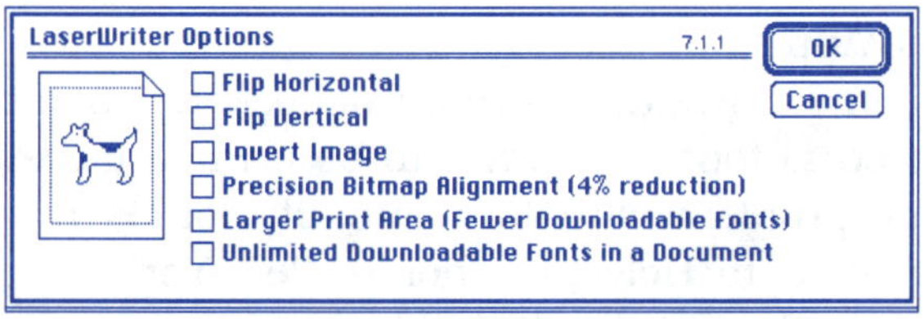

Note The technical term for the animal shown in the Page Setup Options dialog box is *dogcow*, as it resembles both a dog and a cow.

Flip Horizontal and Flip Vertical Flip Horizontal prints text and graphics backward. You will need a mirror to read it, which is fine if you want to emulate Da Vinci's diaries. Flip Vertical flips the page so that it is upside down.

Invert Image The Invert Image option causes black to print as white and vice versa. This option is the all time favorite of the toner cartridge industry, whose motto is "Print early, print often, and invert image."

Precision Bitmap Alignment The Precision Bitmap Alignment option reduces bitmap graphics by 4 percent to ensure proper positioning on the page. This can give you greater control over the appearance of bitmap graphics on the printed page because the standard screen resolution of the Mac—72 dots per inch—is not exactly divisible into the standard resolution of a laser printer—300 dots per inch. By reducing the size of a bitmap by 4 percent, its appearance on the page will more closely resemble its appearance on the screen.

Larger Print Area Choose the Larger Print Area option if you need to set larger margins than are normally supported on your printer. The price for this feature is a reduction in the number of fonts that can be downloaded.

Unlimited Downloadable Fonts There is a limit to the number of fonts that can be downloaded to the printer when printing a document. The exact limit depends on many factors, including the model of the printer, its total memory, and the nature of the specific fonts being downloaded. Checking the Unlimited Downloadable Fonts box removes the limit, but can significantly slow printing of documents with more than a few downloaded fonts.

The LaserWriter Print Command ⌘-P

A number of the options in the LaserWriter Print dialog box are common to other printers as well. MacWrite Pro offers several options that are not available in other programs.

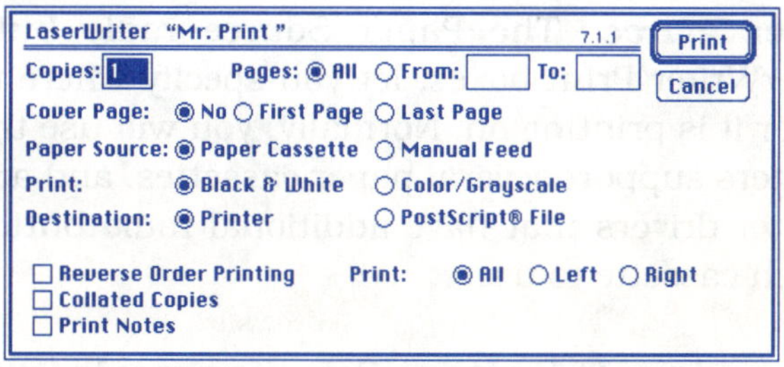

Copies The Copies field, available in all versions of the Print dialog box, tells MacWrite Pro how many copies of the document to print. The default value, 1, is already selected when the screen opens, so you need only type a new number to change this value. Printing multiple copies of a page is very quick; the printer only has to calculate how to print the page once. Succeeding copies of that page are printed at the rated speed of the printer's print engine. See the section on collation later in this chapter for more details.

Pages The Pages option, available to all, has two radio buttons. If the All radio button is checked, the entire document is printed. If you type a number into either the From or To fields, then the From radio button is checked, and only those pages you have specified are printed.

Cover Page The Cover Page option has three radio buttons to let you specify whether a cover page is printed as a first page, a last page, or not printed at all.

The cover page identifies the name of the user who printed the document (which is taken from information entered in the Sharing Setup Control Panel), the name of the program that printed the document, the date and time the document was printed, and the name of the printer.

Note If you are using background printing, the name of the application on the cover page is listed as "PrintMonitor."

If you are a single user, you will not want to print cover pages, since in most cases you already know who you are. However, if you are sharing a printer with a number of other users, the cover page can help identify which documents belong to whom in the printer output tray.

Paper Source The Paper Source radio buttons, available in all LaserWriter Print boxes, let you specify where the printer is to get the paper it is printing on. Normally, you will use the paper cassette. Some printers support several paper cassettes, and are supplied with custom printer drivers that have additional radio buttons that let you specify which cassette to use.

Print: Black & White or Color/Grayscale Printing Most of the time you will select Print Black & White, since it is faster than the Print Color/Grayscale option. Any color bitmap images in your document will be reduced to a single color when printed with this option set to Black & White. This includes text you have colored in MacWrite Pro.

When you check Print Color/Grayscale, the Mac will *dither* (convert to a grayscale pattern) color graphics or colored text in the document to print on a printer that supports, strictly speaking, only black and white. This has results that vary, depending on the type of image you are printing. Colors might not print out in the shade of gray that you expect. Due to the way the human eye works, yellow, for example, looks brighter than it actually is. A 30 percent yellow seems brighter than a 30 percent gray. As a result, when a 30 percent yellow is translated to gray scale, it is darker than the color image indicates.

Of course, if you have a color printer, select the Print Color/Grayscale option.

Destination Most of the time, you print to a printer. However, this radio button lets you save the output of your document as a PostScript file instead. The resulting file can then be downloaded to any PostScript device with a special utility such as the LaserWriter Utility that comes with Apple's LaserWriters. An advantage of printing to a PostScript file is that you only need this utility, not MacWrite Pro itself, to print the document. You may find, for example, that your service bureau (where you print the documents, if not at your home machine) does not have MacWrite Pro yet. Also, you do not have to worry about the service bureau not having the fonts used in a document.

Note Don't print a document that is a PostScript file because that results in a printout of the PostScript code that defines the printed document. Instead, download it to your printer. Also, these PostScript files can become quite large, so for large documents or documents that include bitmap images, plan your disk storage accordingly.

Reverse Order Printing When you select Reverse Order Printing, the last page of the document is printed first, and appears first in the tray of your laser printer. This option is designed primarily for use with older laser printers such as the original Apple LaserWriters and related printers that incorporate the same Canon print engine. On these printers, paper is output face up, so multipage documents are reverse collated unless the Reverse Order Printing option is selected. More modern laser printers, such as the Apple LaserWriter NT family, output pages face down so that the document is automatically collated properly without the use of the Reverse Order Printing option. Reverse Order Printing is a MacWrite Pro exclusive option.

Collated Copies Collated Copies option, another MacWrite Pro option, presents a two-sided choice. If you are printing more than one copy of a multipage document using this option, the printer creates each copy from beginning to end before beginning the next. The advantage of this approach is that at the end of the print run each copy of the document is fully collated. The disadvantage is that printing this is slower because the printer must recalculate each page every time it is printed. If you turn Collated Copies off, printing will be faster, but collating has to be done manually. Decide for yourself which is more convenient.

Print Notes If Print Notes is checked, MacWrite Pro's Notes are printed as they appear within your document. Notes, another feature exclusive to MacWrite, are just that—a screen version of the little Post-its you use to leave notes to yourself (or others) about the document. See Chapter 15 for a discussion of the Notes feature of MacWrite Pro.

Print: All/Left/Right You can specify whether or not All pages of the document are printed, odd-numbered (Right) pages, or even-numbered (Left) pages by clicking the All, Left, or Right radio button. Choose All to print the entire document. The Left and Right options are mainly useful when you need to print on both sides of the paper. This choice, another MacWrite Pro exclusive, only appears in the Print box when you are printing from MacWrite Pro.

Note To print on both sides of the paper, first print the document with the Left option checked, then turn the resulting output over, position it to be fed again to the printer, and print again with the Right option checked. The exact positioning of the paper for the second printing pass will depend on the specific printer you are using. If you are doing this, you probably will want to change margin settings to Inside/Outside margins instead of Left/Right. Chapter 5 tells you how to do so.

PrintMonitor and Background Printing

If you checked Background Printing in the Chooser, a document is not immediately printed after you click the OK box in the Print dialog. Instead, the document is *spooled* or saved to a disk file in a special folder, called PrintMonitor documents (Spool Folder in System 6), which is inside the System Folder. After the entire document has been spooled, a special application called PrintMonitor is launched automatically by the Finder. PrintMonitor then actually sends the document to the printer.

The major advantage to background printing using PrintMonitor is that it allows you to continue to do other work on the Mac while the document is being printed. You can do such things as make modifications to the document being printed, open other documents (and print them), and even start other applications and print from them while PrintMonitor is working (each subsequent print request is lined up in a *queue* to wait its turn). Without background printing, your Mac hands are tied while the Mac concentrates solely on printing.

The convenience of background printing does, however, have its price. Since PrintMonitor is constantly getting data from the spool file to send to the printer, the hard disk is kept fairly busy. As a direct result, you will notice that MacWrite Pro (and other programs) do not open or save documents as quickly as usual while PrintMonitor is working. But compared to doing nothing while waiting for a document to print without background printing, this performance hit is relatively unimportant.

You can check the status of documents waiting to be printed by bringing PrintMonitor to the front. System 6 users can do this on the Apple menu. System 7 users can select it from the Application menu at the upper-right corner of the screen, as shown here:

The PrintMonitor window, shown in Figure 9-3, has three portions. The field at the top shows the name of the document currently being sent to the printer by PrintMonitor. The scrolling field in the middle lists all the documents waiting to be printed. The area at the bottom tells you the exact status of the currently selected document. When you first open the PrintMonitor window, the document being printed is selected, and this area tells you exactly what PrintMonitor is doing with the document:

looking for the printer, preparing data, and printing are common messages you see when a document is being printed. PrintMonitor also tells you how many pages are in the currently selected document. If you click the name of another document in the queue, PrintMonitor tells you what program created the document, when it was queued to be printed, and how many pages the document contains.

Canceling a Print Job

You can remove any document from the print queue by clicking its name and then clicking on the Cancel Printing button. The name of the document will be removed from the list, and the spool file in the PrintMonitor Documents folder will be removed.

Note Canceling a print job—especially one in progress—sometimes takes PrintMonitor a few seconds. Wait until the window is redrawn on the screen before clicking this button again.

Postponing a Print Job

PrintMonitor also permits you to postpone printing of a document until a later time, or even a different day.

FIGURE 9-3 PrintMonitor controls background printing

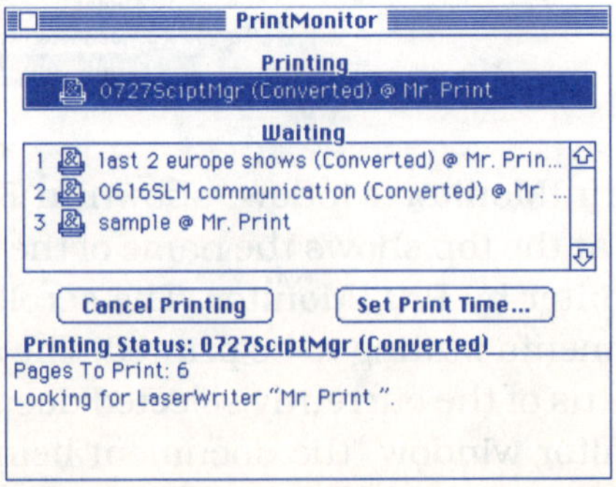

To postpone printing a document, select the name of the document in the PrintMonitor window, and click the Set Print Time button, which summons the Set Print Time dialog box:

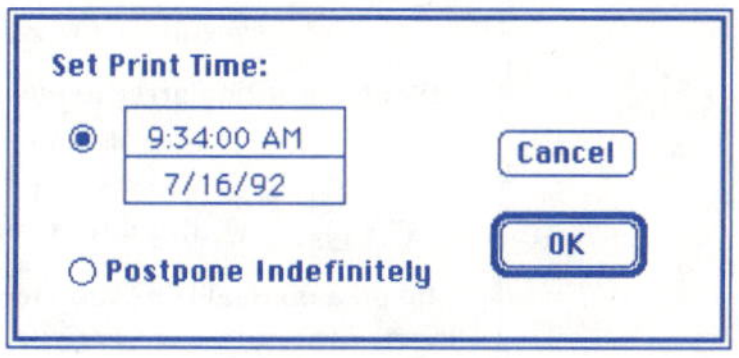

To change the print time, click one of the digits in the time area; arrows will appear to the left (similar to the arrows that appear in the General control panel when you want to set the internal clock on the Mac; consult your user manual). Use the arrows to change the time. You can do the same for the date. Click the OK button to confirm postponing the print job to the time you specify. Postponed printing works like the alarm; if the computer was off when the set time passed, you will be notified when you next start up.

If you click the Postpone Indefinitely button, the document will not be printed at all, but will be held in the PrintMonitor documents folder. You will need to select that document, and Set Print Time again to print it later. The PrintMonitor application is located in the Extensions folder of your System folder; you can start it manually by opening that folder and double-clicking its icon.

Printing Errors and the Preferences Dialog Box

If an error occurs while PrintMonitor is working, it will notify you in one of several ways, depending on settings in the PrintMonitor Preferences dialog box, shown in Figure 9-4, which you can access from the Edit menu.

The first radio button in the PrintMonitor Preferences dialog box lets you specify whether the PrintMonitor window is always visible when the program is printing documents. Many people prefer to have the No option set, as the PrintMonitor window does not really need to be displayed.

FIGURE 9-4 The Preferences dialog box for the PrintMonitor

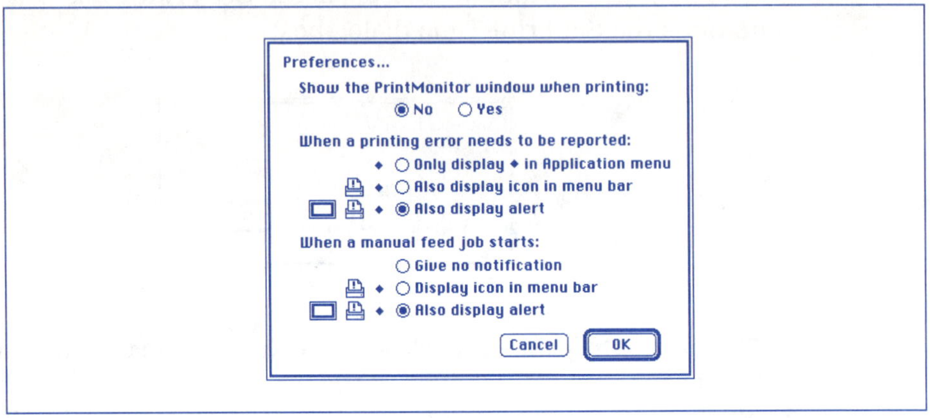

When you choose PrintMonitor from the Application menu, the window will be displayed anyway, and it will disappear when you switch to another application.

The second set of radio buttons lets you specify what PrintMonitor does when an error occurs. This is a matter of personal taste. Some prefer to have PrintMonitor present a dialog box describing the error. This dialog box appears no matter what application you are using. You may find it irritating, though. If the first option is checked, a diamond will appear next to PrintMonitor's name in the Application menu, meaning that you will have to check the Application menu manually to discover if PrintMonitor is having problems.

If the second option is checked, the icon at the top of the Application menu will blink, switching between the icon of the program you are using and the PrintMonitor icon. This might be enough notification for you.

Note These three PrintMonitor error condition options are additive. For example, if the third button is checked, the Application menu item also blinks, and a diamond appears next to the name of PrintMonitor in the Application menu.

The third set of radio buttons lets you specify what PrintMonitor should do when you are printing a document that requires manual paper feed to the printer. If the first button is checked, PrintMonitor will do nothing other than wait for a new sheet of paper; you should probably keep the PrintMonitor window open in this case. If the second is checked, the program will flash the menu bar; if the third is checked, it will display an alert dialog box.

Typical errors that PrintMonitor will warn you about include inability to find the printer (at which time you should make sure that the printer is turned on and, perhaps, check with the Chooser to make sure it is selected and available). PrintMonitor also warns you when the printer is out of paper, or if it has no paper tray.

PrintMonitor defaults to 100Kb of RAM to operate. Sometimes, particularly if you are printing a large document with complicated graphics, the program tells you that it does not have enough RAM. It gives you the option to have it "resize itself." If you say yes, it then quits and restarts with a larger memory partition. In some cases this indicates a problem with the document you are attempting to print. You might be able to solve this problem by canceling the current print job and issuing the print command again.

Sometimes, too, you may have too many applications open to allow PrintMonitor to run. PrintMonitor tells you this, and when you quit from an open application it starts again automatically and then prints the document.

Finally, the PrintMonitor application itself may have become corrupted. If you have repeated printing problems that you cannot solve with any of the techniques above, try printing from another application. If you still cannot print, copy a fresh copy of PrintMonitor from the original System disk to the Extensions folder in the System folder.

Serial Printers

Serial printers are the other family of printers commonly used on the Mac. The members of this growing family share several characteristics in common. They do not support the PostScript page description language; they are usually connected to one of the Mac's two serial ports rather than a network; and they are designed to be less expensive to purchase and operate than the more sophisticated and powerful laser printers.

The most important members of this family of printers are the ImageWriter (I and II), the StyleWriter, the Personal LaserWriter SC, and the Personal LaserWriter LS. There are three lesser members of this family of printers that are not recommended because of their established track record of poor performance: the ImageWriter LQ, the AppleTalk ImageWriter LQ, and the AppleTalk ImageWriter. These printers are not discussed here.

Note When creating documents for use with any of these printers, you should take care to use appropriate fonts. While PostScript printers can scale fonts in both the TrueType and PostScript formats, only TrueType fonts will be scaled well to these "QuickDraw" printers unless you are using Adobe Type Manager. See Appendix D of this book for a discussion of bitmap, TrueType, and PostScript fonts.

Printing to the ImageWriter

The ImageWriter is a relatively inexpensive but serviceable *dot-matrix* (sometimes called impact) printer. It doesn't actually print characters, but instead prints rows of dots in a pattern that, by the time it is finished, is a passable representation of a real printed page. Aside from being a noisy beast, its main drawback is a poorly designed pin-feed input system for traditional fanfold computer paper. The single sheet feeder option, however, works beautifully. If you're using an ImageWriter II and don't have the sheet feeder, get one soon. You deserve it.

The ImageWriter Page Setup Command

The ImageWriter Page Setup dialog box, shown here, resembles a subset of the LaserWriter Page Setup dialog box:

The Paper option contains five choices: US Letter, US Legal, Computer Paper (the fanfold kind with the holes on either side), A4 Letter, and International Fanfold.

The Orientation option has icons that you can click for either regular portrait mode or for landscape mode printing.

The three Special Effects options are Tall Adjusted, 50% Reduction, and No Gaps Between Pages. The Tall Adjusted option changes the ImageWriter 80 dot-per-inch horizontal resolution to the standard Mac screen 72 dot horizontal resolution. Check the Tall Adjusted option to make the printer output match the screen output as closely as possible. Use the 50% Reduction option for thumbnail. Use the No Gaps Between Pages option if you're printing graphics or long, unformatted lists on fanfold paper.

The ImageWriter Print Command ⌘-P

The ImageWriter Print dialog box, shown here, contains options for controlling the quality; range of pages; number of copies; paper feed method; order of printing; printing odd, even, or all pages; collation; and printing MacWrite Pro's Notes.

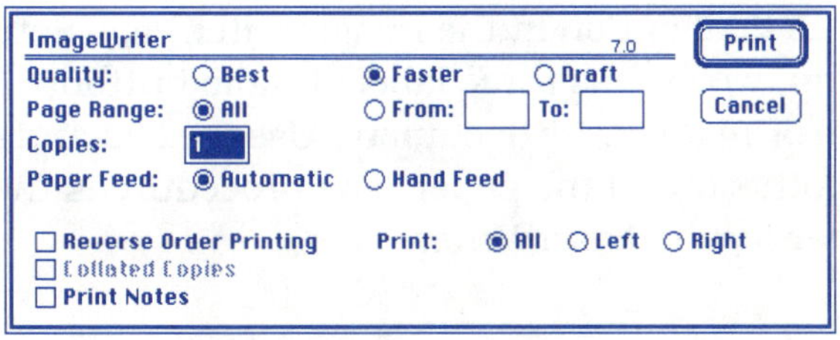

Quality The Quality option lets you select between the ImageWriter's three modes of printing: Best, Faster, and Draft. Best mode is the highest quality, but it is also the slowest mode because it causes the ImageWriter print head to make two passes for each line, with the second pass dots slightly offset from the first to provide a more finished look to the text. Select Faster mode for all but the final printouts of your documents. Draft mode is much faster (up to 250 characters per second, according to the

ImageWriter II documentation) but the price for that performance is a single 10-point Monaco font and no graphics.

Page Range The Page Range option has two radio buttons. Use the All radio button to print the entire document. Use the From/To radio button and the From/To fields to print a specified range of a document.

Copies Use the Copies option to specify how many copies of a document you want to print. The Copies field defaults to 1.

Paper Feed There are two Paper Feed radio buttons: Automatic and Hand Feed. Choose Automatic if you are using either pin-feed paper or individual sheets in the ImageWriter II sheet feeder. Choose Hand Feed for envelopes or printing one-each documents on special letterhead.

Miscellaneous Printing Options Check the Reverse Order Printing box to print from the last page of a document to the first. Check Collated Copies if you are printing more than one copy of a multipage document. Unlike printing collated copies on a PostScript laser printer, there are no performance issues involved on the ImageWriter.

Check the Print Notes box to print MacWrite Pro's special Notes, which you use like Post-its to write notes that are not part of the document to yourself or others. Notes will be discussed in Chapter 15.

The final option in the ImageWriter Page Setup dialog box is the Print option, which has three labeled radio buttons: All, Left, and Right. Click All to print an entire document. Use the Left and Right options for printing on both sides of the paper. The procedure is the same as that described earlier for the LaserWriter.

Printing to the StyleWriter

The StyleWriter is Apple's least-expensive printer for the Mac. It is a relatively easy printer to use, fairly inexpensive, and prints with a good quality.

The StyleWriter Page Setup Command

The StyleWriter Page Setup dialog box, shown here, is relatively simple:

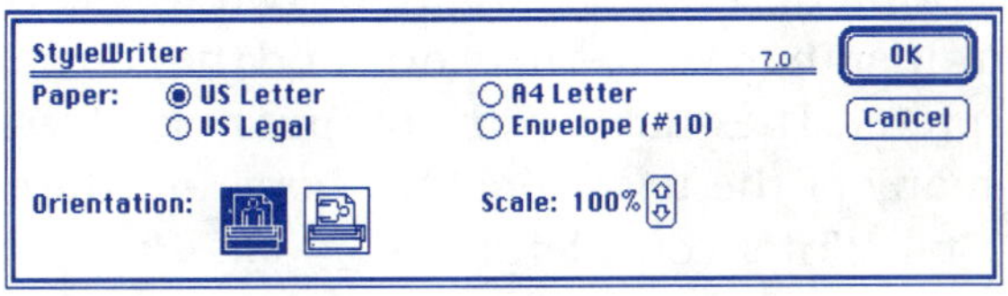

The four Paper options are US Letter, US Legal, A4 Letter, and Envelope (#10). Two Orientation icons let you select standard portrait mode printing or landscape mode printing. The Scale option lets you control scaling in 20 percent increments ranging from 100 percent to 20 percent. Scaling is useful for printing thumbnails.

The StyleWriter Print Command ⌘-P

The StyleWriter Print dialog box is identical to the ImageWriter Print dialog box described previously with only one exception. The Quality option of the StyleWriter Print dialog box has only two options: Best and Faster, as you can see here:

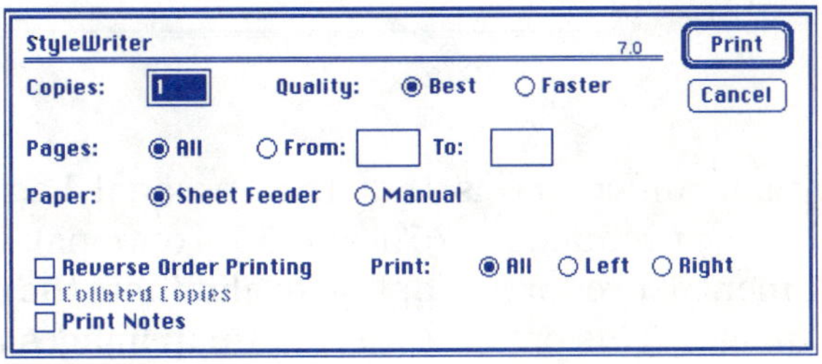

As with the ImageWriter, choose the Best option for the final printout; for printing copies to edit choose Faster.

Printing to the Personal LaserWriters

The Personal LaserWriter SC and the Personal LaserWriter LS are two printers designed for individual (or personal) use. They differ from the laser printers described above in two ways: They connect to the serial port rather than via the network, and they do not incorporate a PostScript interpreter. The quality of the output resembles that of the laser printers, but many of the user considerations are the same as the ImageWriter and StyleWriter considerations.

The Personal LaserWriter Page Setup Command

The Page Setup dialog boxes for the Personal LaserWriter SC and the Personal LaserWriter LS closely resemble the Page Setup dialog boxes for the ImageWriter, as you can see here:

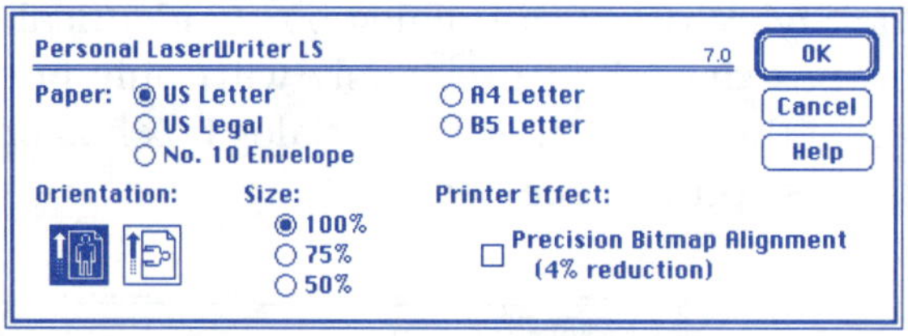

The main difference is that the Personal LaserWriters give you more control over reduction (75% and 50% options). Use the Precision Bitmap Alignment 4% reduction option to eliminate the mild distortion of bitmap-ped images. This option causes bitmap images to print faster, but it also reduces the entire page by 4 percent.

The Personal LaserWriter Print Command ⌘-P

The Print dialog boxes for the Personal LaserWriter SC and the Personal LaserWriter LS are also nearly identical to the Print dialog box for the ImageWriter. The Print dialog box for the Personal LaserWriter LS is shown here:

The major difference is that they lack the ImageWriter's Quality option.

The two Print dialog boxes for the two Personal LaserWriters differ from each other in the Paper Source option. The SC has radio buttons for selecting between the Paper Cassette and Manual Feed. The newer and somewhat more sophisticated LS has radio buttons for selecting the Paper Cassette and LS's Multipurpose Tray.

Note The Personal LaserWriter LS Page Setup and Print dialog boxes are the only ones in this litter equipped with a Help button. System 7 Balloon Help is available for all Print and Page Setup dialog boxes.

Third-Party Printers

Finally, a variety of serial printers are available from third parties. The Hewlett-Packard DeskJet printers, for example, are popular with those who need near-laser quality printing on a budget. Third-party printers designed to work with the Mac include their own drivers. If you have such a printer, consult its documentation for specific Page Setup and Print options.

Summary

The first step in printing documents with the Mac is to use the Chooser desk accessory to select the printer you want to use. Remember to choose Page Setup after switching printers when MacWrite Pro is running.

The sophisticated PostScript-based laser printers, including Apple's family of PostScript LaserWriter printers, are most commonly used in the business environment.

Printer options are accessed with the Page Setup and the Print dialog boxes. Both of these are accessed by commands on the File menu. System 7 Balloon Help is available for all Page Setup and Print dialog boxes.

The LaserWriter Page Setup dialog box contains options for controlling the following:

- Paper size
- Size reduction
- Orientation
- Font substitution
- Text smoothing
- Graphics smoothing
- Faster bitmap printing
- Other options

The LaserWriter Print dialog box contains options for controlling the following:

- Number of copies
- Number of pages
- Cover page
- Paper source
- Black and white or color/grayscale

- File destination
- Reverse-order printing
- Collation
- Print notes option
- Printing odd and/or even numbered pages

The PrintMonitor is an intelligent application that automatically handles background printing so you can continue to use the Mac while pages are being printed. Background printing is available to all network-linked printers and the StyleWriter.

Printers that connect directly to one of the Mac's serial ports are another class of printers. These single-user printers include the ImageWriter, the StyleWriter, the Personal LaserWriter SC, and the Personal LaserWriter LS. The Page Setup and Print dialog boxes for these printers are very similar to the LaserWriter dialog boxes.

Many third-party printers are designed to work with the Mac—these include their own printer drivers.

PART II

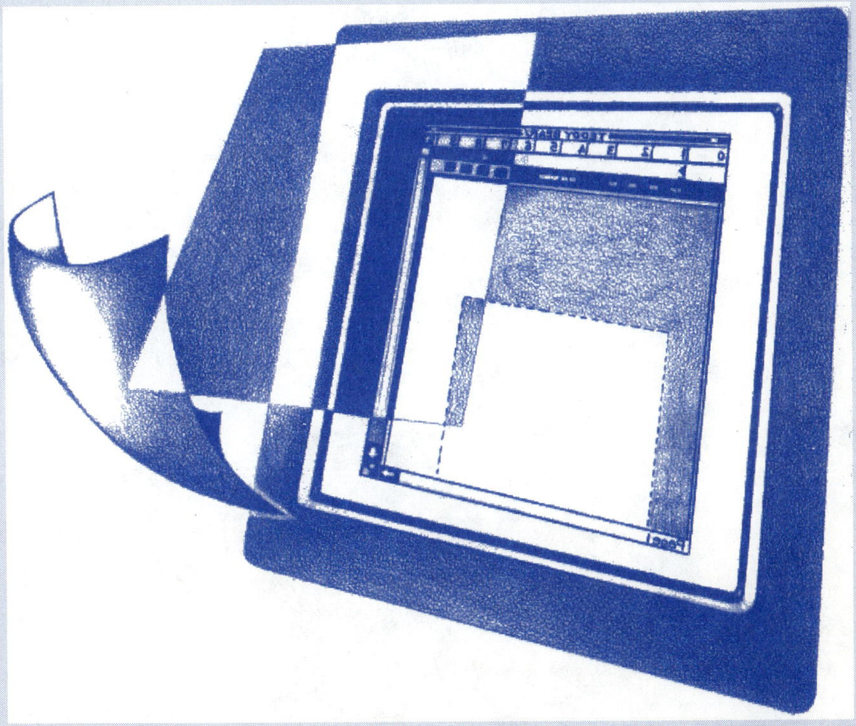

Advanced Topics

CHAPTER 10

Frames

Most of a document's text is placed on the page for you more or less automatically. Aside from setting margins, column widths, line spacing, and the like, you don't have direct control over exactly where on the page something will be located. Most of the time this is how you want your word processing tool to work, leaving you free to concentrate on the content rather than the style.

However, there are times when you do want precise control over the placement of page elements. If you are creating a newsletter, preparing letterhead, or printing an envelope, for example, you might want to place items precisely on the page.

Sometimes you might want to place an item precisely on the page independently of the flow of the surrounding text. Illustrations and tables are examples of this kind of page element.

MacWrite Pro provides you a flexible, powerful tool called *frames* for managing these kinds of page elements.

Kinds of Frames

There are two basic kinds of frames: text frames and graphics frames. Two other types of text frames are the table frame and the note frame. Other types of frames may be available to you via MacWrite Pro AddIts in the Claris Folder in the System Folder.

A *text frame* contains text that you can edit as needed. You might use text frames in documents for notes, picture captions, or sidebars, elements that you do not want to be part of the main text. A *graphics frame*, or picture frame, contains graphics.

Frames can be placed on the page in two ways. *Independent frames* have a specified location on the page. *Anchored frames* are anchored, or attached, to a specific location in the text. If the text associated with an anchored page moves to a different page, the frame moves along with it. Independent frames remain on the page where you created them, regardless of how the surrounding page elements change.

Creating Frames

There are several ways to create new frames. The most basic method is to use the commands on the Frame menu. There are commands for inserting tables (discussed in Chapter 12) and notes (discussed in Chapter 15), and a hierarchical menu for creating text and picture frames.

When you use the Text command on the Insert Frame submenu, a new inline frame is created *at the insertion point.* The new frame is 1 1/2 inches wide. Its height is dependent on the size of the type of the style definition for the default paragraph—text *within* the new frame will have the Default style, regardless of the text around it. Thus if the size of type specified in the Default style is 12 points, the new frame will be 17 points tall. The height of the line containing the new frame is adjusted to make room for it.

Note All frames that you insert with the Frame menu commands are anchored inline frames except for note frames, which are anchored, no-wrap frames. All frames inserted via the Tools palette are fixed (no anchor).

Immediately after you create a new text frame, the insertion point is automatically placed within the frame so you can begin typing in it immediately.

To create a graphics frame, use the Picture command on the Frame menu's Insert Frame submenu. As with text frames, the new graphics frame will be an inline frame. The default size is an inch square. (Pasting a graphic directly from the Clipboard also creates a graphics frame.)

Most of the information in this chapter concerns working with text frames, although many of the tips relate to all frames. For additional details on working with graphic frames, see Chapter 11. For details on working with tables, see Chapter 12; for details on working with notes, see Chapter 15.

Working with Frames

Text in frames can be styled with virtually all the standard text styling tools. The only exception is that the Format Section command is not available, so you can't do things such as have multiple columns within a frame. You can, however, achieve this result by using a table frame. The first text you type into a frame has the Default style.

You have two Frame tools. The Modify Frame dialog box lets you specify some properties of frames: whether they are anchored on the page, how (or whether) text flows around them, and their precise positions. The Tools palette lets you create frames interactively and specify some other frame properties: the color and pattern used to fill the frame and its border, and the width and style of the border.

The Modify Frame Dialog Box

The Modify Frame dialog box is summoned using the Frame menu's Modify Frame command. It is shown here:

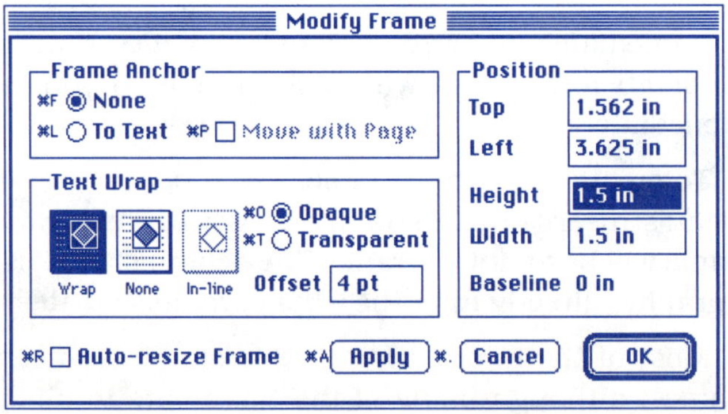

Like most MacWrite Pro dialog boxes, the Modify Frame dialog box displays the ⌘-key equivalents for many of its buttons. These equivalents, which are made visible by holding down the ⌘ key, are shown in the preceding illustration. The various frame properties that you can set with this dialog box are discussed in more detail later in this chapter.

The Tools Palette

The Tools palette is summoned with the Show Tools Palette command on the Frame menu. The Tools palette is shown here:

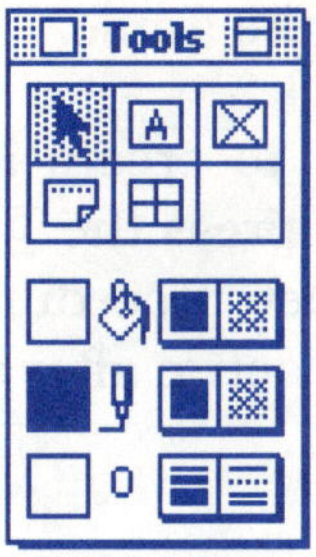

The top portion of the Tools palette provides five tools for creating and selecting frames. These tools, which are Claris AddIts, are shipped by Claris with MacWrite Pro. If you add more AddIts, the Tools palette grows. As you remove AddIts, the Tools palette shrinks to a minimum of three tools.

The first tool, the arrow, represents the standard mouse pointer. Use the arrow to switch to the normal text tool from the frame creation tools. The Tools palette contains tools for creating text, picture, note, and table frames.

To create a frame using one of these tools, click the tool icon you want to use and then move the mouse pointer to the location in the main body where you want to create the new frame. Press and hold the mouse button and drag to form the frame's rectangle. As you move the mouse pointer with your chosen tool, the page number display at the lower-left corner of the document window changes to display the exact coordinates of the location on the page to which you are pointing. Once you hold down the mouse button, and while you are dragging, the display tells you how wide and tall the new frame will be.

If you press the Shift key while creating the new frame, the frame's size will be constrained in two ways. If you are creating a text frame, the frame shape will be constrained to either a square or have its height constrained to that of the line in which you are creating it. This behavior results because if you try to shrink a frame that is smaller than is allowed, either by the default font size or the Autogrid setting, MacWrite Pro assumes that you want it constrained this way. This applies to both axes.

When you release the mouse button, the pointer changes to the default pointer icon. If you have created a text frame, an insertion point will appear within the new frame, and you can start typing immediately. Text in the new frame will have the Default style. If you create a picture frame, the frame will have an X through it, indicating that you have not yet placed a picture in the frame.

Note If you wish to create a number of frames of the same type successively, either press the Option key as you create frames or double-click the tool. Either procedure hard-selects the current frame tool, forcing it to remain active after you finish creating each frame.

Selecting Frames

There is a difference between selecting a frame and selecting the elements contained *within* a frame. You select a frame by clicking on one of its *borders*. When you point to a border, the pointer changes from an arrow to a cross, with arrows pointing in four directions, as shown here:

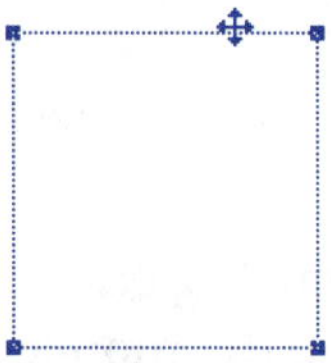

Clicking the frame outline changes the frame's corners to dark squares called *handles*. This is the indication that the frame itself is selected, rather than its contents. When frame contents are selected, the handles at the corners are hollow, as shown here:

Note If you find you are having trouble selecting frames, try one of these techniques. First, zooming in makes the frame, and thus its borders, larger on the screen, so the border is easier to point to. Another trick is to make the borders of the frame larger using the Tools palette, as discussed later in this chapter. Finally, it is sometimes easier to select a frame when contents of the frame are already selected.

Features of the Modify Frame Dialog Box

The Modify Frame dialog box, available by using the Modify Frame command on the Frame menu, is shown here:

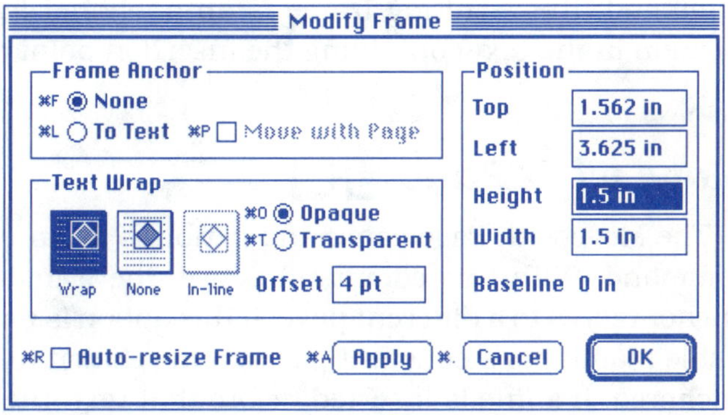

This dialog box lets you change several properties of selected frames. You need not necessarily have the frame selected in order to use this dialog box; if you use the command when a frame's contents are selected, it works just as well. A good time to use this command is immediately after you have created a frame using one of the Insert Frame commands.

As with most dialog boxes, you can use the Apply button to test new settings before casting them in stone with the OK button.

Frame Anchor

Frame anchoring determines how the frame's location is maintained on the page. There are three settings which are discussed in the following sections.

None ⌘-F

If the frame is not anchored, it maintains a fixed position on the page that is specified in the Position portion of the dialog box.

To Text ⌘-L

Anchoring a frame to text places a special anchor character representing the frame in the text. When text containing the frame anchor is moved, the frame moves with it. For example, if text is inserted before text containing the frame anchor, causing that text to move to a different page, the frame will accompany that text to the next page.

When you create a new frame using the Frame menu's Insert Frame command, the resulting frame is an anchored frame, attached to the location in the text containing the insertion point or selection.

Move with Page ⌘-P

The Move with Page command performs as an "Only Move with Page" command. With this command active, the frame will *only* move if the anchor moves to a different page. If this option is not active, the anchored frame maintains a constant position in relation to the text to which it is anchored. If a line is inserted before that text, the frame moves down a line; if a line is removed above it, the frame moves up a line.

Text Wrap

The items in the Text Wrap portion of the dialog box govern how the frame interacts with text and other frames. You have three options for text wrap.

Wrap

With the Wrap option set, text automatically wraps around the frame. You can think of the frame, in this case, as giving the text new margins.

Text will come no nearer the frame than the number of points specified in the Offset field in the Text Wrap section of the box.

None

Setting the None option causes text to flow across the page as if the frame were not there. Since text will then flow "under" the frame, you should also set the frame to be transparent.

Inline

Inline frames are anchored to text; you cannot set this option for nonanchored frames. Users upgrading from MacWrite II will recognize the inline frames technique as identical to the way MacWrite II handled graphics: inline frames are treated as a single character.

Offset

This field determines how close text will come to the border of the frame. The default is 4 points. You can specify different values in different units of measurement, such as 1/4 inch, by typing in the abbreviation of the measurement following the value (for example, type **.25 in**). The default value can be changed in the Preferences panel.

Opaque or Transparent

In the Text Wrap section are two radio buttons that let you choose whether to make a frame opaque or transparent. Transparent is a good choice if text that you want to see flows under a frame.

Position

The four fields in the Position area of the Modify Frame dialog box let you specify the exact location of the frame on the page (from the top and the left), and its height and width. If the frame is an inline frame, the Top and Left fields are inactive.

Auto-Resize ⌘-R

For text frames, the Auto-Resize option constrains the height of the frame to conform exactly to the text contained within it. As you type additional text into the frame, it becomes taller to accommodate the new text; as you delete text, the frame becomes shorter. This button is not available with picture frames.

Setting Frame Properties

The Tools palette gives you several other controls for setting some properties of frames. As discussed earlier, the top portion of the palette includes tools for creating new frames. At the bottom of the palette are three sets of pop-up menus that let you set various properties of frames: patterns and colors for the frame area and the frame line, and the width and style of the frame line.

Note If you set any of these properties with no frame selected, they are automatically applied to any new frames you create. As mentioned earlier, sometimes it is easier to select frames that have heavier borders. You can create a frame with a heavy border using the line style pop-up on this palette.

For the frame area and frame line color and pattern settings, the current settings are shown at the left side of the palette. The controls you use to change them are to the right of the icons that designate the property you are setting. The pop-up to the immediate left of the icon lets you specify the color, as shown here:

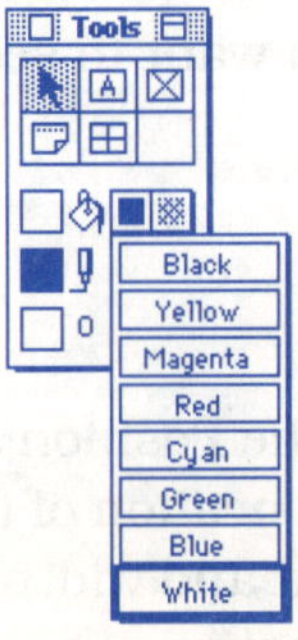

This illustration shows the colors that are available to you if you are using a *black-and-white* system or one with the color depth set to less than eight bits; if you are using a color Macintosh, then up to 81 colors will be available to you.

The next icon to the immediate right of the color icon specifies the *pattern* to be used. When you are using patterns, black areas shown in the pattern pop-up are replaced by the color you select in the color pop-up (you cannot select a color to be used instead of white—no mixing). Here are the standard patterns:

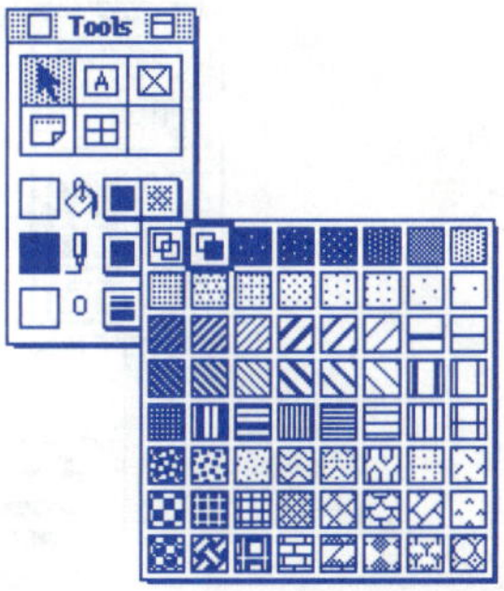

This palette also lets you specify whether a frame is to be opaque or transparent. The square in the top-left corner of the pop-up specifies a transparent frame; the one to its right specifies an opaque frame.

Frame Area, Frame Line, and Line Styles

The *frame area* specifies the color and pattern that is used to fill the frame. For text frames, this means that text will appear with this pattern as the background. For graphics frames, it specifies the color and pattern that will show in areas that are not covered by a graphic.

Note Transparent frames have no frame area setting.

The *frame line* settings determine the color and pattern that are used to draw the border around the frame. This interacts with the next setting, line styles.

Line Styles

The first of the line style settings determines the width of the line used to draw the border. You can also specify that a frame have no border. The Hairline border varies the width of the border depending on the printer. On a 300 dpi printer such as the LaserWriter, the border will be 1/300 inch thick; on a 1200 dpi printer, the border will be 1/1200 inch thick, and so on. Here is the pop-up menu for border settings:

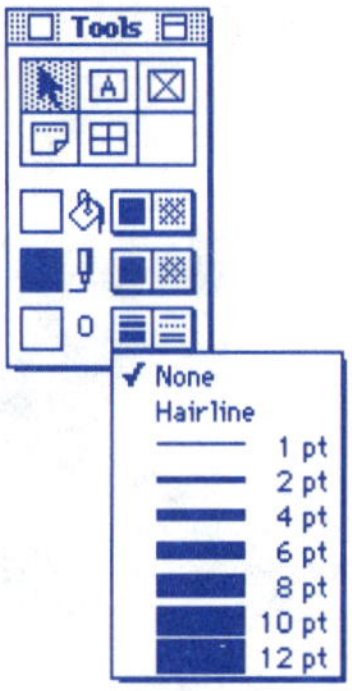

You have four choices of border styles, as shown here:

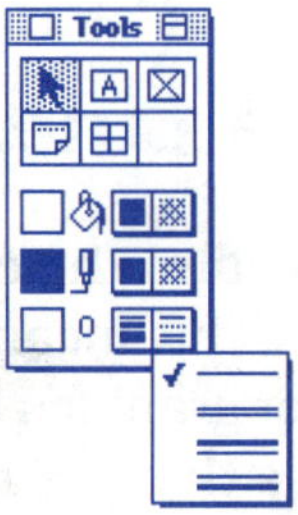

The first option signifies a single line drawn using a width specified in the left pop-up. The second specifies two lines of equal width. The third specifies a fatter external line, with an internal line half the width of the external line—the external line is drawn in the width specified. The fourth choice reverses this.

The Frame Menu

In addition to the tools in the Modify Frame dialog box and the Tools palette, the Frame menu provides tools for managing the layering of overlapping frames. These commands are only available when you have selected a frame that overlaps, either in front of or behind another frame. The Move Forward command moves the selected frame one level closer to the top of the stack. The Move to Front command brings the frame to the very top level. The Move Backward command moves the frame back one level, and the Move to Back command moves the frame so it is behind all the other overlapping frames.

Note Layering frames does not let you position a frame behind text in the main document.

Frame Ideas

As you will see in Chapter 11, frames are particularly useful for inserting graphics into your documents. However, frames have other uses as well.

Column Balancing

One of the most aggravating things with word processors that support multiple columns is there is no way to *balance* columns automatically. Text in columns always flows to the bottom of a column before starting again at the top of the next column. This can be unsightly, as shown in Figure 10-1.

You can manually insert a column break to force text to the next column, but this isn't a good idea unless you are absolutely certain that no further editing of the text will be required. However, you can use a frame to force text in a column to wrap before it hits the bottom of the column. By drawing an empty frame at the bottom of the column and making it a frame around which text wraps, you can balance the columns on the page. It doesn't matter whether you use a picture or text frame

FIGURE 10-1 Unbalanced text columns

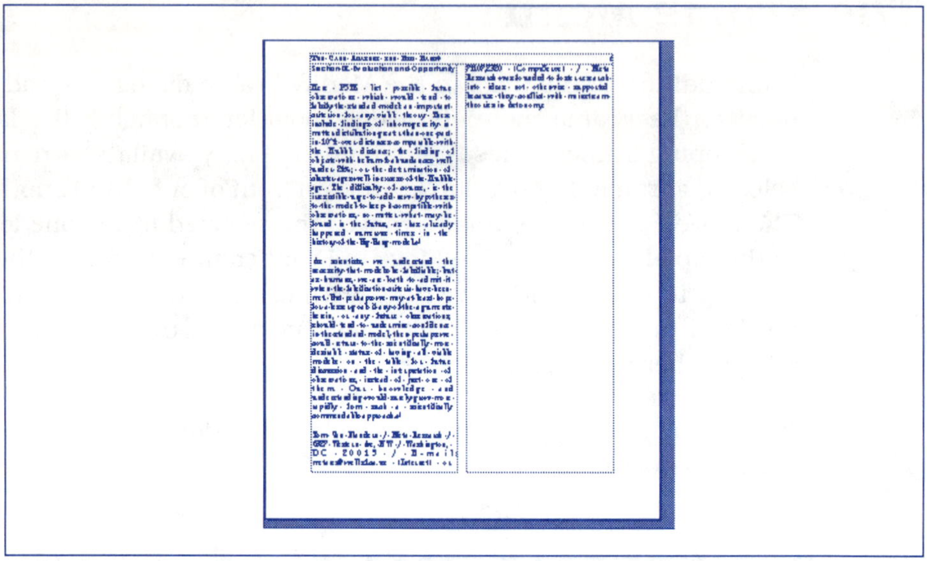

(unless of course you want to put a picture or text into it). This technique will help make your newsletters and other documents containing columns more attractive.

Letterhead

Frames are a useful tool for creating letterhead. To do so, insert a text frame at the top of the first page, and type your address into that frame. You can also insert graphics into the frame (or create another frame to contain the graphics). Letterheads are discussed in more detail in Chapter 16.

Paragraph Borders

Sometimes you need to put a border around a paragraph. Use the Frame menu's Insert Table command to create a table with one cell. Size the frame as needed and enter the text of the paragraph, then use the

Tools palette border width tool to create the border of the thickness you want.

Miscellaneous Tips and Shortcuts

In addition to the many frame features covered in this chapter, MacWrite Pro provides some useful shortcuts that can increase your productivity. Here are a few favorites.

Manipulating All Types of Frames

The following table shows some keyboard and mouse shortcuts for positioning tables on the page:

Action	Shortcut
Override Autogrid with mouse	⌘-drag
Override Autogrid with arrow keys	⌘-arrow key
Move frame by 1-point increments	Arrow keys
Summon Modify Frames dialog box	Double-click frame border or Option double-click frame contents

Manipulating Graphics Frames

The following shortcuts apply to graphics frames only:

Action	Shortcut
Move graphic within the frame	⌘-drag contents
Resize frame and its graphic	Option-drag
Proportionally constrain resize frame and its contents	Shift-Option-drag
Summon Picture dialog box	Double-click picture frame

Summary

MacWrite Pro's frames feature is a powerful tool you can use to position text and graphics precisely on a page.

There are two main types of frames: text and graphics.

Text frames are useful for creating sidebars, letterhead, and many other text objects that are treated differently from the main text.

Graphics frames allow you to control how graphics are treated in a document.

Frames are accessed via the Frame menu and from the Tools palette.

The Modify Frame dialog box gives you precise control over the characteristics of a frame.

The Tools palette lets you quickly create different kinds of frames and control frame fill and border elements.

CHAPTER 11

Graphics

In the pre-Mac days, when it came to microcomputer word processors, text was text, graphics were graphics, and asking an application to combine them into a single document was an impossible task. This changed in 1984, and it was the Mac and the original version of MacWrite that changed it. The Mac's graphical nature and its Clipboard enabled a revolution in word processing. Today, it seems as though inserting pictures, charts, and other graphics into your document is almost expected. It's hard to imagine a newsletter without charts and other illustrations.

MacWrite Pro continues and expands this tradition. It provides you with a variety of powerful, flexible tools to help you add impact to documents with graphics.

Types of Graphics

Before you can take maximum advantage of MacWrite Pro's graphics capabilities, it's important to understand the major different types or formats of graphics that you encounter on the Mac.

On the most basic level, there are two types of graphics: bitmap and object-oriented. *Bitmap images* are composed of collections of dots that may or may not contain different colors: a scanned photograph is an example of a bitmap image, as is a graphic created in a painting application such as Claris MacPaint. *Object-oriented* or *draw-type images* contain information about the shape of the components of the graphics. For example, if you draw an oval in an object-oriented application, the application does not store the locations of the dots that define the oval. Instead it stores the fact that an oval was drawn and its boundaries. You can use both of these types of graphics in MacWrite Pro documents.

Beyond the type of image, there are several file formats that can contain graphics. Here's a rundown of the most common file formats.

MacPaint

The MacPaint file format is the oldest on the Mac; it was defined by the first graphics program to be released for the Mac (for many long months after the Mac appeared, MacPaint and MacWrite were the only applications available). MacPaint images are somewhat rare today, but you might still encounter them.

MacPaint images have only two colors: black and white. Different shades are simulated through different densities and patterns of black dots; and MacPaint documents are limited to 72 dpi (dots per inch), the default screen resolution.

A major benefit of MacPaint graphics is the "what you see is what you get" effect of printed images when you are printing to a lower-resolution device, such as an ImageWriter; a dot on the screen translates directly to a dot on the printed page.

Note You can enhance the appearance of documents containing bitmapped graphics by enabling the Precision Bitmap Alignment and Graphics Smoothing options in the Page Setup dialog box, as discussed in Chapter 9.

PICT

The PICT format is the most common graphic format on the Mac. Most image-editing tools and drawing programs can save files to the PICT format, and files produced by the standard Mac Shift-⌘-3 screen-capture mechanism are in this format. PICT files can contain both bitmap images and object-oriented descriptions of shapes. It is the "second-best" file format: bitmap images are usually better stored and printed as TIFF files (described next), and object-oriented images are usually better handled as EPSF files (described after TIFF). However, given the PICT format's ubiquity on the Mac, you will probably end up using it often. Bitmap images in PICT files are also stored at 72 dots per inch.

As with MacPaint images, you can improve the appearance of printed documents containing PICT images if you enable the Precision Bitmap Alignment and Graphics Smoothing options in the Page Setup dialog box.

TIFF

The Tag Image File Format (TIFF) is a fairly standard format for describing bitmap images. The TIFF "standard" is supposedly the same across a number of different applications on different computers. In practice, however, there are differences between implementations of the TIFF format, and there are times when you might not be able to read a TIFF file created by an application that is not in wide use. However, MacWrite Pro is a very capable TIFF reader and handles the great majority of TIFF files with no problems.

Unlike MacPaint and PICT formats, the TIFF format stores the resolution of the image in the format. Thus, TIFF files can be stored at 300 dpi or 600 dpi resolutions. This makes it the format of choice for scanning, manipulating, and printing high-resolution bitmap images to high-resolution printers.

Note TIFF files at high resolutions, with large numbers of colors, can be quite large, and thus require a hefty amount of both memory and hard disk storage. If you are working with numerous TIFF images in a document, you may have to increase MacWrite's memory. Consult Chapter 1 for instructions on doing so.

EPSF

Encapsulated PostScript Format (EPSF) is the format of choice if you are printing to a PostScript printer. EPSF files are created by applications such as Adobe Illustrator, Aldus Freehand, or Claris' MacDraw Pro. Not all these programs will save as EPSF files by default. Some, such as Adobe

PhotoShop, can save to the EPSF format. However, EPSF is primarily a format for defining shapes, not patterns of dots, so you won't get the advantage of the EPSF format with these kinds of files.

When printing to a PostScript printer, the EPSF format can use the maximum resolution of your printer. Thus, lines will appear smoother when using this format compared to lines drawn in TIFF or PICT image lines. EPSF format files are also more compact than these other formats.

Placing Graphics in Documents

MacWrite Pro graphics are always contained in frames; if you haven't done so yet, read Chapter 10, which explains how to use frames. Graphics files cannot be opened directly by MacWrite Pro; you need to place them into documents either via the Clipboard or with the File menu's Insert command.

The Clipboard

A very easy way to place a graphic into a MacWrite Pro document is through the Clipboard. In the application that created the graphic, select it, or the portion of it you want to bring into MacWrite Pro, and copy it to the Clipboard. Switch to MacWrite Pro and paste the image. A new frame will be created, attached to the text at the insertion point, with the graphic inside it.

While the Clipboard is a useful tool for transferring graphics, it has some limitations. Most applications convert graphics on the Clipboard to PICT format when you leave the applications. If the source image is in TIFF or EPSF format, you get better results by using the File menu's Insert command (described next) to place the picture into the MacWrite Pro document.

Note The Mac Scrapbook is a convenient place to store graphics images that you regularly paste into documents.

The Insert Command Shift-⌘-I

The File menu's Insert command reads a file from disk and places it into the open MacWrite Pro document at the current insertion point. You can insert graphics into existing frames or have MacWrite Pro create a frame for you.

Inserting into a New Frame

To insert a new graphic and have MacWrite Pro create a frame for you, first click at the location in the document where you want the picture to be placed. Then use the File menu's Insert command to insert the file. A standard Insert File dialog box, shown here, will list all the types of files that MacWrite Pro can read; since frames can contain text as well as graphics, this list might include a number of files of types you do not want to import.

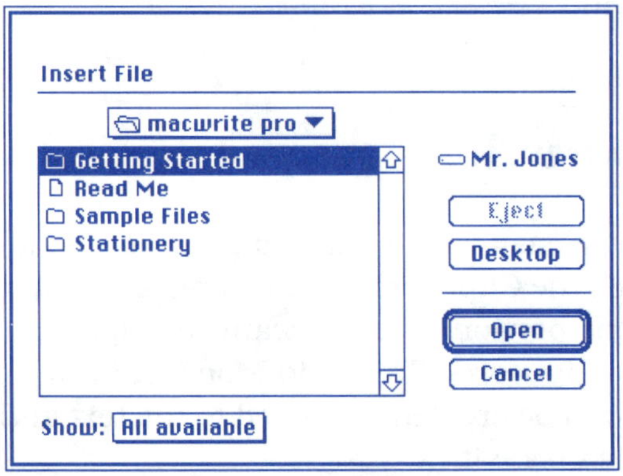

You can use the Show pop-up menu to restrict the list to files of the type you want to open. When you find the file you want and click the Open button (or press Enter or Return), the picture is inserted into your document in a new frame.

This new frame is an inline frame, anchored to the location of the insertion point. The frame automatically sizes to contain the entire picture, providing the picture is no larger than the page, including margins. If the picture is larger than the page, it is automatically cropped, and portions that do not fit on the page are not shown.

Inserting into an Existing Frame

To insert a graphic into an existing frame, first select the frame contents. (Remember that if the frame contents are selected, the handles are hollow; if the frame itself is selected the handles are solid.) Now use the Insert command. If the frame already contains an image, that image is replaced by the one you are placing.

Note If the frame into which you are inserting a graphic contains text, that text is not replaced. Instead, a new inline frame is placed at the insertion point of the text. This is analogous to placing a graphics frame in the body text of a document.

Subscribing to Graphics

You can also insert graphics into a document by using the Publish and Subscribe function that is part of Macintosh System 7. Publish and Subscribe is a mechanism for assuring that data shared between programs is kept up to date. This process is described in Chapter 15. Subscribing to a graphic is functionally equivalent to pasting from the Clipboard: the graphic is inserted into a frame of its own, initially as an inline graphic at the insertion point.

Working with Graphics in Frames

In addition to the standard frame tools discussed in the previous chapter, MacWrite Pro provides tools to control how the graphic is displayed within the frame.

When you select a frame containing a graphic, a new Picture menu appears on the menu bar immediately to the right of the View menu. This menu contains several commands for working with pictures:

Scaling Graphics and Frames

The Picture menu's Scale command summons the Scale Picture dialog box, shown here, which lets you resize the graphic in precise increments:

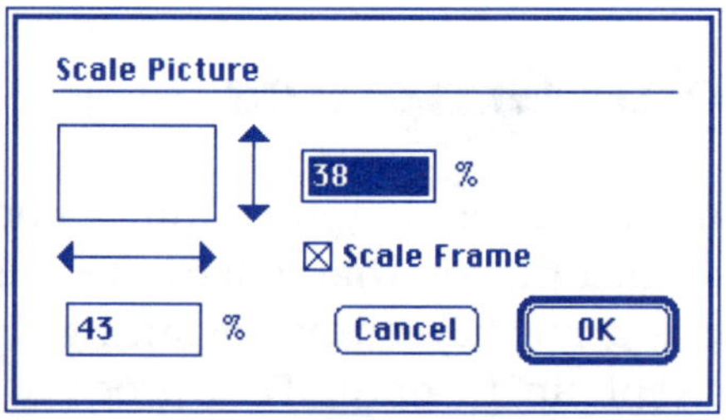

You can also summon this dialog box by double-clicking the graphic. This dialog lets you scale the picture along its two axes and control scaling independently on each axis. To use it, type the percentage by which you want to scale the picture into each field and click the OK button.

By default, the size of the frame is scaled along with the picture inside it. If you want to scale the graphic independently of its frame, click the Scale Frame check box to disable it; you can also use the ⌘-S keyboard equivalent.

You can also scale pictures manually by pressing the Option key and holding it down while you drag from one of the corners of the frame. Both the frame and the picture within it are scaled to the new rectangle that is formed when you release the mouse button. If you press the Shift key along with the Option key, the picture and frame are scaled proportionally. That is, the height and width of the picture and frame after you scale them are proportional to their values before you scaled them.

Note If possible, scale graphics in the application that created them before placing them into MacWrite Pro. Although MacWrite Pro can scale inserted graphics, the results might not be as pleasing, nor do you have as much control, as in the application that created the graphic. A good approach is to insert the graphic into MacWrite Pro and use the Scale Picture dialog to ascertain how it should be scaled. You can then return to the application in which the graphic was originally created and scale it to that size there.

Fit Frame to Contents

The Fit Frame to Contents command on the Picture menu automatically scales the frame so that it exactly encloses the picture contained within it. This is useful when you have created a frame that is larger than the picture it contains.

Fit Contents to Frame

The Fit Contents to Frame command scales the graphic to fit exactly within the frame. This command is useful when the graphic that you are placing is either larger or smaller than the size of the target frame.

After you have scaled the graphic with the Fit Contents to Frame command, you can see the values by which it was scaled using the Scale command; the values in the two fields of the Scale Picture dialog box will show you how much in each direction the graphic was scaled for the frame.

Moving Graphics Within Frames

You can reposition a graphic within its frame by pressing and holding down the ⌘ key while you click and drag the mouse pointer within the frame. This is most useful when the graphic is larger than the frame, and you want to control which portion of the graphic is visible. It is also useful when the graphic is smaller than the frame, and you want to control how it sits within it.

The Picture menu's Center Contents command automatically centers the graphic within the frame. Use this command when the graphic is smaller than the frame containing it.

Hiding Pictures

Graphics within documents slow scrolling, sometimes to a crawl. You can alleviate this by using the View menu's Hide Pictures command. When you hide graphics, only the frame itself shows, and not the graphics within it.

Note Hiding graphics does not affect printing; when you print the document, graphics print, even though they are not displayed on screen.

Summary

The four major kinds of graphics on the Mac are MacPaint, PICT, TIFF, and EPSF.

You can insert a graphic from the Clipboard, with the Insert command, or with the System 7 Subscribe feature.

Graphics can be moved within a frame and scaled. You can scale the frame to fit the size of the graphic, or you can scale the graphic to fit the size of the frame.

Use the Hide Picture command to speed up scrolling on screen.

CHAPTER

12

Tables

Using tabs to create tables in word processing documents was the convention for a long time. Tabs are useful tools for creating and manipulating small, simple tables, but the process of creating and editing larger tables using tab stops can frustrate even the most motivated word processor user.

MacWrite Pro has a table creation tool that is easy to use. Creating tables—and, more important, modifying them after they're created—is a snap. You might find MacWrite Pro's table facility something of a dream come true.

This ease of use in manipulating tables, however, is balanced by a built-in limitation—a MacWrite Pro table can have no more than 100 cells. While this limitation is not onerous for many users, it is for more serious users. We'll discuss ways to work around this limitation later in the chapter. In the meantime, keep the 100-cell limit in mind.

Creating Tables

MacWrite Pro provides three ways to create tables: the Frame menu's Insert Table command, the Frame tool on the Tool palette (refer to Chapter 10 for a general discussion of creating and using MacWrite Pro frames), and conversion of existing delimited text to a table.

Note Bear in mind MacWrite Pro's limitation of 100 cells to a table when using any of these three methods for creating tables; the Insert Table dialog box will not check whether you have created more than 100 cells until you click the OK button to actually create the new table, at which point it will protest.

The Insert Table Command

The Insert Table command on the Frame menu summons the Insert Table dialog box, shown here:

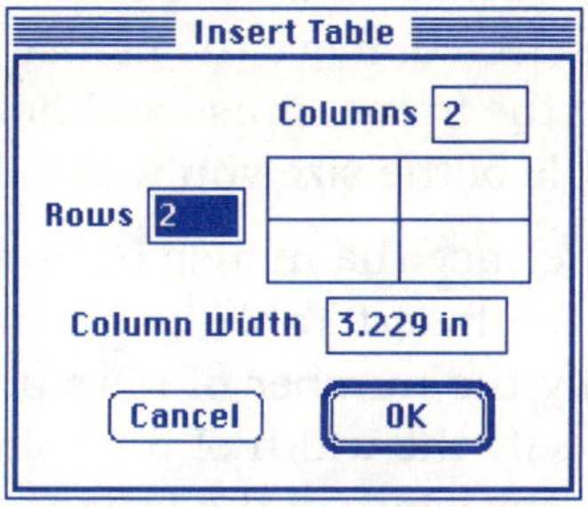

The Insert Table dialog box asks you how many columns and rows you want in the table frame and presents default values of two of each. You can use the Tab key to move between the two fields to type new numbers. The Column Width field is adjusted automatically as you change the number of columns to a value that makes columns of even width across the width of the page. You can also change this value manually. If you set it to a value that would make the entire table too wide for the page, MacWrite Pro will warn you when you click the OK button and tell you what the maximum width for a column can be, based on the number of columns in the frame.

When you click the OK button, the new frame will be created as an inline frame, attached to text at the insertion point. Tables created with the Insert Frame command always extend across the full width of the page.

Using the Tool Palette

The Tool palette also has a Table tool that you can use to directly draw the frame. The Tool palette, with the Table tool selected (shaded) is shown here:

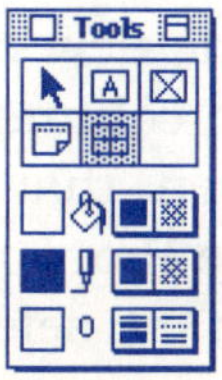

You draw table frames in the same way you draw other kinds of frames. With the tool selected, move the mouse pointer to the location where you want to create the frame, press and hold the mouse button, and drag to form a rectangle of the size you want.

When you release the mouse button, a dialog box similar to the one presented by the Insert Table command is summoned. This dialog box lets you specify the number of rows and columns in the frame. It does *not* let you specify the width of the columns; the columns will be evenly spaced across the width of the frame you have drawn.

Turning Text into Tables

The third method for creating tables lets you transform existing text into table text. The text must be delimited, or separated, with tabs. Here is some text separated by tabs that can be turned into a table:

First Name	Last Name	Address	City	State	Zip
Blair	Miller	1 Highway 61	Duluth	MN	01234
Mick	McQuistion	2 Desolation Row	Hibbing	MN	01234

Note Invisible characters are shown here to illustrate the delimiters; what will appear in a column is separated from other columns with tabs; each row ends with a return character.

To transform this text into a table, select all the text you want to be in the table and choose Insert Table from the Frame menu. As shown in Figure 12-1, MacWrite Pro scans the selected text to determine the number of necessary columns and rows, and presents you with a dialog box to confirm or modify the size of the table.

Note that behind the Insert Frame dialog box, you can see that all the text to be placed in the new table is selected. MacWrite Pro has determined there are seven columns and four rows, and indeed there are. If your tables are not even, that is if some of them contain more columns than others, MacWrite Pro will present you with the *maximum* number of columns that are in the selected text.

When this dialog box appears, you can change the number of columns and rows from the defaults that MacWrite Pro offers you. If you specify a greater number of columns than MacWrite Pro presents, blank columns will be inserted at the end of the text. If you specify a number that is lower than the number it proposes, the excess columns will be grouped together in the final column. In the preceding example, if you specify only four columns, the items in the last three columns are placed together (separated by tabs) in one column.

You can make good use of this capability. For example, when you subscribe to a document created by Microsoft Excel or FileMaker Pro 2.0, the text is placed into MacWrite Pro in a tab-delimited manner. (The System 7 Publish and Subscribe feature is discussed in Chapter 15.) You can use the Insert Table command to format the text into a table, and then you can incorporate it into the document.

Editing Text in Tables

Once you've created a new table, you need to edit or create text in it. As we said at the beginning of this chapter, working with tables in MacWrite Pro is exceptionally easy.

FIGURE 12-1 The Insert Table dialog box

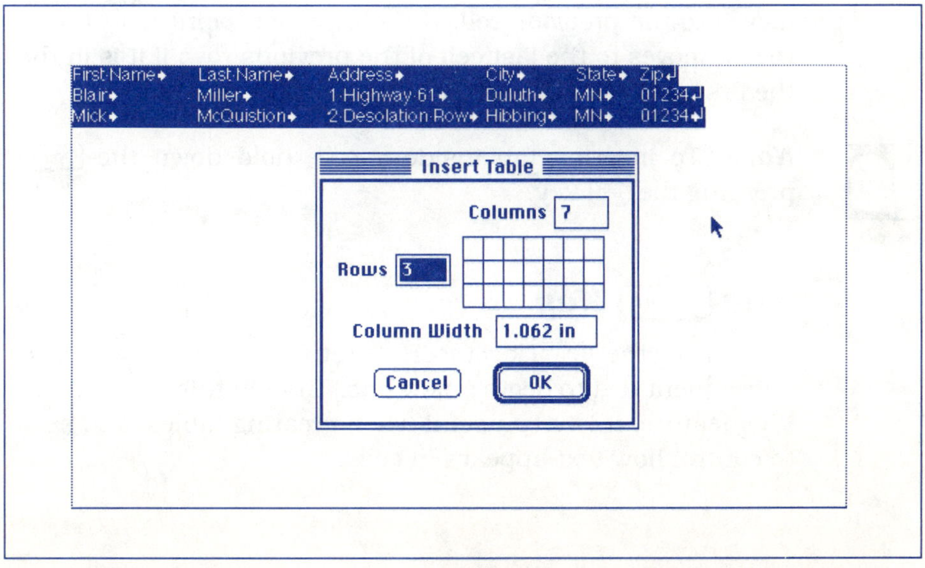

Text in tables is selected using the standard text selection techniques: clicking and dragging and double-clicking. When you are typing text into a cell, the word wrap is based on the borders of the cell: when text reaches the left edge of the cell, it wraps to a new line in the same cell, and the height of the cell is adjusted automatically to make room for the new text. (This is the *default* behavior for the table; later in this chapter you will see how to disable this feature, and the consequences of doing so.)

Navigating in a Table

You can, as always, use the mouse to select text in different cells in the table, but MacWrite Pro also conforms to standard techniques used by database programs and spreadsheets for keyboard navigation in a table.

The Tab Key

Pressing the Tab key moves the insertion point to the next cell. If the insertion point is in the last cell in a row, the Tab key moves the insertion point to the first cell in the next row. If the insertion point is in the last cell in the last row of the table, a new row is added to the table.

If you press the Shift key while pressing the Tab key, the insertion point moves to the *previous* cell. If the insertion point is in the first cell in a row, it moves to the last cell of the previous row; if it is in the first cell of the first row, it moves to the last cell of the last row.

Note To insert a tab inside a cell, hold down the Option key while pressing the Tab key.

The Return Key

Pressing the Return key inserts a return character into the cell, causing subsequent text to begin a new line. Though this isn't strictly a table-editing feature, it is very useful when creating tables, and serves as a tool to control how text appears in cells.

If you hold down the ⌘ key and press Return, The insertion point moves *out* of the table and into the text surrounding it.

The Arrow Keys

You can also use the arrow keys to navigate between cells.

←

The ← key moves the insertion point a character to the left in a cell, unless there is no character to the left; then it moves to the previous cell. If the insertion point is in the leftmost cell of a row, it moves to the rightmost cell of the previous row.

→

The → key moves the insertion point a character to the right, unless there is no character to the right, in which case it moves the insertion point to the next cell.

↑

The ↑ key moves the insertion point up a row; if the insertion point is at the top row, the ↑ moves the insertion point to the same column in the last row.

↓

The ↓ key moves the insertion point down a row; if the insertion point is in the bottom row, the insertion point moves to the same column in the first row. If there are multiple lines in a cell, the ↓ moves first through all the succeeding lines in that cell; then it moves the insertion point to the next row below.

Formatting Tables

You format text within tables in basically the same way you format other text: select it and then use commands on the Font, Size, Style, and Format menus to format it. Just as with other text, specific words or strings of characters within tables can have their own formats. However, tables have their own sets of capabilities as well, which are discussed here.

Selecting Columns and Rows

There are two fundamental ways to select columns and rows: the "traditional" way and the "table" way.

You can select a column or a row by clicking and dragging, just as you select nontable text. To select an entire column, click in the top or bottom cell of the column, hold down the mouse button, and drag to the bottom or top of the column. As you drag, the mouse pointer will turn into a small cross, indicating that you are selecting cells. To select an entire row, click in the leftmost or rightmost cell in the row and then drag to the other end.

The "table" method of selecting a row or a column selects the entire row or column with one click. To select a row, position the mouse pointer at the left edge of the row until the pointer turns into a right-facing arrow. Then click to select the entire row. To select an entire column, position the pointer at the top of the column, find the spot at which it turns into a down-pointing arrow, and click.

Note You can select noncontiguous cells by ⌘-clicking them. You can also select noncontiguous rows and cells with the same ⌘-key technique.

Table Rulers

As you can see in this illustration, Rulers behave somewhat differently when you have a cell or cells in a table selected than they do when the cell or cells are not selected.

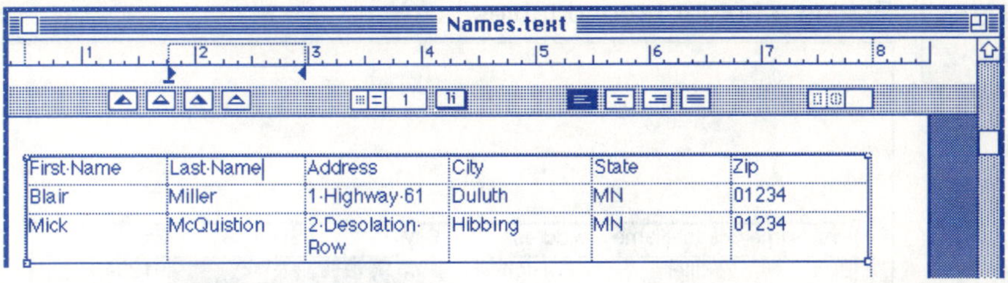

In this example, the insertion point is in the second column. Notice how the Ruler has changed: the first-line indent point, the left indent point, and the right margin are all set separately for each cell in the table. You can change each of these items for any selected cells.

These rulers are similar to regular Rulers, in that changes you make to them affect *only* selected cells. That is, if you select a group of cells in a table, and change a Ruler setting, only those selected cells are changed. For formatting purposes, think of the text in each cell, even though it does not end with a return character, as being *its own paragraph.*

Not all paragraph formatting tools, however, necessarily apply. For example, the Space Before and Space After settings in the Paragraph format dialog box only affect text in a cell when that text is followed by another paragraph in the same cell. This means you cannot use these properties to set the height of rows.

If you have several columns selected, the Ruler is displayed for the *first* column only, but any changes you make to the Ruler affect *all* the selected columns. This is analogous to the way the Ruler works when you have selected more than one paragraph.

Cell Borders

There are two tools for specifying borders around cells.

Using the Tool Palette

The first method of specifying cell borders involves using the Tool palette. First, select the cells around which you want to put a border, as shown in Figure 12-2.

FIGURE 12-2 Putting a border around tables

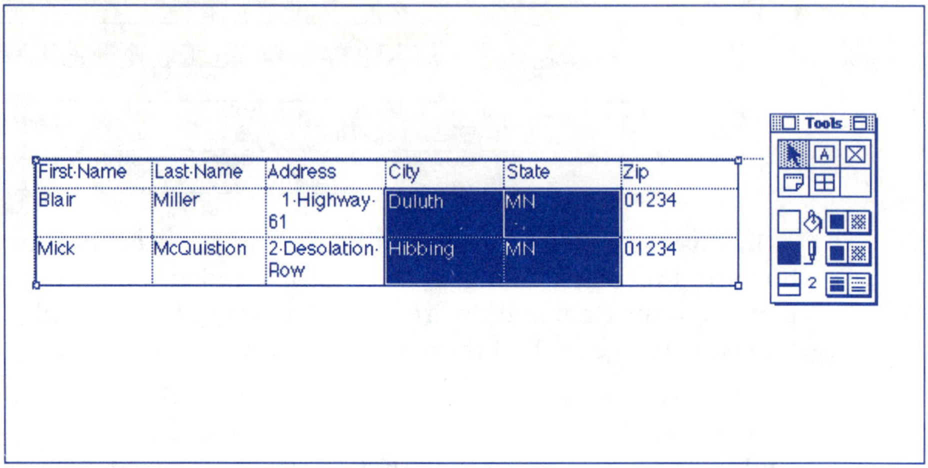

Then, from the Tools palette, choose the Line Width pop-up menu, as shown here:

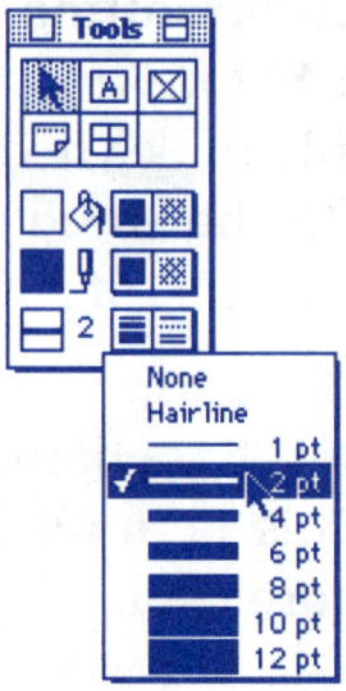

This is the result:

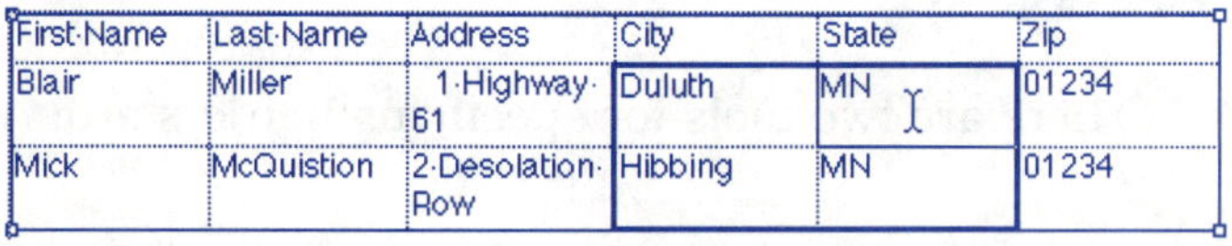

As you can see, the border is drawn around the selected cells, and no border is drawn *between* those selected cells.

Note If you want to apply a border around each of the selected cells, hold down the Option key as you select the border from the Tool palette. This technique works with all the Tool palette cell attributes.

If you just select the table frame without placing the insertion point within any cell (that is, the handles on the corners of the table frame are solid instead of hollow), the entire table takes on the border you specify, and none of the cells do.

Using the Cell Borders Dialog Box

In the previous example, the Tool palette actually applied separate border formatting to each of the four selected cells. For the upper-left cell in the selection, the border was changed for the left and top borders; for the upper-right cell, the border was changed for the right and top borders, and so on.

You can do the same to individual cells (or groups of cells) manually using the Table menu's Cell Borders command. Here is the dialog box that appears when you choose this command with the upper-left cell (in the previous example) selected:

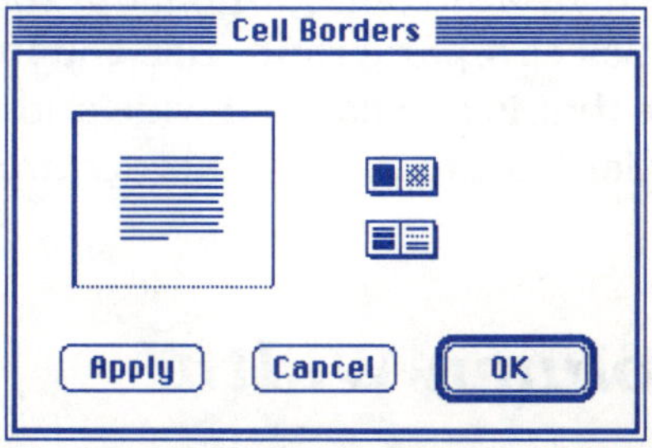

In the midst of this dialog box is a representation of the selected cell. As you can see, the lines showing the top and left edges of the cell are heavier than the others: this illustrates the current borders of the cell. You can format any border of a cell by clicking it and then choosing a new format from one of the pop-ups to the right of the cell representation. In this figure, the top edge has been clicked on:

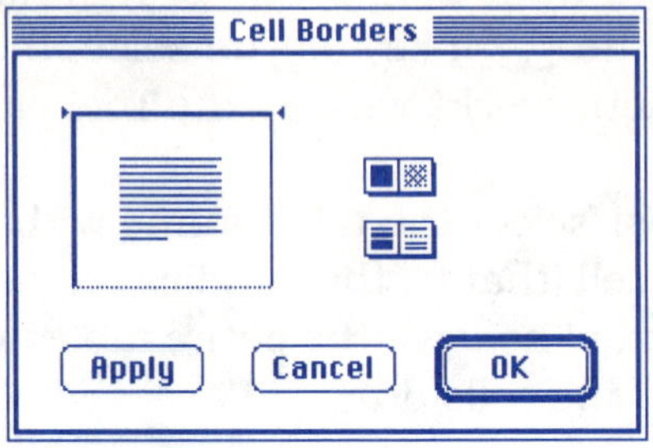

When you click on a border of the cell, handles appear on either side of that border, indicating that changes you make using the pop-ups will affect only that border.

You can select *all* the cell borders, and thus format them all, by clicking in the middle of the cell representation. You can select multiple borders for formatting by pressing the Shift key as you click the different sides.

The pop-up tools to the right of the cell representation work the way the similar tools work on the Tool palette.

Note A good use for boxes around cells is working around one of MacWrite Pro's missing features. MacWrite Pro offers no command to place borders around paragraphs, but there is a way to work around this omission. Select a paragraph, use the Insert Table command to turn it into a table that is one column wide and one row high, and then use the table's border feature to put a border around the single paragraph.

Changing Column Width

There are two ways to do most everything in MacWrite Pro, and changing the width of columns is no exception. There's a direct way and a dialog-driven, precise way.

When you first create a table, all columns are given the same width, but sometimes this isn't satisfactory.

To change the width of a column manually, position the pointer on the border between the *right* edge of the column and its neighbor. The pointer will change, as shown here:

When you hold down the mouse button and drag to the left, the width of that column is reduced; dragging to the right increases its width. When decreasing the width of a column, the width of the column to the right of the selected column is increased; when increasing the width of a column, the width of the column to the right of the selected column is decreased.

Note If you want to change the width of a column *without* affecting the width of surrounding columns, ⌘-drag the column guide. When you change the width of a column using this technique, the width of the entire table is affected accordingly.

The Column Width dialog box, shown here, lets you specify exactly how wide to make the selected columns.

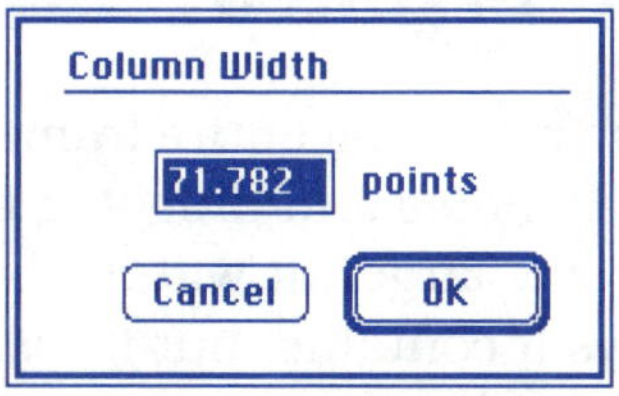

Note Unlike most MacWrite Pro measurement dialog boxes, this one accepts values in points only, not in inches.

Changing Row Height

For most tables, the height that MacWrite Pro sets by default is satisfactory. When you create a new table, the Auto Resize Frame check box in the Modify Frame dialog box is already checked. With this button checked, the height of rows will be adjusted automatically as you enter text into them, and will automatically resize without your intervention as you change the size of text in cells.

The Row Height dialog box, shown below, lets you specify whether you want the height of the row to be handled automatically, and a minimum height (in points) for the row.

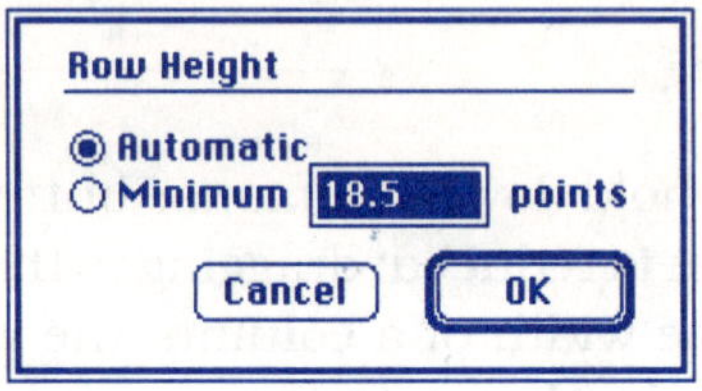

If the Auto Resize check box in the Modify Frame dialog box is checked, the Automatic radio button in this dialog box is disabled.

The field lets you specify a *minimum* height for a row, not an absolute height. Even if the Automatic button is not checked, the height of the row will be adjusted for larger text.

This dialog box accepts numbers in the range of 6.125 (minimum height for a row) to 604.7 points.

Resizing Table Frames

You can also resize the entire frame containing a table by clicking one of the frame's handles and dragging to make it larger or smaller. When you make a frame larger, it will *not* become taller. That depends on the number of rows it contains; but it *will* become wider.

Note When you resize a frame, all columns are resized, and any individual widths you have set are only approximately maintained.

If you make a frame or column too small to contain all its text, text that MacWrite Pro cannot display is represented by a small check box in the lower-right corner of the cell, called an *overflow marker*, as shown here:

The first time this happens during each document editing session, a dialog box appears to alert you. Thereafter, the only indication is the overflow marker.

Working with Tables

MacWrite Pro also lets you add and delete columns after a table has been created. An innovative Merge Cells command lets you combine text from several cells.

Adding Rows and Columns

As mentioned earlier, pressing the Tab key when the insertion point is positioned at the end of a table automatically inserts a new row into the table.

You can also add row(s) using the Table menu's Insert Row command. If you select a single row or if the insertion point is in a cell, the Insert Row command inserts a single row *before* the selected row. If more than a single row is selected, the number of rows inserted before the first selected row is the same as the number of rows you have selected. For example, if you have cells in two rows selected, two rows are inserted before the first selected row. If you want to insert a row *after* the currently selected row, hold down the Option key when you select the Insert Row command.

The Table menu's Insert Column command performs the same actions on columns as the Insert Row command performs on rows. To insert a column before the selected column, use the Insert Column command. To insert a column after the selected column, hold down the Option key when you select the Insert Column command.

Deleting Columns and Rows

The Delete Row and Delete Column commands on the Table menu delete the selected rows or columns.

Merging Cells

You can merge any range of adjacent cells in the table by selecting them and using the Table menu's Merge Cells command. MacWrite Pro combines the contents of the selected cells and puts them into a new cell whose properties (including Ruler settings, font information, and cell area and linefill patterns and colors) are defined by the top-left selected cell. The values in adjacent cells across columns are separated from one another by tabs; the contents of horizontally adjacent cells are separated from one another with returns.

Note Avoid using Merge Cells if you intend to use the Table to Text command to convert a table to tab-delimited text later. The resulting table will reflect the new merged values, not the original columns.

There are a number of uses for this command. The following shows a "before-and-after" approach to a problem that occurs when creating cells:

					Before						
	Winter			Spring			Summer			Fall	
Jan	Feb	March	April	May	June	July	Aug	Sept	Oct	Nov	Dec

After											
Winter			Spring			Summer			Fall		
Jan	Feb	March	April	May	June	July	Aug	Sept	Oct	Nov	Dec

In the frame at the top of the illustration, the seasonal headings above the monthly headings had to be placed carefully into the same cells as the months. This necessitated quite a bit of adjusting; you can see that some months had to be made wider and some narrower to accommodate the names of the seasons. Not only is this time consuming, but if items were added in columns below the month headings, these columns would not be the same width. In the "after" table, the cell to the left of the seasonal heading was merged with the one containing the heading and the one after it. The text in this row was then centered, leaving the heading for the season centered over its months.

Turning Tables into Text

Just as you can transform tab-delimited text into a table, you can reverse the process and turn a table into tab-delimited text. To do so, select the table, or any part of it, and use the Table menu's Table to Text command.

This feature has several practical uses. First, other applications cannot read the tables created in MacWrite Pro. Thus, before saving a MacWrite Pro document into another file format, you should consider "detabling" tables so you can see how they will be transformed when they appear when the document is opened with the target application.

Second, tables are a great tool for editing Merge Data Files for use with MacWrite Pro's merge facility, discussed in Chapter 13. It is much easier to edit text in a table than it is to edit simple tab-delimited text. However, MacWrite Pro *cannot* read text from tables for use in merging. Thus, you can edit a list of names in table frames and then convert the table to tabbed text for use in merging.

Note When converting tables to text, watch for tabs and returns that might be embedded in cells. These will *not* be translated when you convert the table to text. Thus, if a table has seven, columns, but one of its cells has eight columns in it, there will be eight, not seven, tabs on the line. This can scramble merge documents. Similarly, returns in tables are not transformed, and can scramble merge data files.

Sorting

This section covers MacWrite Pro's two methods of sorting.

Sorting Paragraphs

The Edit menu's Sort Paragraphs command sorts the selected paragraphs. It summons this dialog box:

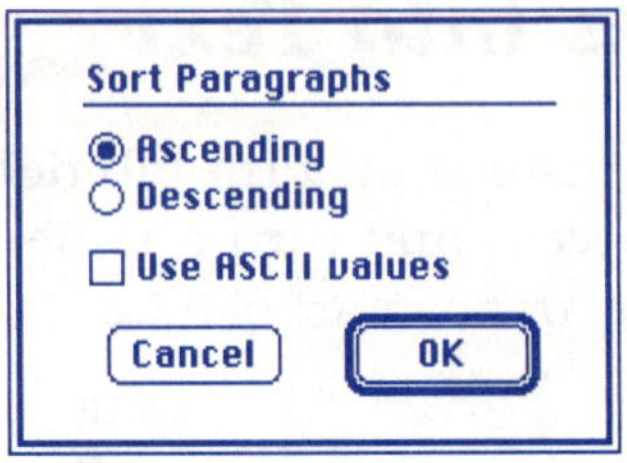

You can sort paragraphs in ascending or descending order. Ascending order sorts in standard alphabetical order (A through Z); descending order does the opposite (Z through A). Paragraphs beginning with numbers come before paragraphs beginning with letters.

Sorting and Invisible Characters

Nonalphanumeric characters at the beginning of paragraphs will affect the sort. Tabs and spaces are the only invisible characters you normally encounter that affect a non-ASCII sort: paragraph, line-break, page-break, section-break, and column-break characters are ignored unless an ASCII sort is specified. (ASCII sorts are discussed in the next section.) If the first character of a paragraph is a tab, then that paragraph will be sorted so it comes before all other paragraphs. Thus, a paragraph beginning with a tab and the letters a b will sort before a paragraph beginning with the letter a.

Sorting and Numbers

Numbers do not necessarily sort in numeric order. If you have eleven paragraphs, numbered 1 through 11 with digits, the sort order will be 1, 10, 11, 2, 3, and so on. Sorting is based on characters, *not* on the values of those characters. Furthermore, numbers always sort before letters.

Note You can assure that paragraphs that begin with numbers are sorted in proper numerical order by prefacing single-digit numbers with a 0, such as 01.

Sorting by ASCII Values

ASCII is a code for numbering individual characters: the ASCII code for an uppercase A is different from the ASCII code for a lowercase a. This is the case for all characters. When sorting, all paragraphs beginning with uppercase letters will sort before all paragraphs beginning with lowercase letters. Normally, this won't affect sorting, since paragraphs will usually begin with uppercase letters.

Note If you anticipate doing an ASCII sort, remember that break characters (line, page, section, and column) are also sorted; sorted documents containing these characters will be relocated accordingly.

Sorting in Tables

To sort paragraphs within a table, select the table cells you want to sort and use the Table menu's Sort Cells command. As with the Sort Paragraphs command, only selected rows are sorted. The Sort Cells command summons this dialog box:

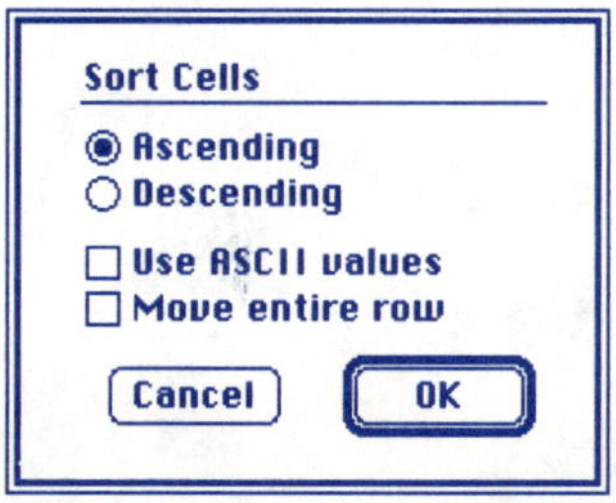

As you can see, there is an additional check box in this dialog box. If the Move entire row box is checked, sorting moves all selected rows of the table according to the sort order of the leftmost *selected column* into the new order; if it is not checked, only those columns selected are sorted. Sorting is based on the columns you have selected. Since moving columns around separately from their rows can scramble a table, you should be careful!

The Move entire row option lets you sort in orders that are different than the first paragraph. Thus, if you have some names and addresses in a table, you can sort them in ZIP code order by selecting the ZIP code column.

Summary

The MacWrite Pro Table frame is a powerful yet easy-to-use tool for creating tables; you need not worry about fumbling with tabs to align columns. Its only real limitation is that tables are limited to 100 cells.

There are three ways to access the table tool: by selecting the Frame menu's Insert Table command, using the Frame tool on the Tool palette, and converting existing tab-delimited text to a MacWrite Pro table.

Most standard text-formatting, editing, and navigation techniques apply to tables. There are a few differences, however.

You can easily add and delete rows and/or columns to and from existing tables.

CHAPTER 13

Merging

Merging, sometimes called "mail merge" is the process of combining text from two different documents into a third document. You've probably received letters prepared in this way, of the type that begins "The Jones family of 1034 Pomona Avenue may have already won $10 million!" We don't encourage you to create this type of letter unless you really *do* have $10 million to give away (if so, give us a call). However, merging documents is a good technique to add a personal touch to a form letter, letting you tailor portions of a letter to different individuals.

In merging, there are two documents involved. The first is the *Merge Data File*, and the second is called the *Merge Template File*. The Merge Template File contains the text, such as a form letter, into which you want to pull data from the Merge Data File. If you are creating a form letter, the Merge Template File contains the text of the letter, and the Merge Data File contains the names and addresses you want to merge into it.

Creating a Merge Data File

The Merge Data File contains a number of *records*. A record contains the items of information in the Merge Data File that will be used to create separate pages in the merged document. Records are separated by one another by return characters in the Merge Data File, so each record is its own paragraph.

Records, in turn, are divided into *fields*. Fields are separate items of information. Let's take a look at an example. Figure 13-1 shows an example of a simple Merge Data File.

This screen shows a Merge Data File containing three records, each ending with a return character (so that's three paragraphs). Within these records, different items of information are separated by tab characters. The first line, or record, contains the names of the individual fields. MacWrite Pro will use this line to determine the names of your data fields.

Creating a Merge Data File with MacWrite Pro

How you create the Merge Data File depends primarily on its size and complexity. You can use MacWrite Pro for creating small, relatively simple

FIGURE 13-1 Simple Merge Data File

First Name	Last Name	Address	City	State	Zip
Blair	Miller	1 Highway 61	Duluth	MN	01234
Mick	McQuistion	2 Desolation Row	Hibbing	MN	01234

Merge Data Files. A good example of this might be the names and addresses of, say, the 100 members of your sales staff. Larger and more complex databases, such as a company catalog that contains several hundred records with many fields, are best handled by a dedicated database management tool such as Claris FileMaker Pro or ACIUS 4th Dimension.

Note Spreadsheet applications such as Microsoft Excel and Claris Resolve have database capabilities, and can export in tab-delimited format for use in a Merge Data File.

In this example MacWrite Pro Merge Data File, there are six fields: First Name, Last Name, Address, City, State, and Zip. The first field, First Name, is followed by a tab, which is followed by the second field, then a tab, and so on. A return character denotes the end of the record.

To create a Merge Data File in MacWrite Pro, first type a line containing the names of the fields, pressing Tab affter each field name. When you have typed all the field names, press Return to mark the end of the first record. (The first record contains the names of the data fields.) Next type the text you want to appear in each of the fields, pressing Tab after every field except the last in each record, after which you press Return. Later in this chapter, you will see exactly how to use this information in the Merge Template File. If the line containing the record wraps over to the next screen line, don't be alarmed; visible screen wraps do not affect the record definition. The end of a record is determined only when you press Return.

Note If you do not have the information for one of the fields, for example, a phone number or a ZIP code, be sure to leave a blank space where the information would normally go. In this example, press the Tab key a second time to skip the field with the missing data.

When you are creating the Merge Data File in MacWrite Pro, it is useful to create the records as a table. Tables make it easier to enter data, letting you move from one field (column) to the next with the Tab key. However, since MacWrite Pro cannot read a table-based file as a Merge Data File, you will need to use the Table to Text command to transform the table into tabbed text before you can use it in merging.

When saving the MacWrite Pro Merge Data File, you don't have to save it in a special file format (such as text only). However, it is important that the first line in the document contain the field names. It is also important that no text other than the data records be in the document. Do *not* save it as a Text with Line Breaks format document; this adds a hard return at the end of each screen line and will detroy your field definitions if they exceed one line.

Creating a Merge Data File with Other Programs

MacWrite Pro is not designed to be a complete tool for managing data. This is as it should be. Many users keep name and address lists in a database (such as FileMaker Pro, FoxBASE, or RecordHolder) or personal information manager (for example, DynoDex, TouchBase, or Connections).

MacWrite Pro can read the contents of several database and personal information manager files directly. Before exporting from one of these programs, take a look at the XTND filter list available to MacWrite Pro to see if the program you are using is supported. This will save you the time and bother of the exporting step.

Almost all database programs and personal information managers have *export* capabilities. This refers to their ability to save records to a text-only format, which can be read as a Merge Data File by MacWrite Pro. Consult the documentation for the program you are using for exact instructions on how to perform this export. Generally, these programs will support one of two formats: tab delimited or comma delimited.

Tab-Delimited Format

The tab-delimited format is the one we have been discussing throughout this chapter. All popular Macintosh database manager and personal information manager programs support the tab-delimited format. If the one you are currently using does not support exporting to tab-delimited format files, it probably suffers from other glaring omissions, and you should therefore consider using a better designed tool for your data-management tasks.

Comma-Delimited Format

The comma-delimited format, which is rooted in the origins of MS-DOS, is another common format. It uses the comma rather than the tab as a field separator within records. This format can be awkward to use because commas might be part of the data within a field, for example, the name "John Jones, Jr." The workaround for this problem is to place quotation marks on either side of each field. So a more accurate definition of the format would be a comma-and-quote-delimited format. MacWrite Pro can work with this format as well as the tab-delimited format. However, it is more troublesome to create manually in MacWrite Pro than the tab format, so if you have a choice, always choose tab-delimited files.

Inserting Field Names

Most databases and personal information managers do not insert a separate field name record at the beginning of the data file when you use them to create a text data file for merging with MacWrite Pro. This is a task you will have to perform manually. The procedure is to open the exported file with MacWrite Pro, position the insertion point at the beginning of the file, then enter the field names (using tabs to separate names) as described above as if you were creating the Merge Data File from scratch. Remember to end the field name record with a return character.

A Simple Merge Template File

The next step in merging is to create the document into which the data from the Merge Data File are to be merged. The Merge Template File differs from regular documents that you might create only in that it contains the field names from the Merge Data File in the location you specify. These field names must be specially demarked, but the Mail Merge palette helps make this a painless process.

The Mail Merge Palette

Use the File menu's Mail Merge command (keyboard equivalent: ⌘-M) to open the Mail Merge palette. MacWrite Pro then asks you to locate and open a Merge Data file. You can use XTND filters to open some files in their native format, or you can open a MacWrite Pro document, such as the one created in the first part of this chapter.

When you have opened the Merge Data File, the Mail Merge palette appears, as shown here:

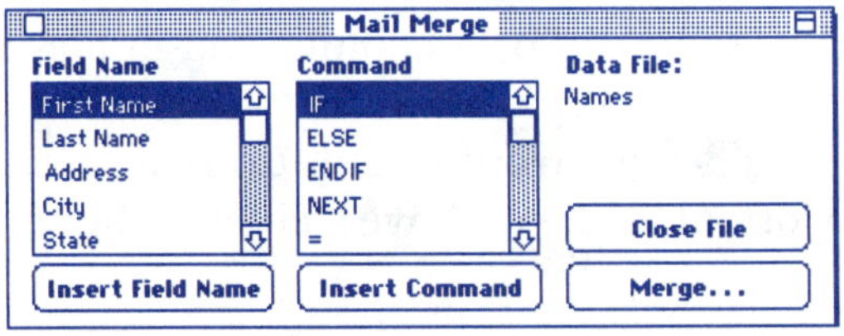

The scrolling field at the left edge of the palette shows a list of all the fields that have been defined in the Merge Data File; the second list shows special merge commands. (These commands are discussed later in this chapter.) You can move this palette (drag it by its title bar) around the screen as necessary to see the document behind it. You are now ready to start creating the Merge Template File itself.

Note If you prefer, you can park the Mail Merge palette by clicking on its zoom box to move it up to the window's title bar, putting it out of the way.

Follow these steps to create a simple Merge Template File based on the Merge Data File created earlier in this chapter.

1. Click the First Name field in the Field name scrolling list.
2. Click the Insert Field Name button below this scrolling list. The first name field is surrounded by the merge delimiters. The « character and the » character are the default (delimiters are discussed in more detail at the end of the chapter).
3. Press the Spacebar to insert a space between the first and last names.
4. Double-click the Last Name item in the Field name list. This is a shortcut for clicking the field name and then clicking the Insert Field Name button.
5. Press Return to create a new line, and then use the techniques in step 4 to insert the Address field.
6. Repeat this procedure to complete the address at the top of the letter. Note the typed comma and space between the City and State fields and the space between the State and Zip fields.
7. Press Return twice to begin the salutation, type **Dear Mr.** and a space, and insert the Last Name field from the Merge Data File.

Note Since all the records in this Merge Data File contain the names of men, we do not need to worry about gender. In real life, you would probably add a field labeled "Salutation" to determine which salutation to use in a letter. Besides indicating Mr. or Ms., this would also let you specify other options such as Dr., Distinguished Senator, or Right Reverend.

8. Press Return twice to begin the body of the letter. Note that the Last Name field is inserted in the first line, as well as the Address field. This is how you can prepare those really irritating Publishers' Clearing House-type letters that grace our mailboxes (sorry, Ed McMahon).

The complete letter is shown in Figure 13-2.

FIGURE 13-2

Simple Merge Template File

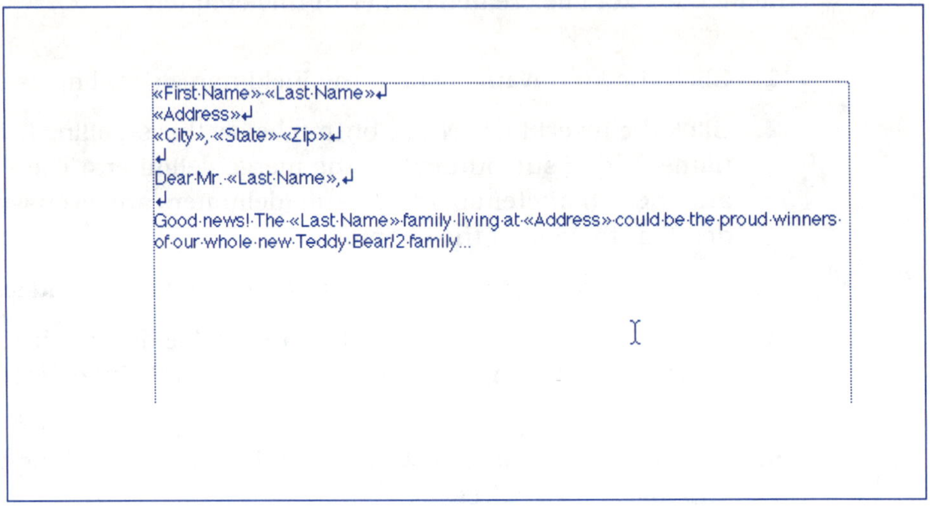

For this illustrative sample, this is as far as we'll go. Feel free to create the body of the letter on your own.

Merging

Creating the documents with the actual field values substituted into the field holders is called *merging*. Click the Merge button in the Mail Merge palette, which summons the Merge dialog box, shown here:

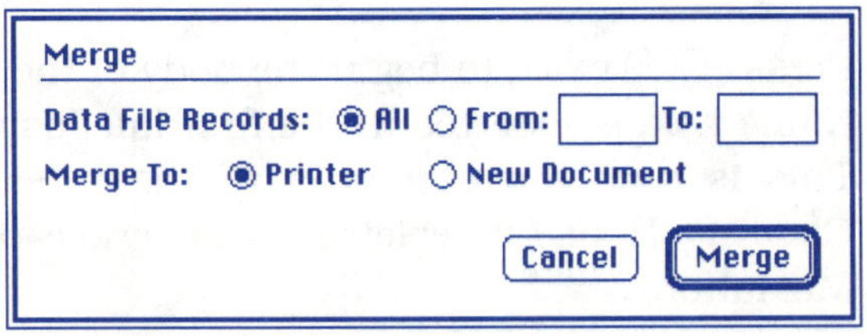

File Records

You can choose to merge all the records in the data file or only a range of records. This portion of the dialog box is analogous to the section of the Print dialog box that lets you choose which pages to print.

Viewing the result of merging only a few records is useful to documents that might contain several hundred records. In this case, print only the first one or two records to judge the results. It is also useful if you have complex combinations of merge commands in your document and want to test them.

Merge Destination

The Merge dialog box also lets you choose between merging directly to the printer or to a new document.

Merging to the Printer

When you merge to the printer, MacWrite Pro first presents you with a standard Print dialog box for the print jobs. To understand some of the options you have here, you need to understand that when MacWrite Pro is merging to the printer, it creates a separate print job for each merged letter. In this sample, the letter that is sent to the first person is a separate document from the one sent to the second person on the list. Thus, some of the choices in the Print dialog box, such as the range of pages to print, apply to each individual document, not to the entire merge print job.

When you have a large number of records to merge and have already tested the merged document, you can safely merge directly to the printer.

Merging to a New Document

When you merge to a new document, MacWrite Pro prepares a special kind of document called a *Working document*. The Working document contains a separate page (or pages, if the Merge Template File is longer than a page) for each record in the data file. A Working document is shown here:

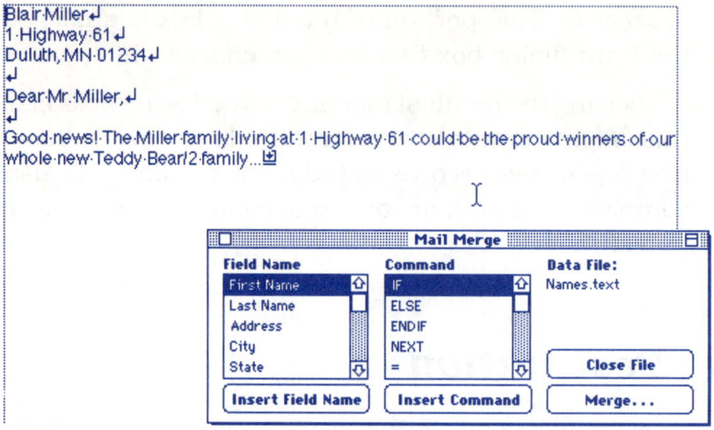

Merging to a new document is a good way to test your Merge Template File before printing a large number of letters. You can use it in conjunction with MacWrite Pro's ability to merge only a few records as a means of testing. Later in this chapter, we'll show you how to use this capability to take merging beyond simple mail merging to create different types of documents.

Merge Commands

The merge features discussed so far show a powerful word processing technique with many uses, but MacWrite Pro also offers additional merging features that add even more power and flexibility to the technique.

Chief among these additional capabilities is the IF condition.

The following illustration shows a modified version of the names the Merge Data File used in the earlier examples. Two fields have been added to this document: Amt Due and Past Due. The Amt Due field shows how much is owed to you by the customer, and the Past Due field shows how many days late the payment is, as shown here:

First Name	Last Name	Address	City	State	Zip	Amt Due	Past Due
Blair	Miller	1 Highway 61	Duluth	MN	01234	100	60
Mick	McQuistion	2 Desolation Row	Hibbing	MN	01234	35	0

Note that in this example, the size of the type is reduced and the margins are widened to make these extra fields manageable on the screen. This isn't necessary; it's just a convenience. You can also use the Page Setup command to switch the layout of your Merge Data File to landscape, so that all fields can fit across the page without reducing the size of the text too much.

Setting Up IF Conditions

You do not necessarily always want to send the same letter to all the people in your list. Sometimes when sending a letter, you might want certain people to get text that is different from that sent to others. For that, you use the IF capabilities of MacWrite Pro Mail Merge. First we'll show you how to use the IF capability; then we'll tell you how it works.

In this sample, you are sending letters to both customers. Use the Past Due field to insert a message to those customers whose accounts are more than 50 days past due. The letter we are preparing is shown here:

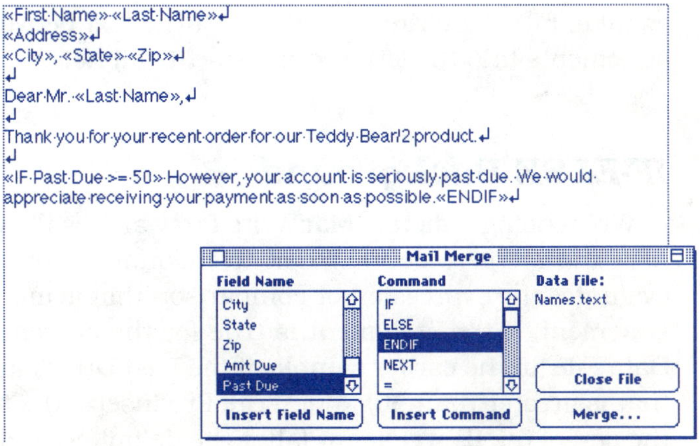

Here's how to do it:

1. Locate the position in the document at which you want to insert the message and click to put the insertion point there.
2. Double-click the IF statement in the Command list in the Mail Merge palette. « IF» is inserted at the insertion point, and the insertion point is positioned between the delimiters.

3. Locate the Past Due field in the Field Name list and double-click it. The field name is inserted between the delimiters, after the IF statement.
4. Scroll to the >= operator in the Command list (it's toward the bottom), and double-click it. It will be inserted between the delimiters, after the field name. (The >= delimiter means greater than or equal to a number, which in this example is 50.)
5. Type **50**, as we want this message to go to those whose accounts are more than 50 days past due.
6. Click to the right of the » delimiter to type the text you want sent to those whose accounts are seriously past due.
7. When you've typed that text, locate the ENDIF command in the Command field in the Mail Merge palette and double-click it to insert it into the text.

When you merge the documents, MacWrite Pro processes these operators for each record. If the value in the Past Due field is greater than or equal to 50, MacWrite Pro will insert the text between the IF and ENDIF statements into the letter; otherwise it will not.

IF-ELSE Background

When doing a merge, MacWrite Pro watches the codes that you insert with the Merge palette. When it encounters an IF statement, it next evaluates the expression or comparison that is immediately after that IF statement. If the statement is true for the current record in the Merge Data File (in the earlier sample, if the Past Due field contains an amount that is greater than 50), MacWrite Pro inserts the text that lies between the end of the IF statement (after the delimiter) and the beginning of the next ENDIF or ELSE statement (which is discussed shortly).

When working with complex merge documents that contain IF tests, we recommend that you merge documents to the screen before printing, to make sure that the logic of your IF statements is working the way you want it to before committing it to the printer.

Other Commands

In addition to the standard IF-ENDIF combination, MacWrite Pro supports two other commands that are useful for merging.

The ELSE Command

The ELSE command lets you specify text to be inserted into the text if a condition is *not* met. In the previous example, you may want to insert different text into the document if the account is not yet 50 days or more past due. Here's how such a statement would look:

«IF Past Due >= 50» However, your account is seriously past due. We would appreciate receiving your payment as soon as possible. «ELSE»Your account is not yet past due, but it could get that way if you don't send payment soon!«ENDIF»

Note that the ELSE command is placed *between* the IF and ENDIF commands.

The NEXT Command

The NEXT command is used when you want to instruct MacWrite Pro to skip a record when a condition is met. In the above example, you may not want to send a letter at all to those whose account is not past due. In that case, the letter would look something like this:

«IF Past Due < 50»«NEXT»«ENDIF»

Put statements of this category at the very beginning of the document. That way the entire process is faster because MacWrite Pro does not have to process the merge fields for the address in letters that it would not print anyway.

Operators

The >= and < tools used previously are called operators. Table 13-1 shows each of MacWrite Pro's operators and what they mean. In this table,

TABLE 13-1 MacWrite Pro Operators and Definitions

Operator	What It Means	Sample
=	Equals or matches	«IF 50 = 50»Fifty equals Fifty! «ENDIF»
<>	Not equal	«IF 1 <> 2»One is not Two! «ENDIF»
<	Less than	«IF 1 < 2»One is less than Two!«ENDIF»
<=	Less than or equal to	«IF 1 <= 2»One is less than or equal to Two!«ENDIF»
>	Greater than	«IF 2>1»Two is greater than One!«ENDIF»
>=	Greater than or equal to	«IF 1>= 0»One is greater than or equal to zero!«ENDIF»
CONTAINS	Contains the following text	«IF abc CONTAINS a»ABC CONTAINS C!«ENDIF»

the Sample column shows a short sample that would evaluate as true during a mail merge. That is, text following the » symbol *would* print.

Compounding Conditions

You can also compound conditions, using three other operators. To compound conditions, embed the compounding operators after the first condition test within the «ref and »brackets.

AND

The AND operator evaluates to true (that is, text after the bracket is inserted) if both the tests are true. Here is a sample of an AND statement.

«IFPast Due >= 90 AND Amt Due >= 100» Our collection agency will contact you soon.«ENDIF»

In this case, if the account is more than 89 days old and the amount due is greater than $200, the phrase after the » is inserted.

OR

The OR operator evaluates to true if *either* of the tested statements is true:

«IF Past Due >= 120 OR Amt Due >= 100» Our collection agency will contact you soon.«ENDIF»

Thus, the collection agency will call if the customer owes more than 100 *or* if the account is 120 days or more past due (regardless of the amount).

AND NOT

The NOT operator evaluates to true if the first IF test is true, but the second is not true:

«IF Past Due >= 120 AND NOT Amt Due <= 10» Our collection agency will contact you soon.«ENDIF»

In this case, the collection agency will call if the account is more than 120 days old, but not if the amount due is $10 or less (the collection agency charges $25 for each account it processes).

Before leaving this topic, remember that if you are processing data managed by a separate database program, it's probable that program can do more sophisticated processing of the records before you export them.

Some Tips

Here are some miscellaneous tips that could make merging easier.

Field Delimiters

When MacWrite Pro is merging your document, it needs a means to distinguish what is to be an item from the Merge Data File, and what is part of the normal text of the document. It does this by looking for a particular set of marker characters, called *delimiters*, that separate the data items.

MacWrite Pro's default delimiter is the «and » pair of characters. The « signifies the beginning of the data item, and the » signifies the end of it. When MacWrite Pro is processing the merge file, it reads the text between these characters and attempts to match them with a named field within the Merge Data File. As you will see later, special merge commands can also be inserted between these characters.

To manually type the first of these characters, press the Option-\ key combination. To type the closing character, hold down the Shift and Option keys while pressing the \ key (Shift-Option-\).

Note The KeyCaps desk accessory is handy for locating infrequently used characters such as these.

You can change these delimiters using the Document tile of the Preferences dialog box, as shown in Figure 13-3. The other choices are the [ ] pair and the { } pair. These characters are easier to type, since they are displayed on the keyboard, and require no Option-key gymnastics. However, it is not uncommon that these characters would actually occur in other contexts within your document. So, unless you know that you will never use them, it's best to stick with the original merge characters. (Once you have typed one of each character in your document, you can always cut and paste them into other places fairly easily.)

Closing the Data File

While you are using the Mail Merge palette with a Merge Data File open, no other users or programs can open that data file. So, if you have the Mail Merge palette open, but are not actively using it to insert fields or commands, you can use the Close File button to free the file for other

FIGURE 13-3 Merge section of the Preferences dialog box

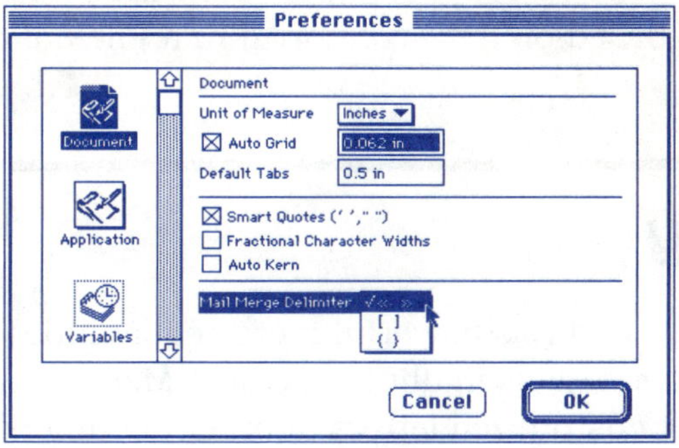

users. There are times, as when using a company's mailing list that is on a file server, that several users may need to access the file.

Standardizing Field Names

While we're giving tips, it's a good idea to mention that you should standardize the field names for all your merge files, whether they are Merge Data files or Merge Template Files. By standardizing field names, such as First Name for the first name, you can save a lot of time. A Merge Template File prepared for use with one merge file will then be more likely to work with a different data file.

Other Document Processing Using Merging

While the traditional use for mail merge capabilities has been to generate letters, as we have shown in this chapter, it is possible to use mail merge to generate other types of documents containing data in structured delimited files. The trick is to delete the special page break character that MacWrite Pro inserts at the end of each letter, or replace it with another character. You can delete it manually by selecting it and pressing the Del key, or use the Find/Change dialog to delete all the records. This technique will be demonstrated in the Document Recipes section of this book in Chapter 20, where we show you how to prepare a catalog based on data contained in a FileMaker Pro (or other) database.

Summary

MacWrite Pro's powerful merge capabilities let you use your Mac and printer as a mass mailing machine. Merging is the processes of creating multiple customized letters or other documents from a template called a Merge Template File with the data records contained in a special file called a Merge Data File.

A Merge Data File consists of individual records, each of which contains information, such as name and address, due dates, and/or similar kinds of data. You can create this data file directly with MacWrite Pro, or you can use information from almost any popular database or spreadsheet application that can export records in a tab- or comma-delimited format for which you have an XTND filer.

The Merge Template File is the master template for the final merged documents. It is identical to a regular document except that it has special placeholders, called field names, which are replaced with actual data during the merge process.

You can fine-tune the merge process with a variety of decision-making commands. The most frequently used include IF, ELSE, and NEXT.

CHAPTER 14

Managing Documents

This chapter discusses the document management features available to you in MacWrite Pro: saving documents, translating them into different formats, opening documents created by other applications, combining documents, and using the Document Info command as an assist in the editing process.

Document Info

The Document Info command on the View menu provides several useful statistics about a document. The dialog box that appears reports the number of characters, words, lines, and paragraphs in the document or the selection.

This information is useful in a variety of situations, but particularly when you are writing for length. Magazines, for example, often specify a length when commissioning an article, either in number of words or number of lines (in which case you will need to make sure that margins and font style and size are specified as well). The Document Info dialog box is shown here:

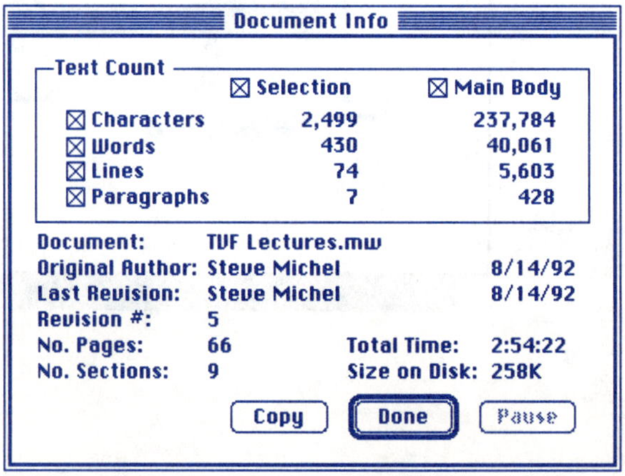

This dialog box can display the number of characters, words, lines, and paragraphs in either the current selection, the entire document, or both. Check boxes determine which items are counted, and whether the selection, entire document, or both are counted.

When you first open the Document Info dialog box, most of the information fields are empty. To have MacWrite Pro perform the counts, click the Count button or press Enter or Return. While MacWrite Pro is counting the characters, words, lines, and paragraphs, the Count button changes to read Pause; clicking it stops the process, displaying the counts "so far."

The amount of time MacWrite Pro needs to count the elements in a document depends on both the length of the document and the range of elements to be counted. With long documents you may find that counting all the elements takes longer than your patience permits. You can speed things up by checking only those elements of interest. For example, if you only need to know the number of words in a document, check only that box and uncheck the others.

As with all MacWrite Pro dialog boxes, this one includes keyboard equivalents for its buttons. Table 14-1 shows those shortcuts.

Selection and Main Body

The two check boxes near the top of the dialog box let you specify whether text in the current selection and/or the entire document (Main Body) are counted.

Although in most cases you will want to check the entire document, there are some uses for checking the selection as well. If you exceed the specified length of a document, you can select paragraphs and count them to determine if deleting those paragraphs will help to reach the specified length.

TABLE 14-1 Keyboard Equivalents in the Document Info Dialog Box

This Key Combination	Is Equivalent to This Button
⌘-S	Selection
⌘-M	Main Body
⌘-H	Characters
⌘-W	Words
⌘-L	Lines
⌘-P	Paragraphs
⌘-C	Copy

Original Author and Last Revision

The Original Author and Last Revision items return the name of the person who created the document, the date it was created, and the date and the name of the last person to edit the document.

The author's name is taken from the name as it is entered in the Application tile of the Preferences dialog box. When you first install MacWrite Pro, the name of the owner of the Mac is automatically entered into this field. This, in turn, is taken from the name of the owner of the Mac as entered in the Sharing Setup Control Panel.

This information is most useful when you are sharing documents between users who work on several different Macintoshes.

Note You can also use this information if several people are working on a document on the same Macintosh—just remember to change the name in the Preferences dialog box before beginning work.

Revision #

The Revision number is increased by one each time a document is opened and saved. A new document has a revision number of 1. Saving it, closing it, and opening it again makes the revision number 2.

As discussed in Chapter 5, you can use the Revision number in headers and footers of a document (or anywhere else, for that matter) by inserting it using the Edit menu Insert Variable command. When the Revision number is inserted as a variable, it is always accurate. Putting it in a header or footer gives you a standard way of making sure that a printed copy of the document matches a computer copy.

Number of Pages and Number of Sections

The No. Pages and No. Sections items display the number of pages and sections in the entire document.

Note The same information is displayed in the Page/Section area at the bottom of the document window if the insertion point is at the end of the document.

Total Time

Total Time displays the total amount of time the document has been edited. This time is incremented when

1. MacWrite Pro is the frontmost application in use on the Mac.
2. The document is the frontmost document opened in MacWrite.

Thus, the time will not be incremented if another application is in front of MacWrite Pro or when the document is open, but you are working on another MacWrite Pro document. It is incremented *only* so long as the document is in the window that is on top of all other windows on the Mac.

This information can be indispensable if you are billing for word processing work by the hour. You can have a fairly exact measure of how long it took you to work on the document and provide a proof of how long you worked on it. (Of course, the proof isn't much good if you open the document, and walk away from your Mac for a couple of hours.)

Size on Disk

Size on Disk displays how much space the document takes up on disk. The number is shown in kilobytes (Kb, also known as K). A kilobyte is 1024 characters.

Note MacWrite Pro documents have a minimum size of 3Kb.

Creating a Table from Document Info

The Copy button at the bottom of the Document Info dialog box copies all of the information in the dialog box to the Clipboard. You can then paste the statistics into the document itself (or into another document, or even into another application).

This information can be useful in some situations on a separate cover page. To make a cover page, place your cursor at the beginning of the document, choose the Section command from the Format | Insert Break submenu.

Opening Documents

There are two ways to open documents with MacWrite Pro: using the Finder and from within the application itself.

From the Finder

The simplest way to open a MacWrite Pro file from the Finder is to double-click the file icon. (You can also select the icon and use the Finder File menu's Open command.)

System 7 provides another way to open documents with MacWrite Pro, even if the document in question was created by another application.

System 7 has a feature called "Drag and Drop." To use this feature, select the icon of a file containing text (for example, one created by TeachText), and drag its icon until the pointer is on the top of the MacWrite Pro icon. If the MacWrite Pro icon darkens when the mouse pointer connects with the MacWrite Pro icon, then MacWrite Pro can open that document. Release the mouse button to open the document. (The procedure is exactly the same as you use when you drag a file to another disk, to a closed folder, or to the trash.)

Drag-and-Drop file opening works whether or not MacWrite Pro is open. It is a handy feature that lets you see quickly whether the file can be opened by MacWrite Pro or not. You will see how MacWrite Pro deals with files that were created by an application other than MacWrite Pro.

From Within MacWrite Pro

Use the File | Open command (⌘-O) from within MacWrite Pro to open files.

The dialog box this command summons is a standard Mac feature. For details on using it to navigate the disks and folders available to you, consult your Macintosh reference manual. MacWrite Pro's Open Document dialog box is shown here:

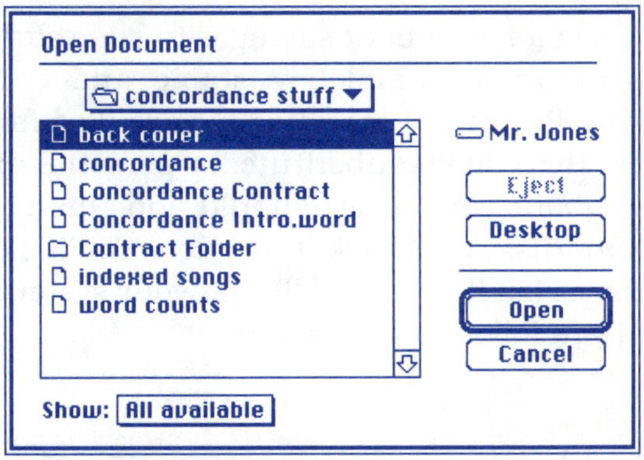

When this dialog box appears, *all* the kinds of documents that MacWrite Pro can open are listed in the middle field; this includes a basic set of five different types of documents, as well as those documents MacWrite Pro can open with its XTND file translators. The XTND translators are discussed in more detail later in this chapter.

Inserting Documents

In addition to opening documents, MacWrite Pro lets you *insert* other documents into a file, using the File menu's Insert command (the keyboard equivalent is Shift-⌘-I). This command displays a dialog box identical to the Open Document dialog box. When you choose a file, the entire contents of that file are inserted into your document at the insertion point or replace any selected text. This is one way of inserting graphics into the body of your text or incorporating boilerplate text.

Note If you hold down the Option key when you choose the Open or Insert commands, MacWrite Pro will display *all* files in the Open File dialog box. This lets you open nearly any kind of file, whether or not

MacWrite Pro knows how to read that file accurately. The text in the file's data fork will be displayed. Use caution with this feature: it lets you open and display files, such as applications and System files, that are best left undisturbed.

Saving

The best advice about saving is to *save early* and save often. No Mac configuration is completely stable and trustworthy. Even though MacWrite Pro will automatically save files for you, and save backups besides, there is no substitute for personal diligence. And while we're talking about saving, we should add this recommendation: *back up your hard disk, and back it up often.* You'll sleep easier, and when the time comes (as it does for all) that your system falls apart on you, you'll be glad you followed this advice.

Save ⌘-S *and Save As* Shift-⌘-S

The File menu's Save command saves the current file. If you have previously saved the document, it is immediately saved, in the same folder and with the same name as before, without showing a dialog box or requiring any further action. If you have not previously saved the file, it works in the same way as the Save As command. This presents you with the dialog box shown here:

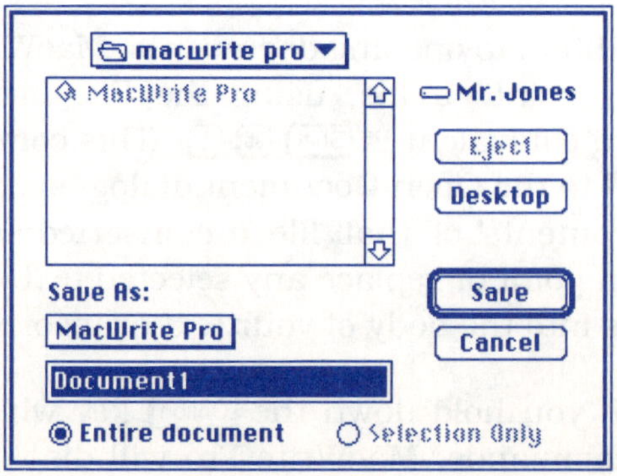

As with the File Open dialog box, this dialog box differs little from standard Mac Save dialog boxes; consult your Mac manual for instructions on navigating through folders and disks.

Above the field where you type the name of the file you want to save is a popup menu that lets you define the type of the file you want to save. Usually you will save in the default MacWrite Pro file format; other file formats are discussed later in this chapter.

Entire Document or Selection Only

At the bottom of the Save As dialog box are two radio buttons that tell MacWrite Pro what to save: the Entire Document or the Selection Only. If no text is selected, the Selection Only radio button is disabled. MacWrite Pro defaults to saving the entire document.

When you save the selection, MacWrite Pro includes in that saved document all *information* about the document, even if it is not necessarily part of the current selection. The complete style sheet for the open document becomes part of the new document, regardless of whether any particular styles were in the selection. Similarly, Document and Section formats (in the latter case, only for the selected section) are saved.

Auto Save and Backup

MacWrite Pro can save documents automatically, and keep backups as well. The Automatic Save/Backup dialog box, shown here, is summoned by the File menu's Auto Save command:

This dialog box contains two check boxes. The first (which has a keyboard equivalent of ⌘-A) enables automatic saving of the current document.

You can also specify the interval (in minutes) at which you want MacWrite Pro to save the current document to disk.

The Keep session backups check box (the keyboard equivalent is ⌘-B) enables automatic creation of backups of the current file whenever the file is saved. When you enable this feature, MacWrite Pro automatically creates a backup of the current file whenever it is saved, whether the save is manual or automatic.

The field to the right of this check box lets you specify how many *session backups* MacWrite Pro will keep. A session starts when you open MacWrite Pro and ends when you quit the program. The backup files have the same name as the file you are saving, with the extra text .BAK and a digit (from 1 to the number of backups you have specified) appended to it.

The Set Folder button at the bottom of the dialog box (the keyboard equivalent is ⌘-S) allows you to specify where the backup files are to be stored. Many people find it convenient to store backup files in a special backup folder. That way it is easy to free up disk space by purging the backup folder of old backups you no longer need. MacWrite Pro uses the MacWrite Pro folder as the default location for storing backup files.

Note You can specify that backups are to be stored on a separate disk, such as a floppy disk or a network disk. If you've had a hard disk crash, you'll understand the impulse to do this.

Revert to Saved

The Revert to Saved command lets you replace the version of the document on your screen with the version you last saved. Not surprisingly, this command is not available if you have not saved your document. Before discarding your changes, it asks for confirmation in this dialog box:

In addition to this command, you can also open previous versions of the file that have been saved by the Automatic Backup feature, if you have enabled it.

File Formats MacWrite Pro Can Use

This section deals with the various *kinds* of files MacWrite Pro can open and save.

MacWrite Pro

The default format for saving a file is the MacWrite Pro "native" format. This file format stores everything in the MacWrite Pro document. MacWrite Pro's creator code is MWPR and files in its normal format have the type code of MWPd.

MacWrite Pro Stationery

Stationery files let you create document templates that assist you in creating standard documents. Stationery files, and tips for using them, are discussed later in this chapter.

MacWrite Pro Options

MacWrite Pro Options is a special stationery file that is stored in the Claris folder inside the System Folder. You need not ever open this file directly; all new documents you create (with the New command on the File menu) automatically have all the same characteristics as those in this file.

Text

The Text format saves all the text in the document, with no formatting information. Besides text itself, it saves tabs and return characters. No information about tab stops, margins, font styles, style sheets, page setup, or any other type of formatting is saved. A return character is placed at the end of each paragraph—exactly where you pressed the Return key when typing the document.

Saving documents as text only is useful mainly when you are saving a file for use on a different kind of computer. However, use this format as the last resort only; make sure that there is not an XTND translator that can do the job for you. It might be the case that there is not a translator that is directly compatible; while there may not be a translator for word processor X, perhaps that word processor can read files in the format of word processor Y for which there *is* a translator.

You should also remember that the Text format does *not* make transformations: curly quotes will not be turned into straight quotes, and ligatures will not be separated into their component letters; you must perform these translations manually if the other program or computer cannot understand these characters.

Text with Line Breaks

The Text with Line Breaks format is similar to the Text format, with one exception: when MacWrite Pro saves a file in the Text with Line Breaks format, a return character is placed at the end of every screen line, not just at the end of every paragraph.

Here's a neat trick to use when *opening* documents. As we mentioned in Chapter 6, many files that you originate on other computers (particularly those that come from online services) are, in effect, in this format: a return is at the end of every line, with two returns at the end of a paragraph. Chapter 6 describes how to use the Find/Change command in MacWrite Pro to transform these files to the correct formatting. However, if you are opening a file that you know is in this format, select the Text with Line Breaks option from the pop-up menu—this tells MacWrite Pro that the file is in this format. When the file opens, the line breaks will be removed, and only one return will appear at the ends of paragraphs.

XTND Formats

MacWrite Pro uses a file-translation architecture called XTND, which allows it to read and write files in a number of different formats. XTND was developed by Claris to facilitate this, and Claris has licensed the technology to other developers so they can write these "filters" for their own programs. In turn, Claris has licensed the technology to Apple, and Apple is making it available to nearly all developers. The goal is to have a common set of filters that all programs can use to read the data of nearly all others. It means that it's relatively easy for MacWrite Pro to be able to read from and write to a wide variety of file formats.

To save a file using an XTND format, use the pop-up menu toward the bottom of the Save As dialog box to specify the format. As you can see here, a number of file formats are supported, both for Macintosh programs and those from other systems.

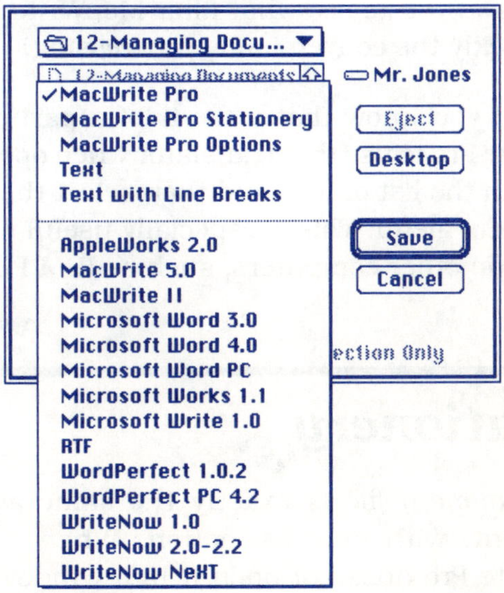

Note Not all the filters shown may be available on your Mac; in turn you may have some filters on your Mac that are not shown in the preceding illustration.

There are more than 50 different file formats supported by XTND. You can also use DataViz' excellent MacLink software to assist you in file translation, should there be an arcane format that XTND does not support.

XTND preserves as much of the original formatting in a document as possible. For example, the AppleWorks 2.0 format may not support graphics; if you save a MacWrite Pro file to the AppleWorks 2.0 format, none of the graphics will be included in the file. The same might be true of features such as tables (which are saved as tabbed text), frames, notes, and the like.

When you open a file that is in a non-MacWrite Pro format, the program will do its best to determine the format of that file, and use the correct XTND filter. The file will be converted to MacWrite Pro format as it is opened, and the program will present this progress dialog box:

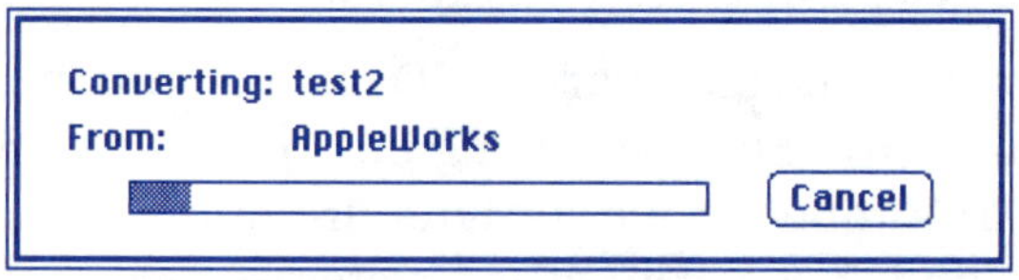

This allows you to see what filter MacWrite Pro is using for the file and how quickly the conversion is progressing.

Note If you know that a file is of a particular format, you can force MacWrite Pro to use that translator when opening the file. To do so, select the file in the list of files and then select the filter you want to use from the pop-up menu. This is especially useful when opening files that were created on other computers, such as IBM PCs.

Using Stationery

A *stationery file* is exactly the same as any other MacWrite Pro document, with one distinction. When you open a stationery file, MacWrite Pro does not open it in a window with the name of the file; instead it opens a new untitled document with all the attributes of the stationery file. Thus, any changes you make to the new file will not automatically affect the stationery pad on your hard disk. Like printed stationery, it is a template on which you place your document.

Stationery documents are very useful. Earlier in this chapter, it was explained how to use the MacWrite Pro Options file to store global settings; the major limitation of this technique is that it affects all new MacWrite Pro documents. On the other hand, you can have as many different kinds of stationery files as you need. While writing this book, for example, we created a stationery file for chapters. This stationery file contained margin settings, style sheets, headers and footers, and more in the format specified by the publisher. In the same way, you can evaluate the various types of documents that you work with and create a stationery document for each one: letters, memos, fax cover sheets, and more. Nearly all the templates described in the Document Recipes section of this book are stationery candidates.

There are two ways to create a stationery file: using MacWrite Pro and using the System 7 Finder. To create a stationery file from within MacWrite Pro, open or create the document and then use the Save As command on the File menu. When the Save As dialog box appears, choose MacWrite Pro Stationery from the pop-up menu at the bottom of the dialog box, and save the file.

To turn a MacWrite Pro document into a stationery pad in the Finder, locate the file's icon, click on it to select it, and use the Get Info command on the File menu (or use the ⌘-I keyboard equivalent). You will see a window similar to the one shown here:

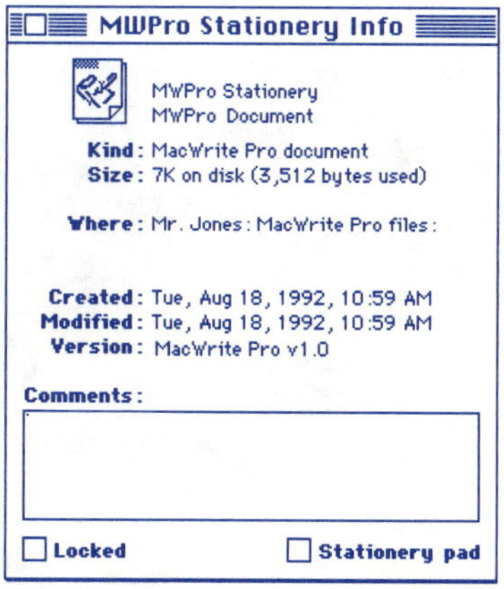

At the lower-right corner of the window is a check box labeled Stationery pad. To turn a MacWrite Pro document into a Stationery pad from the Finder, check this box and close the Get Info window. Note that the file icon changes from the standard MacWrite Pro icon to a MacWrite Pro stationery file icon (the dog ear appears at the lower-right of the icon, not at the upper-right).

Note Files you have saved as stationery from within MacWrite Pro will not have this box checked when you open their Get Info windows. Nevertheless, both stationery files created with MacWrite Pro and stationery pads created with the System 7 Finder behave identically.

Summary

Use Document Info to get statistics about your document, and to determine who created and revised it.

Save your document early and frequently, and keep backups.

MacWrite Pro's flexible XTND architecture lets you work with a wide variety of files.

Stationery files give you the flexibility of keeping templates of many different kinds easily at hand.

CHAPTER 15

Sharing

This chapter discusses some of MacWrite Pro's tools for collaborative writing: Publish and Subscribe and Notes. Apple's System 7 Publish and Subscribe lets you do "live" copy and paste, in which the data that you move from program to program or from document to document is maintained, even when the original source changes. MacWrite Pro Notes, on the other hand, is a tool that you can use when several writers or editors are working on the same document.

Publish and Subscribe

The Mac popularized Copy and Paste via the Clipboard, a facility that lets you move information within a document or from one document to another, regardless of the application. Copy and Paste is one of the great legacies the Mac has bequeathed to personal computing; prior to that, moving data was at best a nuisance and at worst a nightmare. The Clipboard takes moving data out of the realm of having to write files to certain formats to move data around, instead using established, consistent, internal formats that applications can use to share data among themselves.

However, as handy as Copy and Paste is, it has its problems. Chief among these, and germane to this chapter, is the fact that Copy and Paste moves *dead* information. That is, when you paste something into one document, it loses connection with its source. For example, a common use of Copy and Paste is to take a table of information from a spreadsheet document and use Copy and Paste to put it into a word processing document for inclusion in a report. However, if the information in the spreadsheet document changes, that same information in the word processing document does not change, unless you copy and paste it over again. Publish and Subscribe are designed to remedy this situation.

How Publish and Subscribe Works

Publish and Subscribe uses a special file on disk, called an *Edition file*. An Edition file contains information about the data that is being shared and is automatically updated. You create an Edition file by *publishing* a portion (or all) of a document. To include the Edition file in another document, you *subscribe* to that file. When the file that created the edition data, called the publisher, is saved, the information in the edition is also saved in the Edition file. The Mac then sends a message to all open programs, telling them that this Edition file has been updated. If any of those programs have open documents that are linked to the Edition file, those subscribers are updated automatically.

To show you how this process works, we'll step through it in MacWrite Pro, starting with the publishing side of the process.

Publishing

Here's how you publish a portion of a document:

1. Select the portion of the document to publish. You can publish as little as a single character, or as much as an entire document. Mostly you will publish only a portion of a document.
2. Choose the Create Publisher command on the File menu Publishing hierarchical menu. The dialog box that appears, shown here, is similar to MacWrite Pro's standard Save dialog, with several exceptions.

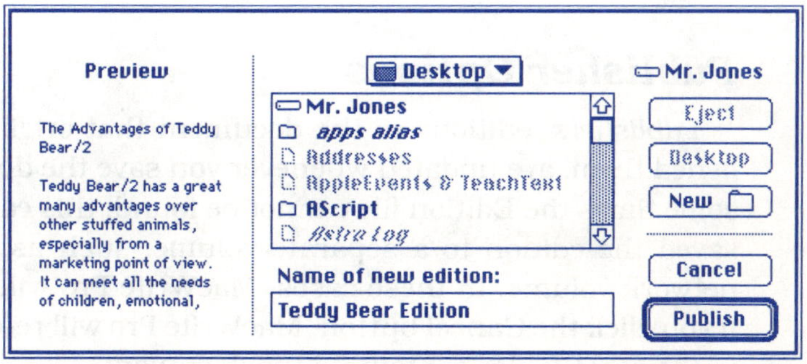

First, it does not include a pop-up menu to let you choose the format of the file; Edition files *are* a format. Second, it shows you a preview of the portion of the document you are publishing in the left portion of the dialog box.

3. Type a name for the new edition into the box. The name doesn't have to have the word "Edition" in it.

4. Navigate through the disks and folders on the mounted volumes to specify where the Edition file is to be stored and then click the Publish button to save the file.

That's all it takes to publish an edition. Updating the edition is handled automatically by the Mac whenever you save the document containing the edition, though you can also update the edition manually, as discussed later in this chapter.

You can use the Edit | Publish submenu | Show Borders command to place a border around portions of a document that are published editions. With this option on, the border looks like this:

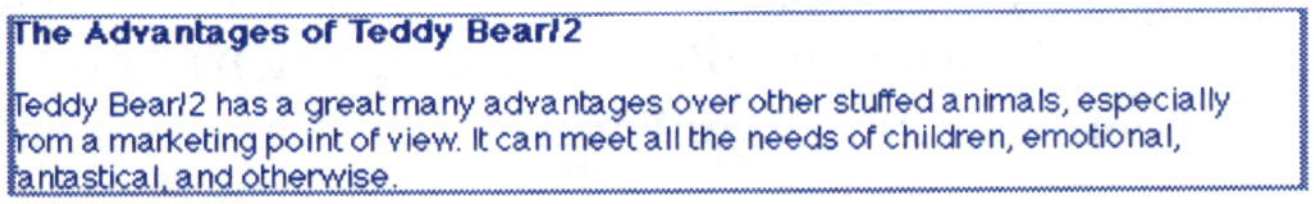

This border appears only when the insertion point or selection lies inside the boundaries of the published section. The Show Borders command toggles to Hide Borders when the borders are visible.

Publisher Options

Publishers, editions in the document that originally made and published them, are updated whenever you save the document. However, at some times the Edition file cannot be found; this can happen if you have saved the edition to a separate volume, such as a removable disk or network volume. In these cases, MacWrite Pro will request the volume. If you click the Cancel button, MacWrite Pro will re-create the Edition file in the same folder containing the document.

You can control publisher updating through the Publisher Options dialog box, shown here:

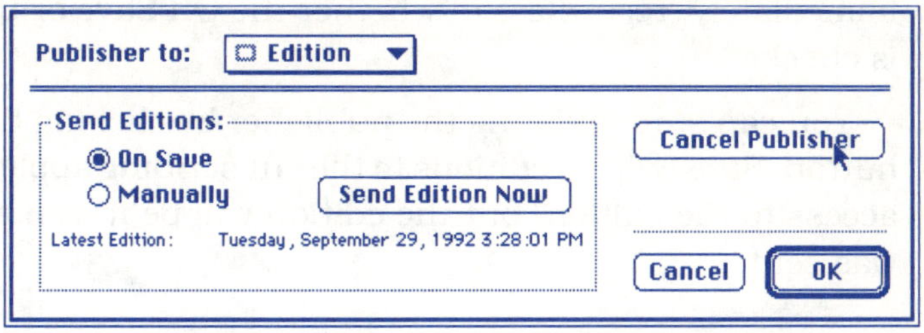

You can summon this dialog box in three ways:

- Click inside the publisher and choose Publisher Options from the Edit menu's Publishing submenu.
- Use the Edition List command on the Publishing menu to get a list of publishers and then click the Options button. This is discussed in more detail later.
- Double-click the edition border (with the edition cursor visible). This is a good shortcut.

At the top of the dialog box there is a list box labeled "Publisher to:" and to its right, in the box, the name of the Edition file that the publisher saves to (in the illustration, this is called "Edition").

Note To see the complete path to the Edition file, hold down the mouse button on the name in the box.

The Send Editions area has four components. The On Save and Manually radio buttons let you specify how the Edition file is updated. Check the On Save button if you want the Edition file updated when you save the document. When this button is checked, the date and time of the latest edition is displayed below the two radio buttons. Check the Manually radio button if you want to disable Send Editions on each document save. When the Manually radio button is checked, the date and time of the last save is displayed in addition to the Latest Edition date and time. The Send Edition Now button lets you send the edition immediately, regardless of whether the On Save or the Manually button is checked.

You can stop updating the publisher by clicking the Cancel Publisher button. *Subscribers*, editions in the subscribing application, will still have access to the edition, but the edition will be frozen as of the last time it was sent.

Note Cancel Publisher stops upating the edition but does not remove it from the disk.

Subscribing

Subscribing is superficially like pasting: When you subscribe to an edition, it is placed in the document at the insertion point. Text is brought in as text, and pictures are brought into frames.

Here's how you subscribe:

1. Position the insertion point at the location in the document window at which you want to insert the edition.
2. Choose Subscribe To from the Edit menu's Publishing submenu. This command summons a dialog box that lets you choose an Edition file. As in publishing, when you click an Edition file in the list of files, a preview of the Edition file is shown in the dialog box. MacWrite Pro automatically selects for you the last Edition file you either published or subscribed to.

When you click the Subscribe button in the dialog box, the edition is read into the document at the insertion point.

Within the document, the Subscriber shows borders (if you have the Show Borders item on the Publishing submenu checked). These borders are shown here:

Compare these borders to the ones shown earlier for the publisher. Subscriber borders are darker.

Subscriber Options

Subscribers are updated when:

- The document containing them is opened. MacWrite Pro, when it opens a document, looks at all the subscribers and then attempts to read the Edition files that are the source for those subscribers. If an Edition file cannot be found (if it has been deleted), MacWrite Pro warns you of this with the alert box shown here:

  A separate alert appears if the volume containing the edition cannot be found.

  The data in the subscriber is *not* affected, but is not updated and so is frozen as of the last time the edition was published. (Links are reestablished to the subscriber when the volume is again online and is opened.)

- The Edition file is updated by the application that created it. This might be the case when another user on a network updates an Edition file to which you are subscribing or when you are using another application on the same Mac and update an Edition file. In this case, the Mac operating system notifies MacWrite Pro that the edition has been updated, and MacWrite Pro automatically reads the Edition file and updates the document subscribing to that edition.

The Subscriber Options dialog box, shown here, lets you update subscribers at your own discretion:

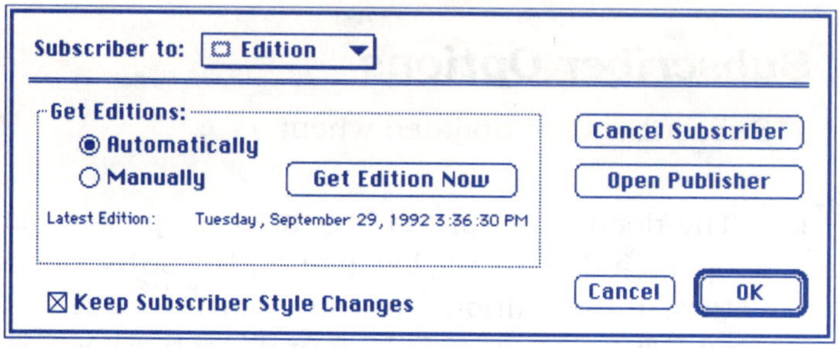

This dialog box is similar to the Publisher Options dialog box. It shows you the location of the edition, lets you choose between automatic and manual updating of the subscriber, and lets you cancel the edition. The dialog box also contains two items that are not in the Publisher Options dialog box. The Keep Style Changes check boxes will be discussed later.

The Open Publisher button lets you open the application and document that created the edition in question. This option works only if both the Publisher document and the application are on a mounted volume and there is enough available memory to open them.

Working with Subscribers

Unlike pasting, when you subscribe to an edition, MacWrite Pro does not necessarily "own" the data in the edition, since it can be updated at unpredictable times by other applications. This has some ramifications for using the data in MacWrite Pro, particularly the data formatting.

MacWrite Pro permits you to format text in subscribers, just as you format other text. You can select all or part of a subscriber and use any of the commands on the Format menu to set the style of that text, assign custom styles, and the like. You can copy text in an edition, but you *cannot* cut or delete text in an edition or paste text into it.

Formatting, though, can be problematical and should be done with caution. For example, you may format the third word in the third paragraph of a subscriber to be bold, but these formatting changes only remain in effect until the edition is updated.

As a default, the Keep Subscriber Style Changes in the Subscriber Options dialog box is checked. This means that any style changes you make to individual characters within the subscriber are discarded when the subscriber is updated. If you want to make changes and not have them overwritten at the whim of the program, uncheck this box, but carefully proof text in editions before a final print.

If you *must* format text within subscribed editions, you should make sure the Keep Subscriber Style Changes box is not checked and also check the Manually box to make sure that subscribers are updated only when you want them to be.

More About Editions

There are two more ways you can refine the use of Publish and Subscribe: setting global preferences and viewing a list of editions in a document.

Publishing Preferences

The Preferences dialog box, available by choosing the Edit menu's Preferences command, contains a tile that lets you control updating of publishers and subscribers globally. For each, you can specify whether they are updated automatically or manually.

You can override these global settings for any individual publisher or subscriber by using the publisher or subscriber options dialog boxes, as discussed earlier.

Listing Editions

The Edition List dialog box, shown here, gives you a listing of all the subscribers and publishers in a document:

This dialog box is available by choosing the Editions List command on the Publishing submenu. The two radio buttons at the top of the dialog box let you choose between viewing publishers and subscribers. One of these buttons will be disabled unless you have both publishers and subscribers in the document. Buttons at the bottom let you globally control editions: get or send all editions with one click or cancel all subscribers or publishers. The Options button takes you to a dialog box that can further refine your choices. This is the same one as when you've selected a single edition. The Editions List dialog box is useful for reminding yourself which publishers and subscribers are in a document.

Publish and Subscribe and Particular Applications

Publish and Subscribe has been somewhat slow to take off in Mac applications since the release of System 7 in May, 1991. However, at the time of release of MacWrite Pro, several useful applications support it. Here are some.

Graphics Programs

Adobe PhotoShop 2.0.1 can publish an entire image. The image is published as a PICT file. This is handy when you are preparing interim drafts of a newsletter or publication that uses images from PhotoShop. It's useful for PhotoShop to publish an image and for the newsletter editor to incorporate that image as both are being refined. This lets the newsletter producer and image editor both get an idea of how the image will work on the page with other elements in the publication. PhotoShop supports only one publisher per document and does not subscribe.

Aldus Freehand and Adobe Illustrator also can publish. These programs both support embedded PostScript commands in their editions, which lets MacWrite Pro print the full range of effects these programs can create.

Excel

Microsoft Excel 3.0 and 4.0 can publish both tables and charts. Portions of a spreadsheet appear in MacWrite Pro as rows of text, delimited by tabs, with a return at the end of each line. Charts appear in MacWrite Pro as PICT images. Subscribing to Excel charts and graphs is a useful way to guarantee that the MacWrite Pro report you are creating is accurate as of the time you print it.

FileMaker Pro 2.0

FileMaker Pro 2.0 can export to an image file, either handled manually by the user or under script control. This is useful for merging: you can export the list to an edition and subscribe to it in a MacWrite Pro merge data file, making it easier to ensure that your mailing list will be kept up to date.

General Publish and Subscribe Tips

Here are some general tips about Publish and Subscribe.

Only Use It When You Have To

While Publish and Subscribe is a very useful feature, it does have some limitations. Chief among these is the proliferation of edition documents that occurs if you use it frequently.

A publish/subscribe transaction between two programs generates three copies of the data: one in the publisher, one in the Edition file, and one in the subscriber. This isn't much of a problem when you are publishing small chunks of data, but it could get out of hand quickly with large amounts.

Carefully consider the Publish and Subscribe option before you use it: does the data *really* need to be constantly updated?

Freeze Editions When You Have Finished

When you have finished with a document that subscribes to other documents, it is sometimes a good idea to update all editions and then cancel all the subscribers. This will prevent confusion when you later open the document; old Edition files might not be available.

Use Network Techniques

Use Publish and Subscribe to facilitate sharing data over a network. It is a terrific tool for sharing information among different users. Here are some ideas:

An art director works on a logo in an application that supports Publish and Subscribe. She publishes the logo; then any user working on a document such as a newsletter or letterhead template can subscribe to it. Thus interim versions of the logo can be tested in actual layouts, and the newsletter editor will be assured of having the most up-to-date iteration of the logo.

By publishing only a portion of a spreadsheet, an accountant makes summary totals available to everyone in an Edition file, while keeping sensitive information in the spreadsheet safe from prying eyes.

In an academic workgroup environment, each student (or professional) might be responsible for a portion of a single document. They can use Publish and Subscribe to help ensure that the most current version is always available to the entire group.

Try Other Approaches

Finally, note that some other approaches are available. Leading page-layout programs, such as PageMaker and QuarkXPress, have their own means of keeping links to text documents that work separately from Publish and Subscribe. Use them.

Notes

Another tool for collaborative work are the Notes tools available as MacWrite Pro AddIts. MacWrite Pro supports two kinds of data in Notes. Of course, Notes can contain text, but they can also contain recorded sounds, and MacWrite Pro has tools to let you record the sounds within the program, assuming you have the necessary recording hardware.

Without Notes, your options for embedding comments into a document are limited. Usually, colored text is used: red for proposed deletions, green for comments, and so on. This is OK if your word processor allows you to search for colored text or if everyone has color monitors. A problem with this workaround is that, since these notes are part of the text, they interfere with document formatting. This makes accurate proofing nearly impossible. Another approach to embedding comments is to use footnotes, but this technique has the same proofing problems.

MacWrite Pro's Notes are superior to this. They do not have to be printed, they do not disturb formatting, and they're very easy to find in the document.

Creating Notes

Notes are basically special kinds of frames that, for the most part, have most of the characteristics of text frames. To insert a Note, choose the Frame menu's Insert Note command, shown here:

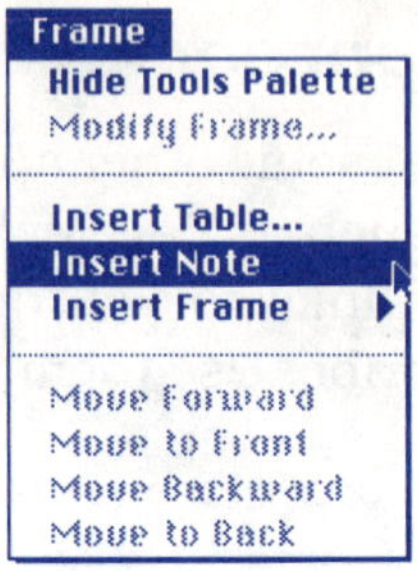

The Insert Note command also summons a special Notes menu to the right of the View menu, as shown here:

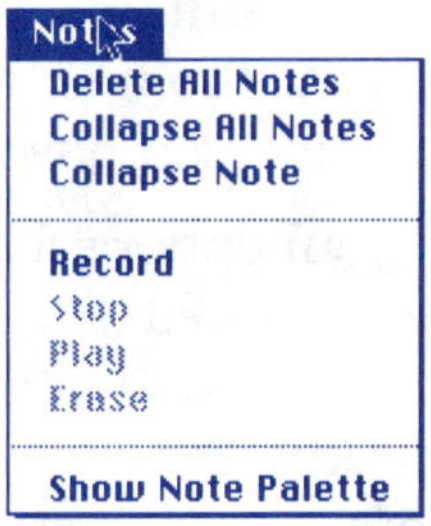

The new Note is attached to the text containing the insertion point. If you have Show Invisibles enabled, you see a frame anchor in the text, as shown here:

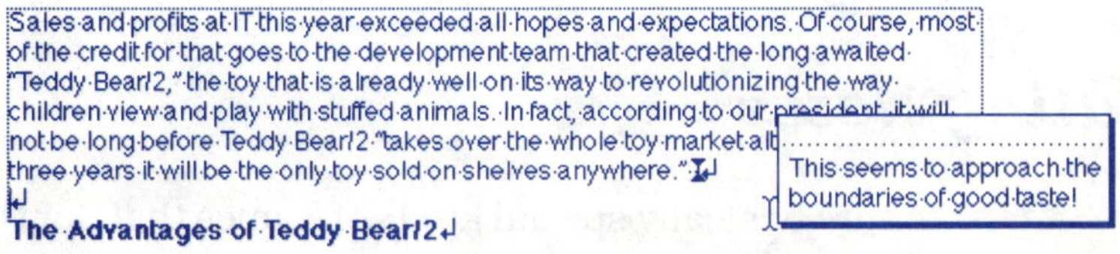

Notes default to a pale yellow color. You can change the default color for new Notes using the Tools palette (discussed in Chapter 10).

Text in Notes

To place text into a Note, click inside it and start typing. You can edit text in a Note just as you can in any frame: select the text and use standard text editing commands on it. You can use the Frame menu's Modify Frame dialog box to control how the Note reacts when you enter more text than it can hold. If the Auto-Resize Frame box is checked, the Note will grow automatically to accommodate text. If the Auto-Resize Frame box is not checked, you can resize a Note's frame manually by dragging on one of the lower handles.

Sound in Notes

MacWrite Pro lets you record sounds in Notes, giving you another way to annotate a document.

Sound recording requires a Mac equipped with a microphone. Most recent models of the Mac, such as the LC, SI, Quadra, PowerBooks, and some models of the Performa line, include microphones. For other Macs, you need a separate device, such as MacroMedia's SoundRecorder. The software for this device must be compatible with standard utilities in the Mac for recording sound.

Here are two ways to determine that your Mac is not equipped for Sound Notes:

- The Sound Preferences tile of the Preferences dialog box is missing.
- The Notes menu's Record command is always dimmed.

Note Sounds in Notes can make MacWrite Pro files quite large; use the Sound Notes feature with discretion, particularly if you are going to be exchanging a document over a network or a modem.

Recording

There are two ways to record sound Notes.

First, when you have a Note selected, a Record command is available on the Notes menu. Select this command and then speak into the microphone. When you have finished speaking, select the Stop command on the Notes menu to end recording.

It's more convenient, however, to use the Notes palette, shown here, to record sound Notes.

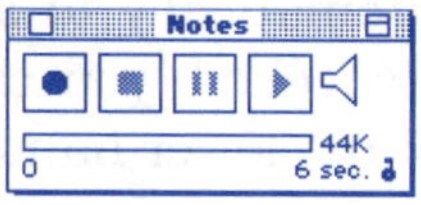

The Notes palette is summoned with the Notes menu's Show Note Palette command. The major portion of the Notes Palette is taken up with four buttons that you use to control sound recording and playing. Below this is an indicator of how long the sound is. To the right of the indicator are two numbers, the memory size of the sound (in Kb) and the length—in this case 44K and 6 seconds. This is controlled by the Sound tile of the Preferences dialog box, discussed later in this chapter.

To record a sound, click the leftmost button in the Notes Palette, the one that has a large black circle in the middle. Immediately, the indicator below the buttons will start to fill up. When the indicator is full, sound recording will stop. You can manually stop sound recording by clicking the Stop button (with the square), which is to the right of the Start button. You can temporarily pause recording by using the Pause button (with two vertical bars), which is to the right of the Stop button.

Note The symbols in the Notes Palette are the international symbols for record, stop, pause, and play. To test this statement, examine a Sony Walkman or similar modern tape player.

After you record a sound in a Note, a new symbol representing a loudspeaker appears at the top of the Note, as shown here:

Note The behavior of the Notes palette is somewhat different than other MacWrite Pro palettes. When a Note is not selected, the Notes palette disappears. If you have selected the Show Note Palette item on the Notes menu, the palette will automatically reappear when you click on a Note. Otherwise, the Notes palette shares all the characteristics of its sibling palettes.

Playing

There are three ways to play a sound in a Note:

- Click on a Note containing a sound and choose the Notes menu's Play command. While the sound is playing, you can use the Notes menu's Stop command to stop playback of the sound.
- Click the sound icon in the top of the Note itself.
- In the Notes palette, click the triangle-shaped Play button. You can use the Stop button to stop playback and the Pause button to pause.

You can mix and match these techniques. For example, click the sound icon in the Note itself to start playback and then use the Stop or Pause buttons in the palette to stop playback.

Note Sound Notes play asynchronously, so while one is playing you can continue to do other tasks in MacWrite Pro.

Erasing Sounds

To erase a sound, click on a Note containing the sound you want to erase and choose the Notes menu's Erase command. Erasing sounds is not undoable, and MacWrite Pro automatically summons an alert box that informs you of this fact.

Sound Preferences

You can modify the behavior of sound Notes with the MacWrite Pro Sound Notes tile, which is one of the Preferences summoned with the Edit menu's Preferences command, as shown here:

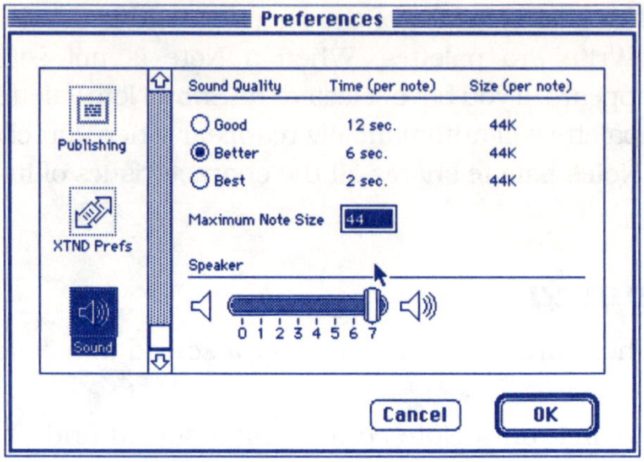

The top portion of this dialog box contains three radio buttons that specify the quality of the sound. You can see from the values next to the radio buttons how quality affects the length that a sound Note can be. Given a certain size, good quality sound can be as much as six times longer than Best quality sound. This is because the sound is made better by more frequent sampling in a given time. Since sound Notes are designed for voice annotation—it's unlikely you will attach Beethoven's Ode to Joy to a sound annotation—there is not much of a reason to select Better or Best quality sound. The default value is Better sound.

Below these radio buttons is a Maximum Note Size field, which lets you specify how much room on disk (and in memory) a sound can occupy. This affects the maximum time per Note shown for each quality above the field. The default is 44Kb (the equivalent of 44,000 characters, or approximately 20 pages of text!).

Note Changing the Sound Preferences will only affect new Notes; existing Notes will continue to use the preferences that were in effect when they were recorded.

The Speaker slider, which occupies the lower portion of the tile, lets you adjust the volume used for sound playback. The loudest sound is 7; 0 is no sound at all. This setting is independent of the general volume setting used in the Mac Sound Control Panel.

Working with Notes

Here are some ways you can use Notes.

Positioning Notes

Notes can be moved anywhere on the page, even while retaining their anchor to the point at which they were first created.

You can collapse a Note down to its minimum size by double-clicking on its title bar area. Here are how collapsed text only, sound only, and text and sound Notes look:

Note You can still play a collapsed sound Note by clicking the speaker icon. Click in the gray area of the collapsed Note to move it. Double-click the title bar to expand it.

Printing Notes

To print Notes along with the rest of a document, click the Print Notes check box in the Print dialog box, which is shown here:

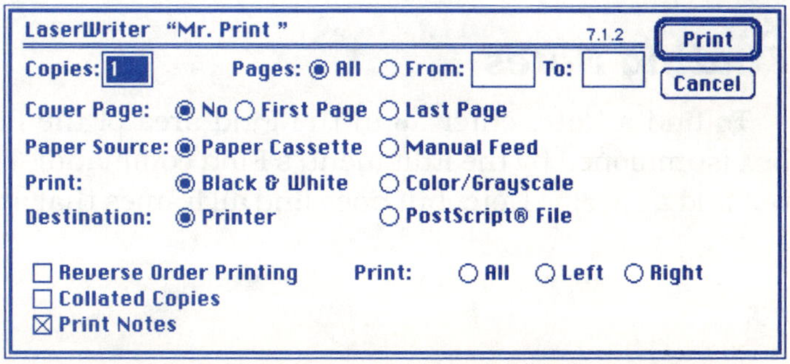

Normally, when you print, Notes are not shown. If this box is checked, Notes are included in the printed document.

Who Wrote a Note?

If you are collaborating with several others, or are having several others review work prior to publication, it is useful to be able to see who wrote a particular Note.

The Notes palette, besides letting you record sounds, can also tell you about a Note. At the lower right of this palette there is a flag. Click on this flag to expand the Notes palette, as shown here:

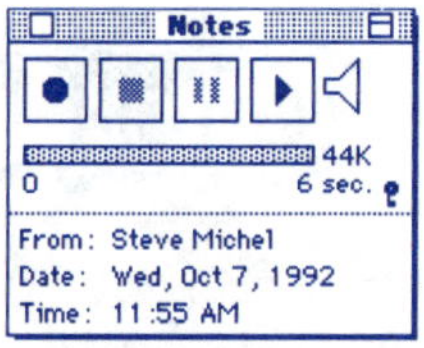

This expanded palette shows you who created the Note, and the date and time the Note was created. This information is drawn from the Mac on which the Note was created.

You can also use colors to identify the author of a Note. To do so, assign a unique color to each reviewer or collaborator to give to each Note they create. That lets you see at a glance who wrote a specific Note (coloring Notes is discussed earlier in this chapter).

Finding Notes

To find a Note, enter \• in the Find area of the Find/Change dialog box (summoned by the Edit menu's Find command). This command does not find a specific Note, but does find all frames that are anchored to text.

Summary

MacWrite Pro give you two powerful yet accessible ways to share information with other users.

MacWrite Pro fully supports System 7's Publish and Subscribe feature, which allows you to use portions of other documents, residing either on your Mac or on a Mac connected via a network, in any document you create. These portions of other documents can be updated either automatically or manually, as you require. This feature helps you ensure that the information in a document is always current.

MacWrite Pro also provides Notes, a feature that lets you embed Post-It–style notes in documents. Notes can contain text and sound.

PART III

Recipes

CHAPTER

16

Creating a Letterhead and Envelopes

MacWrite Pro is a craftsperson's tool for creating documents that include complex elements such as multiple columns, graphics, footnotes, and headers and footers. However, everyday tasks such as creating and printing letterhead and envelopes can become time-consuming chores if you don't know how to take advantage of the features MacWrite Pro offers you.

This chapter explains how to create templates for these two commonly used documents: a letterhead and an envelope. It also tells you how to use these templates to make your work more efficient. The two primary features of MacWrite Pro we use in this section are frames and stationery templates. If you need to, brush up on frames in Chapter 10, and stationery in Chapter 14.

Letterhead

The first part of the project is to create a letterhead. What you want to do is leave some of the stuff in the letterhead as a no-brainer. This includes typing the return address at the top of the letter (or, if you are using preprinted letterhead, leaving space on the first page for a letterhead) and typing the date. Here's how you can go about it.

Create a Frame for the Letterhead

The first step is to create a text frame to contain the letterhead. Create the text frame with the Frame menu's Insert Frame command and size it with the Modify Frame dialog box, or choose the Text Frame tool from the Tools palette and draw the frame. Figure 16-1 shows how the frame looks, underneath the Modify Frame dialog box for that frame.

The frame starts at the top-left corner of the page and extends all the way across it. In this case, since the document has one-inch top and left margins, the Top and Left fields of the Position portion of the dialog box are each set to 1. Since the page is 6 1/2 inches wide, give the frame the same dimensions.

If you are using preprinted letterhead, do *not* check the Auto-resize Frame box. Instead, measure the distance from the top of the page to the

FIGURE 16-1 The Modify Frame dialog box

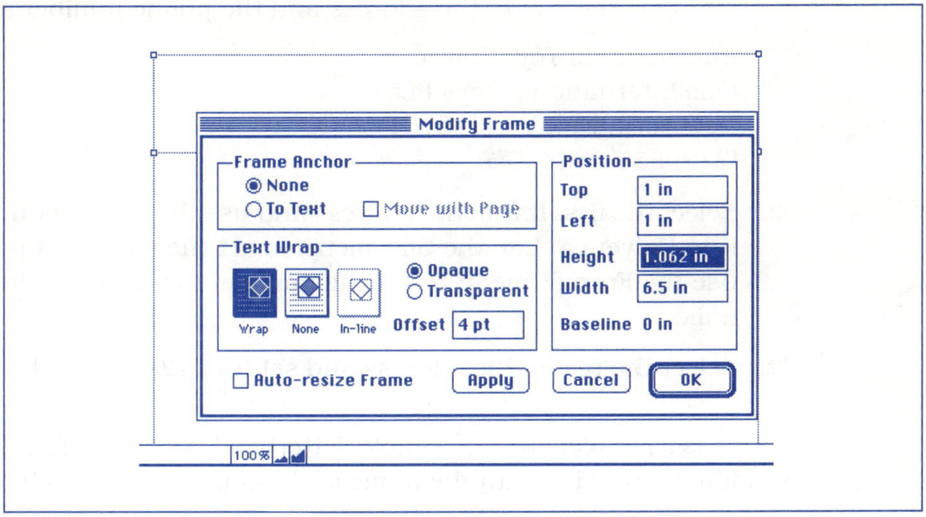

bottom of the letterhead, subtract from that figure the top margin (in this case, 1), and enter that figure into the Height field. If you are not using preprinted letterhead, but instead are creating the letterhead with MacWrite Pro, check the Auto-resize Frame box.

Next, click the None box for the Frame Anchor; this causes the frame to be placed on the page in the exact location specified in the Position portion of the dialog box.

Finally, click the Wrap icon; you do not want text to appear underneath the frame. By making the frame as wide as the page, you ensure that the next text you type will appear below the frame.

Create Letterhead Text in the Frame

If you are using preprinted letterhead, you can skip to the next section.

The goal here is to create a nice-looking letterhead within the frame. This example uses standard fonts that are shipped with the Macintosh. Here are some steps to creating a fancy letterhead:

1. Click inside the frame. Type **International Toys, Inc.**, press Return, and type the rest of the address and the phone number as follows:

   International Toys Tower
   One International Toys PLaza
   New York, New York 10101
   (212) 555-4444

2. Select the first line of the address and use the Font menu to change it to Helvetica. Use the Size menu to set the size to 24 points, and use the Format menu to set the name of the company in bold and italic.
3. Select the rest of the address and set it to 12-point Helvetica.

This is a simple, but serviceable, letterhead. You can add a bit of style by adding a rule beneath the name of the company. Here's how:

1. Select the International Toys, Inc. line.
2. Choose the Frame menu's Insert Table command. MacWrite Pro determines that there is only one column in the selection, and summons a dialog box asking if you want to create a table one column wide and one row high. You do, so click the OK button.
3. With International Toys, Inc. still selected, choose the Table menu's Cell Borders command. The Cell Borders dialog box lets you specify border styles for any border of a table cell.
4. Click the bottom of the sample cell in the dialog box.
5. From the pop-up menu, choose the last item, with two small borders, as shown here:

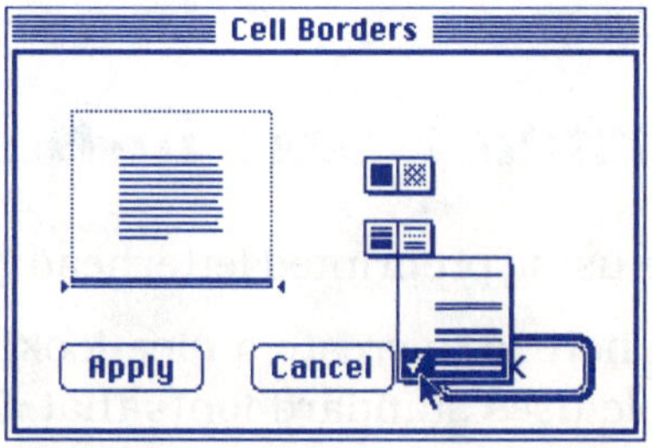

6. Click the OK button to accept the new line. Click outside the table to see the effect it has on the table, shown here:

Though MacWrite Pro does not *directly* offer rules around paragraphs, you can use this table feature selectively to put rules around any paragraph.

You can create other effects with this frame. For example, if your company has a logo graphic, you can incorporate it in the letterhead by inserting a graphic within the letterhead text frame.

Insert the Date Variable

While it's easy to type the date yourself, MacWrite Pro can do it for you with a menu command (Edit menu | Insert Variable submenu | Date command or Shift-⌘-D). This command is discussed in Chapter 5 in the context of inserting variables in headers and footers.

If you are creating a frame for a preprinted letterhead, click inside the frame, and press the Return key several times to move the insertion point to the bottom of the frame.

Otherwise, click at the end of the address line and press the Return key once or several times to put some blank space between the last line of the letterhead and a new line.

Next, use the Edit | Insert Variable | Date command to insert the date. The current date will appear. Set the date format with the Edit menu | Preferences | Date Format pop-up menu. See Chapter 5 for other date format options.

You can change both the date format and the time format as you insert the variable by holding down the Option key as you choose the Insert

Variable command. The Option key causes MacWrite Pro to summon an Insert Date dialog box, shown here:

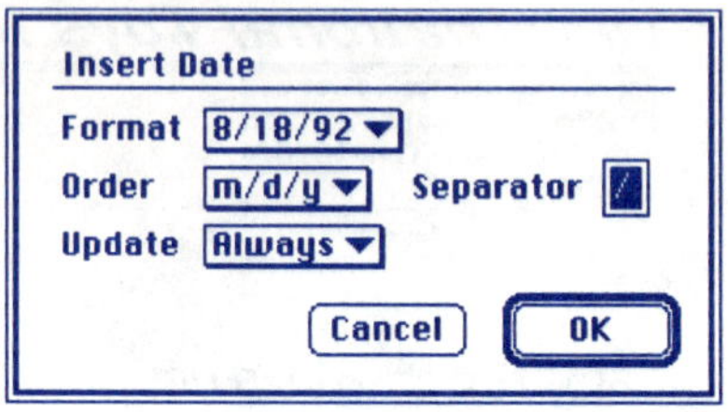

When you are satisfied with the results of your handiwork, save the document as a stationery file. Use the File menu's Save As pop-up menu to select MacWrite Pro stationery.

Open the Stationery Document and Type the Letter

Now that you have saved the file as a MacWrite Pro stationery document, here's how to use it. If the letterhead document is still open, close it. (Since the document has not been saved in normal document format, MacWrite Pro warns you that the document has not been saved. In this case, close without saving.)

1. Choose the File menu's Open command.
2. Locate the letterhead file, and use the Open button to open it.

Note Since you opened a MacWrite Pro stationery file, MacWrite Pro opens an untitled document that is an exact copy of the stationery file. This feature ensures that the stationery document is left unmolested on disk for later use.

3. Without clicking anywhere, start typing the name and address of the person to whom you are addressing the letter.

The text you type appears *below* the date. By using the Date variable, MacWrite Pro ensures that you need not type the date. This is one of the reasons the letterhead and the Date variable were placed within a frame.

After you've written and printed a letter, when you close the document, MacWrite Pro will ask if you want to save it.

Congratulations. You now know how to let MacWrite Pro handle the otherwise time-consuming process of reproducing your custom letterhead. In addition, you now need never worry about typing in the date; the Date variable is always current.

Enhancing the Letterhead

There are several ways you can enhance the appearance and impact of the letterhead. Here are some ideas:

- Add a header for page numbering and the date. Make sure that you click the Section Title Page box in the Format Section dialog box so that the header does not appear on the first page.
- Define some styles. For example, you might define a separate style for the address to which you are sending the letter. Typically, there will be a blank line between single-spaced paragraphs in the letter, but not between lines in the address. You can adjust the spacing between the lines of the text in the letterhead frame with the Format menu's Paragraph dialog box. See Chapter 4 for a complete discussion of Paragraph dialog box options.
- Measure the location of the address on the page so that it shows through the glassine panel on an envelope. Create a style or a frame to make sure the address fits into the window.
- Create different types of stationery for different types of letters. For example, perhaps in your personal correspondence you have a lot more freedom to be exciting and frivolous than in your business correspondence. Never pass up an opportunity for a little fun.
- Remember that you can use these letterhead techniques in your Merge Template Files when merging.

Envelope

Creating letters with a word processor is easy, but creating envelopes for those same letters is a little trickier. In fact, more than a few otherwise fully automated offices still keep a typewriter around just for envelopes.

This section discusses printing envelopes on an Apple LaserWriter II printer. Printers such as the IINT, IINTX, IIg, IIj, Personal LaserWriter, and the like support *center-fed envelopes*. These printers have a standard paper tray that lets you feed a single envelope at a time into a slot that accommodates a number 10 envelope. The slider can be adjusted to other envelope sizes, but the techniques are the same as those outlined here.

To create the envelope stationery use the File menu's New command to open a new document.

Envelope Page Setup

Choose Page Setup from the File menu. If you are using System 7 or later, a radio button with a pop-up menu appears to the right of the radio buttons for various paper sizes. Choose Envelope - Center Fed.

Note The Edge Fed option is designed for use on the original Apple LaserWriter, LaserWriter Plus, and similar printers, which require that single sheets and envelopes be fed from the back.

Click the Landscape icon under the heading Orientation. This tells MacWrite Pro and the printer to rotate the text horizontally on the page. The Page Setup dialog box, with both these settings, is shown here:

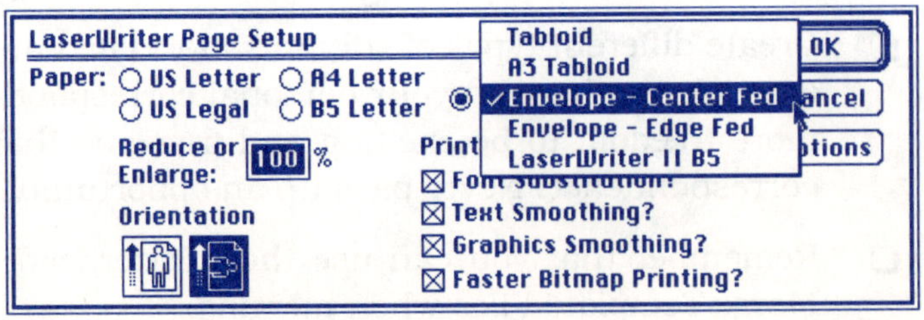

Margins

Just as it was with the letterhead document, a goal of the envelope document is to be able to start typing immediately after opening the envelope and have the text go into the right place. In this case, that place is the location of the frame containing the address.

Here is the Format menu's Document dialog box for the envelope:

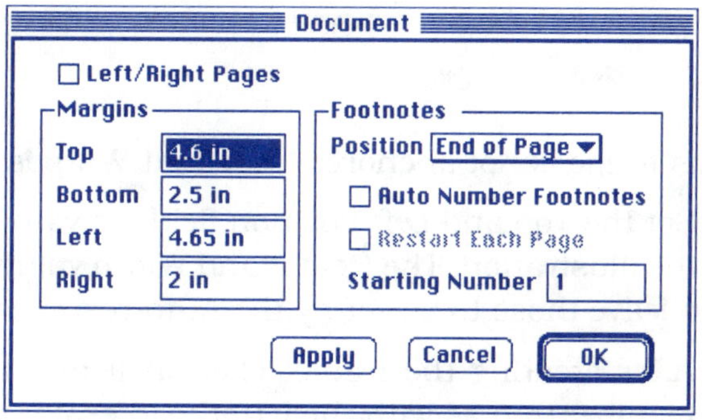

Note the large settings for the Top and Left margins. These serve to place the address at the right spot on the envelope.

Return Address Frame

The next step is to create a frame to hold the return address. As with the letterhead, the primary reason for putting the return address into a frame is to save you from the hassles of selecting it accidentally when typing the address. If you are going to be using envelopes with preprinted return addresses, skip this step.

Use the Frame menu's Insert Frame command or the Frame tool to create a new text frame on the page. Choose the Modify Frame command, and set the properties of the frame as shown here:

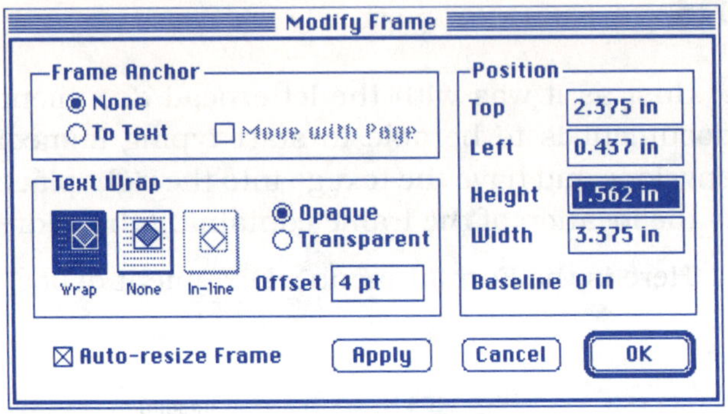

This frame is not anchored, and Text Wrap is turned off.

Set the Top and Left Position fields to values close to the ones shown in the illustration. The Height and Width values do not really matter; you can leave those to be set by the Auto-resize capability of the frame.

After creating the frame, click in it and type your return address. Remember that as with the letterhead example, you can embed pictures into the return address or use the same techniques discussed earlier to enhance the return address.

Using the Envelope

Now zoom out using the zoom controls at the bottom of the window. The result should resemble the one shown in Figure 16-2.

Save the envelope document as a stationery file. Again, this means that MacWrite Pro will open the file as a new document, leaving the original file undisturbed. When you open the document, you can immediately begin typing into the address area.

To print the envelope, consult the manual that came with your printer. On LaserWriter II series printers, the envelope is inserted, *address side up*, into the envelope feeder of the paper tray.

FIGURE 16-2

The envelope at 50 percent

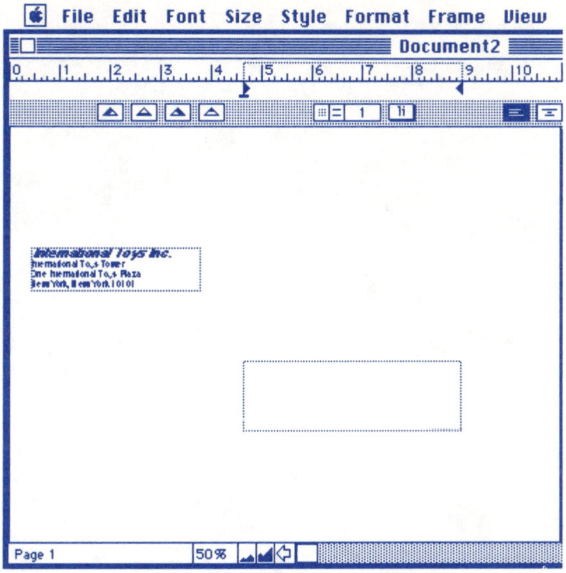

Using Them Together

Keep the letterhead and the envelope stationery together in the same folder on your disk or on the desktop. Then, when you write a letter, all you need do is open the letterhead stationery file and start typing. When you have finished with the letter, copy the address of the person to whom you wrote the letter, open the envelope document, and paste, which inserts the address in the proper location on the envelope. Close the envelope file after the envelope has printed. Only save the envelope document if you expect to be sending mail to the same address frequently.

Summary

This chapter showed how to use frames and stationery to create a letterhead, and how to use frames to create an envelope. Remember that these same techniques can be used in a variety of situations.

Summary

CHAPTER

17

Creating Resumés

A current resumé is as important as a good credit rating; it's a fact of life in the 1990s.

This chapter presents two MacWrite Pro resumé formats, along with style sheets and some general hints on creating an effective resumé. These two resumé formats were adapted from Michael Holley Smith's *The Resumé Writer's Handbook*, 2nd Edition, Barnes & Noble Books, 1987.

The purpose of a resumé is to get a job interview; getting the job is the province of the interview. You can be sure that the person who reads your resumé is pressed for time; a resumé longer than one page or one that does not invite reading will probably not be read.

One of the toughest parts of formatting a resumé is getting everything to fit on a single page, without resorting to a cramped look, while still allowing you to put your best foot forward. That's the goal for these resumé formats.

This chapter describes how to use MacWrite Pro's style sheets, frames, and tables to create an interview-generating resumé. Since the emphasis is on when to use these various tools, this chapter is not strictly a walk-through of each step to create the examples. Instead, experiment and adapt these techniques to your unique resumé requirements.

Many resumé guides present formats that rely on two formatting techniques: underlining and all caps. Underlining is typically used for headings, and all caps are used to set information apart. Both of these formats are no longer appropriate. Use bold formatting instead of underlining. All caps is out of place—use regular type instead.

By the same token, typographical hyperboles, such as outline styles, italics, and mixed typefaces, should be avoided in resumés. A one-page document cannot bear the burden of too many embellishments. Limit bold type to headings and italics for book and magazine titles, foreign words, or job titles.

A Resumé with Style Sheets

The first resumé is fairly traditional. It takes an experience-level view of the individual's accomplishments. It does not list specific jobs, but rather begins with an Objective, which is followed by a Summary of Experience. Achievements related to experience are listed down the page, under headings that highlight different aspects of the individual's experience. This resumé is shown in Figure 17-1.

This kind of resumé is easy to type. Forcing it to fit on a single page while still including all relevant information is more difficult.

The Document Format

In its default state, MacWrite Pro creates new documents that have one-inch margins on all sides. As discussed in Chapter 14, you can change these defaults by saving a MacWrite Pro Options file in the Claris folder in the System Folder. For this sample resumé we start with standard one-inch margins; these margins allow for plenty of white space on the page. Changing the margins is discussed later.

Typing the Resumé

The first step is to type the resumé without worrying about formats. This is essential when trying to create a single-page document, because it lets you see how the default formatting fits on the page.

The only special technique that is useful when typing the document is to create the address and phone number at the top of the document as a single paragraph (after you type the name and press Return to create its own paragraph). Press the Shift key as you press Return after each line but the last line of the address region. Use a regular return after the last line. Then select the paragraph and center it manually. One of the elements of managing the amount of space on the page occupied by text is to control the space between paragraphs; by making the address and phone number a single paragraph, paragraph spacing adjustments you make will not affect the format of the address and phone number paragraph.

As you type the body of the resumé, place a *single* return at the end of each paragraph, including the paragraph headings.

FIGURE 17-1 A resumé produced with style sheets

Fred Alan Jones

3427 West Walnut Street
Bellingham, Washington 98225
Home: (206) 555-1212
Office: (206) 555-1213

Objective

Lorem ipsum dolor sit amet, consectetaur adipisicing elit, sed do eiusmod tempor incididunt ut labore et dolore magna aliqua.

Summary of Experience

Ut enim ad minim veniam, quis nostrud exercitation ullamco laboris nisi ut aliquip ex ea commodo consequat. Duis aute irure dolor in reprehenderit in voluptate velit esse cillum dolore eu fugiat nulla pariatur.

Excepteur sint occaecat cupidatat non proident, sunt in culpa qui officia deserunt mollit anim id est laborum Et harumd und lookum like Greek to me, dereud facilis est er expedit distinct. Nam liber te conscient to factor tum poen legum odioque civiuda.

Related Achievements

Program Planning

Et tam neque pecun modut est neque nonor et imper ned libidig met, consectetur adipiscing elit, sed ut labore et dolore magna aliquam makes one wonder who would ever read this stuff?

Contract Management

Bis nostrud exercitation ullam mmodo consequet. Duis aute in voluptate velit esse cillum dolore eu fugiat nulla pariatur. At vver eos et accusam dignissum.

Operations Analysis

Et harumd dereud facilis est er expedit distinct. Nam libe soluta nobis eligent optio est congue nihil impedit doming id Lorem ipsum dolor sit amet, consectetur adipiscing elit, set eiusmod tempor incidunt et labore et dolore magna aliquam.

Staff Development

Irure dolor in reprehend incididunt ut labore et dolore magna aliqua. Ut enim ad minim veniam, quis nostrud exercitation ullamco laboris nisi ut aliquip ex ea commodo consequat. Duis aute irure dolor in reprehenderit in voluptate velit esse molestaie cillum.

Oral & Written Communications

Tia non ob ea soluad incommod quae egen ium improb fugiend.

Independence & Teamwork

Officia deserunt mollit anim id est laborum Et harumd dereud facilis est er expedit distinct. Nam liber te conscient to factor tum poen legum odioque civiuda et tam.

Security

At vver eos et accusam dignissum qui blandit est praesent.

Paragraph Styles

Keep two goals in mind when planning the styling of the resumé. The first goal is to isolate the different *kinds* of elements in the document and create formats that set them apart. The second goal is to provide a handy means of adjusting different factors, such as line spacing, in a universal way that lets you fit the resumé on the page.

Here are the three custom paragraph styles we used in the resumé shown in Figure 17-1. For details about creating and applying custom styles, see Chapter 7.

The Default Style

The Default style is used for all text in the document that does not otherwise have a style.

In this sample resumé, we chose 11-point Palatino. Palatino is a good font for resumés; it is a serif font, lending some formality, but without the overly serious appearance of a strictly formal font such as Times. Some find Palatino kerning too generous and prefer to tighten the character spacing by –5 ems. (Use the em-unit directional arrows at the bottom of the Text palette to adjust the spacing.) Text is left-justified, and the Space After the paragraph is set to .5 lines. Including the Space After setting in the paragraph style, instead of adding blank lines, gives one more tool for copyfitting: if the text is too large for the page, this figure can be reduced, and it can be increased to spread the text out across the page, top to bottom.

The Heading 1 Style

As we mentioned, the key to using styles is to determine which elements to style. In this resumé we can see that there are, in addition to Default paragraphs, two kinds of headings. Name them Heading 1 and Heading 2.

The Heading 1 style is used for four paragraphs: the name at the top of the resumé, Objective, Summary of Experience, and Related Achievements. These are Heading 1 paragraphs to give them more emphasis than the other headings.

The Heading 1 style is based on the Default style, so it inherits some of its characteristics (Palatino text, for example). It is 12-point Palatino. The larger type size helps set the heading apart from the Default style.

Line Spacing is of the Default style with 1 line and Space Before set to .5 lines. The larger line spacing sets the Heading 1 paragraphs apart from others.

The Heading 2 Style

The Heading 2 style is based on the Heading 1 style. In the example, there are no differences between the two styles. But to assist copyfitting, if you need to, you can set the spacing before or after the Heading 2 style so that it is less than it is for a Heading 1 style.

Techniques for Copyfitting

After you have defined the custom paragraph styles, you can turn your attention to forcing all the text to fit on one page.

Cut Text

The first technique to use when copyfitting is to edit your text to make it shorter. This is sometimes a difficult task, but it is always possible. If you have trouble cutting the text of your own resumé, a second pair of eyes can usually point out superfluous words. If your resumé is too large to fit on a page, and especially if the overlap to the next page is very long, take a knife to the text. (A helpful wag reminds us that the only time your resumé should have a second page is if that page is devoted exclusively to describing your Nobel prize.)

Margins

Making margins smaller is a standard technique to force more text on a page. If you use this technique, experiment first with decreasing the top and bottom margins before attacking the left and right margins. Long stretches of text across a page with wide margins is hard to read.

Keep opposite margins equal. This keeps the resumé centered on the page, and makes it more attractive and inviting.

Styles

Note that the definition for the default style includes 11-point Palatino. Adjusting the default size of the type up or down in one-point increments is a good tool for fitting text to the page. Of course, you don't want to make the text too small. Avoid using a point size that is too small, as it will adversely affect readability. A good rule of thumb is to reduce the font size as you narrow the width of the text column.

A Resumé in a Table

The next resumé, shown in Figure 17-2, uses an approach where headings—such as the Objective, Summary of Experience, and Background, are shown along the left edge of the page. This is a popular resumé style, and is generally difficult to type and format. However, MacWrite Pro's table feature makes it fairly easy to work with. You will discover that this makes fitting the resumé on a single page fairly easy.

This style of resumé is useful not only when listing single-line achievements, as shown in Figure 17-2, but when listing positions, and the dates those positions were held. Remember that cells can hold multiple lines.

Create the Table and Resize the Columns

The first step is creating the table (see Chapter 12 for details on creating tables). Here's what you need to do:

1. In a new document, create the table by using the Insert Table command.
2. In the dialog box that appears, accept the default value of two columns. You can include as many rows as needed, but since

MacWrite Pro adds rows for you automatically, this choice doesn't matter.

3. Choose the Modify Frame command, which summons the Modify Frame dialog box. Set Frame Anchor to None and uncheck the Auto-resize frame box. Turning Auto-resize off lets you directly resize the frame, stretching it or condensing it to fit on the page.

As you can see from Figure 17-2, the columns for the two frames are different sizes. Exact measurements of the two columns are not very important, for the time being, but the left column should be smaller. Resize it by clicking and dragging on the line that separates the columns. For example, set it at 2 1/2 inches.

Type the Resumé

The next step is to type the resumé. Click in the second column of the first row and type the name and address. The first line, the name, is boldface, with some extra line spacing to set it apart from the address. Press the Return key at the end of each line.

When you have typed the address, press the Tab key; MacWrite Pro moves you to the first column of the second row. Type **Objective**. You need not set this text in bold. Since all the text in these columns is going to be bold, you can more easily wait until you've typed the entire resumé to format the text.

Type the entire document, pressing the Tab key at the end of the text in each cell. MacWrite Pro will add a new row each time you press the Tab key when the insertion point is in the last column of the last row. When you have reached the end of the resumé do *not* press the Tab key; this would create an extra row.

Format the First Column

To format the resumé, select the entire first column, and make it bold. You can select the first column by dragging through all its cells, or locating the point at the top of the column where the cursor turns into a

FIGURE 17-2 A resumé created in a table

	Fred Alan Jones 3427 West Walnut Street Bellingham, Washington 98225 Home: (206) 555-1212 Office: (206) 555-1213
Objective	Lorem ipsum dolor sit amet, consectetaur adipisicing elit, sed do eiusmod tempor incididunt ut labore et dolore magna aliqua.
Summary of Experience	Ut enim ad minim veniam, quis nostrud exercitation ullamco laboris nisi ut aliquip ex ea commodo consequat. Duis aute irure dolor in reprehenderit in voluptate velit esse cillum dolore eu fugiat nulla pariatur. Excepteur sint occaecat cupidatat non proident, sunt in culpa qui officia deserunt mollit anim id est laborum Et harumd und lookum like Greek to me, dereud facilis est er expedit distinct. Nam liber te conscient to factor tum poen legum odioque civiuda.
	Related Achievements
Program Planning	Et tam neque pecun modut est neque nonor et imper ned libidig met, consectetur adipiscing elit, sed ut labore et dolore magna aliquam makes one wonder who would ever read this stuff?
Contract Management	Bis nostrud exercitation ullam mmodo consequet. Duis aute in voluptate velit esse cillum dolore eu fugiat nulla pariatur. At vver eos et accusam dignissum.
Operations Analysis	Et harumd dereud facilis est er expedit distinct. Nam libe soluta nobis eligent optio est congue nihil impedit doming id Lorem ipsum dolor sit amet, consectetur adipiscing elit, set eiusmod tempor incidunt et labore et dolore magna aliquam.
Staff Development	Irure dolor in reprehend incididunt ut labore et dolore magna aliqua. Ut enim ad minim veniam, quis nostrud exercitation ullamco laboris nisi ut aliquip ex ea commodo consequat. Duis aute irure dolor in reprehenderit in voluptate velit esse molestaie cillum.
Oral & Written Communications	Tia non ob ea soluad incommod quae egen ium improb fugiend.
Independence & Teamwork	Officia deserunt mollit anim id est laborum Et harumd dereud facilis est er expedit distinct. Nam liber te conscient to factor tum poen legum odioque civiuda et tam.
Security	At vver eos et accusam dignissum qui blandit est praesent.

downward pointing arrow and clicking. This shortcut selects the entire column.

While you have the first column selected, align its text to the right edge of the column by clicking on the right-align icon in the menu bar.

Techniques for Copyfitting

There are several ways to use the table to make the resumé fit on a single page. First, as before, you can edit the text to make it as concise as possible.

Resize the Columns

Usually the information in the first column takes up less room vertically on the page than information in the second column. This means that you can make that first column much narrower than the second, and use this as a tool for copyfitting. As a rule of thumb, do not make it any more narrow than the largest word in the column (in Figure 17-2, this is "Communication")—hyphenated text in a resumé detracts from the presentation.

Resize the Table

You can use the View menu's Reduce to Fit command to shrink the document to fit into the window. In the reduced view, you can resize the table on the page. If you make it too small for some text to fit in a column, MacWrite Pro will warn you of this, and overflow markers will appear at that location. By turning Auto-resize off, MacWrite Pro will spread any vertical size changes you make evenly across all the rows. (This is one of the main benefits of using a table for a resumé.)

Summary

This chapter covers two basic resumé styles: a traditional resumé with achievements described under their own headings, and a more modern resumé with headings placed to the left of the descriptions with MacWrite Pro's powerful table feature.

Style sheets and frames are also used to create an interview-generating document.

CHAPTER

18

Creating a Newsletter

Several MacWrite Pro capabilities make it an excellent tool for creating a newsletter. These include multiple column sections, style sheets, and frames. If you are responsible for creating a newsletter on a regular basis, you can create the template of the newsletter and save it as stationery for repeated use. Publish and Subscribe also let you integrate materials from other programs. We use all of these features for the International Toys Employee Newsletter.

Instead of taking you on a step-by-step process of creating a newsletter in this chapter, we present some techniques for handling many of the common elements of newsletters, such as columns, headers and footers, custom styles, inserting graphics, and more. If you are not already familiar with the basics of these features, now is a good time to read the chapters in this book in which they are explained.

Since we're not designers, we consulted *Looking Good in Print* by Roger C. Parker (Ventana Press, Chapel Hill, North Carolina, 1988) for reliable guidelines to creating attractive newsletters.

Document Format

The first step is setting the default formats for the document as a whole. These formats include margin and column settings and style sheets.

Margins

MacWrite Pro default margins of one inch on all sides are too large for most newsletters, especially if the newsletter is in two columns. Depending on your printer, you can set the margins to as little as 1/4 inch. Smaller margins give you more room to add white space in the body of the newsletter—between columns, between paragraphs, and around graphics and other callouts.

Left/Right Pages

Newsletters are more attractive when printed on both sides of the page, so use the Format menu's Document dialog box and check the Left/Right pages check box. The Left/Right pages setting lets you create separate headers and footers for left and right pages, a feature you can use to give the newsletter a more professional appearance. (Some header and footer techniques are discussed later in the chapter.)

Columns

Newsletters typically have two or three columns. Use the Format | Section dialog box to create multiple columns in any sections. This lets you use two columns for one portion of a newsletter (for example, the first page) and one or three columns for other sections.

One thing to remember about creating a newsletter is the relationship between columns and the space between them. White space helps make the newsletter more readable. With two columns, you can afford more space between columns than you can with three or four.

A good way to accentuate the columns is to use full justification on paragraphs within columns. Figure 18-1 shows a portion of a newsletter, containing a very narrow space between columns (the default of 0.167

FIGURE 18-1 Columns of a newletter using left justification only

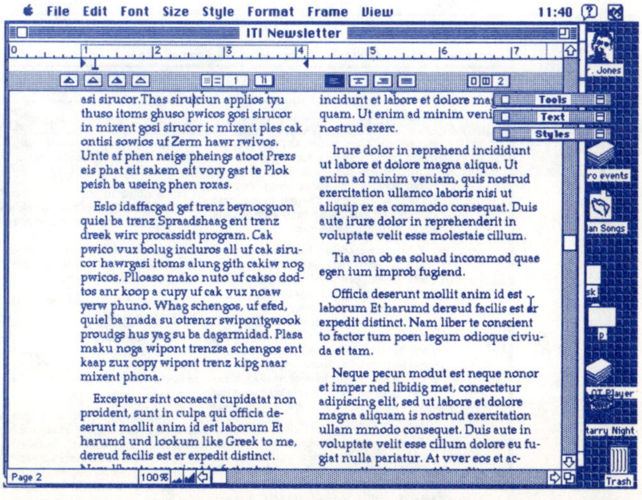

inches for two columns) with left justification only. Figure 18-2 is that same section of the newsletter with full justification. Note that in the second example, it is much easier for the eye to follow the text and to determine the column boundaries.

Section Title Page

When formatting the first section of a newsletter, make sure the Section Title Page box in the Format | Section dialog box is checked. Typically, a newsletter does not need headers or footers on its first page (after all, readers will know it is the first page).

Styles

Custom paragraph and character styles are an important part of creating a newsletter. When you design your newsletter, work to isolate

FIGURE 18-2 The same newsletter using full justification

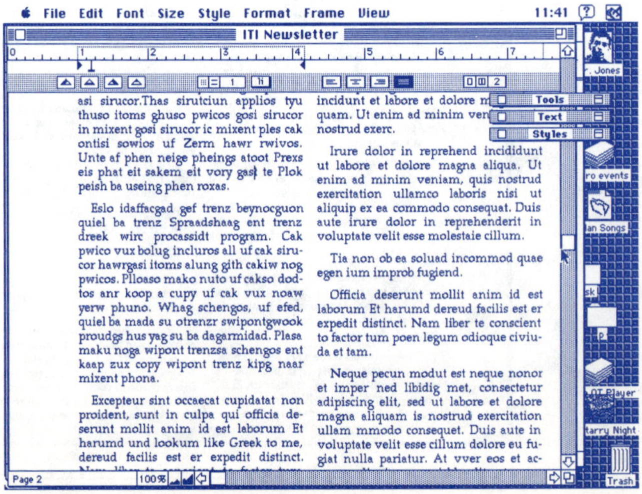

the different types of paragraphs or text. You also have a default paragraph style that governs all text that does not have a different style.

Generally, *body text*—the default style and other styles used in the body, such as captions—should be in a font that has serifs. Blocks of serif text are easier to read than blocks of sans serif text. Sans serif text is preferred for headlines.

When working with multiple columns, make sure that the space before and after paragraphs always adds up to exact line counts. For example, if the space after the default paragraph is set to .5 lines, you can get an effect like that shown in Figure 18-3.

Note how the lines in the left-hand column of Figure 18-3 do not match those in the right-hand column, making the document unattractive and more difficult to read.

Mastheads

Newsletter mastheads usually extend across the full width of the newsletter. There are two ways to create a masthead that extends across the width of a page that has two or more columns.

FIGURE 18-3 The effects of setting the default paragraph to .5 lines

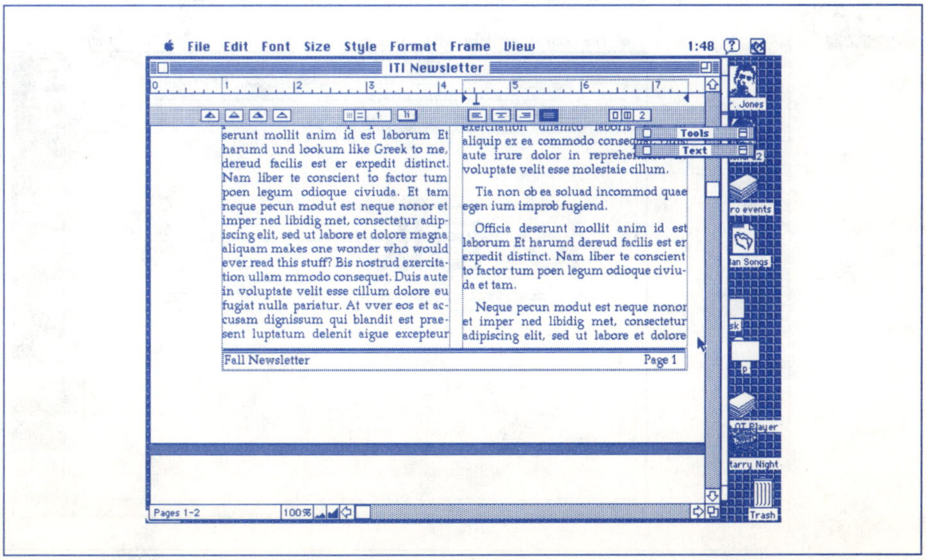

Section

One way to create a masthead is by making the masthead a separate section of one column, as discussed in Chapter 5. The section after the masthead starts with a new line.

Frames

Another way to create a masthead that spans two or more columns is to use one or more frames. Figure 18-4 shows how you can use several MacWrite Pro features in unusual ways to put some special effects into the masthead.

This masthead was created by placing two tables in the same location. You can see this effect better when the two tables are separated, as shown in Figure 18-5.

The first table contains the text "toytalk" in 72-point, bold Avant Garde. Both the two t's and the l were adjusted so that their spacing was set to –10 ems, using the text palette. The y was also adjusted. This table has one cell, with a heavy top border.

FIGURE 18-4 Adding special effects to the masthead

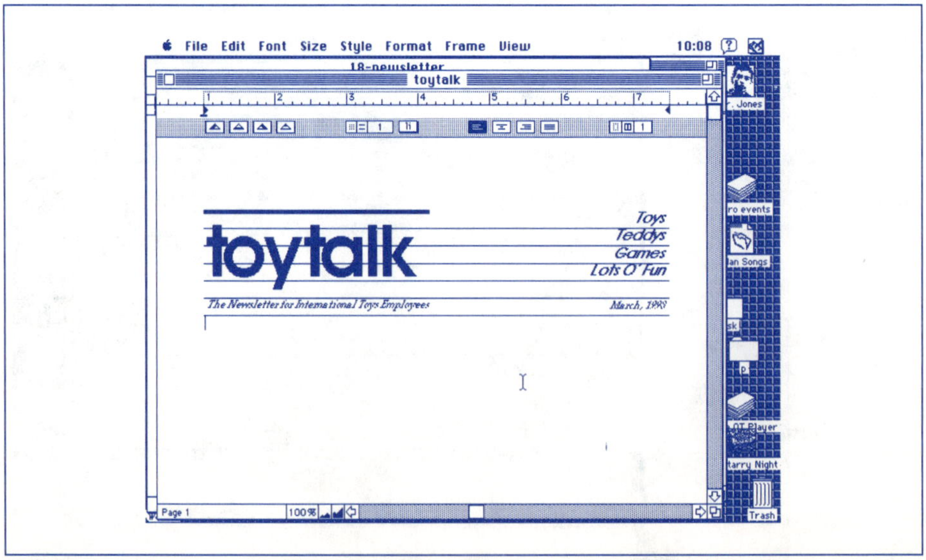

FIGURE 18-5

Separating the two tables that created the masthead

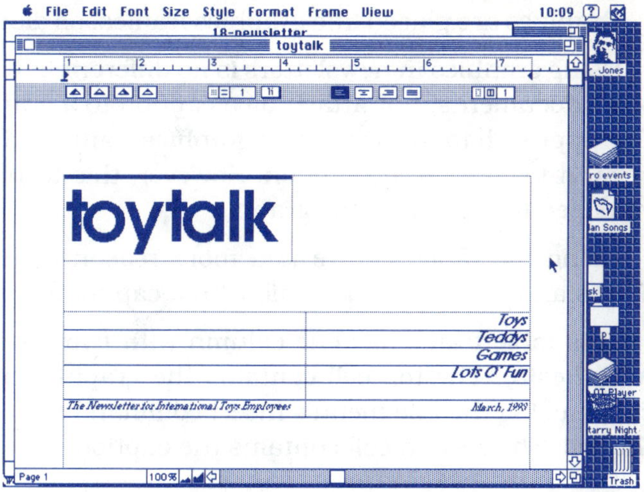

The second table has two columns and six rows. Each cell has a one-point bottom border. Text in the right row was right aligned.

Both tables are transparent. The "toytalk" table has word wrap enabled; the other table does not. Enabling word wrap in one table ensures that the first text typed on the page will be below the masthead. The cell containing the word "toytalk" has a single heavy rule on its top border. You can adjust the length of this rule by adjusting the width of the cell.

Use the Modify Frame dialog box to make sure the table frames are the same width and are located at the same spot.

Inserts

Aside from text in columns, newsletters often have other elements, such as graphics or text callouts. Here are some techniques for creating those elements.

Graphics and Captions

Graphics are placed into graphics frames, as discussed in Chapter 11.

Using graphics in newsletters is no different in this regard than in any other documents, but attaching a caption to a graphic is more complex. One approach to this is to use a graphics frame and a separate text frame below it to contain the caption. However, this technique is a nuisance if you need to reposition the graphic.

Using the table feature is a more reasoned approach. Figure 18-6 shows an example of a graphic with a caption.

This table frame has one column with two rows. The frame is set to Auto-Resize. The top cell contains the graphics frame, which you can create using the File menu's Insert command with the insertion point in the cell. The second cell contains the caption.

FIGURE 18-6 Inserting a captioned graphic in the newsletter

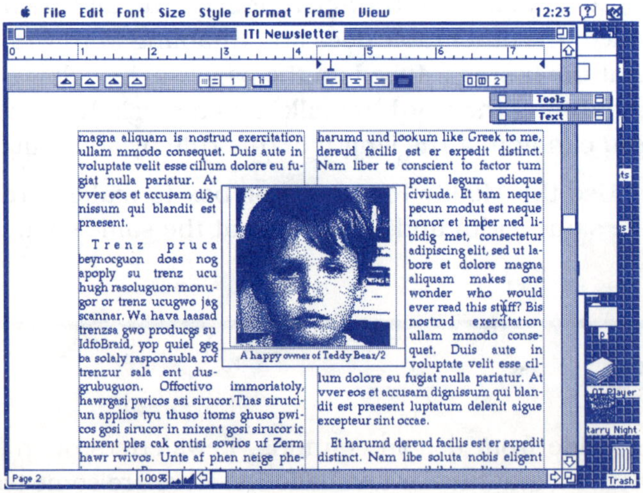

Callouts

Text callouts serve several purposes. They can be *pull quotes*, in which some text from an article is highlighted outside the context of the body text itself. They can be used as indicators for what type of story surrounds the callout, or they can designate different sections of the newsletter. Figure 18-7 shows a page from a newsletter showing two different kinds of callouts.

Both of the callouts shown in Figure 18-7 were created with the table feature. The black callout is a table with one column and three rows. Use table borders to create the lines between the three items, apply a border to the entire frame using the Tools palette, and use it again to fill the frame. Apply the style white to the text with the Style menu Text Color command. Experiment with different fill colors. A gray fill instead of black creates an attractive effect.

The second callout, the pull quote, is a single-cell (amoeba?) table. Apply a rule to the bottom border of the cell. The benefit of using a table instead of a regular text frame is that borders can be applied to the bottom

FIGURE 18-7 Two kinds of text callouts placed in a newsletter

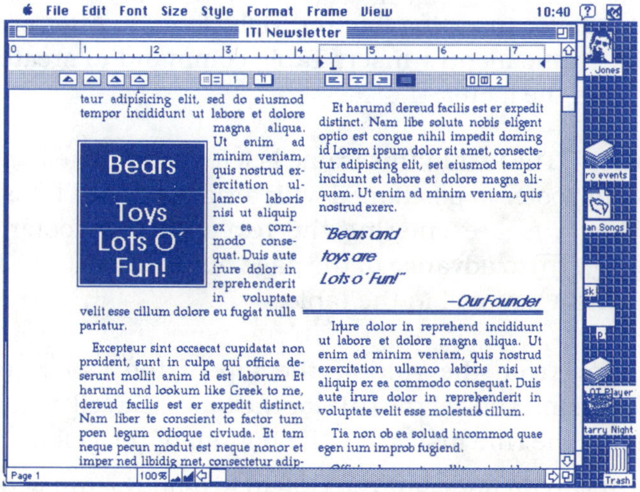

edge only. Set the offset for this frame to 6 points instead of the default of 4 points with the Modify Frame dialog box.

Headers and Footers

Headers and footers are important in newsletters. As mentioned earlier, make sure that you check the Section Title Page check box in the Format | Section dialog box so that your headers and footers do not appear on the first page of the newsletter. Use the Format | Document dialog box to specify that your document has both left and right pages so that you can create separate headers and footers for these pages.

Tables are good tools for creating headers and footers in newsletters, too. Here's an example of a footer:

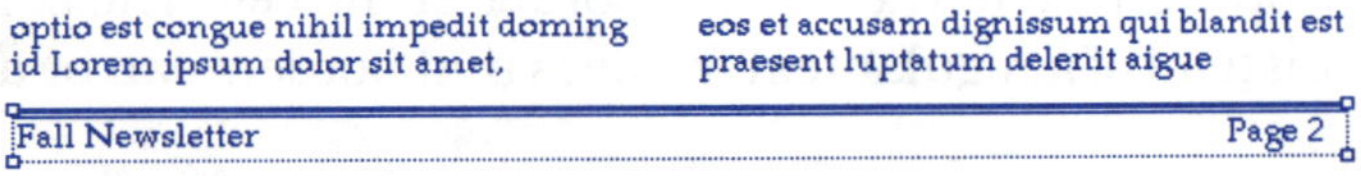

To create this footer, choose the Format menu's Insert Footer command; if you have specified left/right pages, there are separate commands for inserting left and right footers. After creating the footer, use the Frame menu's Insert Table command to create a single-celled table within the footer.

Note The text in this frame is left aligned; the Page number at the right of the footer is positioned with a right-aligned tab set at TK on the ruler. When you are entering the text into this footer, remember to press Option-Tab to advance to the page number location. The Tab key alone will create a new cell in the table.

To create the rule at the top of the footer, use the Cell Borders command and set the rule for the top of the cell; when you create a header, apply the rule instead to the bottom of the cell.

If you do not want the rule to extend the full width of the page, create two or three columns, rather than a single column, and give only some of the cells borders.

CHAPTER 19

Forms

Almost every business uses forms that are meant to be filled out by hand. This is distinct from forms that are to be filled out on the Mac screen. MacWrite Pro is not a database program, and for filling out forms you should use such a program. But MacWrite Pro is an excellent tool for creating printed forms.

In search of a form, we turned to *Webster's Secretarial Handbook* (G. & C. Merriam Co., Springfield, Mass.). We selected an employee earnings record from page 439 of the 1976 edition of this handbook. Creating this form involves several techniques that you can use when creating a variety of form types using MacWrite Pro. The key to creating a printed form with MacWrite Pro is to make good use of the table feature.

The Employee Earnings Record

Figure 19-1 shows the finished form.

FIGURE 19-1 Finished earnings record form

Name ____________	Social Security # ____________
Address ____________	Date of Birth ____________
____________	Marital Status ____________
No. of Exemptions ____________	Hourly Rate ____________

Line No.	Week Ended	Hours Wkd.	Earnings			Deductions			Net Pay	Check No.	Year-To-Date
			Reg.	Over-Time	Total	FICA	FWT	Total			

The top portion of the form contains areas for writing employee information including the name, address, number of exemptions, and social security number. The lower portion of the form is devoted to 12 columns, each with its own heading. The two superheadings "Earnings" and "Deductions" are separate from the 12 headings.

This chapter describes how to create this form with MacWrite Pro.

Create the Table

The form is divided visually into two parts, and the best technique to create it is to use two distinct tables. (The observant reader will quickly realize that the form contains eight cells over the 100-cell table limit anyway, so using two tables is your only option.)

The first table includes all the heading information: the cells at the top and the headers for the columns. Thus, the table will have 12 columns and three rows. Here's how you create the table:

1. If the Tools palette is not open, open it by choosing the Frame menu's Show Tools Palette command.
2. Click the Table tool in the palette.
3. Point to the top-left corner of the page guide (margin), hold down the mouse button, and drag to the right. Release the mouse button when you reach the right margin.
4. The Insert Table dialog box appears. Type **3** for the number of rows and **12** for the number of columns. Click the OK button. The table should look like the one in Figure 19-2.
5. Choose the Modify Frame command from the Frame menu (or Option-double click anywhere in the table frame). Make sure that the Auto-Resize Frame check box in the Modify Frame dialog box is checked. This ensures that each cell will automatically expand to accommodate all the text you type. Click the OK button to close the Modify Frame dialog box.

FIGURE 19-2 The results of using the Insert Table dialog box

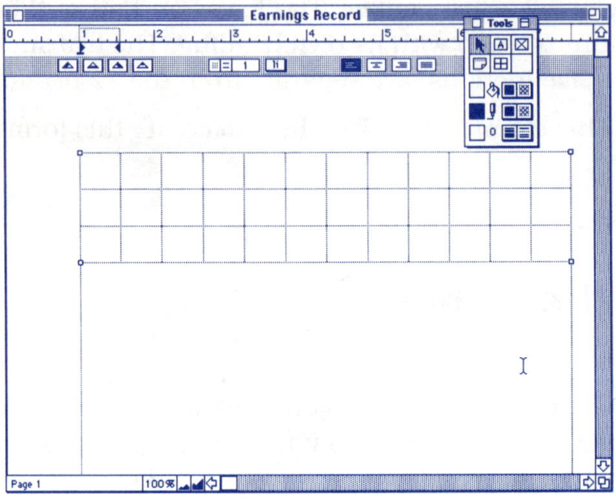

Font and Size

Select the entire table by clicking and dragging from one corner to the opposite. Set the font and size to 10-point Courier.

Note If you find Courier too conservative or unattractive, experiment with other fonts. Good candidates include 10-point Palatino with –5-em spacing, Goudy, Garamond, or Helvetica.

Centered Paragraphs

Most of the text is centered, so click the center icon on the Ruler to make the standard paragraph centered. Later in the form creation process you can easily change the alignment of the exceptions.

The Top Row

The next step is to use the Merge Cells command to turn the 12 columns in the first row into two columns. Here's how:

1. Select columns 1 through 6 in the first row by clicking in column 1 and dragging to column 6, so it looks like this:

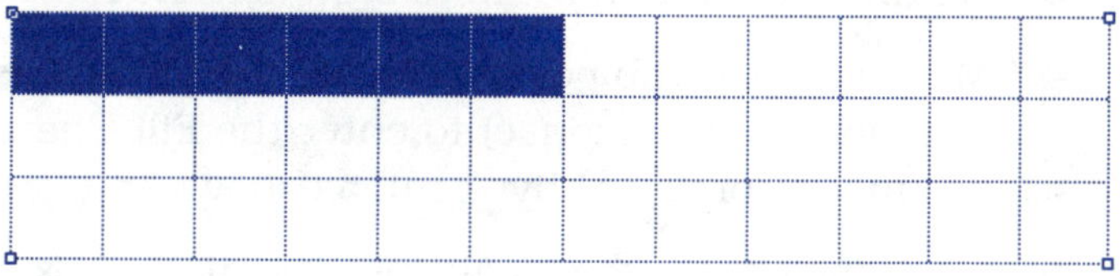

2. Choose the Table Merge Cells command. This command merges the six selected cells into one wide cell. The result looks like this:

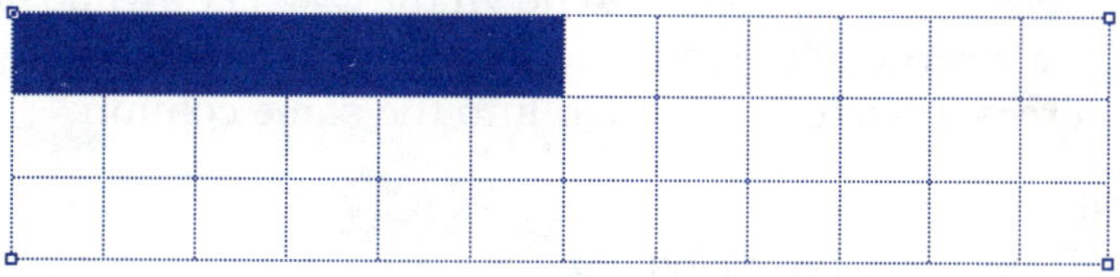

3. Repeat the process, selecting the second group of cells in the top row and merging them. When you are finished, the table should look like this:

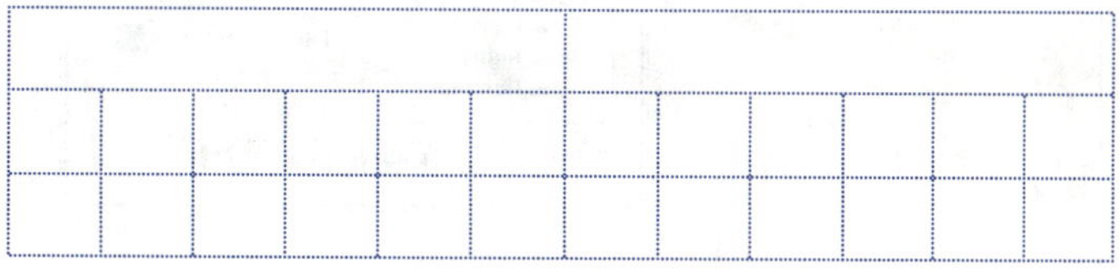

In the next set of steps, you type the text into the top two cells, and create the blank lines:

1. Click in the first cell in the top row to position the insertion point. Click the left-align icon on the Ruler, so that text in the cell is not centered.
2. Drag a right-align tab to 4 1/8 (4.125) inches on the Ruler. (As you drag the tab icon, its exact position is displayed in the Page Number box at the bottom-left corner of the document window.) Alternatively, you can use the Insert Tab dialog box to position the tab.
3. Double-click the new tab to summon the Format Tabs dialog box.
4. Make sure the tab position is set to 4.125 inches, press the Tab key once (or use the mouse) to enter the Fill Character field, and type an underscore (Shift-hyphen), as shown in Figure 19-3.
5. Click the OK button to dismiss the dialog box.
6. Type **Name**, then hold down the Option key while you press the Tab key. A leader is inserted, extending to the 4.125-inch position.

Note If you do not hold down the Option key while pressing the Tab key, the insertion point advances to the next cell. Holding down the Option key forces a tab to be inserted into the same column.

FIGURE 19-3 Filling in the Tab dialog box

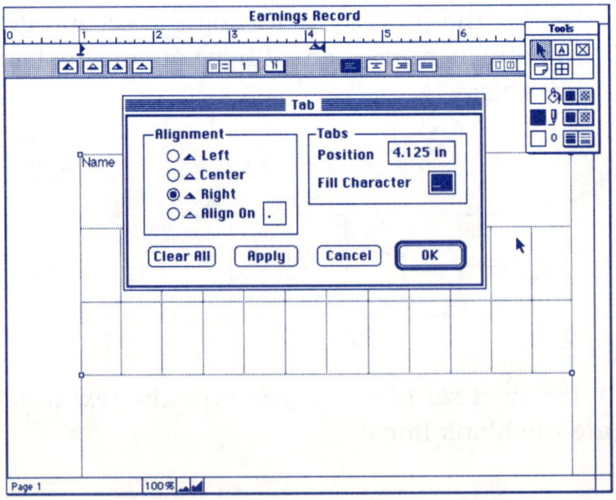

7. Press the Return key to insert a new line. Type **Address**, followed by Option-Tab and a Return.
8. This next line contains no text, so insert a tab with the Option-Tab key combination and press Return.
9. Type **No. of Exemptions** and press Option-Tab.

That's it—the text in the first cell has been entered. The only thing left to do with this text is adjust the line spacing, but it's more efficient to enter the text for the second cell, then adjust the line spacing in both cells at the same time.

Here's how to enter the text into the second cell (the one with Social Security, and so on, in it):

1. Press the Tab key to move into the second cell, or click in it.
2. Click the left align icon on the Ruler so that text in the cell is not centered.
3. Set a right align tab at the 7 1/4-inch mark. The simple way to do this is to copy the Ruler from the left cell. Place the insertion in the left cell, use the Format menu's Copy Ruler command (Shift-⌘-C), and then place the insertion point in the right column and use the Format menu's Paste Ruler command (Shift-⌘-V). You can also place this tab by dragging the tab icon to the new position and double-clicking the new tab to summon the Tab dialog box to specify the underscore fill character, but the Copy Ruler technique is much more efficient.
4. Type the text into the cell, pressing Option-Tab and Return after each line. Type **Social Security #**, **Date of Birth**, **Marital Status**, and **Hourly Rate**.

The next step is to adjust the spacing of the text in both of the cells in the top row to allow enough room to fill in the blanks.

1. Select the top row by dragging through both its cells.
2. Click the line spacing indicator on the Ruler to set the line spacing of the top row to 2.

Note Using the underscore as a tab fill character is a good technique to use when creating a variety of forms. It is far better than the technique of typing multiple underscores until they line up; tabs let you alter the width of the line, and ensure that even if you change fonts, the lines will remain consistent.

Merging Cells

Compare the finished table in Figure 19-1 with the following table, which shows the progress so far.

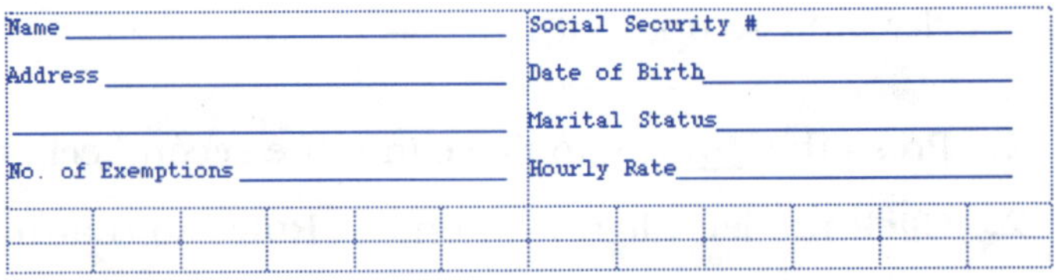

The next step is to create the centered Earnings and Deductions heads:

1. Select cells 4, 5, and 6 in the second row, as shown here:

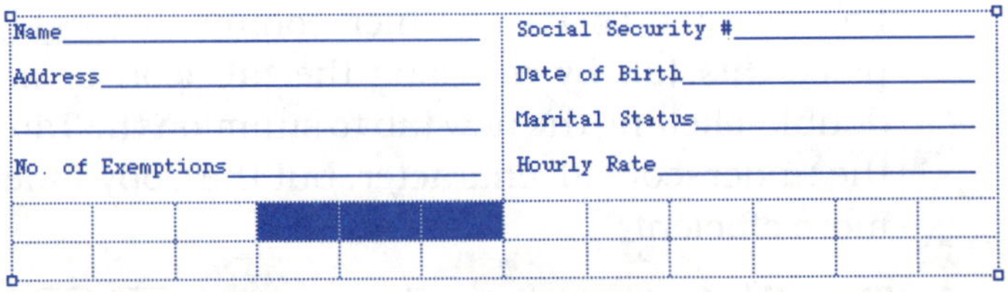

2. Choose the Merge Cells command from the Table menu. The resulting single cell occupies the position formerly held by the three selected cells.
3. Without clicking anywhere else, type **Earnings** into this newly merged cell.

Merge the next three cells to the right, and type Deductions into the newly merged cell. The result should look like this:

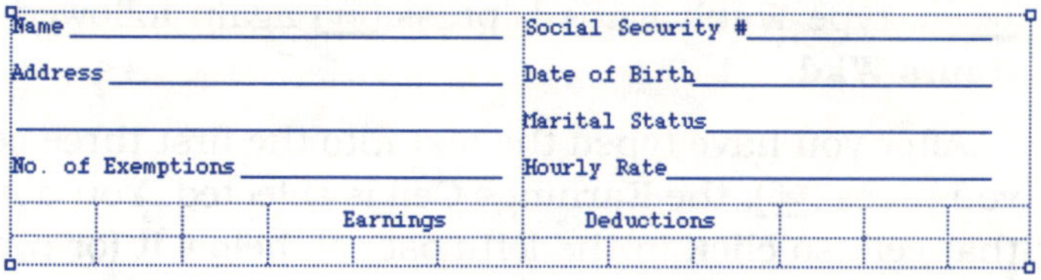

This is a good technique for creating headings that cover several cells in a table.

The next step is to merge the remaining six cells in the third row, three to the left of the Earnings cell, and three to the right of the Deductions cell, and merge them with the cells below in the fourth row.

1. Select the first cell of the third and fourth columns, like this:

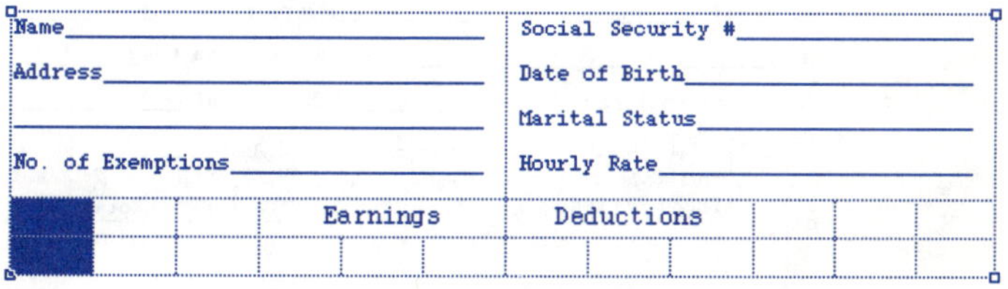

2. Choose Merge Cells from the Table menu.

Repeat these steps for the remaining cells on either side of the Earnings and Deductions cells. If you inadvertently merge the wrong cells, choose Undo from the Edit menu. When you are finished, the result should look like this:

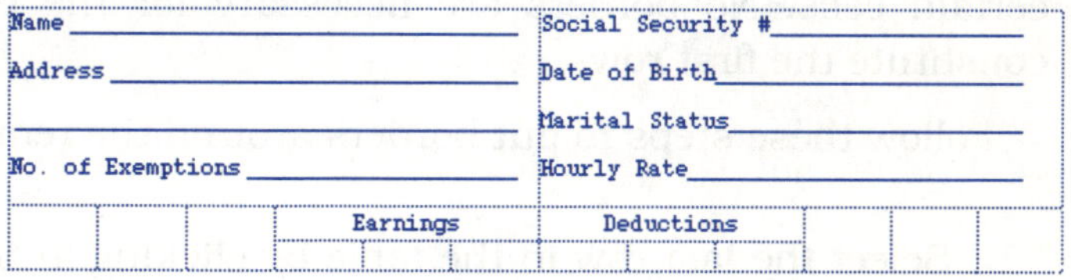

Next enter text into the cells. Click in the leftmost cell in the second row, press Return, and then type **Line No.** Pressing Return causes the text to line up with the bottom of the cell. Note that word wrap takes care of moving "No." to the second line. Press Tab to move to the next cell, press

Return, type **Week Ended**, press Tab again followed by Return, and type **Hours Wkd.**

After you have typed the text into the first three cells, note that when you press Tab, the Earnings Cell is selected. You don't need to type into that cell, so click in the leftmost cell below it (or press the keyboard ↓ twice). Press Return, type **Reg.**, press Tab, type **Over-Time**, and so on, until you have typed **Total** in the third cell under the Deductions cell, as shown in the following illustration. If you press Tab after typing Total, another row will be added below these cells. If this happens, choose the Table menu's Delete Row command or the File menu's Undo command to kill that new row. Then click in the cell to the immediate right of the Deductions head and type **Net Pay**. Finish the second two heads. Here is how the form looks after filling in all these cells:

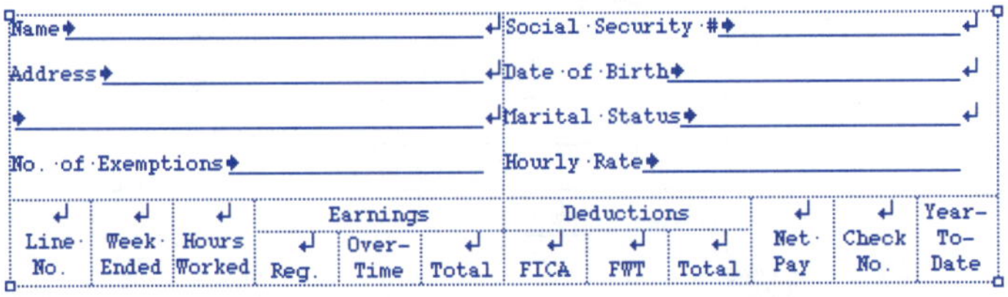

For this illustration, we have enabled Show Invisibles, so that you can see where the Return characters were inserted into the fields.

Formatting Borders

The next step in producing the form is providing borders around certain cells. No borders are necessary for the two large cells that constitute the first row.

Follow these steps to put borders around the remaining cells.

1. Select the last row in the table by clicking in the first column and dragging to the left. Include the Earnings and Deductions cells:

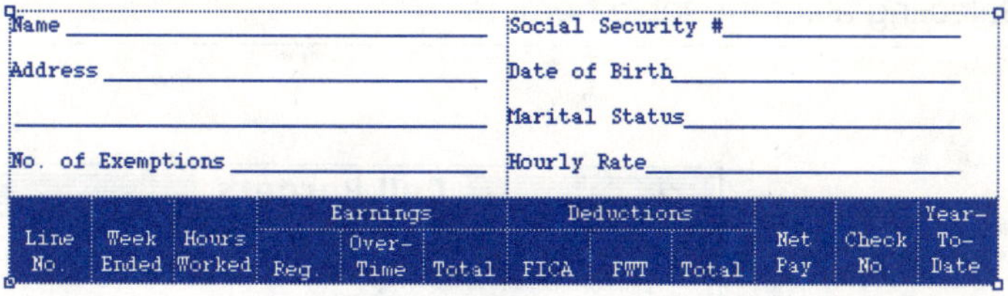

Name ______ Social Security # ______
Address ______ Date of Birth ______
______ Marital Status ______
No. of Exemptions ______ Hourly Rate ______

Line No.	Week Ended	Hours Worked	Earnings			Deductions			Net Pay	Check No.	Year-To-Date
			Reg.	Over-Time	Total	FICA	FWT	Total			

2. Choose the Table menu's Cell Borders command, which summons the Cell Borders dialog box.
3. In the cell representation in the left portion of the dialog box, click in the middle of one of the cells to select all the borders, as shown in Figure 19-4.
4. From the pop-up, choose a 1-point border to apply a 1-point black border to the cells.

Note You can experiment with other cell border options in the Cell Border dialog box. As you try new line patterns, colors, styles, and cell fill patterns, use the Apply button to see what effect your choices have on the table. No effect is permanently applied to the table until you click the OK button.

5. Click the OK button to apply the new borders.

After these steps the form should look like this:

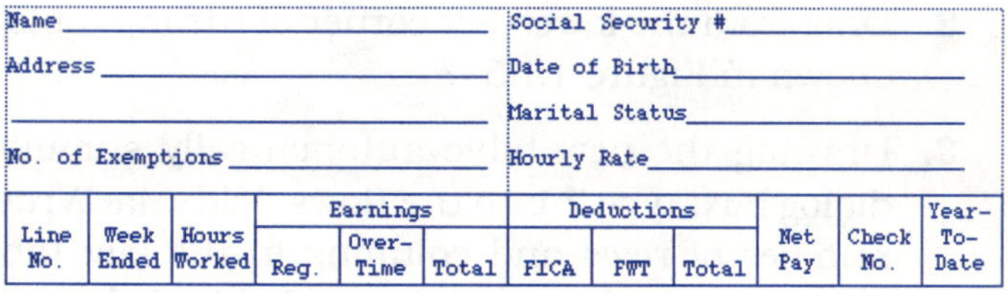

Name ______ Social Security # ______
Address ______ Date of Birth ______
______ Marital Status ______
No. of Exemptions ______ Hourly Rate ______

Line No.	Week Ended	Hours Worked	Earnings			Deductions			Net Pay	Check No.	Year-To-Date
			Reg.	Over-Time	Total	FICA	FWT	Total			

FIGURE 19-4 Selecting all of the table borders

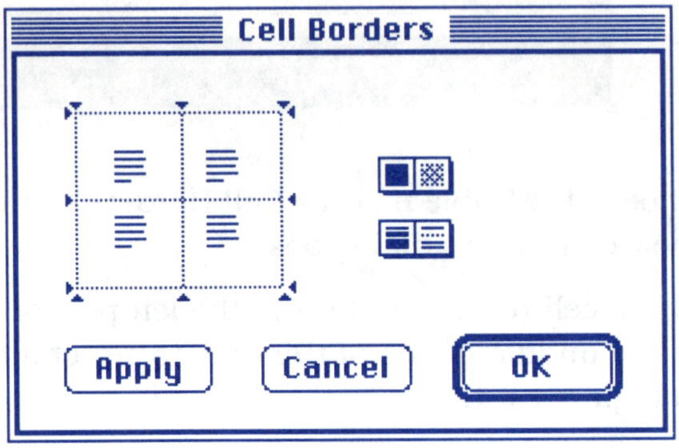

Completing the Form

The next step is to create a table to hold the cells for the remainder of the form:

1. Choose the Table tool from the Tools palette.
2. Drag from the lower-left corner of the top table to the right edge, as shown in Figure 19-5.
3. Drawing the new table automatically summons the Insert Table dialog box; type **7** into the Rows field. MacWrite Pro remembers the number of rows and columns in the last table created, so 12 is already entered in the Columns field. Click the OK button to dismiss the dialog box. The form should now look like Figure 19-6.

If the cells look too small, you can adjust the height of the rows by making the table as a whole taller by dragging the handle at the bottom-right corner of the new table.

FIGURE 19-5

Creating a table to hold the remainder of the cells

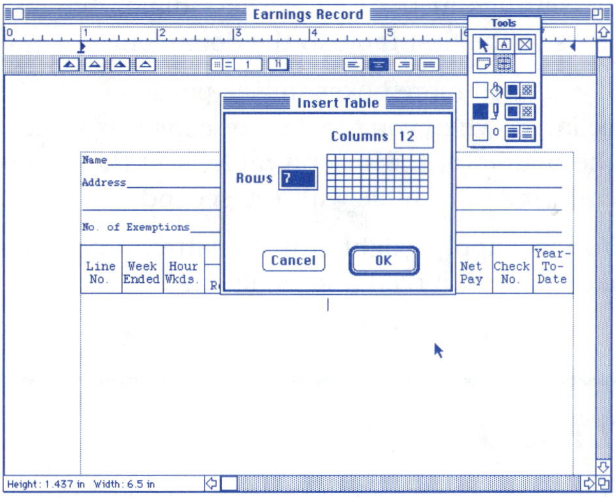

FIGURE 19-6

The form near completion

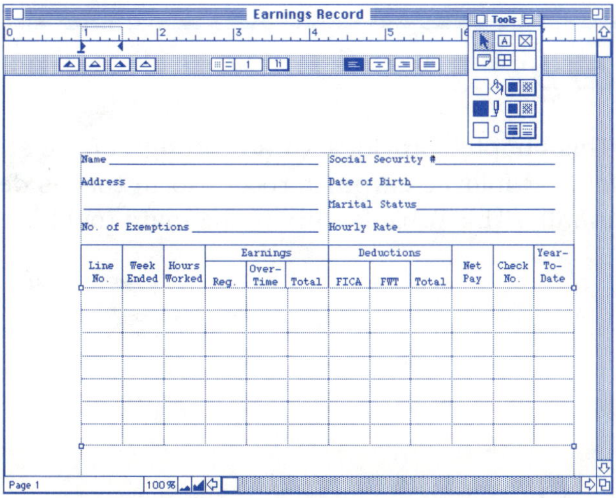

To apply cell borders, select all the cells in the table, and use either the Tools palette or the Table menu's Cell Borders command. Use the same settings in the Cell Borders dialog box as you used in applying borders to the first table in the document.

If you need more boxes in this portion of the form, you can make the table larger when you create it or copy this table to the Clipboard, paste at the bottom of the second table, and then reposition as necessary to line up this third table with the second.

You can apply a light gray fill pattern to alternate rows of the table to make it easier to read and to fill out.

Using This Form

Although this form is designed to be filled out manually, you can use an existing database together with the MacWrite Pro Mail Merge feature to fill in parts of it. For example, you might merge records from an employee database file to create forms with the employee information automatically printed in the top portion of the form. Merging is discussed in Chapter 13.

Summary

This chapter provides a walkthrough of the steps needed to create a printed employee earnings record form that is designed to be filled out manually. The Table feature is the main tool for creating this form.

CHAPTER

20

A Catalog

This chapter discusses preparing a product catalog using MacWrite Pro together with a database application. Claris FileMaker Pro 2.0 is used to prepare the catalog, but other database applications can be used as well, so long as they can export database records to a delimited file for use as a MacWrite Pro Merge Data File.

This technique makes use of several MacWrite Pro features, including multiple-column sections, character styles, mail merge, and Find/Change. A text frame is used in the footer to create reversed type.

At the end of the chapter, we will suggest some other, similar uses of merging for automatic document production.

The Database

The contents of the catalog depend on the information in the database. This example uses a simple database that contains four fields. The Item field contains the name of the catalog item, the Description field contains a textual description of the item, the Item# field is for a product number, and the Final field contains the price. Here's how the database looks in FileMaker Pro 2.0:

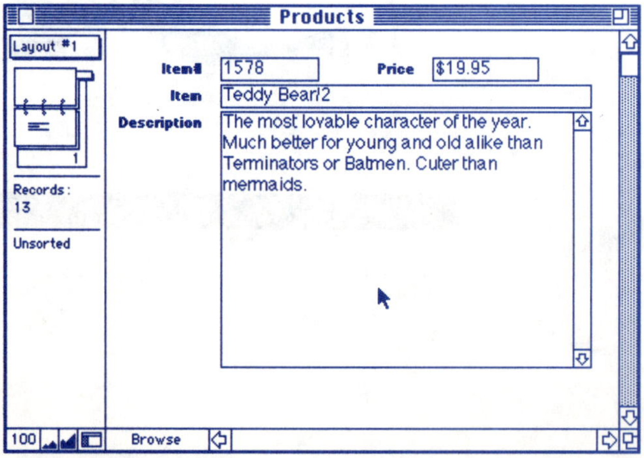

After adding some records to the database, the next step is to create the merge data file. Consult the documentation for the database you are using. FileMaker Pro 2.0 has an Export command that saves the record to either a tab-delimited text file or to a specific merge data file. The merge data file is called, in this example, Teddy Bear Products.

The MacWrite Pro Catalog Template

Before creating the merge data file, refer to Figure 20-1, which shows the final output of a single page of the catalog.

As you can see, the catalog is in two columns, with a reversed message at the bottom of each page.

Format the Section

The first step is to format the document into two sections. To do so, choose the Section command from the Format menu. Here are the settings we used:

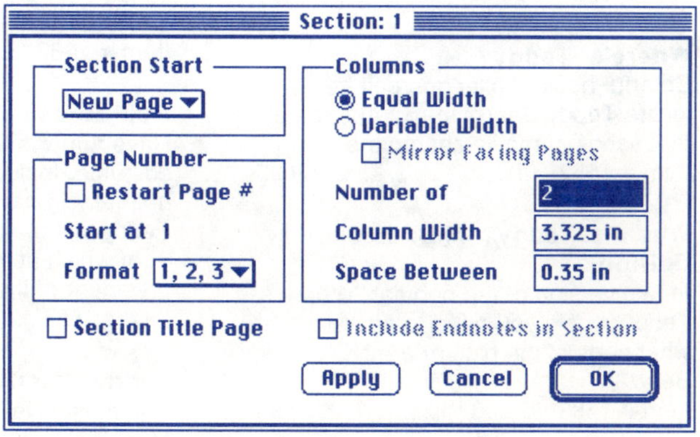

As you can see, the section is formatted into two columns. The space between has been doubled from its default of .167 inches to .35 inches. This will make the catalog a little more readable.

FIGURE 20-1 The final output of a catalog page

Teddy Bear/2
The most loveable character of the year. Much better for young and old alike than Terminators or Batmen. Cuter than the Little Mermaid.
Item # 1578 ....$19.95

Teddy Bear/2 Morphing Model
Watch this Teddy Bear/2 turn into a wide variety of other animals before your very eyes!
Item # 1579 ....$39.95

Teddy Bear's Dream House
Put Teddy in his place with this dream home! Complete furnishing include peopleskin rug, mounted salmnon trophies on wall. Wet bar included!
Item # 1580 ....$49.95

Teddy and the Pirate
Teddy Bear/2 Game. Can you help Teddy avoid the clutches of the evil pirates?
Item # 1581 ....$11.95

Where's Teddy?
Colorful book challenges children to locate Teddy Bear/2 in pictures featuring thousands of movie characters.
Item # 1582..................................$9.95

Where's Teddy? M.C. Escher Edition
In this version of the popular "Where's Teddy" book, you need to figure out what parts of the picture are NOT Teddy Bear/2?
Item # 1583 ....$10.95

Teddy Bear/2 Karaoke Machine
Is it live or is it Teddy? Lets you sing along with all Teddy's big hits: The Teddy Bear's Picnic, Teddy Went A-Courting, I Am I Said, and more.
Item # 1584 ....$89.95

Teddy Meets Godzilla
Excellent live-action video pits Teddy Bear/2 against the monstor who has challenged continents. Whatever the outcome of this challenge, you can trust Teddy's motto: I'll Be Back.
Item # 1585 ....$19.95

Teddy's Greatest Hits, Volume II
Teddy plays and sings his favorite songs: Fur Elise, Fur He's a Jolly Good Fellow, Bear With Me, The Paws that Refresh, and many more!
Item # 1586..................................$8.95

Tightrope Teddy
Hours of fun with this Teddy Bear circus set! Teddy teaches humans to stick their heads in his mouth, balance on balls, jump through hoops of fire (may not be suitable for children under 3), and ride bicycles.
Item # 1587 ....$59.95

Bull Moose Teddy
Have fun with this Teddy Bear/2 costume. Includes pince-nez, pith helmet, big game rifle, safari geer. Teddy will really enjoy is bully pulpit from which he launches a run for president of the United States!
Item # 1588..................................$9.95

Teddy Bear/2
The most loveable character of the year. Much better for young and old alike than Terminators or Batmen. Cuter than the Little Mermaid.
Item # 1578 ....$19.95

International Toys **Call 1-800-555-1212**

Insert the Merge Codes

The next step is to insert the merge codes into the document. As you read in Chapter 13, the tool for doing this is the Merge palette, which you access with the File menu's Mail Merge command. When you use this command, MacWrite Pro first asks you to locate and open the merge data file and then presents the Merge palette, as shown here:

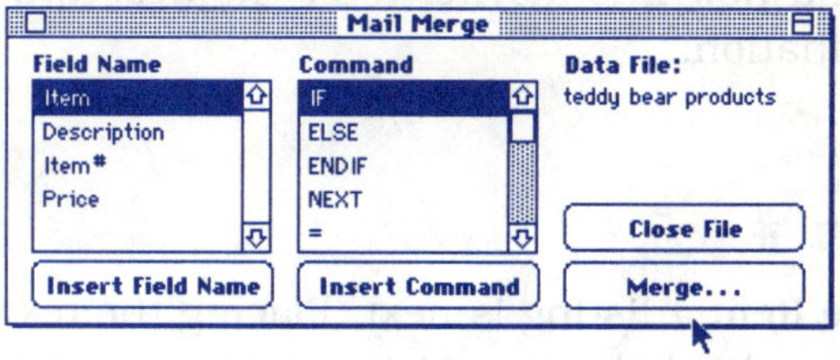

The Merge palette shows the names of the fields in the data file. The field names in the Merge Document must also be formatted, so when you insert the merge characters, also create custom character styles for each of the fields. This makes it easy for readers to distinguish the different elements of each listing in the catalog. Custom character styles are not absolutely necessary to create the catalog—you can also use the menus or the Text palette, but by using custom character styles, you can quickly fine-tune the overall appearance by modifying the custom character style.

Item

The first field to insert into the file is the Item field, which contains the name of the product:

1. Make sure the insertion point is at the top-left corner of the first column and that there is no other text in the column.
2. Double-click the Item field in the scrolling field list in the Merge palette. MacWrite Pro automatically inserts the Item field, with its delimiters.
3. Press and hold the Shift key while pressing the Return key.

This third step inserts a "newline" character, which tells MacWrite Pro that you want to end the line with the Item field, but do not want it to be considered as a paragraph separate from the text after it. This technique also makes formatting the entire catalog listing easier.

Description

On the new line created by the newline character, insert the Description field by double-clicking it in the Merge palette's scrolling field list. Insert a new line marker after the description with the Shift-Return key combination.

Item

The Item # listing is next. Placing the text "Item #" before the actual item number helps the reader understand the organization of the catalog. Type **Item #** on the line after the Description field. Press the Spacebar and then insert the Item # field.

Price

Inserting the Price field is the next step, but this is a good place to apply some formatting. The price field should be aligned with the right margin, with a leader (a line of periods) between the item number and the price, as shown here:

At the top of the illustration you can see that a right-align tab has been inserted at the right edge of the margin.

Here's how to do this, assuming the cursor is located immediately after the Item # field:

1. From the tab well on the ruler, click a right-align tab and drag it up to a position on the ruler just to the left of the right margin. (Review the previous illustration if you aren't sure which tab is a right-align tab. It's the icon with the wide right side.)

2. Summon the Tabs dialog box with the Format menu Tabs command. (You can also summon this dialog box by double-clicking one of the four tab wells or by the keyboard equivalent: Option-⌘-T.)
3. When the Tabs dialog box appears, click the tab you just created. The Position field then changes to represent the location of the new tab mark.
4. Press the Tab key to move into the Leader field, and type a period. The result should look like Figure 20-2.
5. Click the OK button to accept changes to the tab, and dismiss the dialog box.

   This process sets the paragraph format to contain the right tab at 4 inches and to provide the leader.

The next step is to insert the tab itself and the Price field:

1. Make sure the insertion point is directly after the Item # field delimiter.

FIGURE 20-2 Formatting the Price field

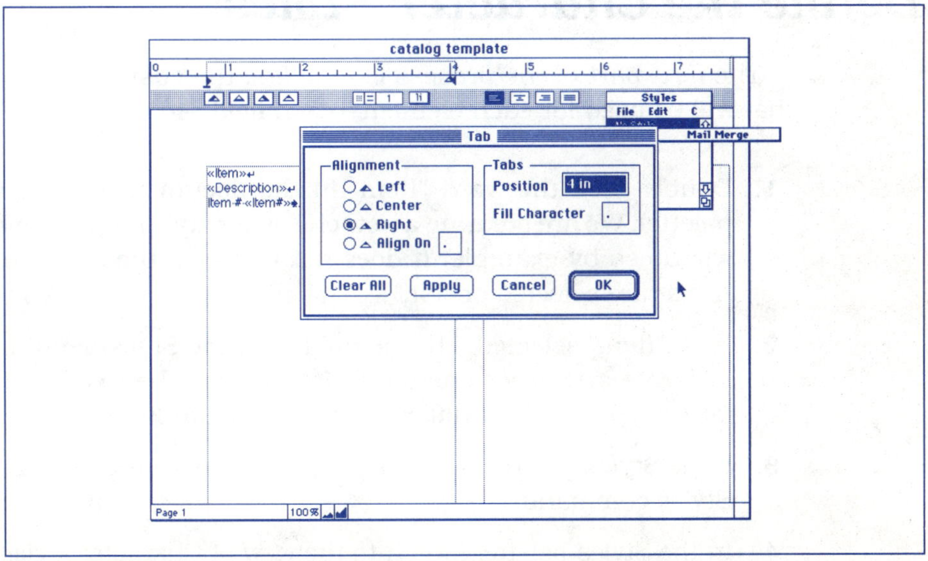

2. Press the Tab key. The leaders are inserted, and the insertion point moved to the 4-inch point.

3. Type **$** (since the next item will be price, and a dollar sign is not included in the merge data file).

4. Double-click the Price field in the Merge palette to insert the Price field into the document.

5. From the scrolling Command list, double-click the Next command. The Next command is inserted within delimiters into the record. This causes MacWrite Pro to jump to the next record in the merge data file when performing the merge.

When you are finished with this process, the Merge palette is no longer needed, so you can either close it or collapse it. (Closing the Merge palette also closes the merge data file.) Later, after defining the custom character styles, you will use Copy and Paste to propogate this definition down the page.

Define the Character Styles

The next part of the process is to define the custom character styles that will be used for each element—each field—in the catalog.

1. Double-click the word "Item" in the document (not in the Merge palette). We are creating a new character style for the Item field, and will do so by example. It does not matter if the delimiters around "Item" are selected or not.

2. With "Item" selected, choose Bold from the Style menu. If you want to create any other custom formatting for the Item field—such as larger type or a font different from the default, do so now.

3. If the Styles palette is not visible, open it with the Style menu Show Styles command.

4. In the Styles palette, switch to the view of Character styles using the menu in the top-right corner of the palette. A letter C should be visible, indicating that the palette is displaying custom character styles.

5. From the Styles palette's File menu, choose New Character Style. MacWrite Pro asks if you want to define a new character style based on the selection, and asks for its name. Type **Item** and click the OK button.

Repeat the process for each of the fields, omitting step 2 (unless you want the entire listing to be bold) and substituting any other character formatting you want to apply. For example, you might want to italicize the Item # and Price fields. Give the Item # text you typed and the dollar sign before the price the same styles as the Item # and Price fields.

Propogate the Records

Once the styles have been defined, you can copy and paste the record definition down the page. Here's how you do it:

1. Click to the right of the <<price>> field definition.
2. From the Merge palette, click on the Next command in the scrolling list of commands. "<<NEXT>>" is placed on the line.
3. Press the Return key. The completed field definition now looks like this:

The <<NEXT>> command, remember, tells MacWrite Pro to print the data from the next record. The Return was inserted to leave a blank line after the record.

The next set of steps tells MacWrite Pro to print a number of records on the same page:

1. Select the record. The easiest way to do this is with the Edit menu Select All command or its keyboard shortcut, ⌘-A.
2. Use the Format Paragraph dialog box to set the Space after this paragraph to one line.

3. Copy the text using the Edit menu's Copy command (⌘-C).
4. Click at the end of the text and Paste the text. Repeat this process until both columns are filled with the record definitions (but do not overlap to the next page). The screen should look something like Figure 20-3. Of course, depending on the styles you use, your mileage may vary.

Create the Footer

The next step is to create the reversed footer. In this sample document, we are ignoring left and right pages. In a real catalog, you would probably want to create separate footers for left and right pages; see Chapter 5 for instructions.

FIGURE 20-3 Setting up your file to print a number of records on the same page

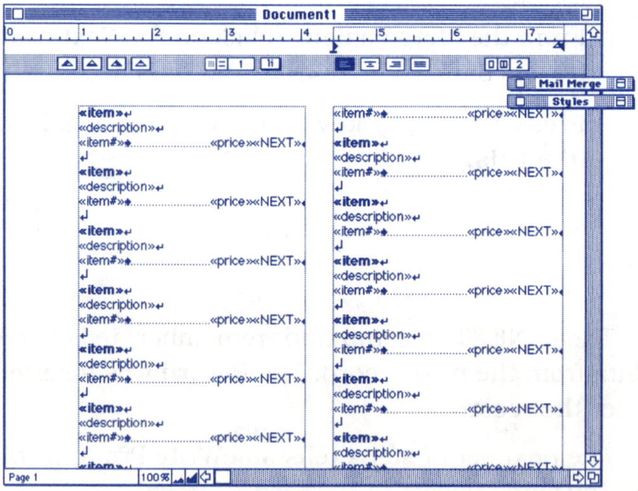

In this instance, we are using a text frame embedded in a footer to create the reversed text, as shown here:

Here are the steps for creating the reversed footer.

1. Choose Insert Footer from the Format menu. MacWrite Pro creates the new footer and places the insertion point within it.
2. Choose Text from the Frame menu's Insert Frame submenu. MacWrite Pro creates the new frame within the footer, and makes it exactly as high as the footer and one inch wide.
3. Resize the frame by dragging the handle in its lower-left corner to the lower-left corner of the footnote.
4. Click inside the frame and type International Toys, press Tab, and type **Call 1-800-555-6789**.
5. Drag a right tab to close to the right margin. If a character appears in the Fill Character field (which it may, inheriting it from the tab set earlier), select that fill character, and press the Del key to get rid of it.
6. Select all the text in the footer (that is, "International Toys" and the phone number).
7. Format the text: set the font to Avant Garde, the size to 14 points, and the style to bold.
8. From the Text color menu on the Style menu, choose white. The text in the footer will disappear.
9. If the Tools palette is not visible, choose Show Tools Palette from the Frame menu. If the palette is collapsed, expand it.
10. Set the fill color of the frame to black by choosing that color from the fill pop-up on the Tools palette, as shown here:

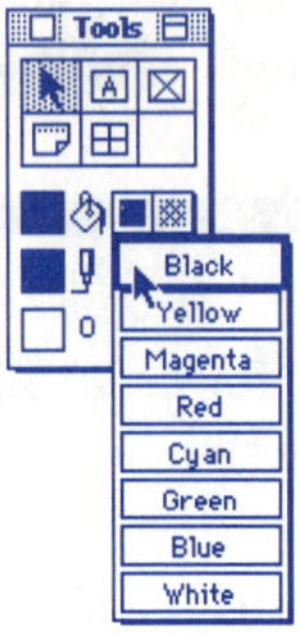

If you haven't done so throughout this process, now is a good time to save the document. Our sample is called "Catalog Template."

Merging

The next step is to merge the data from the Teddy Bear Products merge data file into the new template. First, make sure the Catalog Template file is open.

If the Merge palette is not open, open it by using the File menu's Mail Merge command and select the Teddy Bear Products file. If the Merge palette is collapsed, zoom it open.

With the Merge palette open, here are the steps for merging and creating the product catalog:

1. Click the Merge button on the Merge palette.
2. In the dialog box that appears, click the New Document radio button, as shown here:

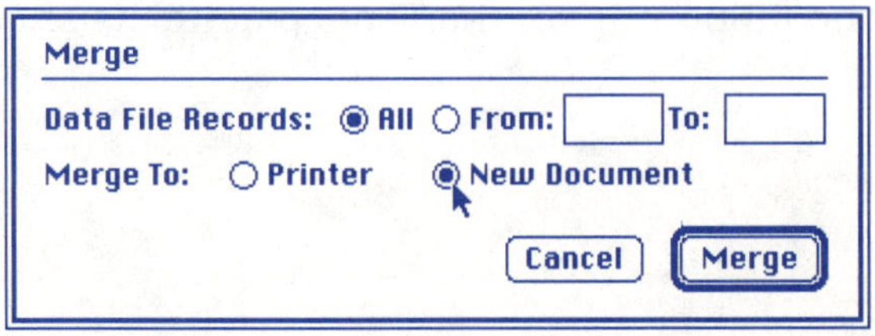

Now click the Merge button to start the merge process. A progress window appears as MacWrite merges the new document. When the process is complete, a new document named WorkingDoc_merged1 appears on the screen. Since you no longer need the Merge palette, collapse or close it.

Suggestions for Other Uses

This example shows that Mail Merge need not be used only for annoying letters and junk mail. Here are some other uses for the same techniques:

- ☐ An employee telephone list, in two or three columns, based on information stored in a corporate database
- ☐ Merging data into forms, as discussed in Chapter 19
- ☐ Address labels for a mailing list

Use System 7 Publish and Subscribe to keep information current. This technique works both when you create the data file in MacWrite Pro and when you use a database such as FileMaker Pro to create the data file.

Summary

MacWrite Pro's powerful Mail Merge tool can be used for more than creating mailings. In this chapter, Mail Merge is used to create a product catalog. The advantage of this technique is that it's easy to update the catalog.

The step-by-step instructions include use of multiple-column sections, character styles, and footers.

CHAPTER

21

Academic Papers

This chapter covers academic outlining and styles for term papers. It discusses outlining as an organization technique and how to evolve an outline into a finished paper. The general style sheet for term papers and other academic writing is easy to modify to accommodate almost any academic style.

Outlining

Outlining is an integral part of the way many people write. Others shun outlining altogether. If you are a member of the latter group, don't skip over this section. The outline styles presented here are useful not only for those who rigorously outline everything they write, but also for managing the final preparation of documents.

Creating Outline Styles

Figure 21-1 shows a sample outline for a humanities paper. The outline text is taken from *Writing in the Disciplines to Accompany the Rhinehard Handbook for Writers*, Second Edition, by Bonnie Carter and Craig Skates (Fort Worth: Holt, Rhinehard and Winston, 1989). This book does not take computer-based word processing into account, so its styles rely on underlining rather than the preferred italics. Check with those for whom you are preparing your materials to see if italics are suitable.

In Figure 21-1, the second head is selected; you can see from the accompanying Styles palette that this paragraph has the style Level 2. There are four styles, one for each level of the outline. Here is how you can create those styles in a new document:

1. On the Ruler, drag the left-indent triangle to the 1 1/2-inch position. The indent marker is the one shaped like a triangle facing to the right.
2. Drag the first-line indent marker (the inverted t) back to the left margin.
3. Drag a left tab marker from the tab well to the 1 1/2-inch position on the Ruler so the screen looks like Figure 21-2.

FIGURE 21-1 A sample outline

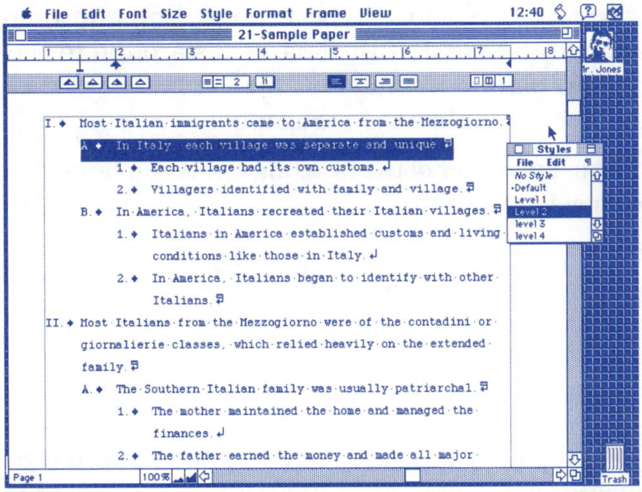

4. If the Styles palette is not open, open it with the Style menu's Show Styles command. Choose New Paragraph Style from the Styles palette File menu to summon the Custom Paragraph Style dialog box.

FIGURE 21-2 Changing the tab to 1 1/2 inches

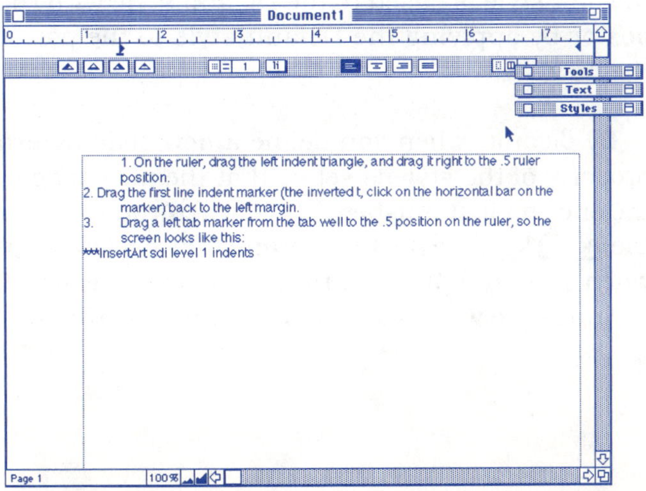

5. Name the new style Level 1; then click the OK button.

To type a heading, type **I**, press Tab, and then type the text of the paragraph. Note that the text wraps around to the left to the left-indent marker. Setting the tab and the left indent at the same position makes it easier to number the paragaphs.

The remainder of the heading levels can be created in the same manner so they look like this:

```
I.◆ Level·1
    A.◆ Level·2
        1.◆ Level·3
            a.◆ Level·4
```

Each paragraph is indented 1/2 inch from the one preceding it, and each has a tab stop set 1/2 inch to the right of the first-line marker.

Note When you create a new paragraph by example, the Based On portion of the style definition is picked up from the style the paragraph had before you defined it. Thus, if you follow the steps above and then press the Return key to create a new paragraph, that new paragraph will have the Level 1 style. When you create the Level 2 style, it is based on Level 1. While this might be acceptable, it is preferable to have the style based on the Default style. You can change the style on which the new style is based to the Default style with the Define Styles dialog box or by applying the Default style to the paragraph before defining the new style.

By default, when you define a new style by example, the Next Style property of the style is set so that the next style created is the same as the one you just finished. Thus, when you type a Level 2 style and press the Return key, the next paragraph is also a Level 2 style. This has benefits when you are outlining, but you may want to make the Next style the Default style when you are not typing an outline.

Modifying the Styles

There are several ways to modify these styles. For example, if you are not using a numbering scheme for outlining, you should change the position of the left-indent marker so that it is the same as the first-line marker.

You can also apply different styles to the various heading levels. These styles might include a larger type size for the Level 1 or Level 2 styles than for the others. Level 3 and Level 4 styles might include underlined or italicized text. Level 1 and Level 2 styles might benefit from increased Space Before, too.

Using the Styles

When you work on the outline, you can use keyboard shortcuts to apply styles. As discussed in Chapter 7, styles are automatically added to the Style menu's Paragraph submenu, as shown in Figure 21-3.

FIGURE 21-3 Styles are automatically added to the Style menu's Paragraph submenu

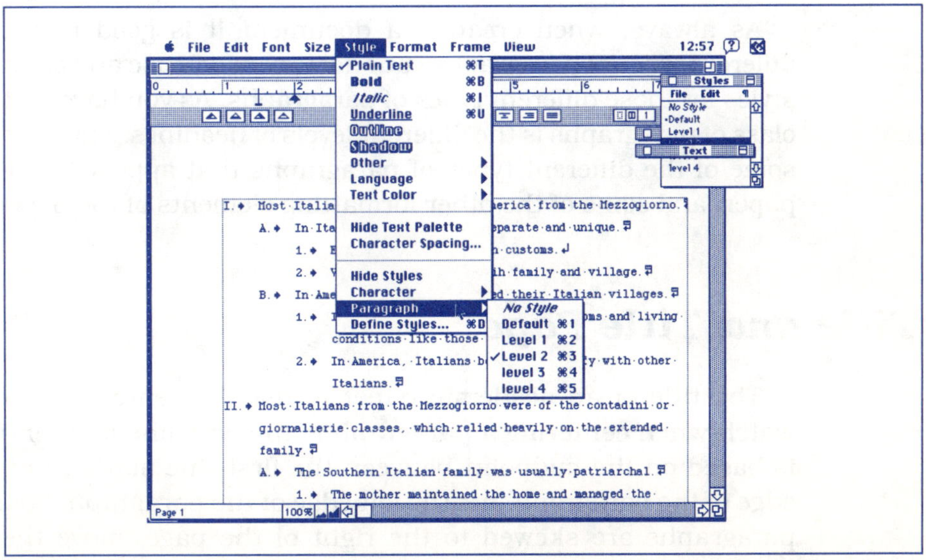

Thus, to change a paragraph to the Level 1 style, press ⌘-2 (the Default style is always ⌘-1); to change a paragraph to the Level 3 style, press ⌘-4.

You can also use the command keys and the levels of styles to "promote" or "demote" the various headings. Cutting and pasting lets you reposition the topics in the outline.

Once you have created the topics, you can start writing by placing the cursor at the end of the heading paragraph, pressing the Return key, and then creating the paragraphs that fill out the heading. Before you do this, you might want to change the Next Style property of each of the paragraphs so that the Next style is Default. Do this with the Define Styles dialog box.

Preparing an Academic Document

This section examines some elements of the academic paper, again based on *Writing in the Disciplines to Accompany the Rhinehard Handbook for Writers* mentioned at the beginning of this chapter.

As always, when creating a document it is good to consider the different types of paragraphs your document will use and create different styles for those different types of paragraphs. As you have just seen, one class of paragraphs is the different levels of headings. This section covers some of the different types of paragraphs that appear in an academic paper, and some of the other formatting elements of the paper as well.

Title and Title Page

The title of an academic paper is usually centered. One thing to watch when centering a paragraph is the first-line marker. Centering is based on the midpoint between the first-line marker and the right edge of the paragraph, *not* the left edge of the paragraph. So if centered paragraphs are skewed to the right of the page, move the first-line marker to the left margin.

If you need a title page, you must use [Return] to control the vertical position of the title on the page; there is no command to center text vertically on the page. Be sure to insert a Page Break after the title to ensure that the body text begins on a new page.

Headers and Footers

Headers for academic papers are generally fairly simple—your last name followed by the page number. Here's a simple header:

The last name appears in this version flush to the left margin, and a right-align tab is inserted at the right margin to align the word "Page," followed by a space and the Page number, with the right margin. Use the Edit menu's Insert Page Number command to number pages automatically.

Quotations

Long quotations should be set apart from the main text by indenting them about a half inch on the left. You can also indent them on the right, though most style guides do not so specify a special right indentation for quotations. You may also single-space quotations and add space before and after the paragraph to help set them apart.

The best way to manage quotations is to use a custom paragraph style. You may discover that if you add space before the paragraph in the style definition there is too much white space between paragraphs in the quotation. If this is the case, add a second custom style for the second paragraph of a quotation, with no space before.

Notes

Depending on your style guide, notes can be placed as either footnotes or endnotes.

Footnotes

Footnotes at the bottom of the page are managed automatically by MacWrite Pro, as discussed in Chapter 5. Remember that MacWrite Pro defines one custom paragraph style for the footnote itself, and two custom character styles—one for the marker (the location in the text at which you inserted the footnote) and one for the reference (the marker at the bottom of the page). You cannot select the footnote reference number directly, so modifying the custom style is the only way to change the appearance of the footnote reference.

When MacWrite Pro inserts the footnote text, the footnote reference is placed at the position of the first-line marker in the footnote itself. The rest of the style—margins, spacing, and so on—is based on the Default style. Figure 21-4 shows an example of a modified footnote style that helps make it easier to differentiate the footnote reference from the footnote text.

Note that the left-indent marker on the Ruler is positioned to the right 1/8 inch, and the first-line marker is flush with the left margin. If there are numerous footnotes on the page, this makes it easier to differentiate them visually.

FIGURE 21-4 A modified footnote style

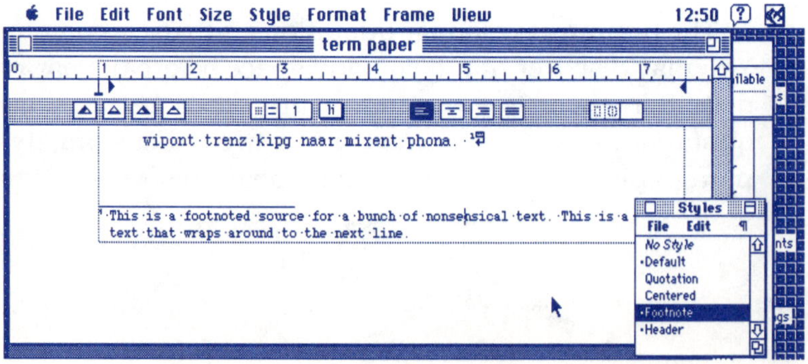

Endnotes

Endnotes are placed at the end of a document, usually on a page of their own. Here's the best way to create endnotes:

1. Choose the Format menu's Document command.
2. Choose End of Document from the Footnote Position pop-up menu, as shown here:

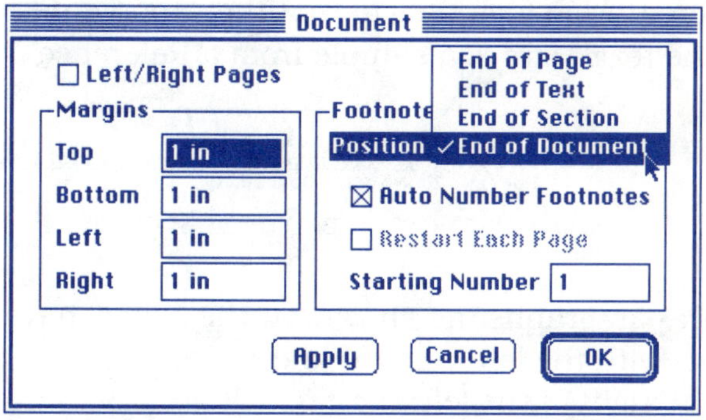

This places the footnotes at the end of the document, in a separate section of their own.

As you type the document, use the Insert Footnote command. When you have typed the text of the footnote, press ⌘-Return to have MacWrite Pro return the insertion point to its original position in the body of the text.

The next step is to create a heading for the Notes page:

1. Scroll to the end of the document and click in one of the notes to place the insertion point.
2. Use the Insert Header command. A new header is created for this separate section.
3. Type **Notes** into the Header area and center the text.

If you are using endnotes, you should modify the custom Footnote Reference style. Notes on a separate page do not need to have their references in the Superior style. To do this, choose Define Styles from the Style menu, click on the Footnote Reference style, and click on the

Character button. Uncheck the Superior box to remove this style. You can also uncheck the boxes for size and font name so that the footnote references assume the default character style.

References

References are usually placed at the end of the paper. They are different from footnotes in that they are not necessarily cited specifically in the text. Here is a sample from a Reference page:

References

Miller, Perry. The American Transcendentalists: Their Prose and Poetry. New York: Doubleday, 1983.

Langer, W.C. (1972). The Mind of Adolph Hitler. New York: Basic.

Both paragraphs, as shown on the Ruler, have their first-line markers flush with the left margin, and the left-indent markers are set 1/2 inch to the right of the left margin.

The first reference follows the style from the *Chicago Manual of Style*, and the second is from the APA Format.

Stationery

If you intend to create more than one paper using the same style, create a stationery file to store the settings. The best way to handle all this stuff is to create stationery files. After you have created all the settings you need—styles, margins, and so on—save the document in MacWrite Pro Stationery, giving it a meaningful title such as "stationery template." You can delete nearly all the text from the document before saving it. If you have formatted different sections differently, keep the section break characters in the stationery template.

PART IV

Appendixes

APPENDIX

A

Installing MacWrite Pro

This appendix discusses the ins and outs of installing MacWrite Pro, including what the Installer places into the Claris folder in your System Folder. It tells you which files are placed where in the default installation, the various customization options, and which files you can safely get rid of if you are short of hard disk space.

Installing MacWrite Pro

To install MacWrite Pro on your hard disk, insert the disk labeled Install. When the disk appears on the desktop, double-click the Install program to launch the installer.

Note MacWrite Pro requires a minimum of System 6.04.

There are two main options for installing MacWrite Pro: Easy Install and Customize Install.

Easy Install

Easy Install installs the complete MacWrite Pro package on the hard disk you specify. It is the option to choose unless free space on the hard disk is limited. To perform the Easy Install, click the Install button on the opening installer screen, shown in Figure A-1.

Note If you have more than one hard disk on your Mac, you can use the Switch Disk button to switch to another disk. When you run the Install program, it assumes that you want to install it on the disk from which the Mac is booted.

If you choose the Easy Install option, skip to the "Personalizing" section.

FIGURE A-1 The Easy Install dialog box

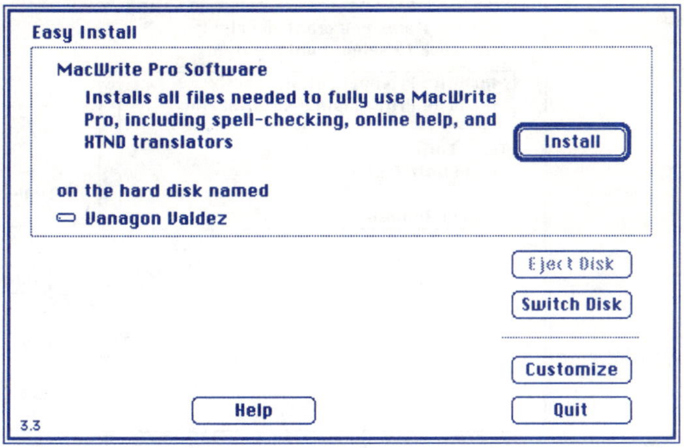

Customize Install

The Customize Install option lets you choose which of the various MacWrite Pro components you want to install. You can use Customize Install to load only those components you absolutely need, to conserve disk space. You can also use Customize Install to reinstall any MacWrite Pro files that you might have inadvertently deleted.

To customize the installation, click the Customize button in the installer opening screen. This summons a new window, with a scrolling list of the optional components, shown in Figure A-2.

Click to select an item on this list; Shift-click to select multiple items. As you click individual items in the list, a window describing your selection appears below the scrolling list. Here the Install program lists the size, date, version, and a brief description of the item you have selected, as shown in the section describing each option. If you Shift-click to select two or more items, the window displays a bulleted list of the names of the selected items only, as shown in Figure A-3.

FIGURE A-2 The Customize Install dialog box

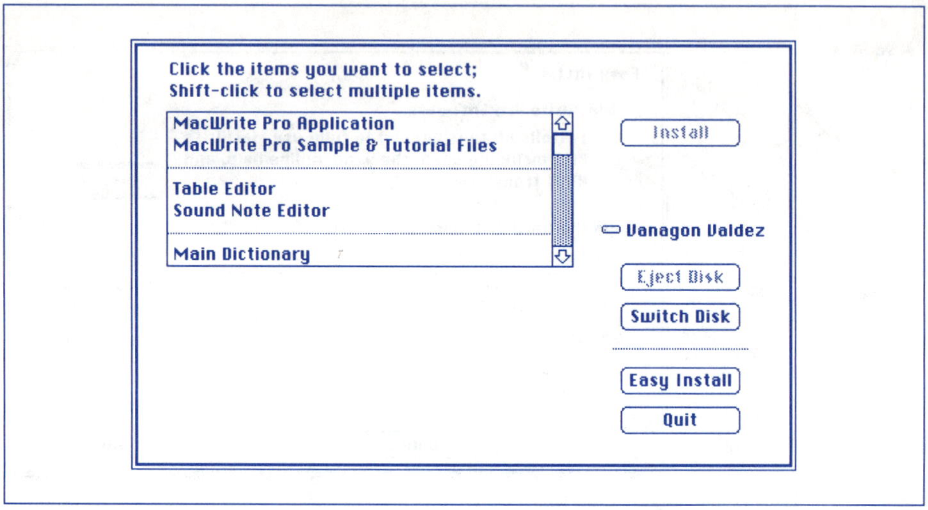

FIGURE A-3 A list of the selected items

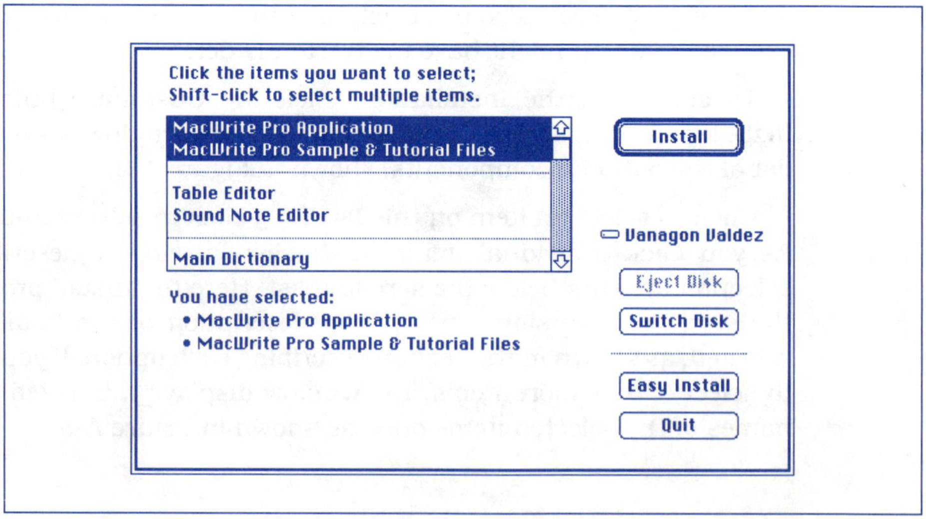

Note Since this book was written while Claris was applying the final polish to MacWrite Pro, the actual statistics for the items you select may vary from those shown in the illustrations used in this chapter.

Here is a list of all the Customize Install options with a brief description of each.

MacWrite Pro Application

The MacWrite Pro Application item installs just the program itself, without any of the other files, as shown in Figure A-4.

MacWrite Pro Sample & Tutorial Files

The MacWrite Pro Sample & Tutorial Files item installs the sample documents, sample stationery, and the tutorial documents, as shown in Figure A-5. If you are learning MacWrite Pro, these files are worth the two or three hundred Kb of space on your disk. You can remove them at any time by dragging them into the trash.

FIGURE A-4 Installing the MacWrite Pro Application item

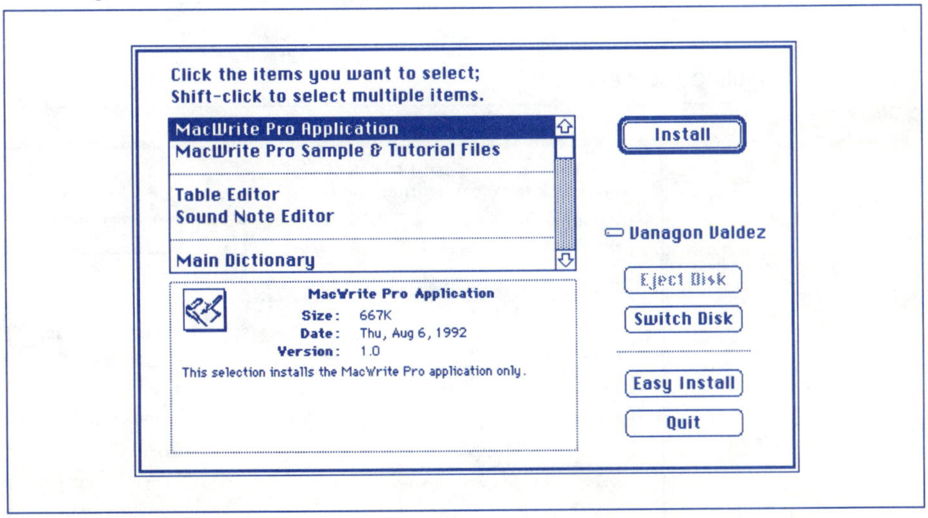

FIGURE A-5 Installing MacWrite Pro Sample & Tutorial Files

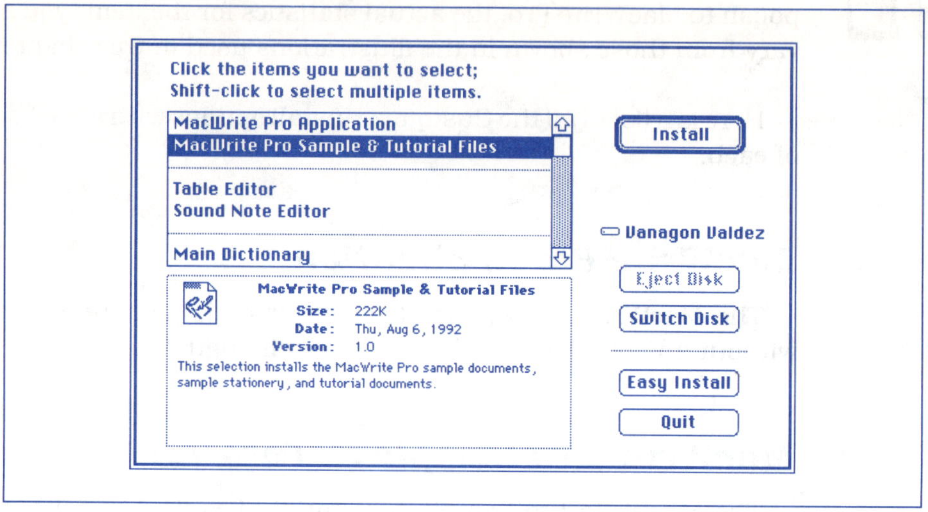

Table Editor

The Table Editor item, shown in Figure A-6, installs the table ADDit. Tables are great time-savers, and the table ADDit takes up very little disk space.

FIGURE A-6 Installing the Table Editor

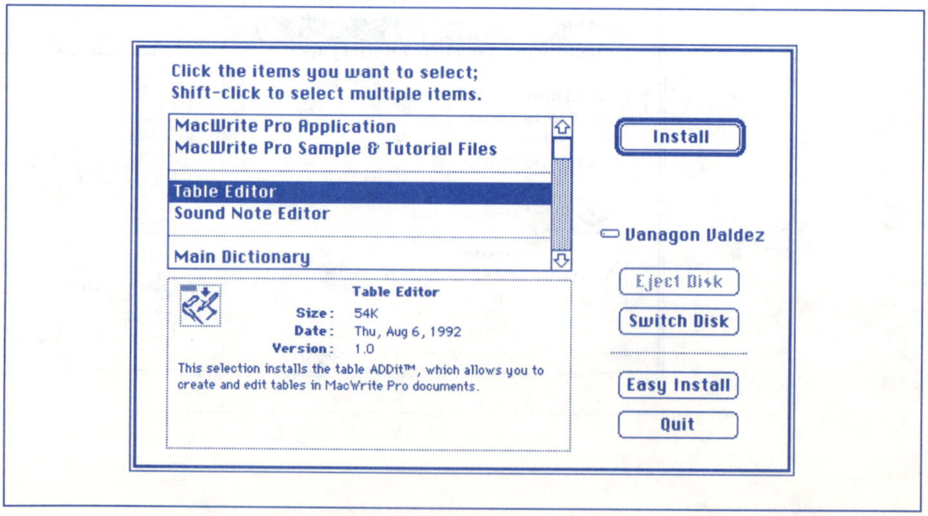

Sound Note Editor

The Sound Note Editor item, shown in Figure A-7, installs the sound note ADDit, which lets you embed sound notes in a document. If your Mac is not equipped with a microphone, you can safely skip installing the Sound Note Editor. It is extremely small, however, so if your Mac has a microphone, you should install it anyway, if only to show your coworkers what a great word processor decision maker you are.

Main Dictionary

The Main Dictionary item, shown in Figure A-8, installs the MacWrite Pro Main Dictionary. One of the chief benefits of modern word processing for those among us with questionable spelling and/or typing skills is the ability to spell-check our work. Install the Main Dictionary.

User Dictionary

The User Dictionary item, shown in Figure A-9, installs an empty User Dictionary. MacWrite Pro will create an empty User Dictionary for you automatically whether or not you install this 1Kb file.

FIGURE A-7 Installing the Sound Note Editor

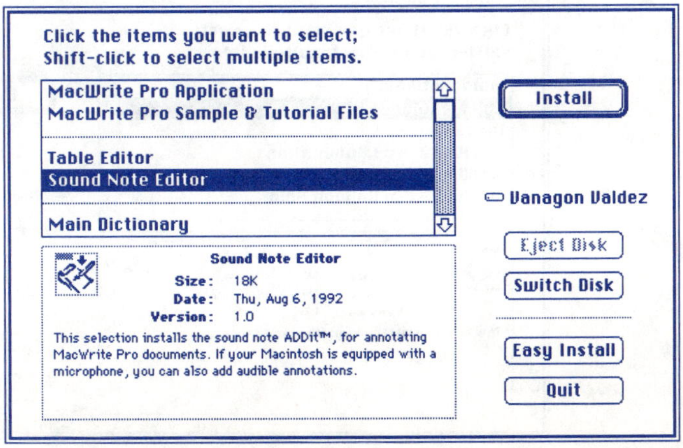

FIGURE A-8 Installing the Main Dictionary

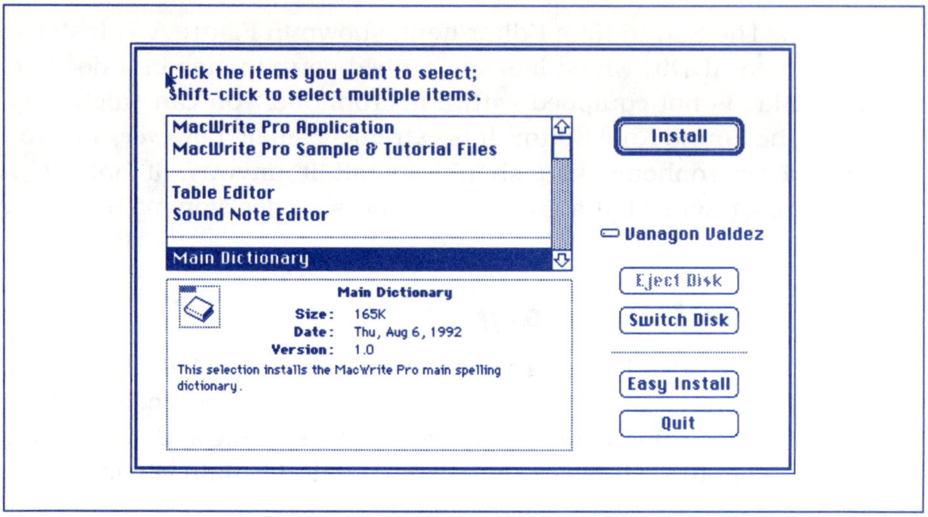

Thesaurus

The Thesaurus item, shown in Figure A-10, installs the Microlytics Thesaurus desk accessory. If you ever find yourself at a loss for a

FIGURE A-9 Installing the User Dictionary

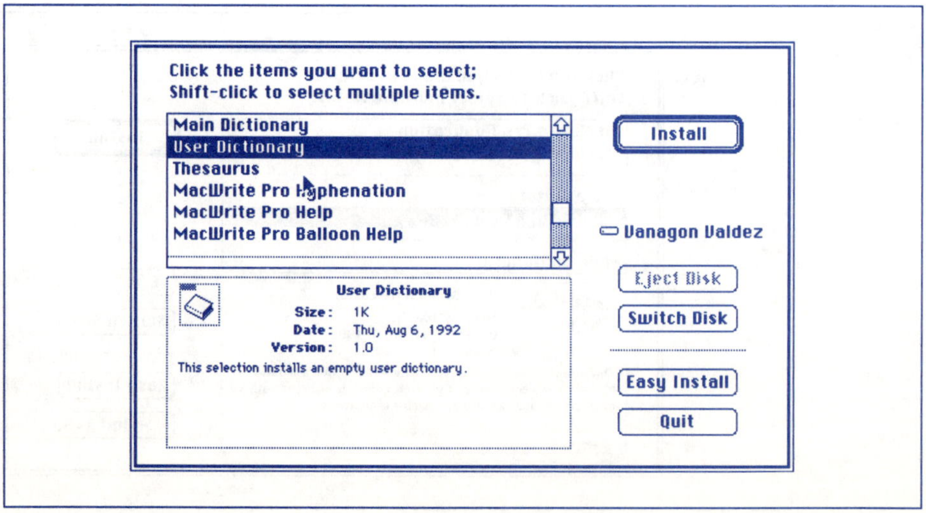

FIGURE A-10 Installing the Thesaurus

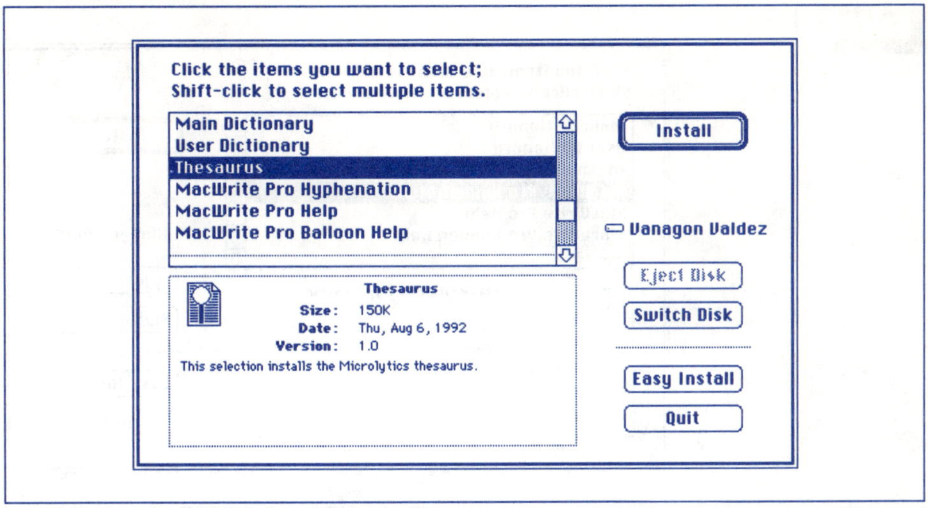

synonym or antonym, the small amount of disk space the Thesaurus requires is well worth the price.

MacWrite Pro Hyphenation

The MacWrite Pro Hyphenation item, shown in Figure A-11, installs the hyphenation package. It requires a very small amount of disk space, and your documents will look better properly hyphenated.

MacWrite Pro Help

The MacWrite Pro Help item, shown in Figure A-12, installs the main MacWrite Pro help system, but not Balloon Help. It requires a few hundred Kb of disk space, but when you need assistance with a particular command or procedure, you won't regret the expenditure.

MacWrite Pro Balloon Help

The MacWrite Pro Balloon Help item, shown in Figure A-13, installs Balloon Help, which is only available if you are using System 7.0 or later.

FIGURE A-11 Installing Hyphenation

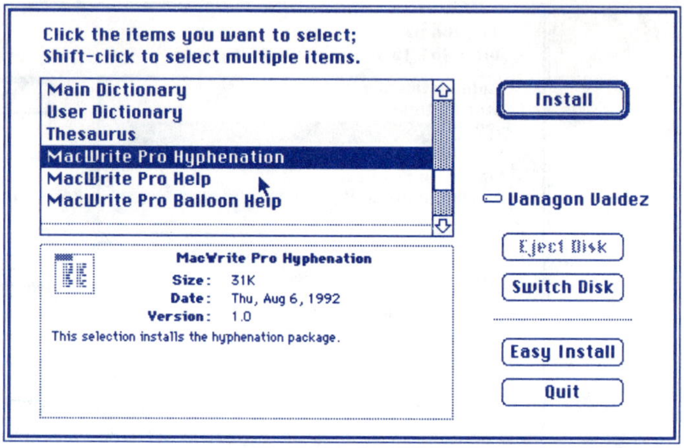

If you are using an earlier version of the Mac operating system, you might consider upgrading now.

FIGURE A-12 Installing Help

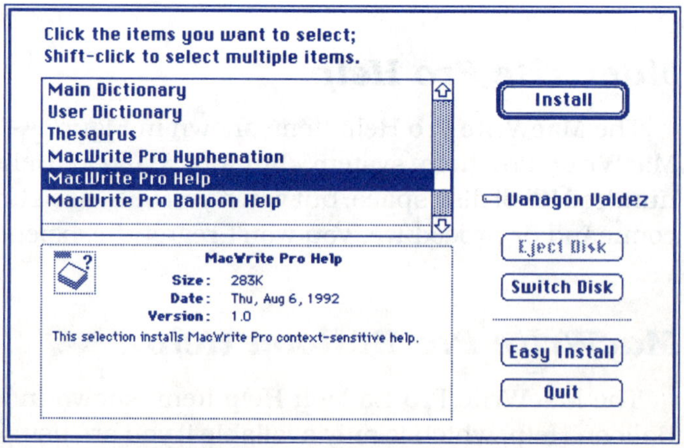

FIGURE A-13

Installing Balloon Help

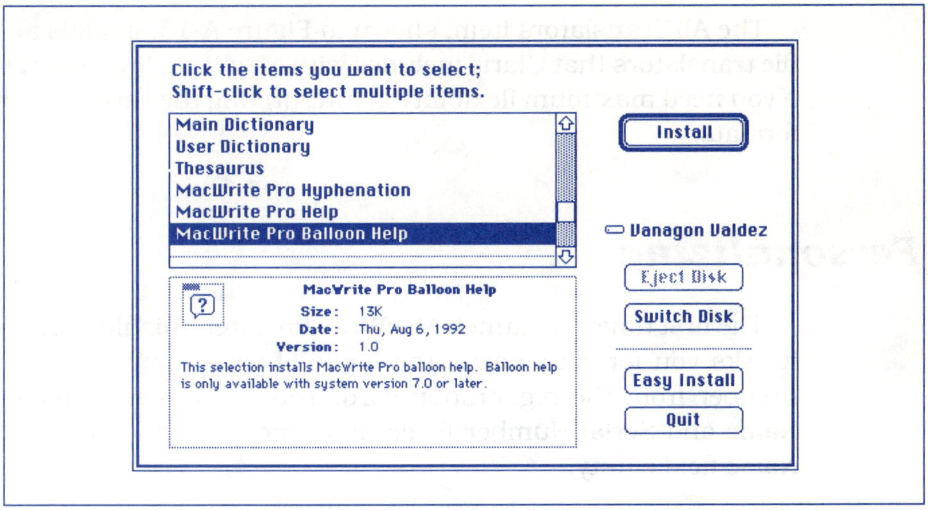

Minimum Translator Set

The Minimum Translator Set item, shown in Figure A-14, installs a subset of the available XTND file translators.

FIGURE A-14

Installing the Minimum Translator Set

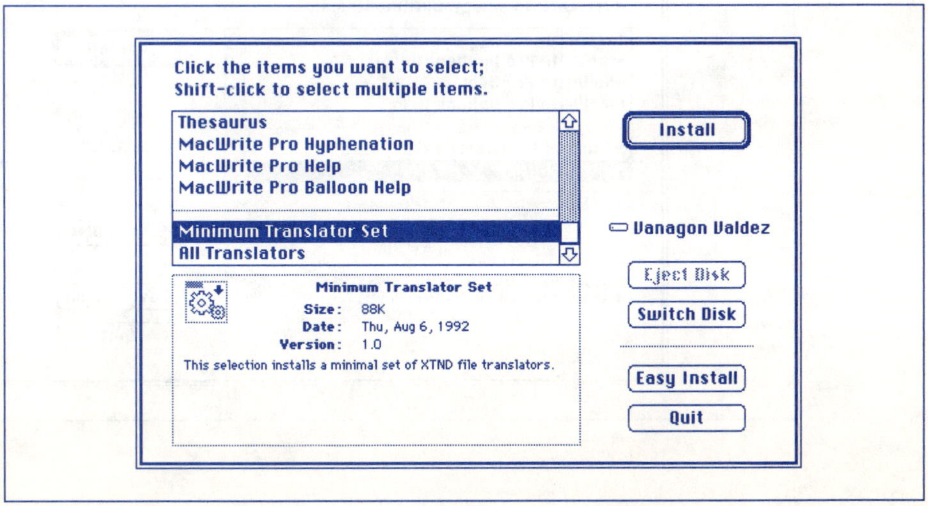

All Translators

The All Translators item, shown in Figure A-15, installs all the XTND file translators that Claris includes with MacWrite Pro. Select this option if you need maximum flexibility in interpreting the various supported file formats.

Personalizing

The first time you launch MacWrite Pro after finishing the installation, it asks you for your name, the name of your company, and the serial number from the registration card. You must enter something in the Name and Serial Number fields; however, you can leave the Company Name field empty.

Note It's not absolutely necessary that you type the exact serial number; just about anything will do. However, when you call Claris for technical support, you are asked for the serial number, and this is a handy place to store it.

FIGURE A-15 Installing All Translators

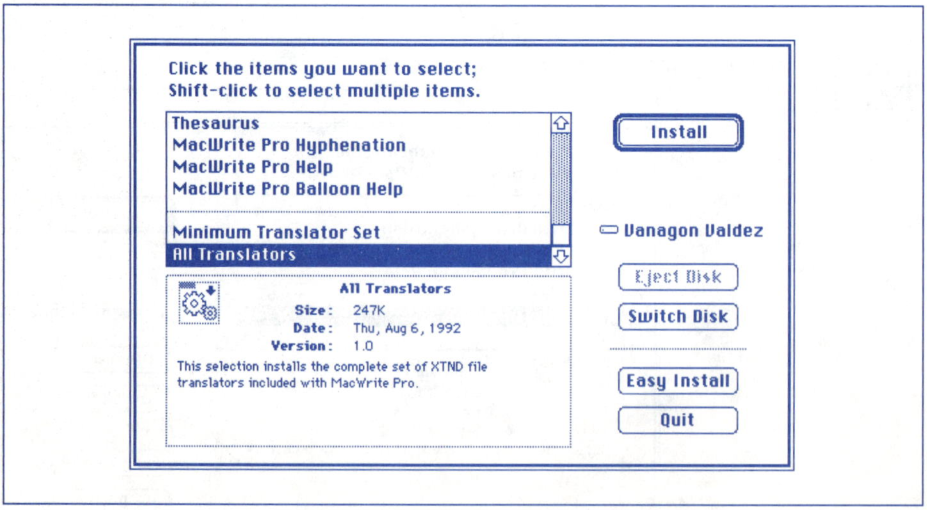

Folders and Files

This section explains the contents and consequences of each of the files and folders the installation process creates.

MacWrite Pro Folder

The Installer places MacWrite Pro into a folder called MacWrite Pro Folder at the top level of your hard disk. The folder contains these files and folders:

MacWrite Pro

The MacWrite Pro file is the MacWrite Pro application itself.

Read Me

The Read Me file contains information about MacWrite Pro that was too late to include in the documentation. After reading it (and perhaps printing a copy), feel free to delete this file.

Tutorial Folder

The tutorial folder contains the files used by the tutorial in the MacWrite Pro documentation. Once you are familiar with the basics, you can delete this folder.

Sample Files Folder

The Sample Files folder contains the MacWrite Pro sample files. It's a good idea to keep these files around as a source of new ideas and techniques for creating your own documents.

Claris Folder

If the hard disk onto which you install MacWrite Pro has a System Folder, then MacWrite Pro creates a special folder inside the System Folder called the Claris folder. If the disk onto which you install MacWrite Pro does *not* have a System Folder, the Claris folder is instead placed into the MacWrite Pro folder.

If you have other Claris products, or other products that include XTND translators, you probably already have a Claris folder in your System Folder. In this case, the MacWrite Pro installer *updates* the contents of this folder. That is, if there is a translator for, say, WordPerfect 5.0 files in your Claris folder, this translator will be updated with the newer version. The installer has no effect on translators for which it does not have a newer version.

Files in the Claris folder that have the word "Claris" in them are shared between different Claris products. For example, if you use both MacWrite Pro and FileMaker Pro 2.0, you do not need (or have, if you have used the installer) separate versions of these files.

The Claris folder may have some other files in it as well. These other files will include help files for other Claris products as well as any non-English dictionaries you have installed.

ADDit Folder

The ADDit folder contains the special programs that can be created for MacWrite Pro. Two ADDits are shipped with MacWrite Pro: editors for sound notes and tables. If you will absolutely not be using either of these features, you can discard the files. However, since the two files together take up less than 200Kb, we recommend that you look for other things to delete first.

If you later acquire other ADDits, they will probably include installers that place them into this folder automatically; otherwise, you can drag them into it yourself.

Claris Fonts

The Claris Fonts file contains a list of all the fonts installed in your system, as well as small bitmap images of the fonts themselves. These bitmap images are used when MacWrite Pro is building the Fonts menu, so it can more quickly show you the names of the fonts using the fonts themselves.

Deleting this small (depending on how many fonts you have) file serves no purpose, as MacWrite Pro recreates it the next time you launch it.

Claris Help System

The Claris Help System file contains the actual programming code that MacWrite Pro (and other Claris products) uses when it is displaying its help. In reality, this is kind of a stripped-down version of HyperCard, as all Claris help is actually created in HyperCard.

If you never want help with the program or are creating a stripped down version of MacWrite Pro for use on a PowerBook with a small hard disk, you can save approximately 60Kb of disk space by deleting this file; the big gains come when you delete the MacWrite Pro file discussed later in this section.

Claris Translators Folder

This folder contains the actual translators used by the XTND system. These translators are used by MacWrite Pro—and other programs that use XTND—when opening or saving files in a non-native format.

Generally, each XTND translator is less than 50Kb, so there's not much to be gained from deleting individual translators. But if there are translators for programs you will never need to read or write (you know which ones they are), delete them.

If you are building a stripped system for a PowerBook, and will never need to translate files, delete the entire contents of this folder, as well as the file described next.

Claris XTND System

This file contains the programming code that MacWrite Pro and other XTND-compatible products use when translating files with XTND. You can delete this file if you are sure you will never need it.

When installing MacWrite Pro, you might have already seen a file by this name in your System Folder. Don't worry about the different versions; this file is always downward-compatible with previous versions.

MacWrite Pro Balloon Help

Not surprisingly, this file contains the information that is displayed when you turn on Balloon Help. It's not a bad idea to have Balloon Help available when first using MacWrite Pro, but once you are familiar with the program, or if you need the extra 133Kb of disk space, delete the file.

MacWrite Pro Help

This file contains the detailed MacWrite Pro help. As with Balloon Help, you can delete it to save over 500Kb of disk space. However, this help is so useful, we recommend that you keep it around for those times when you need help with a procedure that you use infrequently.

This file is actually a HyperCard stack, and can be edited by HyperCard. You need to open it from *within* HyperCard by using the Open Stack command. (Always work on a copy of this file so that if your enthusiastic hacking fails, you can restore the original.) If you are a competent HyperCard scripter, use this capability to add new information to the Help stack. For example, if your work group uses several custom style sheets, you can add a complete description of each style sheet to the Help stack.

Main Dictionary

The Main Dictionary contains the spelling dictionary used by MacWrite Pro and other Claris programs when checking spelling.

MacWrite Pro Preferences

The MacWrite Pro Preferences file records settings that you set in the MacWrite Preferences dialog box, as well as the locations of certain files, such as dictionaries, special dictionaries, and hyphenation files, that MacWrite Pro uses.

MacWrite Pro Hyphenation

The MacWrite Pro Hyphenation file contains code used by MacWrite Pro when you have autohyphenation turned on. Hyphenation uses the US Hyphenation file, as well as any other hyphenation files for foreign languages you may have installed.

US Thesaurus

The US Thesaurus file contains the code for MacWrite's Thesaurus function, as well as the text of the Thesaurus.

User Dictionary

The User Dictionary file contains those words you "teach" MacWrite Pro when checking spelling.

Summary

The MacWrite Pro Installer installs MacWrite Pro and all of its collateral files with the click of one button.

If you want to install only some of the collateral files to save disk space, or if you need to reinstall files you may have accidentally deleted, use the Customize Install procedure.

APPENDIX

B

Useful Utilities

This appendix contains a brief discussion of some other products that complement MacWrite Pro. Of course, there are thousands of programs available for the Macintosh, and most can be used with MacWrite Pro in one or more ways. This is a sampling of products that are particularly germane to the task of word processing.

Commercial Programs

When we envisioned this appendix, we originally planned on including only public-domain or shareware programs. However, two commercial programs are so useful, we feel we have to include them.

QuicKeys

QuicKeys is a keyboard macro program. It lets you record a sequence—such as choosing a menu item with the mouse, or typing a string of text—and save that sequence so that it can be executed with a single keystroke. For example, if you are using a fax modem, you can create a QuicKey that chooses the fax modem from the Chooser, opens the Page Setup dialog box, clicks the OK button, prints the document to the fax modem, and then switches back to your standard printer. This could all happen with one keystroke. Our only reservation about QuicKeys is that its interface seems somewhat confusing. Nevertheless, it's a supremely useful program.

QuicKeys is a product of CE Software of Des Moines, Iowa.

DynoPage

DynoPage lets you print MacWrite Pro documents (or those of virtually any other program) to a wide variety of unusual paper styles. Most useful is the "book format," in which DynoPage automatically paginates the document and prints on both sides of the paper; when the document is finished printing, you simply fold it in half and staple it to form a book. This results, by the way, in a 75 percent savings of paper. You can also print to a variety of papers that are perforated for portable organizer pages (such as DayTimer or FiloFax pages). The DynoPage package includes paper stock compatible with a variety of popular organizers. We use this utility often, and it's hard to imagine how we would do without it.

DynoPage is published by Portfolio Systems, Inc., of Brooklyn, New York.

Freeware, Shareware, and Public-Domain Utilities

A large number of freeware, shareware, and public-domain utilities have been available almost from the day the first Macintosh shipped. Before getting into the recommendations, two issues need to be addressed.

Definitions

The three terms are often confused, and sometimes erroneously used interchangeably. *Freeware* denotes a software program that is free; the author has written it and decided to allow others to use it as much as they want and distribute it to others. The author retains the copyright to the program and may place conditions on its distribution. *Shareware* means that the author has made the program available to others, but asks that if you use it, you send him or her a nominal amount (typically, this is less than $25). If you *do* use a shareware program, you are morally obligated to send payment to the author. This often has practical value as well; shareware registration generally means that the author will send you the latest version of the program, along with a printed or disk-based manual. You will also probably be notified of newer versions as they appear. Finally, *public domain* means that the author has distributed the program and relinquished all rights to it.

Sources

The second issue regarding noncommerical utilities is how to acquire them. Generally, there are three sources for those programs: friends and colleagues, user groups, and online sources. There's not much that we can say about getting software from friends and colleagues, except to remind you that you should make sure any software you get this way is *not* commercial software. If you do get commerical programs from friends, you are legally obligated to purchase your own copy before you use it.

User Groups

There are several hundred Macintosh-related user groups, and there's probably one near you. Apple Computer maintains a list of Macintosh user groups, and you can find the name of the one nearest you by calling 1-800-538-9696. The two largest user groups in the United States are the Boston Computer Society (BCS) and the Berkeley Macintosh User Group (BMUG). Here are their addresses and telephone numbers:

Berkeley Macintosh User Group
1442-A Walnut Street #62
Berkeley, CA 94709
(510) 849-3684

Boston Computer Society
One Center Plaza
Boston, MA 02108
(617) 367-8080

Both of these groups publish newsletters and have libraries of disks that can be purchased at low cost. The Fall 1992 BMUG newsletter, for example, lists several hundred disks, including 79 disks of fonts alone!

Online Services

If you have a modem and communications software, the world of online services is open to you. The most popular online services are CompuServe, America Online, and Prodigy. CompuServe, being the oldest of the three, has the largest collection of software, as well as the most labyrinthian user interface (unless you use a program such as CompuServe Navigator or CIM). America Online and Prodigy are both easier to use, but lack the depth of CompuServe.

Finally, if you are at a university or other site with access to the vaguely defined Internet, the best selection of public domain Macintosh utilities can be had by anonymous FTP (file transfer protocol) at the address *Sumex-aim.stanford.edu.*

Utilities

With that in mind, here's a discussion of some noncommercial utilities we use.

TypeIt4Me

You may have noticed as you read this book that the words "MacWrite Pro" appear several hundred times. Thankfully, we did not need to type all those occurrences, we relied instead on TypeIt4Me.

TypeIt4Me lets you create *glossaries*—shortcuts for frequently typed words or phrases. For example, in our glossary, we assigned "MacWrite Pro" to "mwp". Thereafter, when we typed the text "mwp" TypeIt4Me automatically backspaced three characters and typed "MacWrite Pro".

TypeIt4Me can be a real time saver, but you need to be careful when you assign a glossary entry that the text you assign is unique. In the case of "mwp", we were confident that those characters would not be used in another context. If, on the other hand, you assign "MG" to mean Mikhail Gorbachev, you will experience problems writing intelligently about the history of the British sports car industry.

TypeIt4Me was written by Riccardo Ettore, and its shareware price is $30.

SmartKeys

Chapter 2 discusses some common desktop publishing keystrokes that contribute to more professional-looking documents. These include smart quotes and ligatures. SmartKeys is a Control Panel application that, like TypeIt4Me, watches what you type, and substitutes the proper characters for the characters you type. For example, SmartKeys can automatically substitute a single space each time you type two spaces; it can also substitute an em-dash each time you type two dashes.

You can disable SmartKeys features that you don't need. MacWrite Pro has its own smart quotes, so SmartKeys' smart quotes are redundant. In HyperCard scripts, two dashes have a specific meaning, so you can disable the SmartKeys' em-dash substitution when running HyperCard. You can also disable SmartKeys completely on an application-by-application basis.

SmartKeys was created by Maurice Volaski, who asks no shareware fee for the program—what could be a better bargain?

Fonts

There are, literally, hundreds and hundreds of different fonts available on the Macintosh. As mentioned earlier, the BMUG catalog lists 79 *disks* full of public domain and shareware fonts!

The leading providers of commercial fonts are Adobe Systems, Inc., and Cassady & Greene. Font designs themselves cannot be copyrighted; only font *names* can be copyrighted. This means that what one person can design with a font program, another can reproduce. Thus, if there is a commerical font you like, chances are that you can find a shareware or public domain font based on that design. However, commerical fonts do tend to look better than shareware or free versions. Nevertheless, public domain and shareware channels are good sources for such things as unusual display fonts or foreign character sets.

Disinfectant

The threat of computer viruses is a fact of automated life, though it's not a word processing problem per sé.

Disinfectant is an antivirus utility with two components: an extension that watches for viral activity, and an application that can scan a disk for viruses.

Disinfectant has two main advantages over its competitors. First, it can detect all *known* viruses that were around at the time the most recent version was created. The Disinfectant Extension watches for the behavior of these viruses and nothing else. This means that it never gives a "false hit." It also does not waste time scanning floppy disks each time you insert one.

Secondly, there is the satisfaction that comes from the realization that the author is not cashing in on the problem.

Disinfectant is freeware and is produced by John Norstad of Northwestern University.

McSink and MiniWriter

It may seem peculiar to mention two small text editors as complements to a word processing program. However, you may find yourself needing to type in some text only to realize that you do not have enough memory currently free to launch MacWrite Pro. Both McSink and MiniWriter are desk accessories and therefore are available in all but the most cramped memory conditions.

Note In addition to these two products, there are probably at least a dozen such text editors available. MiniWriter is useful because of its simplicity. McSink is useful because of its wide range of features.

David Dunham's MiniWriter has been around for nearly as long as the Mac itself. It doesn't have a lot of features, but those it has are well implemented. (As a historical aside, MiniWriter was the first text editor featuring smart quotes.) You can create and edit files as large as 32,000 characters (32K) with MiniWriter. The program is shareware and costs only $12.

McSink is a shareware version of a more powerful commercial utility called Vantage, a product of BaseLine Publishing. McSink probably got its name because it includes almost everything but the kitchen sink. It can transform spaces to tabs (and do the opposite), add or strip linefeeds, add returns to the ends of lines, and a variety of other handy feats. McSink's shareware price is $45. The shareware package includes an order form to purchase Vantage for $90.

FontView

FontView is a desk accessory that displays all the characters in a particular font (Figure B-1 shows the FontView display for the Chicago font), tells you what key combination is necessary to produce each one, and lets you click on them to type them. It is somewhat like the KeyCaps

FIGURE B-1 The FontView window

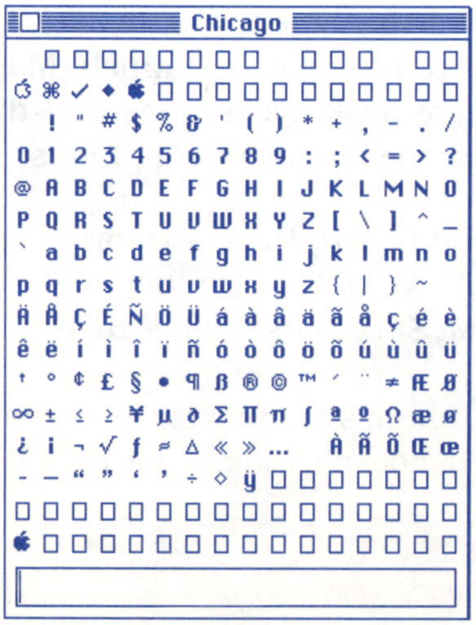

desk accessory, but shows you all characters at once. It is especially useful when using a font such as Zapf Dingbats.

FontView's ShareWare asking price is a very reasonable $8.

Other Products

Two other products aren't software, but we have found both to be useful and can recommend them.

PaperDirect Catalog

PaperDirect is a mail-order paper source that provides a full range of types of paper and accessory products for your printer. The Fall 1992 catalog includes everything from stationery to card stock to labels to cleaners for your laser printer to certificates. Your first order of $30 or more gets you a "PaperKit" containing hundreds of sample papers. To get the catalog, call PaperDirect at 1-800-A-PAPERS (1-800-292-9377).

Mouse Topper

The Mouse Topper is an unusual, inexpensive utility for the Mac mouse. It is an ergonomic replacement for the top portion of the standard Apple ADB mouse. It takes only a few minutes to install (or remove), and has a clearly written manual.

Many mouse users find that the Apple mouse forces the button finger into an uncomfortable positon. Because the Mouse Topper is wider, it can be more comfortably grasped, and the position of the button means that the button finger *lays* on the button rather than being bent above it. A more comfortable mouse is a more productive mouse and a kinder mouse. If you have experienced pain in your wrist or elbow while using the Apple mouse, you owe it to yourself to investigate this product.

The Mouse Topper is a product of Contour Designs of Los Altos, California, and has a list price of $19.95.

APPENDIX

C

File Translators

This appendix covers using the many file-format translators that come with MacWrite Pro. Every word processor has its own unique file format. MacWrite Pro can translate files created by the most widely used word processors, including those on the Mac and files created by word processors on the IBM-PC and compatibles that run the MS-DOS operating system.

Claris Translators

As the sentient cartoonist Eli once observed, no Mac is an island. Some Mac users with whom you share documents are forced by circumstance or corporate dictate to use other word processors. Others use computers that run the MS-DOS operating system. Without some way to translate these foreign file formats, you are reduced to exchanging printed copies of your MacWrite Pro documents with your less fortunate fellows.

Claris Corp. has developed a clever system of integrating file translators with MacWrite Pro (and the company's other applications, as well). This system is called XTND, and is composed of two parts: the translation engine itself and individual translator files. These files are automatically stored in the Claris Translators folder when you install MacWrite Pro. Figure C-1 shows the contents of the Claris Translators folder.

Note When you install MacWrite Pro, you have the option of installing the Minimum Translator Set, which includes MacWrite 5.0, MacWrite II, and Microsoft Word 4 and 5 word processing file translators, plus PICT and RTF graphics file translators. Use this option only when you are absolutely certain that you will never need any of the other translators. The translator files are relatively small. See Appendix A for MacWrite Pro installation options. MacWrite Pro has four internal translators that are always available. These are Text, Text with Line Breaks, MacWrite II (import only), and MacWrite Pro stationery.

FIGURE C-1 The individual translators

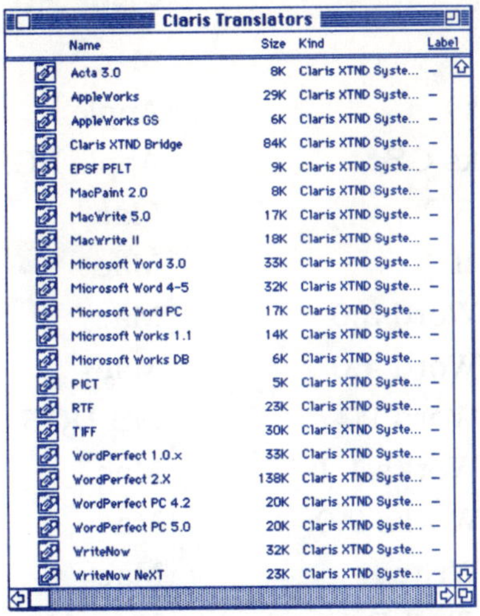

Translator File Formats

MacWrite Pro supports an extensive list of file formats, as shown in Table C-1.

Exporting to Another File Format

Since the XTND file translation system is always available, saving an open document in another format is an easy process. Here's how:

1. With the document open, choose the File menu's Save As command (Shift-⌘-S) to summon the Save As dialog box.

TABLE C-1 Word Processing Formats MacWrite Pro Recognizes

Format	Platform	Import	Export	Insert
Acta 3.0	Mac	Yes	No	Yes
AppleWorks	Apple II	Yes	Yes	Yes
AppleWorks GS	Apple IIGS	Yes	No	yes
MacWrite 5.0	Mac	Yes	Yes	Yes
MacWrite II	Mac	Yes	Yes	Yes
Microsoft Word 3.0	Mac	Yes	Yes	Yes
Microsoft Word 4.0	Mac	Yes	Yes	Yes
Microsoft Word PC	MS-DOS	Yes	Yes	Yes
Microsoft Works 1.1	Mac	Yes	Yes	Yes
Microsoft Works 2.0	Mac	Yes	Yes	Yes
Microsoft Write	Mac	Yes	Yes	Yes
RTF (Rich Text Format)	Mac, MS-DOS	Yes	Yes	Yes
Microsoft Word for Windows	MS Windows	Yes	Yes	Yes
Text	All	Yes	Yes	Yes
WordPerfect 1.0.2	Mac	Yes	Yes	Yes
WordPerfect 2.0	Mac	Yes	Yes	Yes
WordPerfect 4.2	MS-DOS	Yes	Yes	Yes
WordPerfect 5.0	MS-DOS	Yes	No	Yes
WriteNow 1.0, 2.2	Mac	Yes	Yes	Yes
WriteNow Next	Next	Yes	Yes	Yes

2. Choose the file format you need from the Save As pop-up menu. This pop-up menu includes all of the available XTND file translators, as shown here:

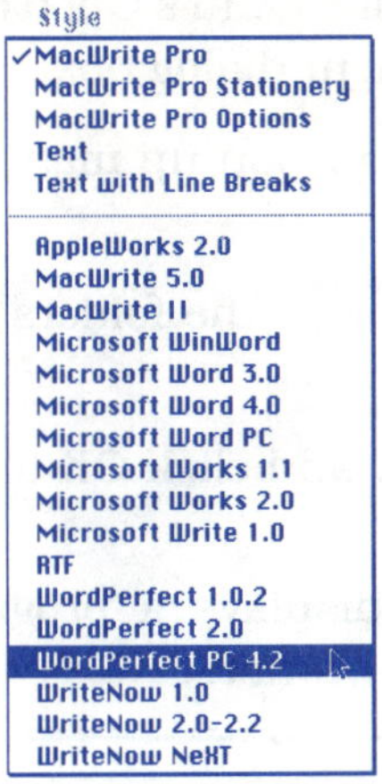

Note Whether or not you are saving in another format, you have the option of saving the entire document or a selection of the document only with the radio buttons at the bottom of the Save As dialog box.

3. Give the document a name different from the existing document name and click the save button.

Importing from Another File Format

You have two ways to read a file created by other applications: the Open command and the Insert command.

Importing with the Open Command

You can directly open files that are stored in any of the available formats. Here's how:

1. Choose the File menu's Open command (⌘-O), which summons the Open Document dialog box.
2. From the Show pop-up menu, select the file format of the file you want to open.
3. Navigate through the folders and files on disk to find the file you want to open.
4. Select the file and click OK to open it.

MacWrite Pro displays a progress status box as the file is being translated, as shown here:

Importing with the Insert Command

You can insert a file in a foreign format directly into a MacWrite Pro document with the File menu's Insert command (Shift-⌘-I). After you have selected the Insert command, the procedure is exactly the same as importing with the Open Command just described.

Inserting Graphics

You can use the Insert command together with the XTND translator to insert graphics files directly into a MacWrite Pro document. The supported formats are listed in Table C-2.

The EPSF (Encapsulated PostScript File) format is a standard file format for graphics files created by applications such as Adobe Illustrator and Aldus FreeHand that can take advantage of PostScript printers' capabilities. The MacPaint 2.0 file format is a bitmap graphics format that is rarely encountered today. The PICT format is an object-oriented graphics standard in wide use. TIFF (Tagged Image File Format) is a high-resolution (greater than 72-dpi) format commonly used in scanner applications.

TABLE C-2 Graphics Formats MacWrite Pro Recognizes

Format	Platform	Import	Export	Insert
EPSF	Mac, MS-DOS	No	No	Yes
MacPaint 2.0	Mac	No	No	Yes
PICT	Mac	No	No	Yes
TIFF	Mac, MS-DOS	No	No	Yes

Special Considerations

The XTND file translation system is easy to use and quite powerful, but it does have a few limitations. When you open or insert a file you can expect to have to do some manual reformatting. As a rule of thumb, the simpler the format of the document in question, the less reformatting you will have to do. If the document contains formatting features not available in MacWrite Pro, those features will be lost. For example, if you import a Microsoft Word document that contains indexing and table of contents entries, those entries appear in the new MacWrite Pro document, but the links used by Microsoft Word to create those entries are lost because MacWrite Pro does not support those features.

The same limitations apply to saving a document in another file format. MacWrite Pro frames, for example, are not translated, so those fancy tables and sound Notes are lost when the file is translated.

Text and Text with Line Breaks

Two translator formats, Text and Text with Line Breaks, deserve special consideration. Both of these formats represent the lowest common denominator of word processing files.

Text

A document saved in Text format contains no formatting other than returns between paragraphs; all font information, Ruler settings, and other niceties found in the original document are stripped out.

Use the Text format when you need to create a file for which no translator is available. For example, if you are exchanging a file with someone using a totally outdated computer, the Text file format may be the only feasible option. Fortunately, you will rarely encounter this situation. All popular Mac word processors can read, at the least, MacWrite or Microsoft Word format files, so you can use one of these formats as an intermediate file. The MS-DOS Word 5.0 file format can be read by Microsoft Word for Windows, so you can easily exchange files with those using that product and still retain all major formatting.

Text with Line Breaks

The Text with Line Breaks format is identical to the Text format except that the word-wrap of the original document is retained. Use this format when you compose a message to be uploaded to a bulletin board or other text-only electronic services.

Files from Other Platforms

Sharing files with other Mac users is very straightforward. If the users' Macs are not networked but are in the same vicinity, you can always exchange the physical media, usually a common floppy disk or a removable Syquest or Bernoulli cartridge. Files can also be exchanged by using a commercial electronic service such as AppleLink, CompuServe, or America Online.

Sharing Mac files with MS-DOS users is almost as easy. All the options available for Mac-to-Mac file transfers are also available for Mac-to-MS-DOS file transfers, although transferring files to and from an MS-DOS disk is a bit more complex. All modern Macs are equipped with a 1.44Mb floppy drive called the SuperDrive. Consult the manual that comes with your Mac for details. Any Mac with a SuperDrive can access 3 1/2-inch disks from MS-DOS by using a utility such as Apple's Macintosh PC Exchange, Insignia's AccessPC, or Dayna's DOS Mounter.

If the Mac and the PC are physically near enough, you can hook up the serial ports directly with a null modem cable and use a transfer program such as LapLink Mac III or MacLink to move the files very quickly between machines.

If your Mac is networked via AppleShare or Novell Network, you can transfer files with connected MS-DOS machines over the network.

Acquiring Additional Translators

The file translators supplied with MacWrite Pro are probably adequate for the needs of the majority of users. If you find that you need to translate files in a format not supported, you have a variety of options.

XTND Translators

Claris Corporation develops additional translators from time to time. These are available free to registered MacWrite Pro users from Claris Public Relations. The phone number is (408) 727-8227.

DataViz offers an extensive set of XTND translators that are compatible with MacWrite Pro. DataViz is at (203) 268-0030.

Other Translators

If you can't find an XTND translator that suits your needs, you may want to investigate one of the commercial file translation products. The three best known products in this category are

- Word for Word/Mac from The Software Toolworks at (415) 883-3000
- LapLinkMac III from Traveling Software at (206) 483-8088
- Software Bridge/Mac from Argosy Software at (212) 274-1199

APPENDIX

D

Macintosh Fonts

An understanding of how the Mac works with fonts can help you in several ways. First, understanding the ins and outs of the three kinds of fonts used on the Mac can help you choose fonts that print best to a particular printer so that your documents look as good as their design permits. Second, using the correct kinds of fonts in a document can help ensure trouble-free print sessions. Finally, different kinds of fonts require different hard disk file organization schemes. This appendix explains the different kinds of fonts available for the Macintosh and tells you how to manage fonts on your system.

Fonts Versus Typefaces

The meanings of some important font terms varies, depending on context. In traditional typography, a font is a set of characters having the same size and style. Thus, 9-point Courier is a different font than 9-point bold Courier, which is a different font than 10-point bold Courier. To traditional typographers, a typeface, in contrast, is a family of different fonts that share a common design but vary in size and style. On the Mac, font means a family of fonts of the same design of varying sizes and styles. In other words, the typographer's typeface is the Mac user's font. This discussion, not surprisingly, uses the Mac meaning of the word font.

Note If you ever have to deal with traditional typography, use the original definitions of "font" and "typeface."

Three Kinds of Fonts

There are three kinds of fonts used on the Macintosh: bitmap fonts (sometimes called screen fonts), PostScript fonts, and TrueType fonts.

Bitmap Fonts

The Macintosh screen display is composed of a grid of small squares called *pixels*. Images on the screen are created by turning different combinations of these pixels "off" (in which case they are white) or "on," in which case they are black (if you have a Mac with a color monitor, this is not strictly the case). Most Mac screens have a resolution of 72 × 72 pixels per inch. A bitmap of a character includes a definition of which pixels within a grid are turned off or on.

All fonts, when printed or displayed on the screen, are actually bitmap fonts, since the term "bitmap" refers to a means of drawing images by placing dots in a pattern to form the object. (The Mac's monitor, by the way, was the first personal computer monitor to be exclusively "bitmapped." This means that instead of relying on hardware to place images on the screen, everything on the screen is placed there by graphics programming in the Macintosh ROMs.) The difference between the kinds of fonts used is in how those bitmaps are generated.

PostScript and TrueType fonts (described in the following two sections) use software technology to generate bitmaps of a particular size. On the Mac, *bitmap font* refers to the kind of font that uses specific sizes of predefined bitmaps to create the image for each character.

Fonts are stored in the System 7 System file, discussed below in "Managing Fonts." Font names that include a trailing number, such as Geneva 9 and Geneva 12, are bitmapped fonts. That is, the bits that form the shape of that character are "hard-wired" into that font in the System file. These bitmap fonts are nearly always shown in outline views on MacWrite Pro's font Size menu.

Bitmap fonts offer several benefits. First of all, the design of the fonts has been "tuned" to the monitor on which they are used. This means that the designer of the font has precisely laid out the array of dots to make the font readable on the screen. Bitmap fonts display quickly when you change from one size to another because the Mac does not have to calculate the new size.

Bitmap fonts also have a few disadvantages when printed if not augmented by the PostScript or TrueType complementing fonts. Because they are tuned to screen displays of 72 dots per inch, bitmap fonts alone do not print attractively on a printer capable of higher resolution, such as a LaserWriter at 300 dots per inch (and as a result are not particularly WYSIWYG). Bitmapped fonts printed at higher resolutions yield jagged type, commonly referred to as "the jaggies."

Bitmap fonts can also take up a lot of room on disk: this is less of a concern with small font sizes (10 to 24 point), but with larger sizes (48 points and up), fonts can become quite large and begin to impact available disk space accordingly.

The final (and biggest) problem with bitmap fonts is in font scaling. With bitmap fonts, when you want to use a font size for which there is no bitmap font available, the Mac has to scale an existing size. This is inconsequential if there is a bitmap available that is twice the size you want (for example, 18-point type looks acceptable if you have a 36-point bitmap installed, but 19-point does not). The jaggies is the result of requesting a size that cannot be easily scaled (in the previous example, 18-point type does not look good if there is no 36-point bitmap available).

PostScript Fonts

When Apple released the LaserWriter in 1985, the new printer included PostScript, a new kind of font technology developed by Adobe Systems, Inc. PostScript enables the LaserWriter to produce type of almost any size. Requiring bitmaps for every conceivable size would be exceedingly cumbersome and overload the operating system. The solution that Adobe developed and that Apple adopted is called PostScript.

PostScript is a device-independent page description programming language that is built into LaserWriter printers (and many other printers released in the six years since the advent of the LaserWriter). PostScript is designed for printing and displaying both fonts and graphics on devices with differing resolutions. One of the key features of PostScript is a means of describing fonts in a way that allows the font to be scaled to a specific size. This means that when you ask the printer to print, for example, 47-point Times, the printer can use the description of the Times font to create a bitmap of the characters in the Times font at 47 points and use those bitmaps to print.

The availability of the original LaserWriter with PostScript helped make possible the birth of a new enterprise that became known as "desktop publishing." It also marked the beginning of the end of the letter-quality (daisy wheel) printer. It gave printer manufacturers a set of software tools they could include in their printers without forcing them to develop a set of custom printer commands (and the inevitable compatibility nightmare that results when each application must be aware of a large number of essentially incompatible printers). The availability of PostScript has encouraged software developers to produce a variety of tools that help users create attractive printed materials, and numerous third parties have created a body of fonts that users can purchase off the shelf and install by themselves.

Although PostScript is an excellent solution to many font-related problems on the Mac, it is not an all-purpose remedy for all of them.

First, the Mac screen itself still requires the use of bitmap fonts of a particular size for optimal results. This means that all the problems of bitmap text screen display still apply to the screen display, even when you use a PostScript printer. While text of differing sizes can be attractively scaled on a laser printer by PostScript, the appearance of text on the screen can vary considerably from that of printed text. Not only will it not be as attractive or accurately reproduced on the screen, spacing between characters can be displayed inaccurately. This is not a problem with long text-only documents; but accurate screen display and character spacing is crucial when you create advertising materials, artwork, typeset documents, or other kinds of documents in which appearance is paramount.

PostScript users can (and most certainly should) circumvent this problem by using Adobe Type Manager (ATM) from Adobe Systems, Inc. ATM uses PostScript font descriptions to create bitmaps of fonts for the screen. This technique helps reduce the jaggies, but it leads to a second problem relating to PostScript fonts.

If the PostScript font you want to use is not built into your printer, or if you use ATM, you must have a PostScript description of the font located on your hard disk in addition to the bitmapped font in the Mac System file. This font file scheme has drawbacks. First, the PostScript font file must be in the correct location for it to be found by the System when you print, or when ATM uses it to create a bitmap of a specific size. Also, because these fonts must be "downloaded" (the Macintosh sends the information to the printer), printing can take longer than with a document that contains fonts already available in the printer.

The third problem with PostScript fonts has fortunately been solved. Adobe originally offered two different kinds of PostScript fonts. It created a "Type 1" font for its proprietary use. Type 1 fonts have embedded *hints* that allow font designers to fine-tune their designs for different sizes.

Hints are part of the font definition, invisible to the user, that assist the printer in scaling the font to different sizes.

Type 3 fonts are similar to the Type 1 fonts, except they do not have these hints, and are therefore less desirable. For a long time Adobe refused to release the formula for creating Type 1 fonts. As a result, it was very difficult for third parties to develope Type 1 without licensing Adobe's technology. This problem was solved in early 1990 when Adobe (largely as a result of the Apple TrueType announcement described in the next section) published the Type 1 font specifications.

Note Type 3 fonts are incompatible with ATM. If you are one of the few holdouts still using ancient Type 3 fonts, you really owe it to yourself to upgrade to Type 1 versions.

TrueType Fonts

Apple announced its TrueType technology in mid-1989 when it announced plans for System 7. TrueType defines yet a third standard for Macintosh type.

TrueType works similarly to Adobe Type Manager, insofar as it also uses a mathematical description of a specific font character to generate bitmapped characters of specific sizes. It does this by encoding the mathematical description of the character within the font resource in the System itself.

TrueType was introduced in part as a response to the proprietary nature of Type 1 fonts and as a way for Apple to gain control over the font technology used on the Mac. As a counterresponse to TrueType (Microsoft licenses it for use in Windows) Adobe made public the Type 1 font specifications. Although ATM was released after the announcement of TrueType, its timing suggests that it was in development long before TrueType was announced.

There are some benefits to TrueType. As with PostScript Type 1 fonts, TrueType allows font designers to embed hints in its font designs to improve their appearance in different sizes. Another advantage of TrueType fonts is that they only require one representation on the Mac: the

TrueType font resource that is stored in your System file. PostScript fonts require both the bitmap definition and the PostScript definition, which is stored in a separate file. This makes managing and using TrueType fonts somewhat easier than PostScript fonts.

Note A future release of System 7 (although not System 7.1) will include a feature functionally similar to Adobe Type Manager that will make working with PostScript fonts easier; in the meantime, as discussed later, Macintosh users can purchase ATM inexpensively.

Managing Fonts

The preceding discussion may be somewhat academic, but the history of how fonts have evolved on the Mac has a bearing on how you use them with System 7, which is what is covered here.

Before System 7, bitmap fonts were stored in the System file inside the System Folder. PostScript fonts were stored in the top level of the System Folder, which usually resulted in a cluttered folder. With versions of the System prior to System 7, you had to use a utility called Font/DA Mover to install fonts (you could also use SuitCase II or MasterJuggler to manage fonts under System 6). If you are still using System 6, you should upgrade to System 7 if for no other reason than the satisfaction of dragging Font/DA Mover to the trash. System 7 exacts a price, however—it requires 2MB of RAM just to operate. This could pose a problem for users with only 2MB on their machines.

Managing Fonts Using System 7.0

This section deals with managing fonts using System 7.0 only; if you have upgraded to System 7.1, skip to the next section. With System 7.0, bitmap and TrueType fonts are stored in the System file, and PostScript fonts (called System Extensions) are stored in the Extensions folder.

In System 7, you can double-click to open the System file as if it were a folder. The following shows an open System file window viewed by name:

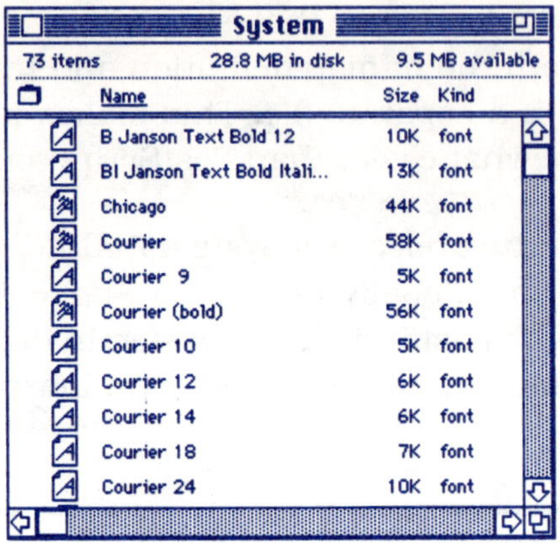

There are two types of fonts listed, although the Kind column does not reflect this fact. Some of the fonts, Courier 9, Courier 10, and Helvetica 9, for example, are shown with numbers after their names, and some are not. The distinction is important. Those files that have the numbers appended to their names are bitmap fonts; the number represents the size of that font. The file called Geneva 9 is the 9-point Geneva bitmap font. Files without numbers after their names are TrueType fonts.

The distinction is also apparent when you double-click one of these files. Double-clicking a bitmap font shows a sample of type in that size, as shown here, in the case of 24-point Times:

The sentence shown, by the way, includes all the letters of the U.S. alphabet.

Double-clicking a TrueType font summons a similar window, but the sample sentence is displayed in three sizes: 9, 12, and 18 points. The Times TrueType font window is shown here:

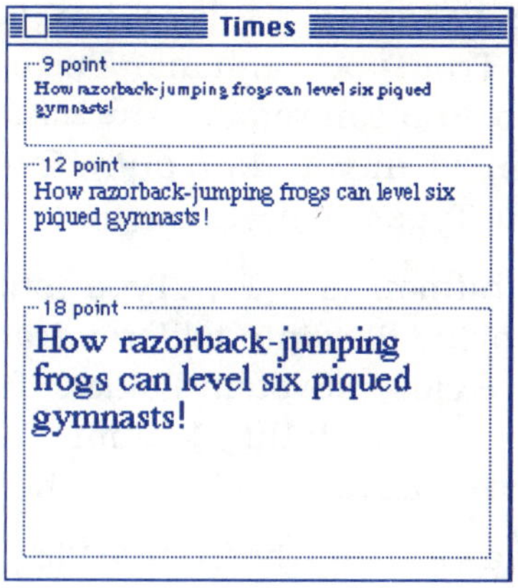

Note This sample does not reflect the actual quality of the TrueType font as it appears when printed on a LaserWriter or other high-resolution PostScript device; this figure is a graphic, captured from a standard 72-dot-per-inch Macintosh screen and is limited to the resolution of the screen (72 dpi). When printed on a LaserWriter, it will be seen at 300 dpi.

If you view the System file by icon, you will see that, in addition to the differences in the way fonts are named, the icons for the two types of fonts differ. The TrueType icon shows a letter A in three different sizes, while the bitmap icon shows the letter A in only one size, as shown here:

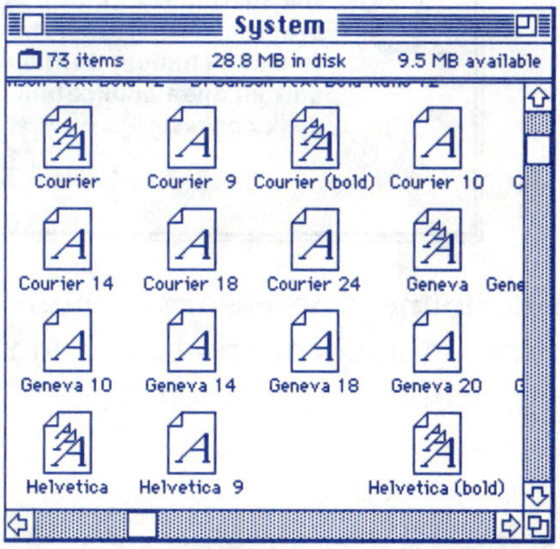

The System 7 installer places both TrueType and bitmap versions of some of the fonts into the System file. As fast as TrueType is, it is still faster for the system to display a font in its actual size using a bitmap than scaled TrueType versions. The appearance of bitmap fonts is superior, also. You can remove any bitmap versions of sizes that you do not use often; when you do require a font size for which no bitmap is available, TrueType will scale the font for you automatically.

Installing bitmap and TrueType fonts into the System file is very similar to copying files into folders: drag the font into the open System file or into the closed System Folder. If the font is in a suitcase (of the type that was used with the old Font/DA Mover utility), the suitcase file will be converted as it is copied into the System file.

To remove a font from the System file, use the reverse of the installation technique: select the icon of the font you want to remove, and drag it to another location (such as the Trash).

Note To copy a font file to another location without disturbing the copy in the System file, hold down the Option key while dragging.

There is a caveat to installing and removing fonts from the System file: All applications, including MacWrite Pro, must be closed before you begin. If you try to install or remove a font while an application is running, the Finder will display an error alert, shown here, telling you to quit all open applications before modifying the System file:

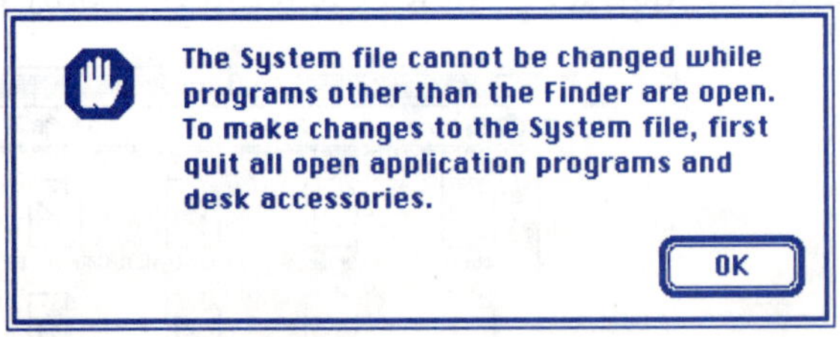

This bit of discipline is necessary because there is no way for the System to notify running applications that a font has been added or removed since the application was launched.

Installing Printer Fonts

Printer fonts are files that contain the PostScript definitions of fonts. Printer fonts are downloaded to the printer automatically when you print a document. You do not need to worry about printer fonts for TrueType fonts, nor for any fonts that are built into your PostScript printer.

A problem might arise when you print a number of different documents, all of which contain the same downloadable font or fonts. Since the downloadable fonts are associated with the document in which they are used, the fonts are needlessly downloaded each time one of the documents is printed. This situation can slow down the printing process. For faster printing you can use the Apple LaserWriter Utility (included with the LaserWriter) or a similar utility to download fonts "permanently," that is, until the printer is reset or turned off.

System 7 designates printer font files as Extensions and stores them in the Extensions folder in the System Folder. If you drag a printer font file into the closed System Folder, the Finder will place it in the Extensions folder automatically.

Managing Fonts Using System 7.1

System 7.1 changes font management from the model used in System 7.0. With System 7.1, you do not need to store fonts within the System file itself; instead, a special Fonts folder resides in the System Folder (much like System 7.0's Apple menu items, Control Panels, and Extensions folders). To install a font in System 7.1, drop the font suitcase on the closed System Folder, and it will be placed into the Fonts folder automatically. Alternatively, you can place font suitcases directly into the Fonts folder yourself. PostScript fonts, which were called System Extensions in System 7.0 and placed in the Extensions folder, are also placed into the Fonts folder in System 7.1.

Note System 7.1 imposes a limit of 128 different font files in the Fonts folder. If you have more than 128 fonts installed, you should combine them together into suitcases or use a utility such as Suitcase or Font/DA Juggler.

You can easily combine fonts from different suitcases into one suitcase using System 7.1. When you double-click a suitcase icon, it opens exactly as if it were a folder. This means that you can open a font suitcase and drag other suitcases into it. You can also drag fonts out of a suitcase. To create a new suitcase, select an existing one and duplicte it using the Duplicate command on the Finder's File menu.

Acquiring Adobe Type Manager

In October 1991, Apple and Adobe announced an "interim" arrangement for delivering Adobe Type 1 fonts to Apple customers. As part of this agreement, Apple includes a coupon for a free copy of Adobe Type Manager with each new Apple PostScript printer and models of the Macintosh that contain 4MB or more of RAM. (In addition to ATM, the coupon also entitles you to the Adobe Garamond font.) Macintosh System 7 users who do not have it can acquire ATM by calling 1-800-521-1976 ext. 4400. There is a $7.50 shipping and handling charge for the software and fonts. If you do not have ATM, avail yourself of this opportunity. The offer is scheduled to be in effect until Apple delivers a version of System 7 that includes the functionality of Adobe Type Manager to support the display of PostScript fonts on screen. Apple has not announced a release date for this version of System 7.

Which Font Type Should You Use?

Given the contrasting font technologies, you need to decide which one to use. Making a prudent decision depends on several factors, including the type of printer you use, your existing library of fonts, and the availability of new fonts that meet your needs.

Avoid Mixing Font Technologies

Even though System 7 automatically installs TrueType versions of Times, Helvetica, Symbol, and Courier fonts, it is prudent to remove them from your System file, leaving only the bitmap versions. This is especially true if you are using Adobe Type Manager. When working on the screen, the system uses the TrueType version of the font for display, but the PostScript version for printing. In most cases, the differences between the two kinds of fonts will be minor, but if you are doing exacting work, it is possible that line breaks will be different between the screen display and the printed document.

Note Since Courier is not a proportional font, the differences between the two versions will be minor, and you can leave the TrueType version of Courier installed (thereby saving a little disk space, since all TrueType fonts do not require separate printer files). On the other hand, if you are creating documents destined for a high-end imagesetter, stick with the PostScript version.

Specific Printer Options

If you use a PostScript printer, it is best to use PostScript fonts and rely on Adobe Type Manager to handle font screen display. Documents containing PostScript fonts print faster on a PostScript printer than do documents with TrueType fonts.

Note If the final destination of a document is a high-end PostScript-compatible typesetting machine, make of policy of using only PostScript fonts.

On the other hand, if you use a dot-matrix printer or other non-PostScript printer such as the Apple StyleWriter or the Hewlett-Packard DeskWriter, you might find that TrueType works well for you. TrueType fonts are easier to manage (there are fewer files associated with each one), and they print fairly well to lower-resolution printers.

Note Neither Adobe Type Manager nor TrueType is particularly proficient at rendering fonts in small sizes (smaller than 9 point, for example) on low-resolution devices, but both TrueType and ATM-rendered fonts look good on these printers at medium (9- to 12-point) and larger sizes.

Your Library of Fonts

If you have an existing library of PostScript fonts, you can ignore TrueType because TrueType fonts offer no significant printing advantages compared to PostScript fonts. Also, PostScript fonts and Adobe Type Manager will continue to be compatible with System 7 as Apple upgrades the Mac operating system and the way it handles fonts.

Index

C

D

E

F

G

H

I

K

L

M

N

O

P

Q

R

S

T

THE

MacWrite Pro Inside/Out
COMPANION DISK

This disk will save you hours of work! In addition to templates that come right from this book, we've scoured shareware and public domain software libraries locating utilities that will make MacWrite Pro® more powerful and easier to use. The *Companion Disk* will help you be more productive and create documents that look better!

Just $25.00

Sample Files
Right from the book, *Sample Files* includes templates for each of the document recipes in part three.

Combiner
This handy utility combines multiple text files. Much simpler than coping and pasting to combine files.

FontView 1.32
Displays a font so that you can quickly locate each character's keyboard position.

Fraction Fonts
Custom versions of PostScript fonts (Helvetica and Times) for printing true fractions. Includes detailed instructions.

Print2PICT
Send a "postcard" of your formatted documents to those who don't have MacWrite Pro. This utility is a Chooser device—so MacWrite Pro thinks *Print2PICT* is a printer!

The Font Well
Paste *The Font Well* into your MacWrite Pro document and apply any font to display or print samples of the entire character set. Keep a copy in your Scrapbook to use on the fly!

Marker Felt Fonts
Enhance your next publication with the look of felt pen! These two fonts come in thin and wide versions, as well as both PostScript® and TrueType® formats. **Great for newsletters, invitations and correspondence.**

SmartKeys 2.1
This keyboard utility will transform your current typing habits into good desktop publishing skills (see chapter two). *SmartKeys* keeps you from double spacing after sentences, substitutes ligatures for "fi" (ﬁ) and "fl" (ﬂ), turns double hyphens into "em" dashes (—), and can be fully customized to meet your specific needs.

StuffIt Expander
This terrific utility decompresses the files you download from on-line services.

Super NotePad
A desk accessory to replace Apple's Note Pad. Great for taking notes or composing when you don't have MacWrite Pro open.

TypeIt4Me
Let this keyboard macro utility make short work of long bunches of text! You type short abbreviations and *TypeIt4Me* substitutes the complete text.

— See Over For Ordering Information —

Yes! *Please send my MacWrite Pro Inside/Out* COMPANION DISK from Steve & Dale

Name ______________________________

Company ______________________________

Address ______________________________

City ____________________ State __________ Zip __________

Daytime Phone *(in case of questions)* (   ) ____________________

MacWrite Pro Inside/Out **Companion Disk** (#80-0035)	**25.00**
California residents please add appropriate sales tax	
Shipping & handling *(US/Canada $3.00 • International $7.00)*	**3.00** *or* **7.00**
TOTAL	

☐ **CALL TOLL FREE: 800-943-7667** ext. 239 *(credit card orders only)*
International: **510-943-7667**

☐ **FAX: 510-943-6882** *(credit card orders only)*

☐ **Check or money order** *(US dollars)*, payable to Heizer Software, enclosed.

☐ MasterCard / American Express / VISA

Credit Card No. ______________________________ Exp. ______

Signature ______________________________

☐ **MAIL YOUR ORDER TO:**

Heizer Software
P.O. Box 232019
Pleasant Hill, California 94523